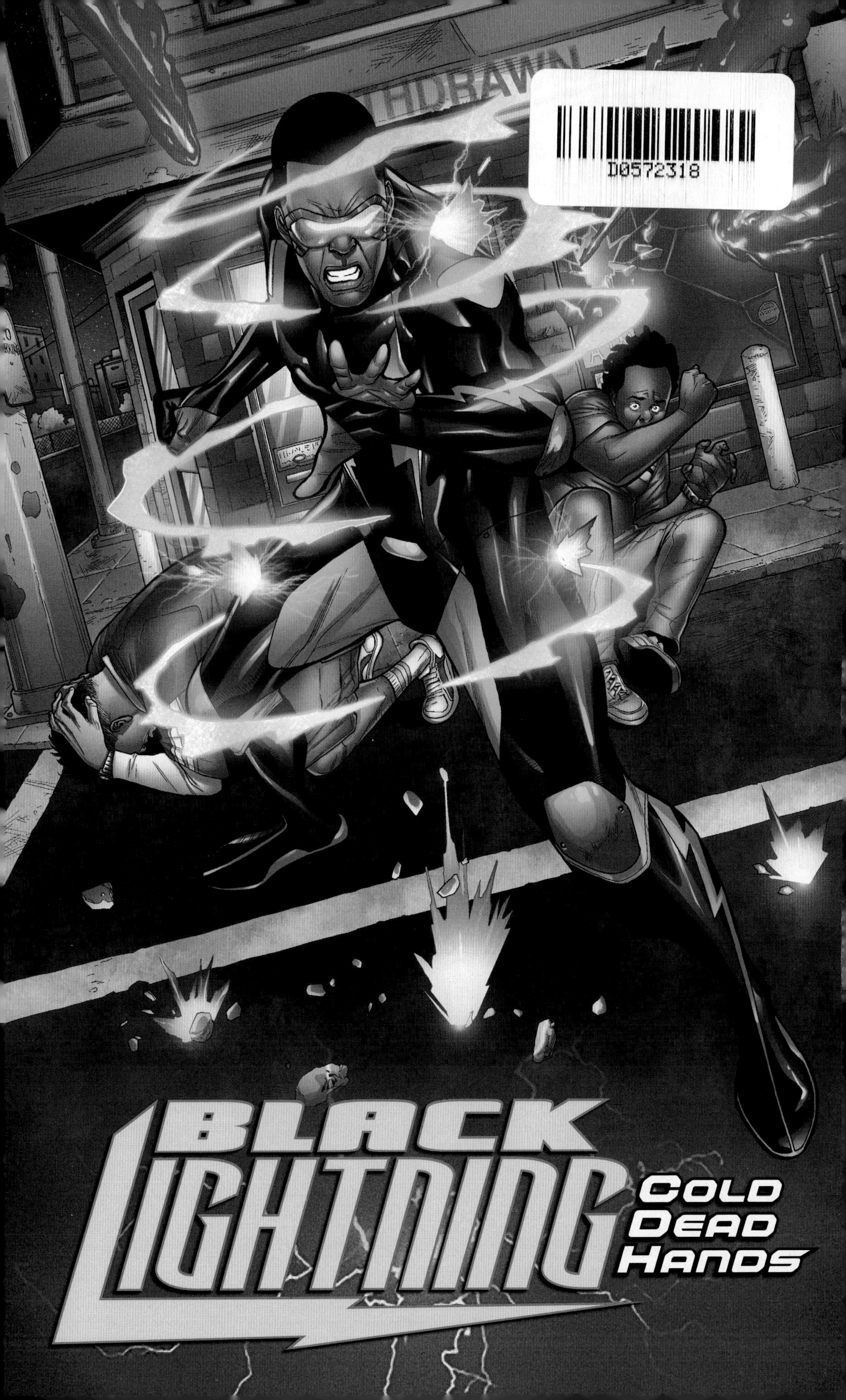
HDRAWN
BLACK
LIGHTNING
COLD
DEAD
HANDS

BLACK LIGHTNING

COLD DEAD HANDS

TONY ISABELLA
writer

CLAYTON HENRY
YVEL GUICHET
artists

PETE PANTAZIS
colorist

JOSH REED
letterer

CLAYTON HENRY, MARK MORALES
and TOMEU MOREY
collection cover artists

BLACK LIGHTNING created by
TONY ISABELLA with **TREVOR VON EEDEN**

SUPERMAN created by **JERRY SIEGEL** and **JOE SHUSTER**
By special arrangement with the Jerry Siegel family

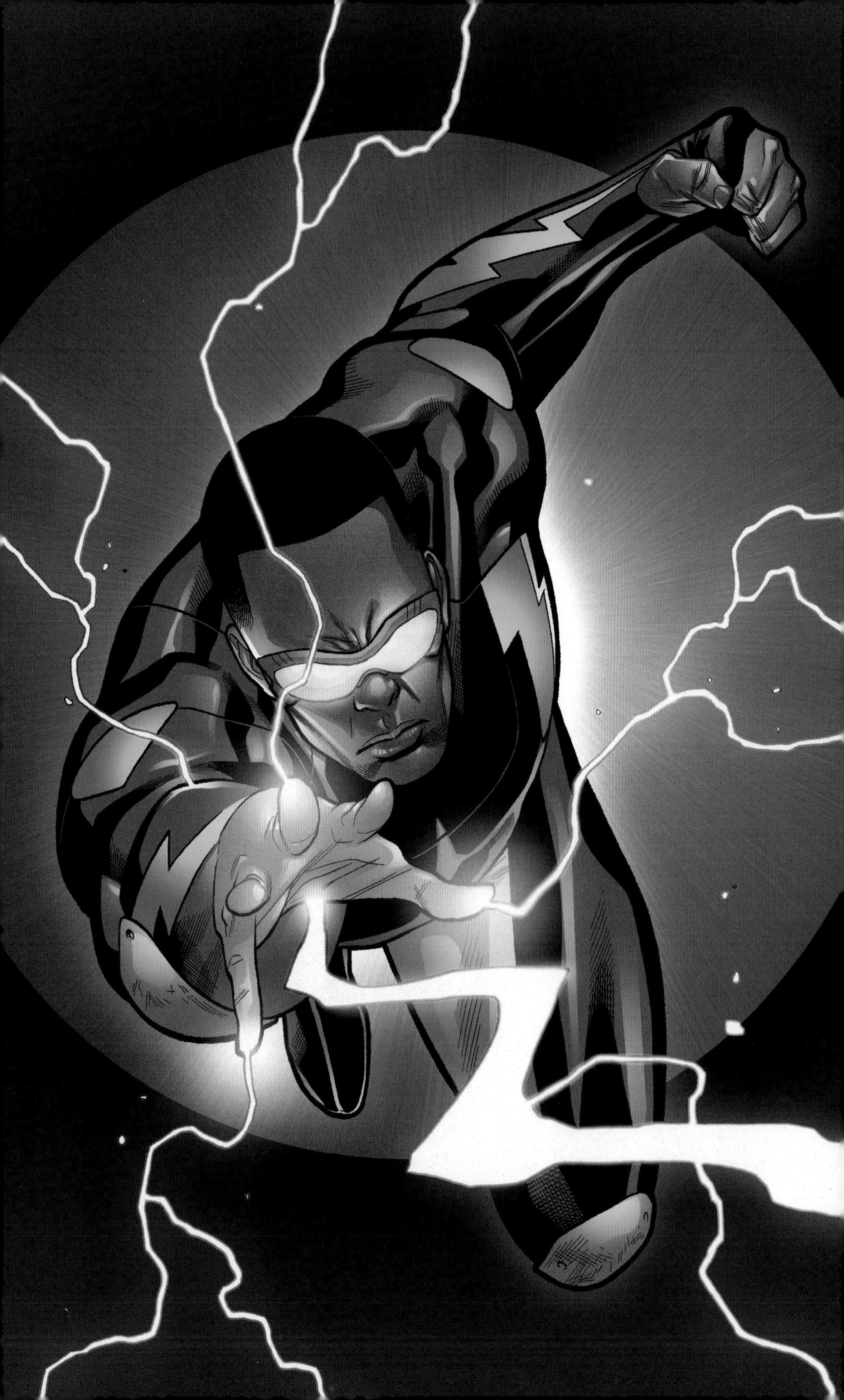

JIM CHADWICK
Editor - Original Series
HARVEY RICHARDS
ROB LEVIN
Associate Editors - Original Series
JEB WOODARD
Group Editor - Collected Editions
TYLER-MARIE EVANS
Editor - Collected Edition
STEVE COOK
Design Director - Books
CURTIS KING JR.
Publication Design

BOB HARRAS
Senior VP - Editor-in-Chief, DC Comics
PAT McCALLUM
Executive Editor, DC Comics

DAN DiDIO
Publisher
JIM LEE
Publisher & Chief Creative Officer
AMIT DESAI
Executive VP - Business & Marketing Strategy,
Direct to Consumer & Global Franchise Management
BOBBIE CHASE
VP & Executive Editor, Young Reader & Talent Development
MARK CHIARELLO
Senior VP - Art, Design & Collected Editions
JOHN CUNNINGHAM
Senior VP - Sales & Trade Marketing
BRIAR DARDEN
VP - Business Affairs
ANNE DePIES
Senior VP - Business Strategy, Finance & Administration
DON FALLETTI
VP - Manufacturing Operations
LAWRENCE GANEM
VP - Editorial Administration & Talent Relations
ALISON GILL
Senior VP - Manufacturing & Operations
JASON GREENBERG
VP - Business Strategy & Finance
HANK KANALZ
Senior VP - Editorial Strategy & Administration
JAY KOGAN
Senior VP - Legal Affairs
NICK J. NAPOLITANO
VP - Manufacturing Administration
LISETTE OSTERLOH
VP - Digital Marketing & Events
EDDIE SCANNELL
VP - Consumer Marketing
COURTNEY SIMMONS
Senior VP - Publicity & Communications
JIM (SKI) SOKOLOWSKI
VP - Comic Book Specialty Sales & Trade Marketing
NANCY SPEARS
VP - Mass, Book, Digital Sales & Trade Marketing
MICHELE R. WELLS
VP - Content Strategy

BLACK LIGHTNING: COLD DEAD HANDS

DC Comics
2900 West Alameda Avenue, Burbank, CA 91505

Printed by Times Printing, LLC, Random Lake, WI, USA. 9/7/18.
First Printing. ISBN: 978-1-4012-7515-0

Library of Congress Cataloging-in-Publication Data is available.

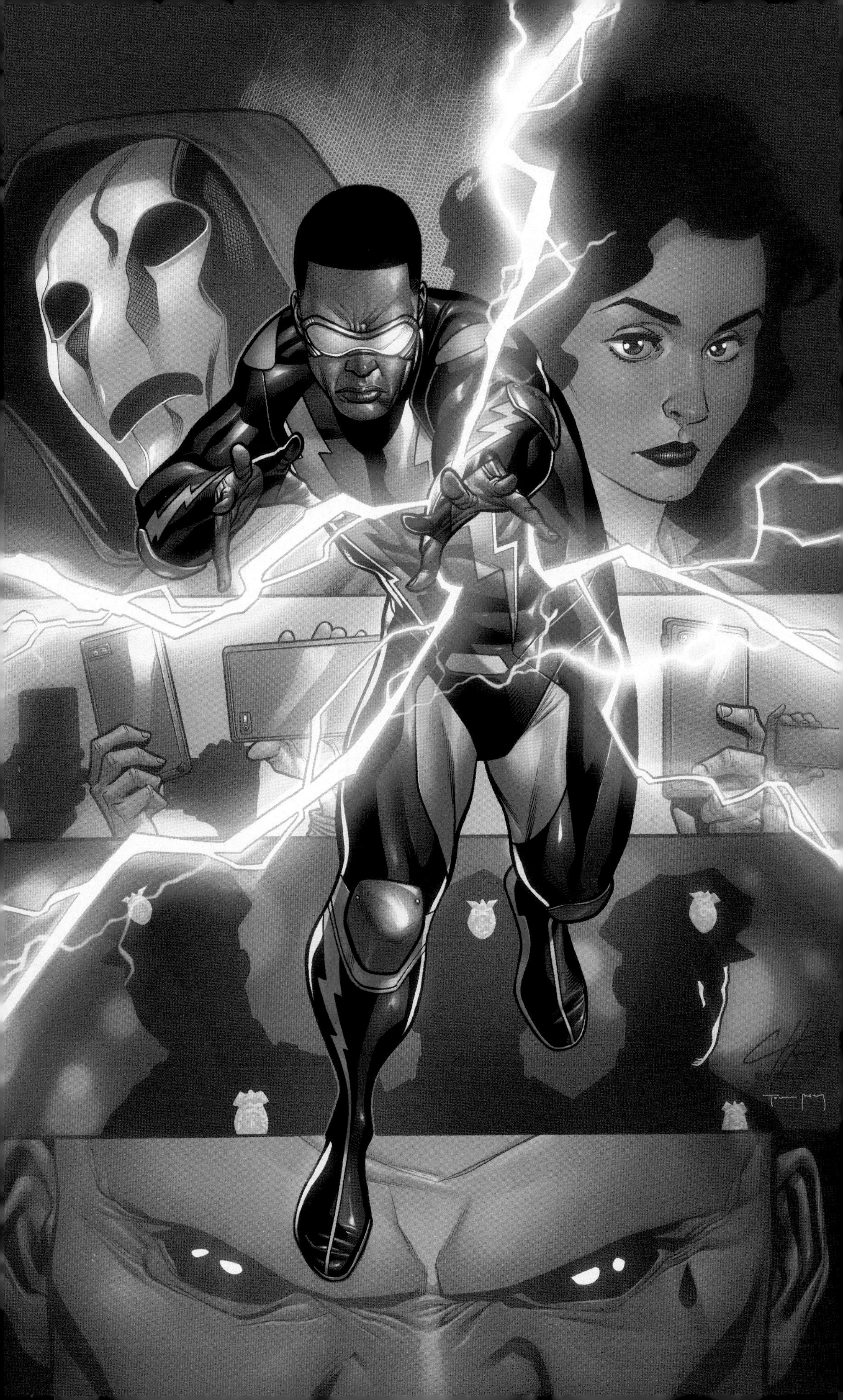

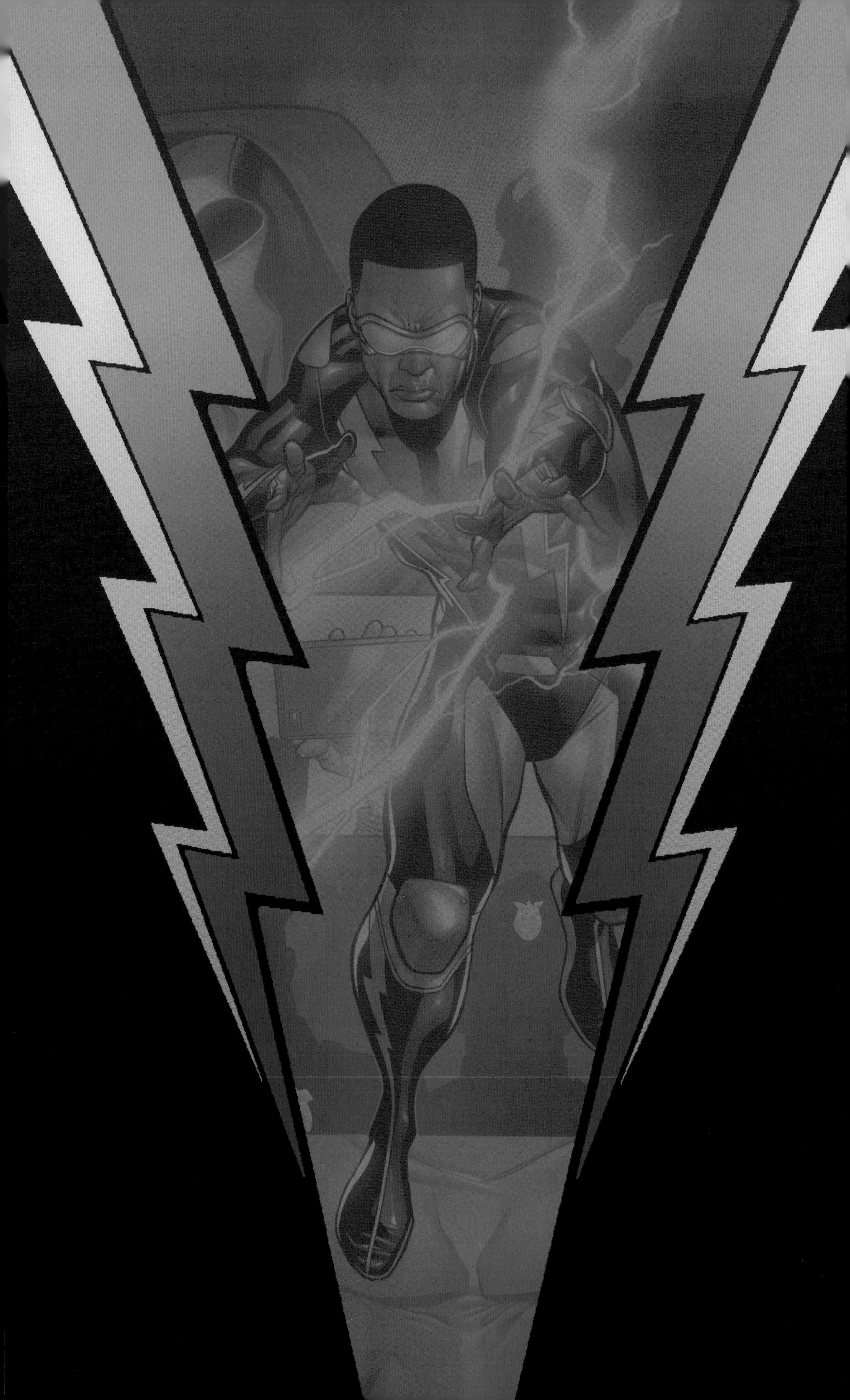

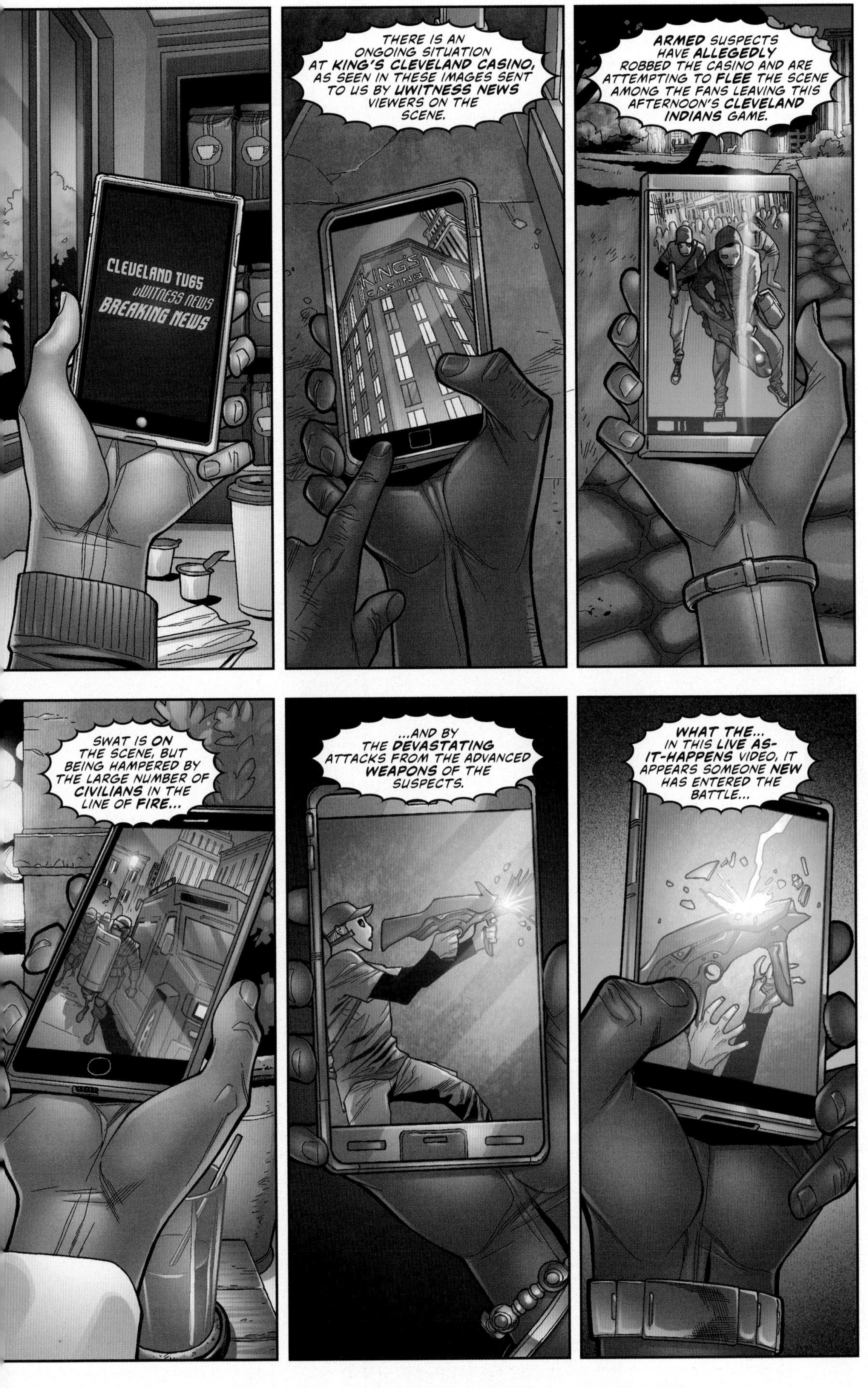

CLEVELAND TUGS
uWITNESS NEWS
BREAKING NEWS
THERE IS AN ONGOING SITUATION AT KING'S CLEVELAND CASINO, AS SEEN IN THESE IMAGES SENT TO US BY UWITNESS NEWS VIEWERS ON THE SCENE.
KING'S CASINO
ARMED SUSPECTS HAVE ALLEGEDLY ROBBED THE CASINO AND ARE ATTEMPTING TO FLEE THE SCENE AMONG THE FANS LEAVING THIS AFTERNOON'S CLEVELAND INDIANS GAME.
SWAT IS ON THE SCENE, BUT BEING HAMPERED BY THE LARGE NUMBER OF CIVILIANS IN THE LINE OF FIRE...
...AND BY THE DEVASTATING ATTACKS FROM THE ADVANCED WEAPONS OF THE SUSPECTS.
WHAT THE... IN THIS LIVE AS-IT-HAPPENS VIDEO, IT APPEARS SOMEONE NEW HAS ENTERED THE BATTLE...

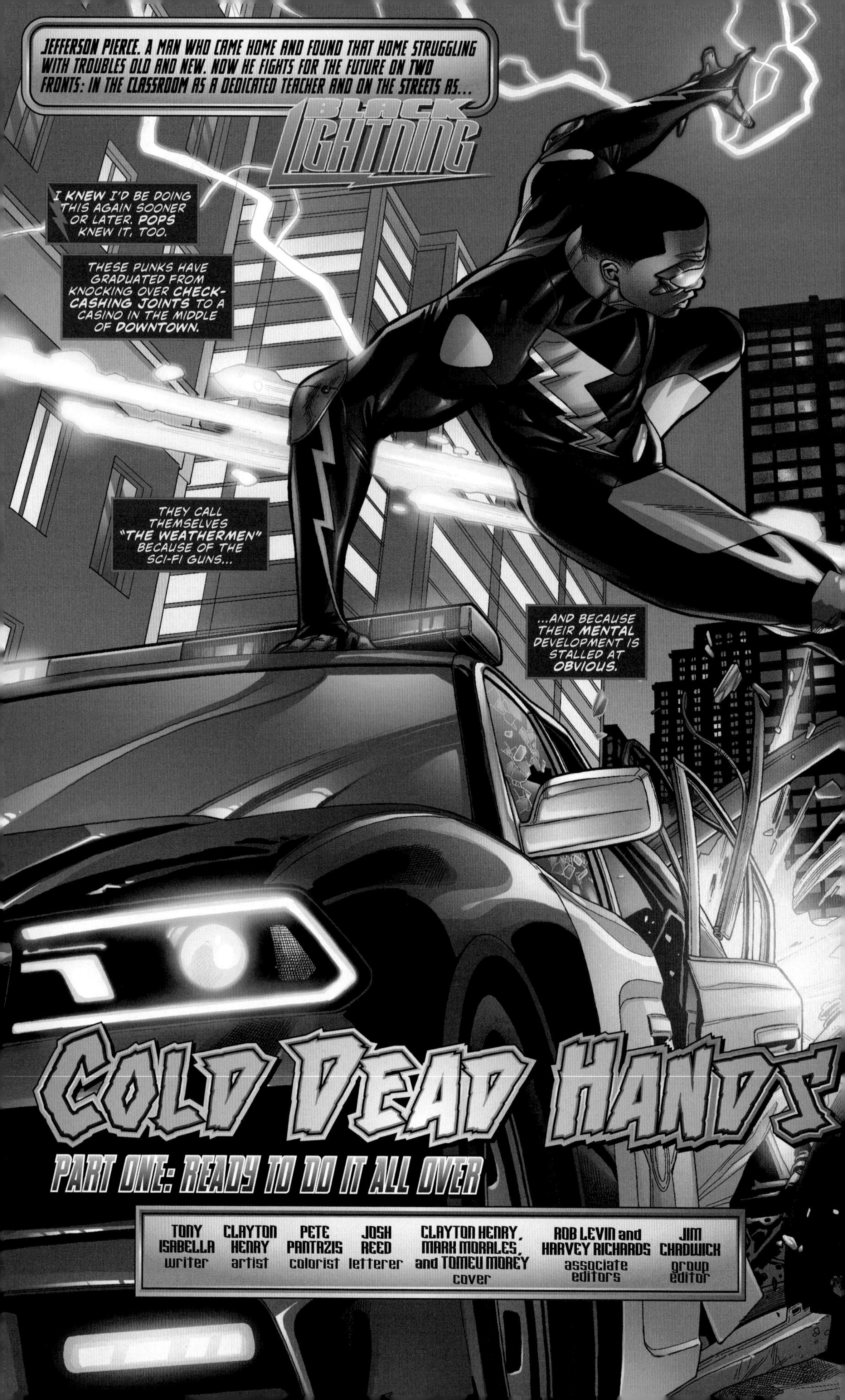
JEFFERSON PIERCE. A MAN WHO CAME HOME AND FOUND THAT HOME STRUGGLING WITH TROUBLES OLD AND NEW. NOW HE FIGHTS FOR THE FUTURE ON TWO FRONTS: IN THE CLASSROOM AS A DEDICATED TEACHER AND ON THE STREETS AS...
BLACK LIGHTNING
I KNEW I'D BE DOING THIS AGAIN SOONER OR LATER. POPS KNEW IT, TOO.
THESE PUNKS HAVE GRADUATED FROM KNOCKING OVER CHECK-CASHING JOINTS TO A CASINO IN THE MIDDLE OF DOWNTOWN.
THEY CALL THEMSELVES "THE WEATHERMEN" BECAUSE OF THE SCI-FI GUNS...
...AND BECAUSE THEIR MENTAL DEVELOPMENT IS STALLED AT OBVIOUS.
COLD DEAD HANDS
PART ONE: READY TO DO IT ALL OVER
TONY ISABELLA writer
CLAYTON HENRY artist
PETE PANTAZIS colorist
JOSH REED letterer
CLAYTON HENRY, MARK MORALES, and TOMEU MOREY cover
ROB LEVIN and HARVEY RICHARDS associate editors
JIM CHADWICK group editor

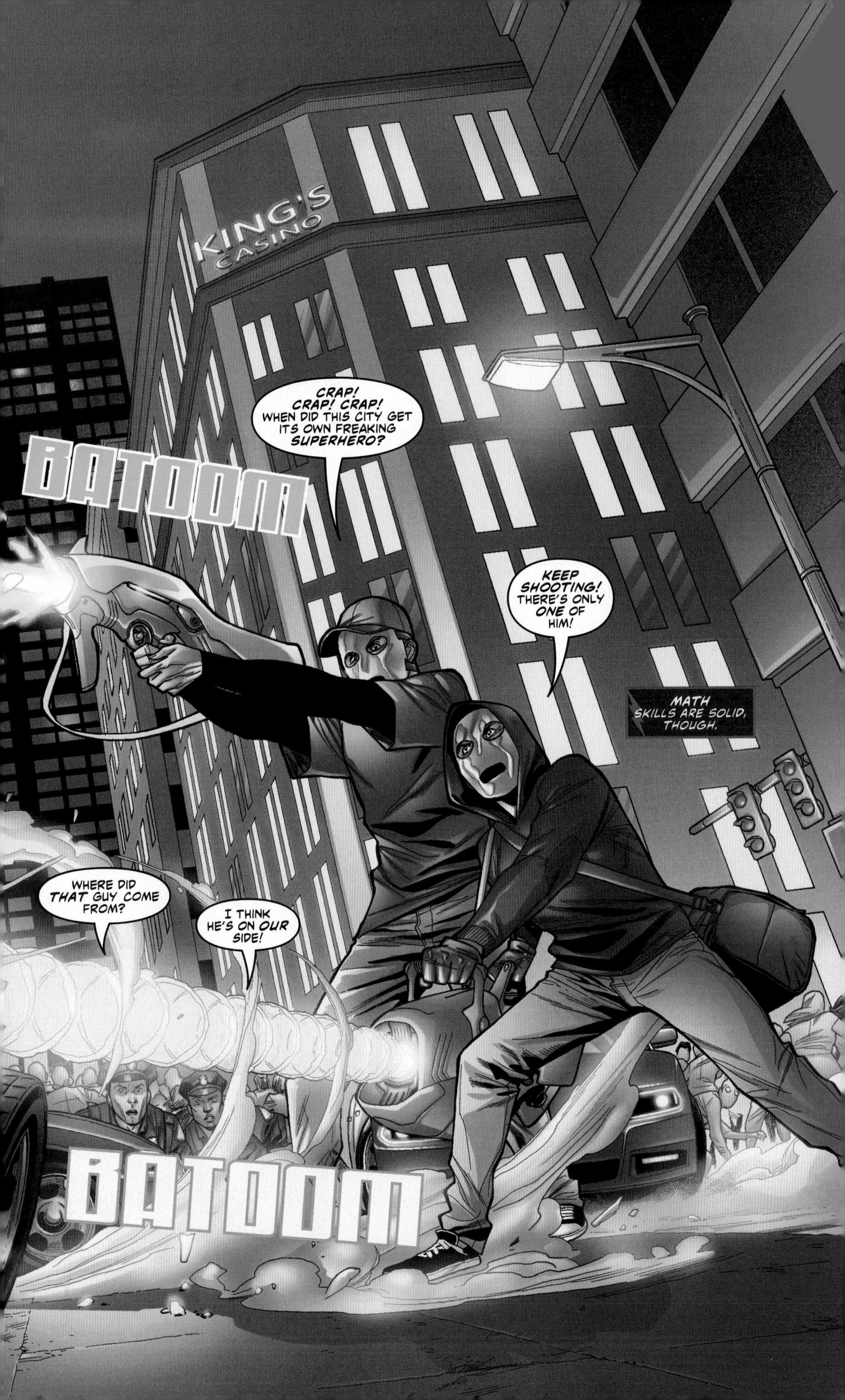
KING'S CASINO
BATOOM
CRAP! CRAP! CRAP! WHEN DID THIS CITY GET ITS OWN FREAKING SUPERHERO?
KEEP SHOOTING! THERE'S ONLY ONE OF HIM!
MATH SKILLS ARE SOLID, THOUGH.
WHERE DID THAT GUY COME FROM?
I THINK HE'S ON OUR SIDE!
BATOOM

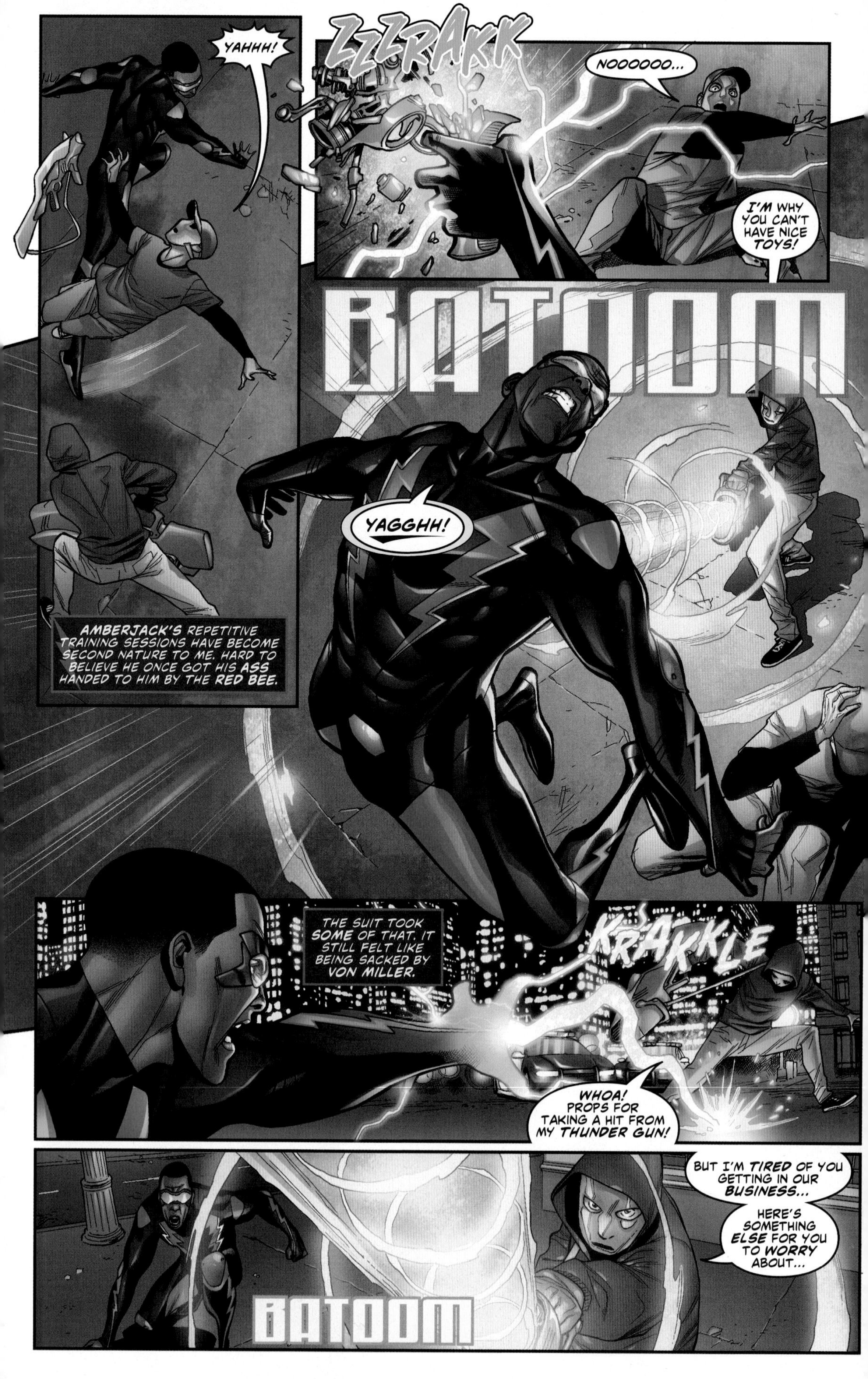
YAHHH!
ZZZRAKK
NOOOOOO...
I'M WHY YOU CAN'T HAVE NICE TOYS!
BATOOM
AMBERJACK'S REPETITIVE TRAINING SESSIONS HAVE BECOME SECOND NATURE TO ME. HARD TO BELIEVE HE ONCE GOT HIS ASS HANDED TO HIM BY THE RED BEE.
YAGGHH!
THE SUIT TOOK SOME OF THAT. IT STILL FELT LIKE BEING SACKED BY VON MILLER.
KRAKKLE
WHOA! PROPS FOR TAKING A HIT FROM MY THUNDER GUN!
BUT I'M TIRED OF YOU GETTING IN OUR BUSINESS...
HERE'S SOMETHING ELSE FOR YOU TO WORRY ABOUT...
BATOOM

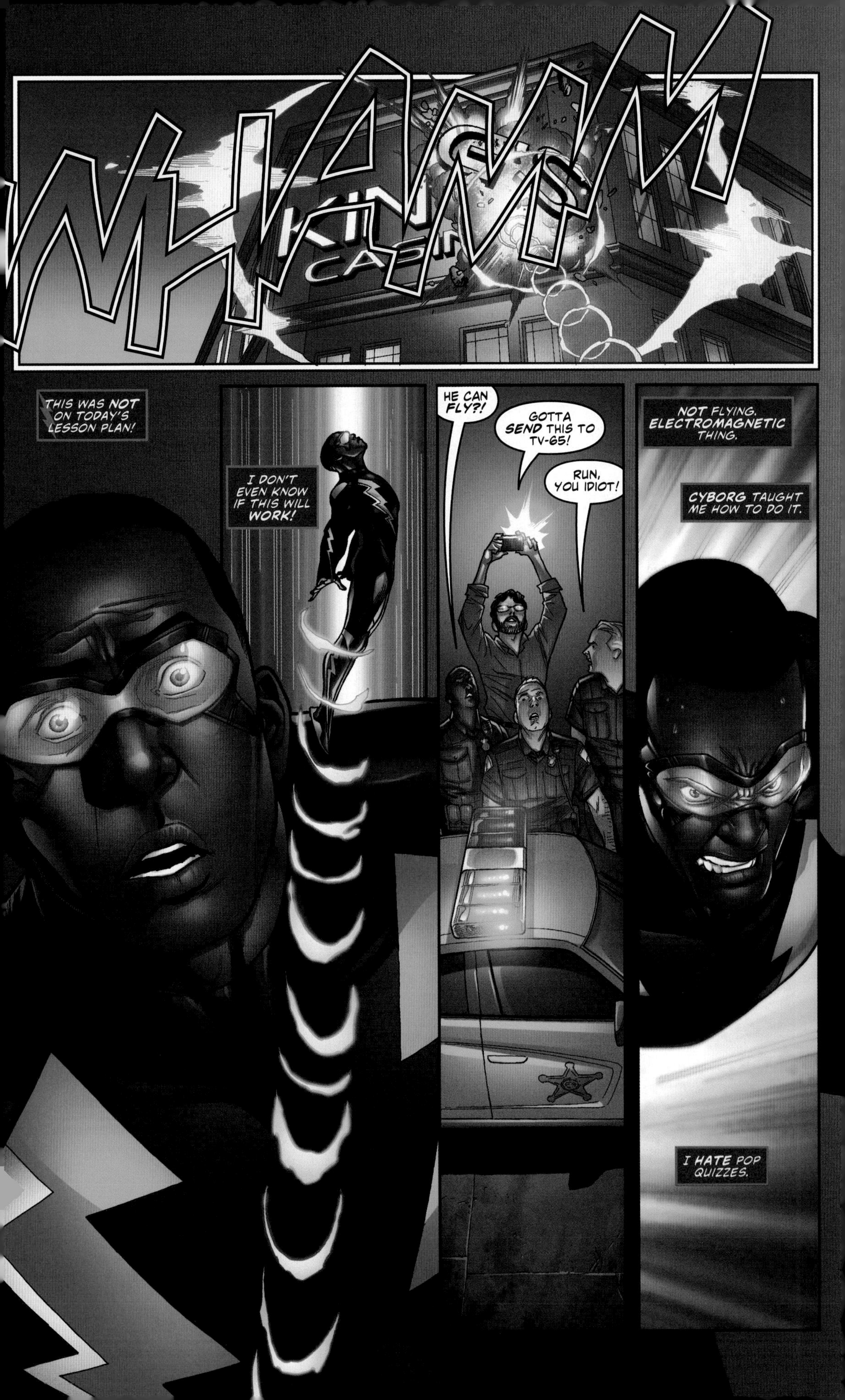
WHAMM
THIS WAS NOT ON TODAY'S LESSON PLAN!
I DON'T EVEN KNOW IF THIS WILL WORK!
HE CAN FLY?!
GOTTA SEND THIS TO TV-65!
RUN, YOU IDIOT!
NOT FLYING. ELECTROMAGNETIC THING.
CYBORG TAUGHT ME HOW TO DO IT.
I HATE POP QUIZZES.

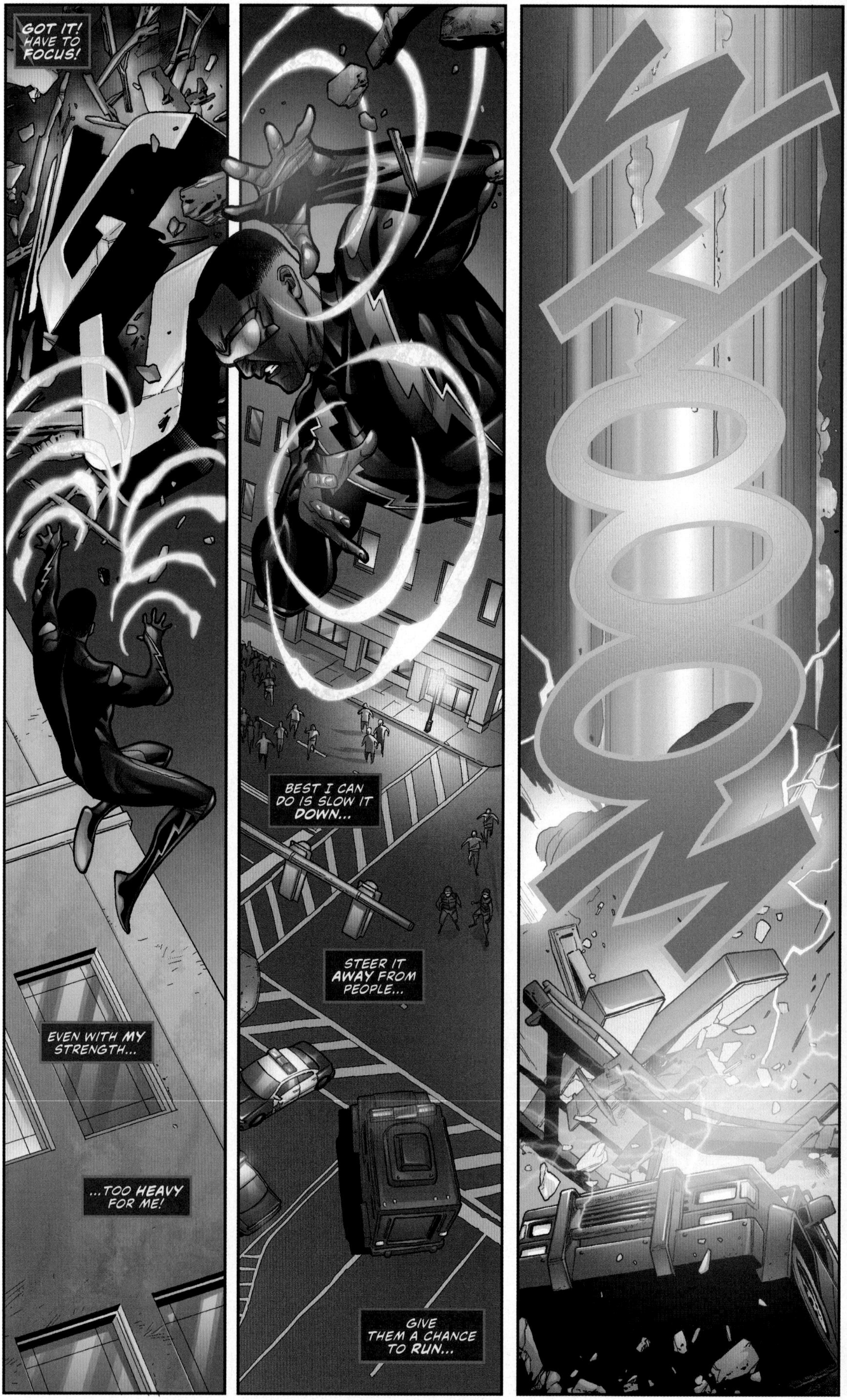

GOT IT! HAVE TO FOCUS!
EVEN WITH MY STRENGTH...
...TOO HEAVY FOR ME!
BEST I CAN DO IS SLOW IT DOWN...
STEER IT AWAY FROM PEOPLE...
GIVE THEM A CHANCE TO RUN...
SHOOOM

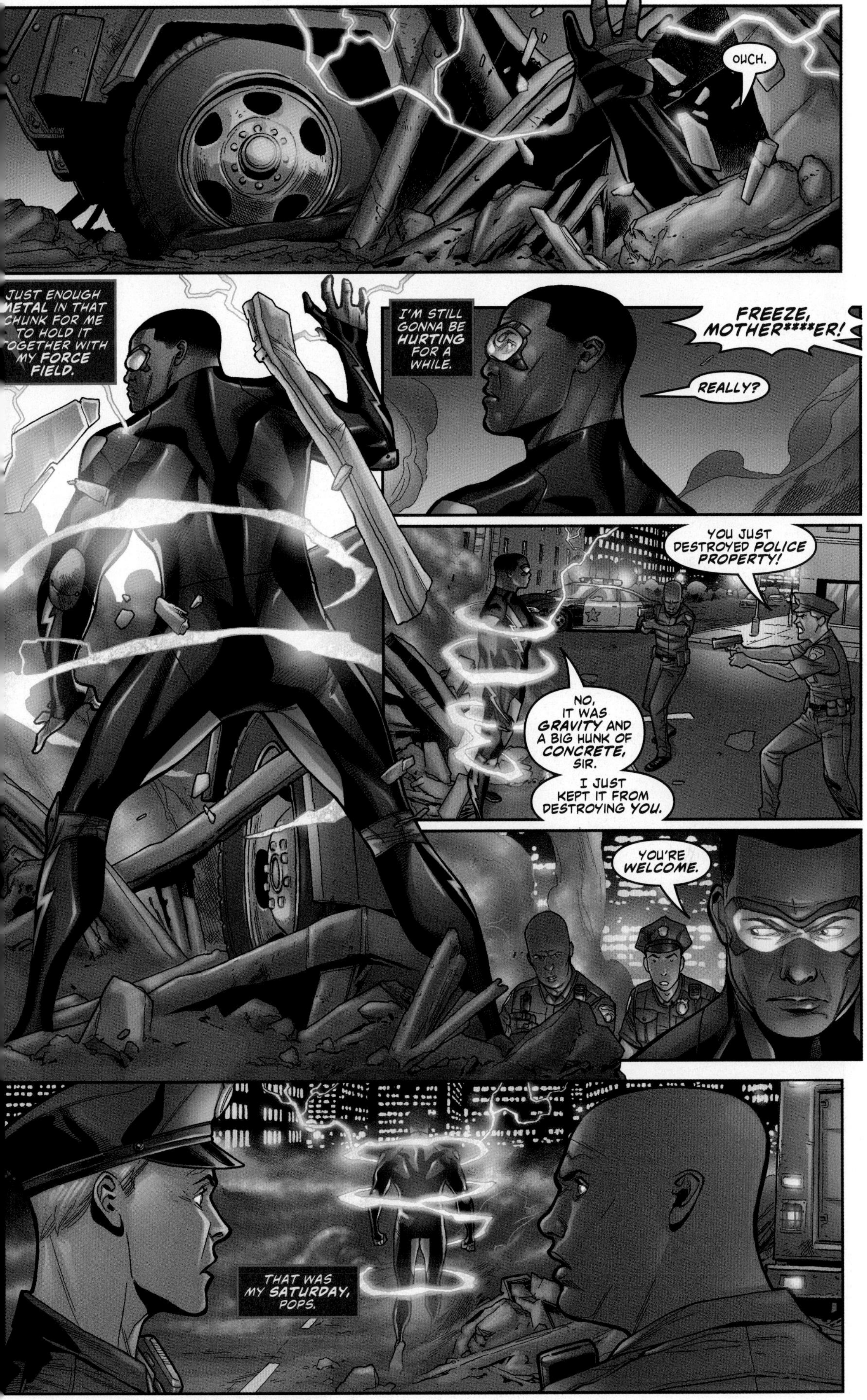
OUCH.
JUST ENOUGH METAL IN THAT CHUNK FOR ME TO HOLD IT TOGETHER WITH MY FORCE FIELD.
I'M STILL GONNA BE HURTING FOR A WHILE.
FREEZE, MOTHER****ER!
REALLY?
YOU JUST DESTROYED POLICE PROPERTY!
NO, IT WAS GRAVITY AND A BIG HUNK OF CONCRETE, SIR.
I JUST KEPT IT FROM DESTROYING YOU.
YOU'RE WELCOME.
THAT WAS MY SATURDAY, POPS.

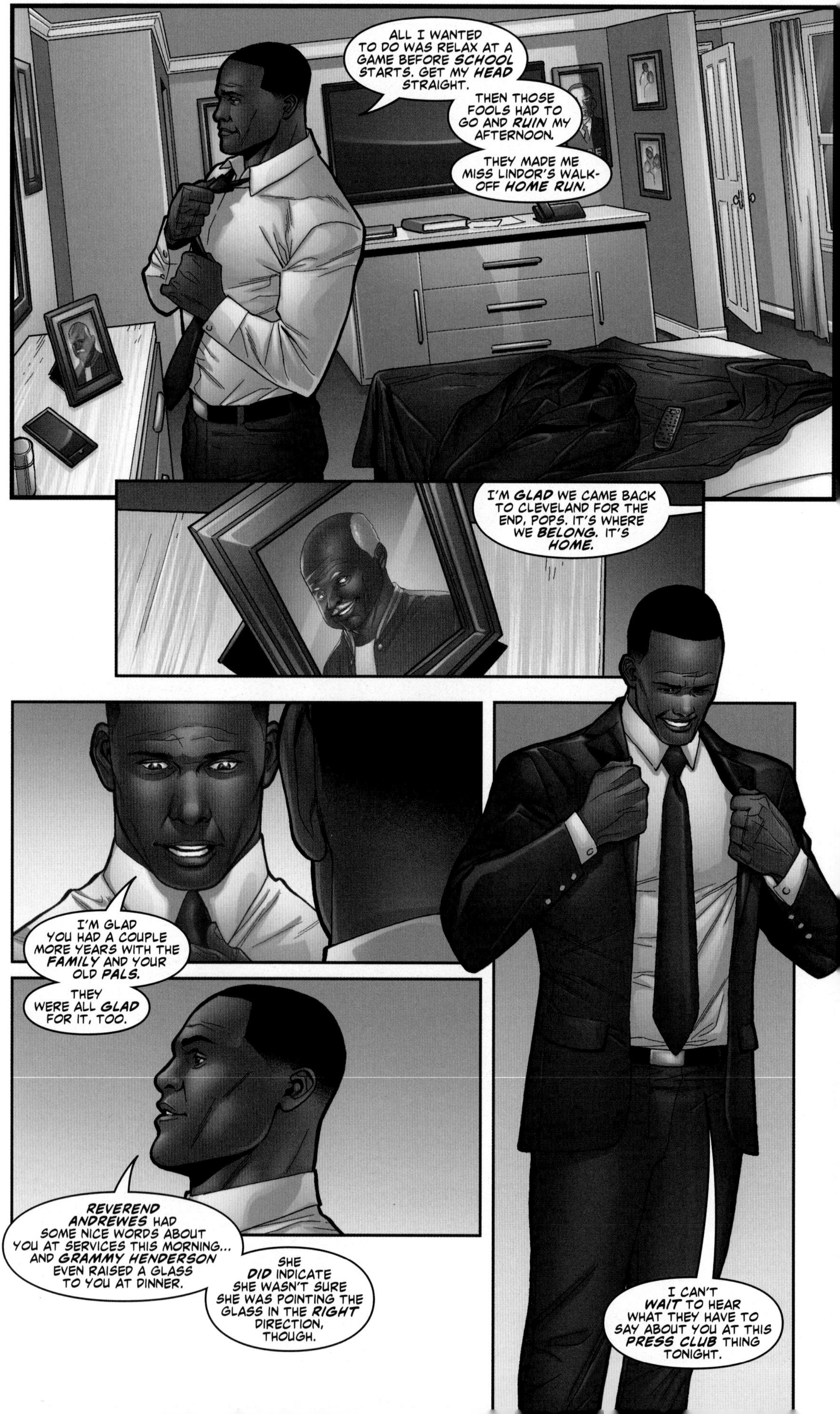
ALL I WANTED TO DO WAS RELAX AT A GAME BEFORE SCHOOL STARTS. GET MY HEAD STRAIGHT.
THEN THOSE FOOLS HAD TO GO AND RUIN MY AFTERNOON.
THEY MADE ME MISS LINDOR'S WALK-OFF HOME RUN.
I'M GLAD WE CAME BACK TO CLEVELAND FOR THE END, POPS. IT'S WHERE WE BELONG. IT'S HOME.
I'M GLAD YOU HAD A COUPLE MORE YEARS WITH THE FAMILY AND YOUR OLD PALS.
THEY WERE ALL GLAD FOR IT, TOO.
REVEREND ANDREWES HAD SOME NICE WORDS ABOUT YOU AT SERVICES THIS MORNING... AND GRAMMY HENDERSON EVEN RAISED A GLASS TO YOU AT DINNER.
SHE DID INDICATE SHE WASN'T SURE SHE WAS POINTING THE GLASS IN THE RIGHT DIRECTION, THOUGH.
I CAN'T WAIT TO HEAR WHAT THEY HAVE TO SAY ABOUT YOU AT THIS PRESS CLUB THING TONIGHT.

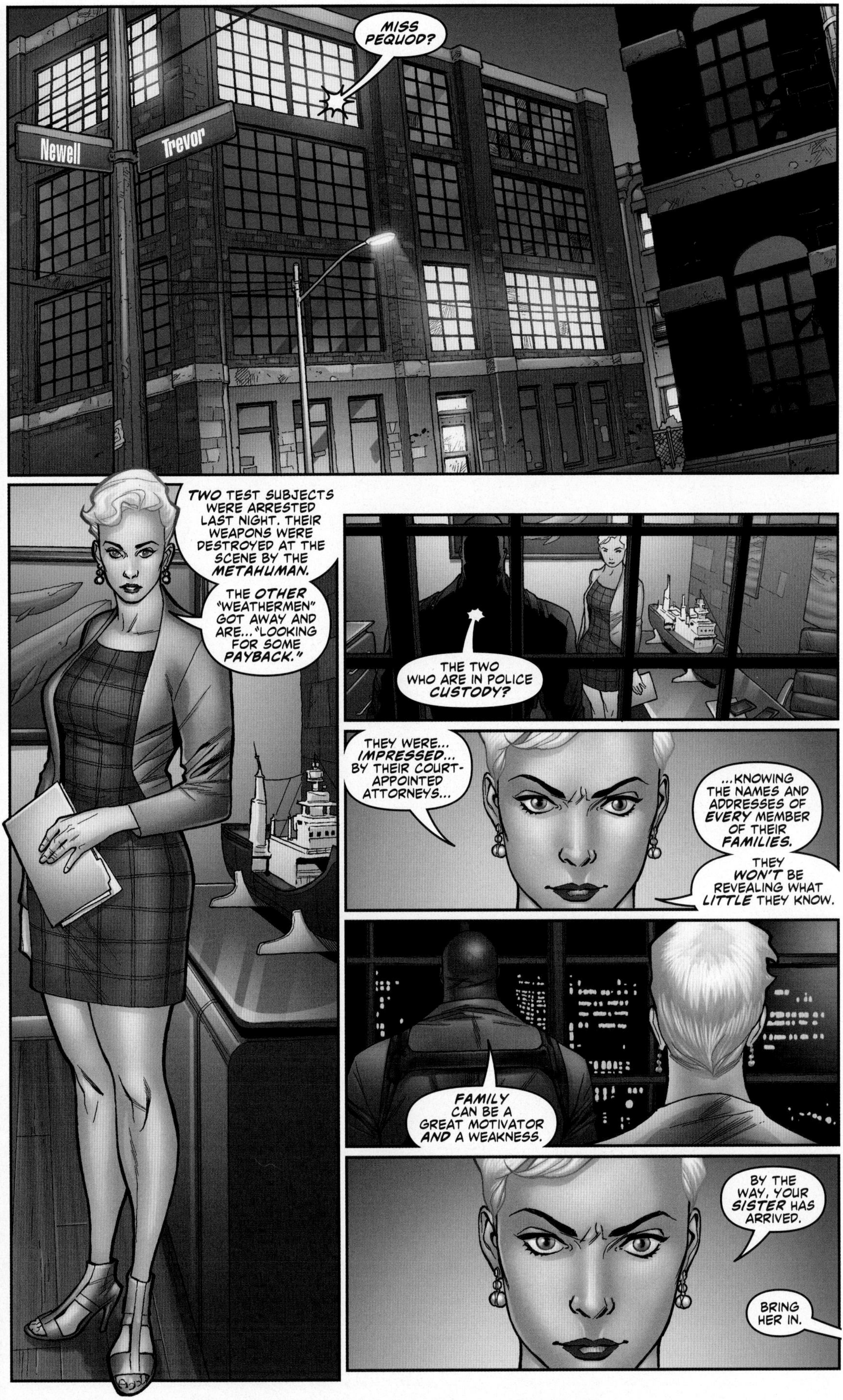

MISS PEQUOD?
Newell
Trevor
TWO TEST SUBJECTS WERE ARRESTED LAST NIGHT. THEIR WEAPONS WERE DESTROYED AT THE SCENE BY THE METAHUMAN.
THE OTHER "WEATHERMEN" GOT AWAY AND ARE... "LOOKING FOR SOME PAYBACK."
THE TWO WHO ARE IN POLICE CUSTODY?
THEY WERE... IMPRESSED... BY THEIR COURT-APPOINTED ATTORNEYS...
...KNOWING THE NAMES AND ADDRESSES OF EVERY MEMBER OF THEIR FAMILIES.
THEY WON'T BE REVEALING WHAT LITTLE THEY KNOW.
FAMILY CAN BE A GREAT MOTIVATOR AND A WEAKNESS.
BY THE WAY, YOUR SISTER HAS ARRIVED.
BRING HER IN.

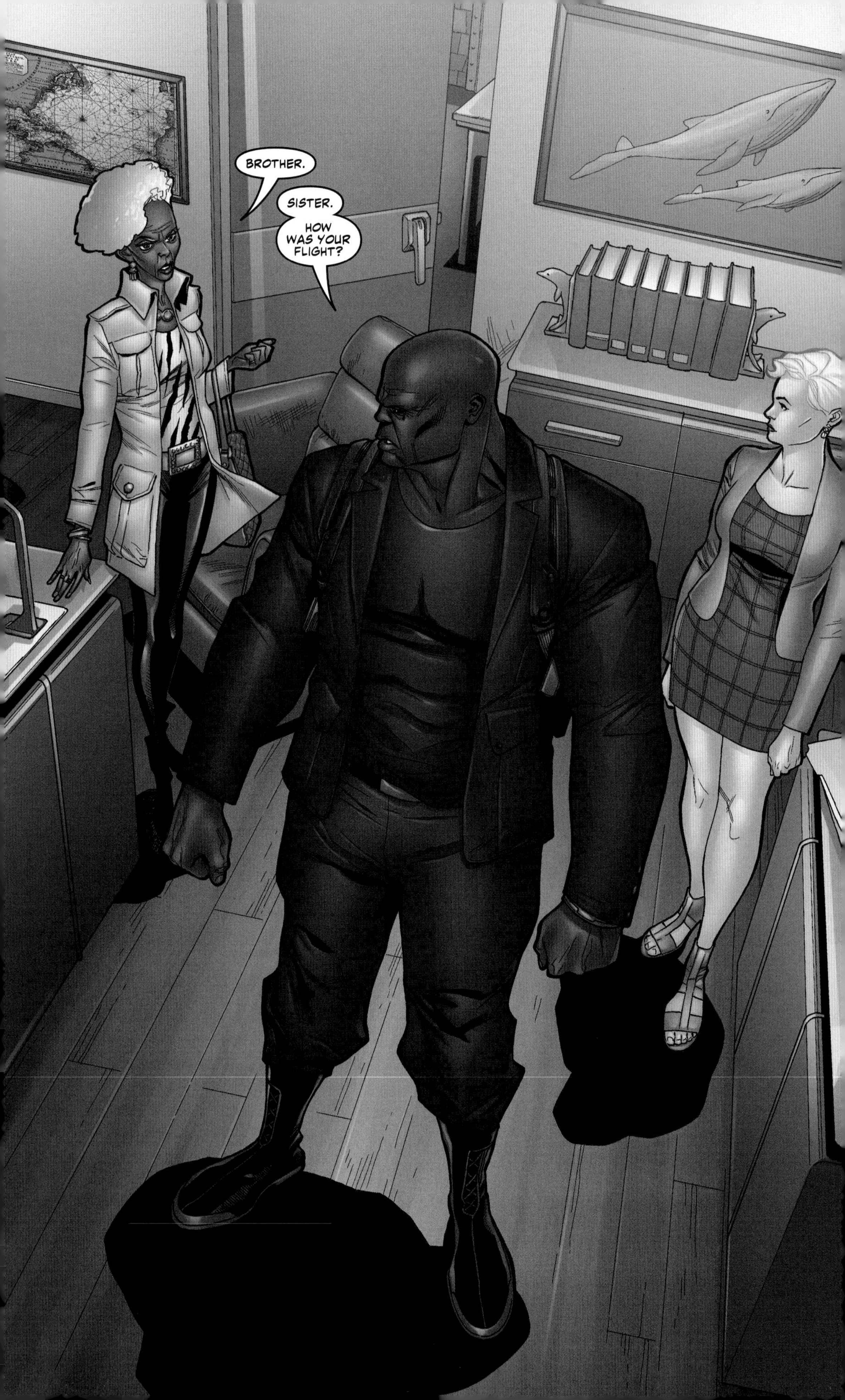
BROTHER.
SISTER.
HOW WAS YOUR FLIGHT?

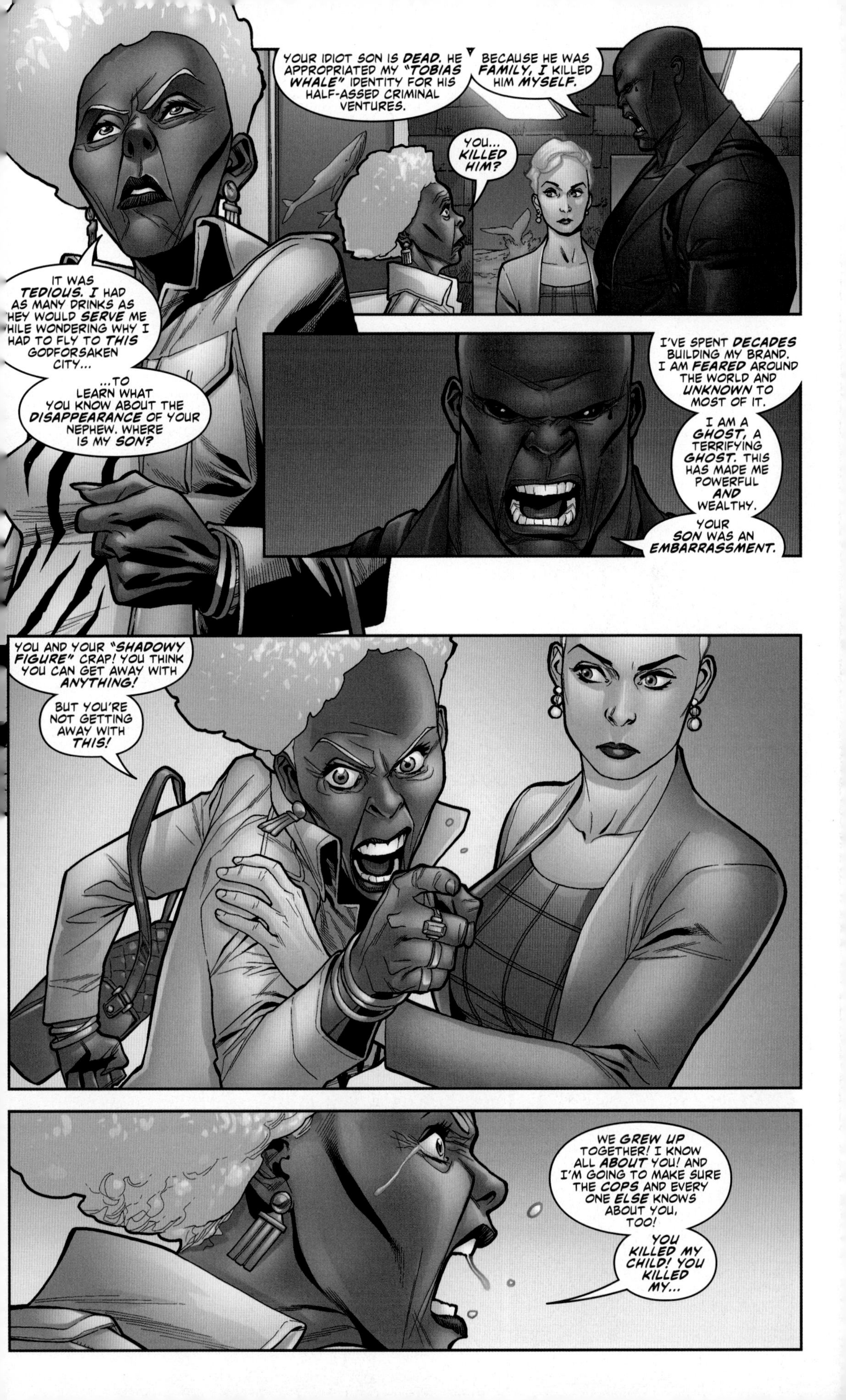
YOUR IDIOT SON IS DEAD. HE APPROPRIATED MY "TOBIAS WHALE" IDENTITY FOR HIS HALF-ASSED CRIMINAL VENTURES.
BECAUSE HE WAS FAMILY, I KILLED HIM MYSELF.
YOU... KILLED HIM?
IT WAS TEDIOUS. I HAD AS MANY DRINKS AS HEY WOULD SERVE ME HILE WONDERING WHY I HAD TO FLY TO THIS GODFORSAKEN CITY...
...TO LEARN WHAT YOU KNOW ABOUT THE DISAPPEARANCE OF YOUR NEPHEW. WHERE IS MY SON?
I'VE SPENT DECADES BUILDING MY BRAND. I AM FEARED AROUND THE WORLD AND UNKNOWN TO MOST OF IT.
I AM A GHOST, A TERRIFYING GHOST. THIS HAS MADE ME POWERFUL AND WEALTHY.
YOUR SON WAS AN EMBARRASSMENT.
YOU AND YOUR "SHADOWY FIGURE" CRAP! YOU THINK YOU CAN GET AWAY WITH ANYTHING!
BUT YOU'RE NOT GETTING AWAY WITH THIS!
WE GREW UP TOGETHER! I KNOW ALL ABOUT YOU! AND I'M GOING TO MAKE SURE THE COPS AND EVERY ONE ELSE KNOWS ABOUT YOU, TOO!
YOU KILLED MY CHILD! YOU KILLED MY...

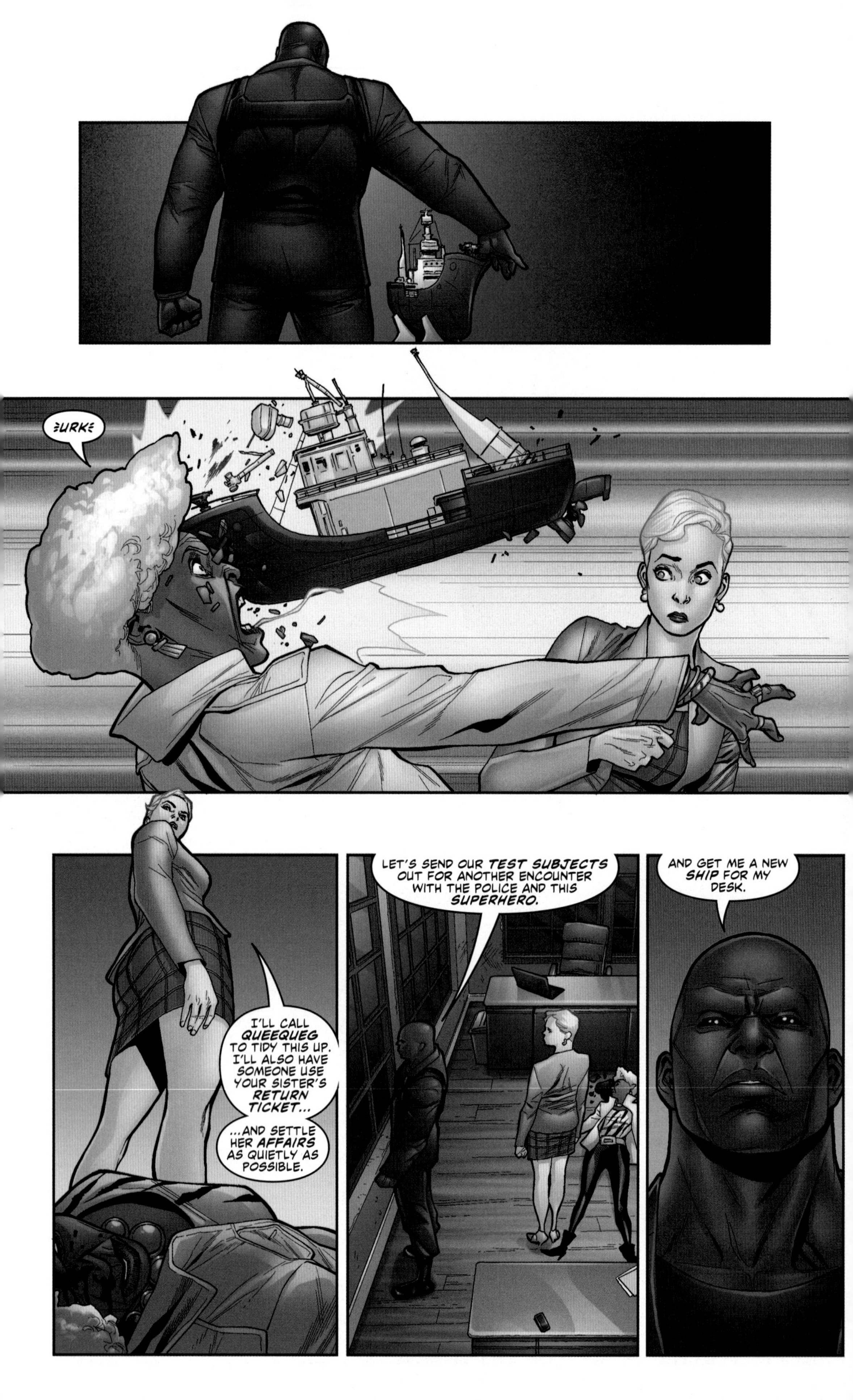
URK
I'LL CALL QUEEQUEG TO TIDY THIS UP. I'LL ALSO HAVE SOMEONE USE YOUR SISTER'S RETURN TICKET...
...AND SETTLE HER AFFAIRS AS QUIETLY AS POSSIBLE.
LET'S SEND OUR TEST SUBJECTS OUT FOR ANOTHER ENCOUNTER WITH THE POLICE AND THIS SUPERHERO.
AND GET ME A NEW SHIP FOR MY DESK.

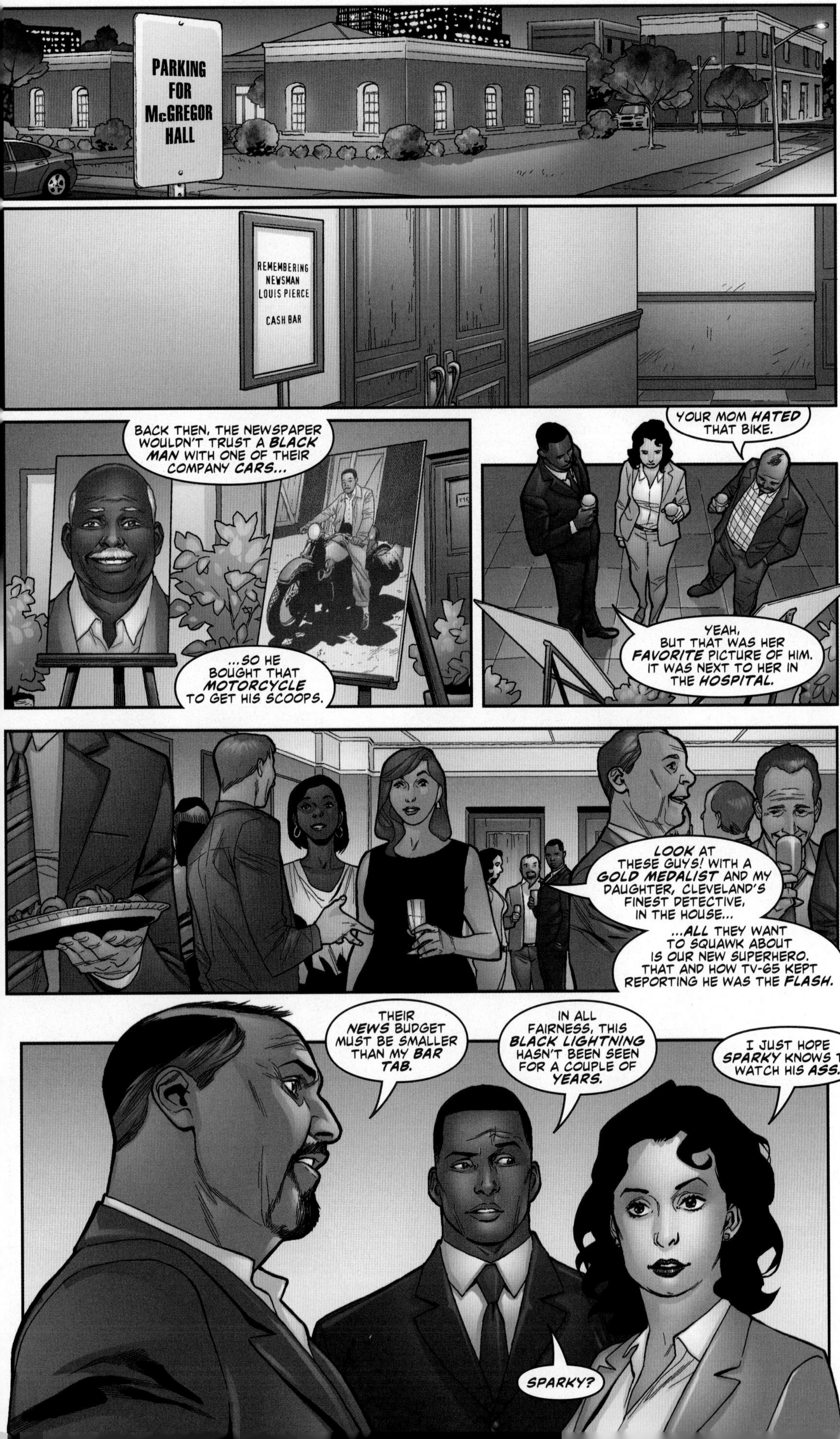
PARKING FOR McGREGOR HALL
REMEMBERING NEWSMAN LOUIS PIERCE
CASH BAR
BACK THEN, THE NEWSPAPER WOULDN'T TRUST A BLACK MAN WITH ONE OF THEIR COMPANY CARS...
...SO HE BOUGHT THAT MOTORCYCLE TO GET HIS SCOOPS.
YOUR MOM HATED THAT BIKE.
YEAH, BUT THAT WAS HER FAVORITE PICTURE OF HIM. IT WAS NEXT TO HER IN THE HOSPITAL.
LOOK AT THESE GUYS! WITH A GOLD MEDALIST AND MY DAUGHTER, CLEVELAND'S FINEST DETECTIVE, IN THE HOUSE...
...ALL THEY WANT TO SQUAWK ABOUT IS OUR NEW SUPERHERO. THAT AND HOW TV-65 KEPT REPORTING HE WAS THE FLASH.
THEIR NEWS BUDGET MUST BE SMALLER THAN MY BAR TAB.
IN ALL FAIRNESS, THIS BLACK LIGHTNING HASN'T BEEN SEEN FOR A COUPLE OF YEARS.
I JUST HOPE SPARKY KNOWS TO WATCH HIS ASS.
SPARKY?

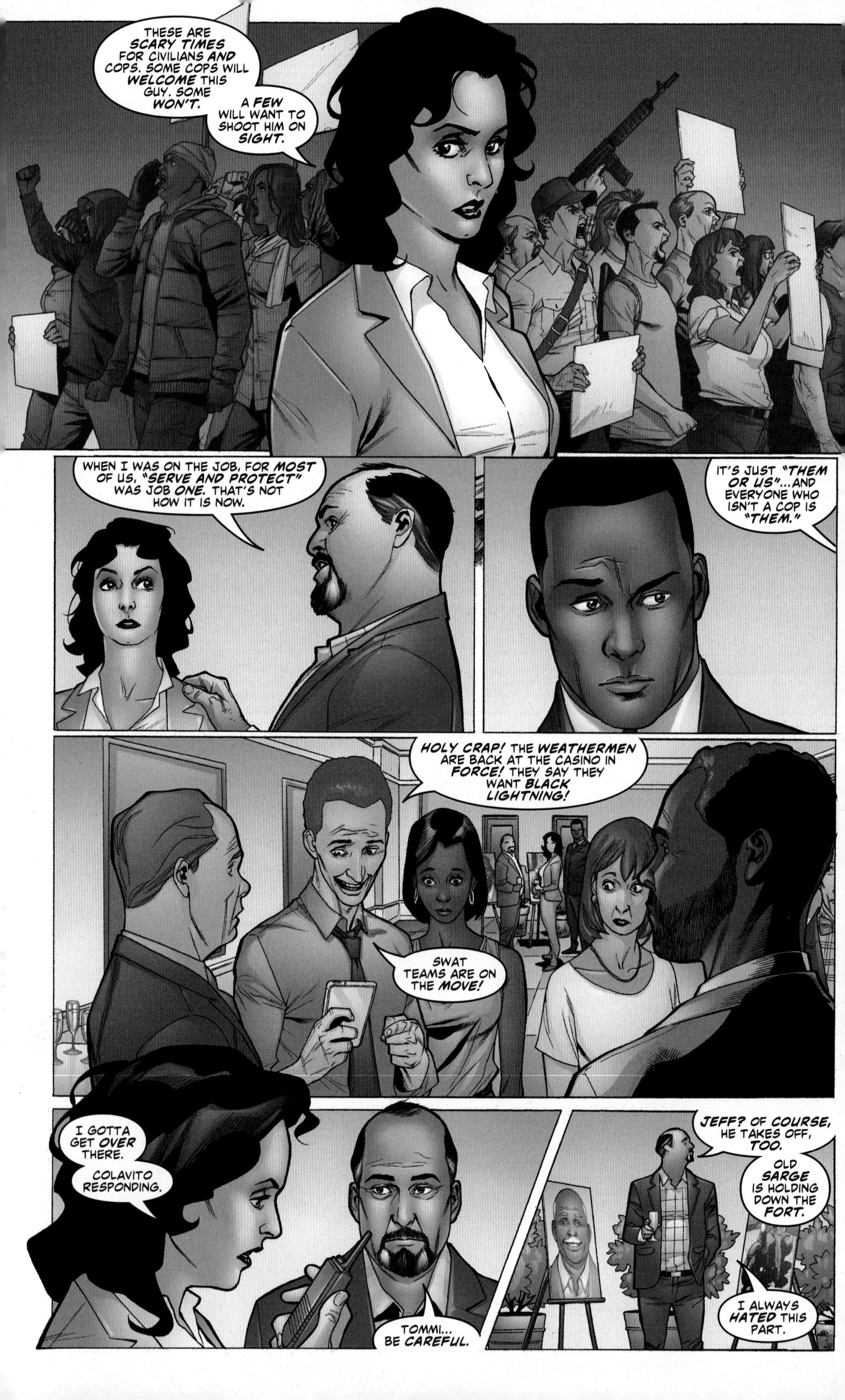
THESE ARE SCARY TIMES FOR CIVILIANS AND COPS. SOME COPS WILL WELCOME THIS GUY. SOME WON'T.
A FEW WILL WANT TO SHOOT HIM ON SIGHT.
WHEN I WAS ON THE JOB, FOR MOST OF US, "SERVE AND PROTECT" WAS JOB ONE. THAT'S NOT HOW IT IS NOW.
IT'S JUST "THEM OR US"...AND EVERYONE WHO ISN'T A COP IS "THEM."
HOLY CRAP! THE WEATHERMEN ARE BACK AT THE CASINO IN FORCE! THEY SAY THEY WANT BLACK LIGHTNING!
SWAT TEAMS ARE ON THE MOVE!
I GOTTA GET OVER THERE.
COLAVITO RESPONDING.
TOMMI... BE CAREFUL.
JEFF? OF COURSE, HE TAKES OFF, TOO.
OLD SARGE IS HOLDING DOWN THE FORT.
I ALWAYS HATED THIS PART.

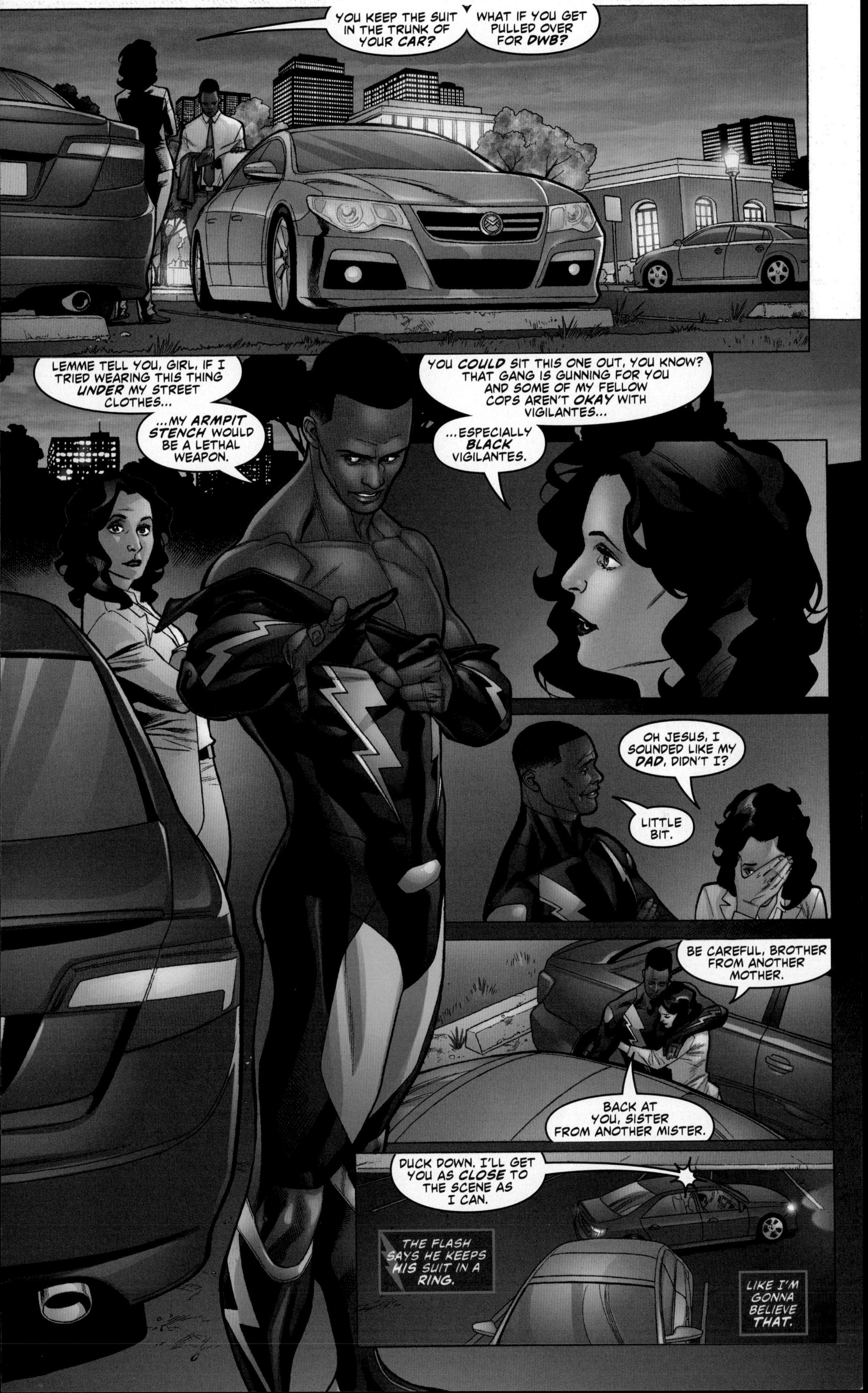

YOU KEEP THE SUIT IN THE TRUNK OF YOUR CAR?
WHAT IF YOU GET PULLED OVER FOR DWB?
LEMME TELL YOU, GIRL, IF I TRIED WEARING THIS THING UNDER MY STREET CLOTHES...
...MY ARMPIT STENCH WOULD BE A LETHAL WEAPON.
YOU COULD SIT THIS ONE OUT, YOU KNOW? THAT GANG IS GUNNING FOR YOU AND SOME OF MY FELLOW COPS AREN'T OKAY WITH VIGILANTES...
...ESPECIALLY BLACK VIGILANTES.
OH JESUS, I SOUNDED LIKE MY DAD, DIDN'T I?
LITTLE BIT.
BE CAREFUL, BROTHER FROM ANOTHER MOTHER.
BACK AT YOU, SISTER FROM ANOTHER MISTER.
DUCK DOWN. I'LL GET YOU AS CLOSE TO THE SCENE AS I CAN.
THE FLASH SAYS HE KEEPS HIS SUIT IN A RING.
LIKE I'M GONNA BELIEVE THAT.

STAND DOWN, *LADY COP.* THIS IS *SWAT'S* SHOW.

YOU'RE SO *CUTE* WHEN YOU PRETEND YOU HAVE *STONES.*

DENISE, NOW WHAT HAVE I *TOLD* YOU ABOUT TEASING THE FELLAS? WE MIGHT *NEED* THEM SOMEDAY.

I NEED *YOU* WAY BEHIND OUR FRONT LINES.

LET ME *EXPLAIN* THINGS, OFFICER. I'M *DETECTIVE TOMMI COLAVITO* AND I *OUTRANK* THE HELL OUT OF YOU.

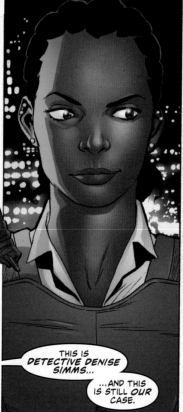

THIS IS *DETECTIVE DENISE SIMMS...*

...AND THIS IS STILL *OUR* CASE.

BECAUSE YOU'RE MY BROTHER IN BLUE, I'M GOING TO *FORGET* WHAT A *JERK* YOU'RE BEING.

WE'VE GOT *SERIOUS* WORK TO DO HERE.

YES, M'AM.

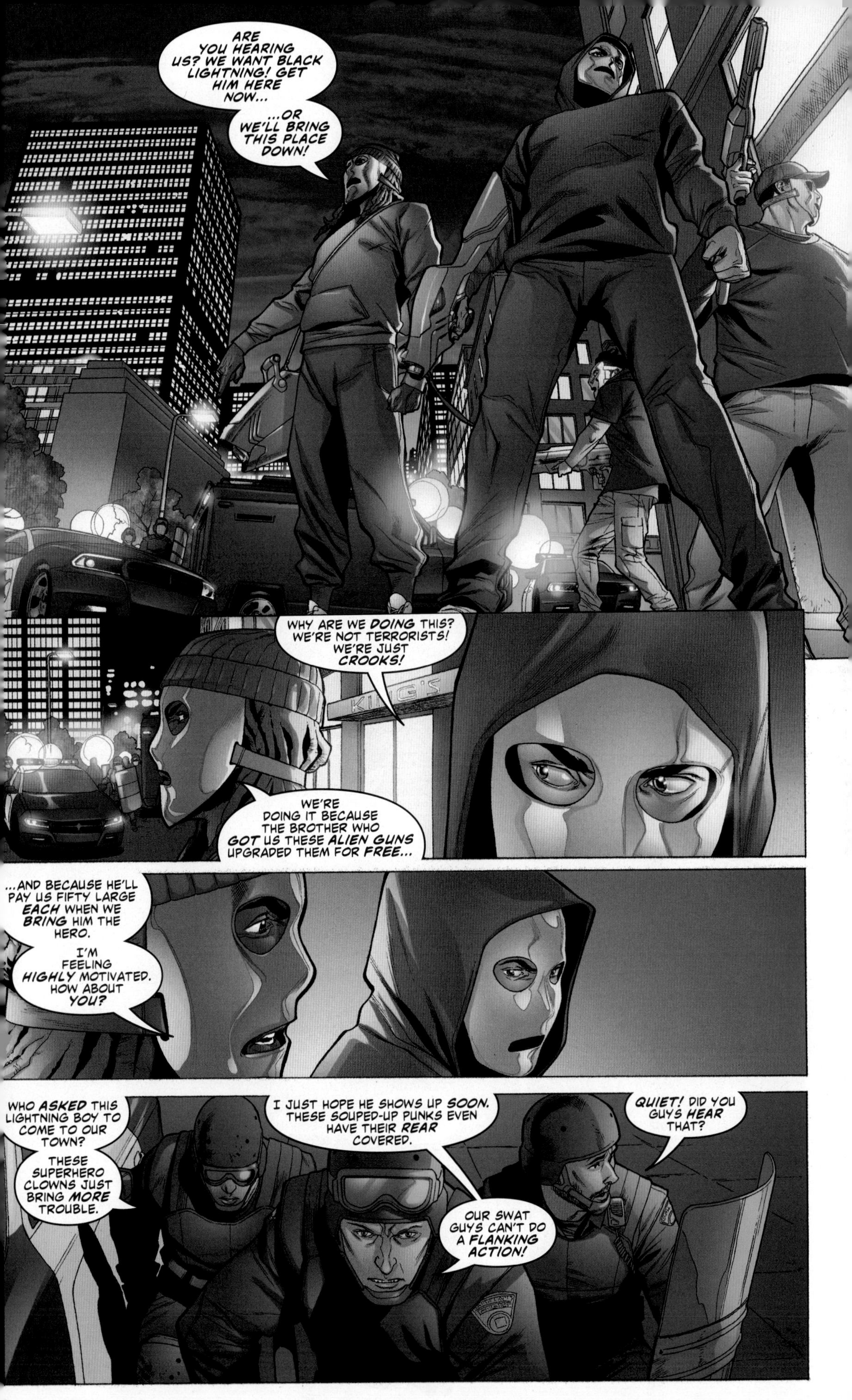
ARE YOU HEARING US? WE WANT BLACK LIGHTNING! GET HIM HERE NOW...
...OR WE'LL BRING THIS PLACE DOWN!
WHY ARE WE DOING THIS? WE'RE NOT TERRORISTS! WE'RE JUST CROOKS!
KING'S
WE'RE DOING IT BECAUSE THE BROTHER WHO GOT US THESE ALIEN GUNS UPGRADED THEM FOR FREE...
...AND BECAUSE HE'LL PAY US FIFTY LARGE EACH WHEN WE BRING HIM THE HERO.
I'M FEELING HIGHLY MOTIVATED. HOW ABOUT YOU?
WHO ASKED THIS LIGHTNING BOY TO COME TO OUR TOWN?
THESE SUPERHERO CLOWNS JUST BRING MORE TROUBLE.
I JUST HOPE HE SHOWS UP SOON. THESE SOUPED-UP PUNKS EVEN HAVE THEIR REAR COVERED.
OUR SWAT GUYS CAN'T DO A FLANKING ACTION!
QUIET! DID YOU GUYS HEAR THAT?

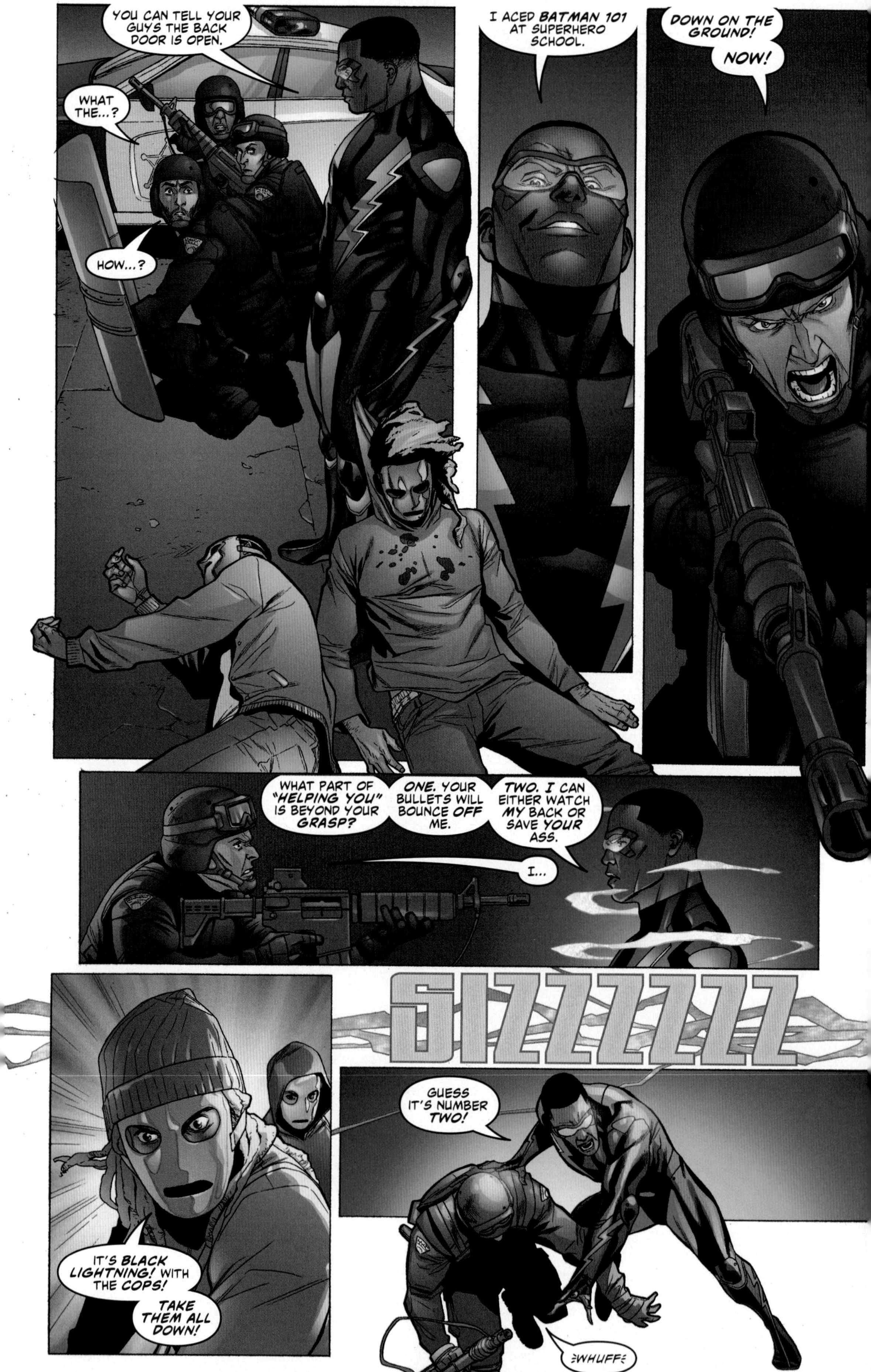
YOU CAN TELL YOUR GUYS THE BACK DOOR IS OPEN.
WHAT THE...?
HOW...?
I ACED BATMAN 101 AT SUPERHERO SCHOOL.
DOWN ON THE GROUND!
NOW!
WHAT PART OF "HELPING YOU" IS BEYOND YOUR GRASP?
ONE. YOUR BULLETS WILL BOUNCE OFF ME.
TWO. I CAN EITHER WATCH MY BACK OR SAVE YOUR ASS.
I...
SIZZZZZZ
IT'S BLACK LIGHTNING! WITH THE COPS!
TAKE THEM ALL DOWN!
GUESS IT'S NUMBER TWO!
WHUFF

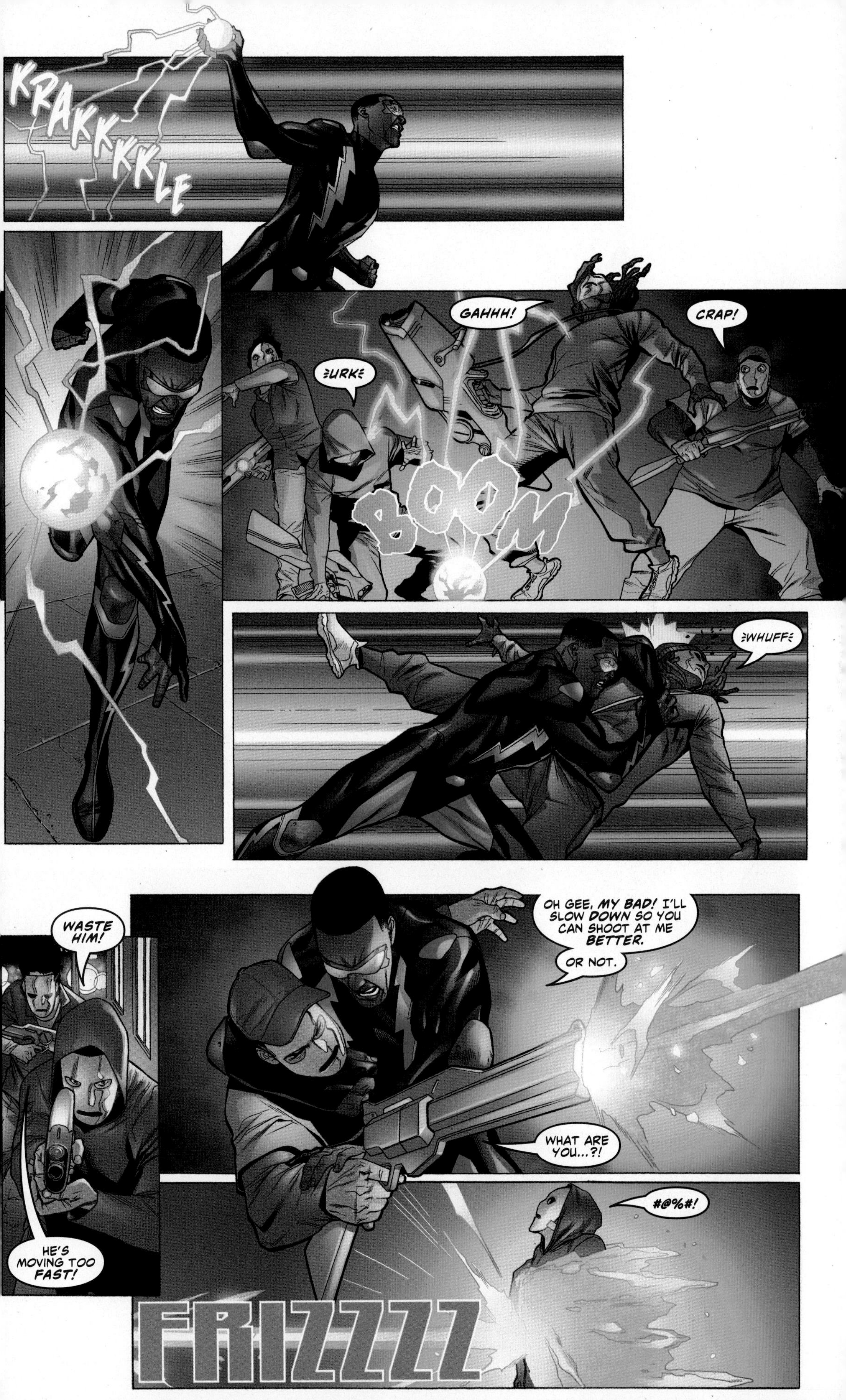
KRAKKKKLE
GAHHH!
CRAP!
URK
BOOM
WHUFF
WASTE HIM!
OH GEE, MY BAD! I'LL SLOW DOWN SO YOU CAN SHOOT AT ME BETTER.
OR NOT.
WHAT ARE YOU...?!
HE'S MOVING TOO FAST!
#@%#!
FRIZZZZ

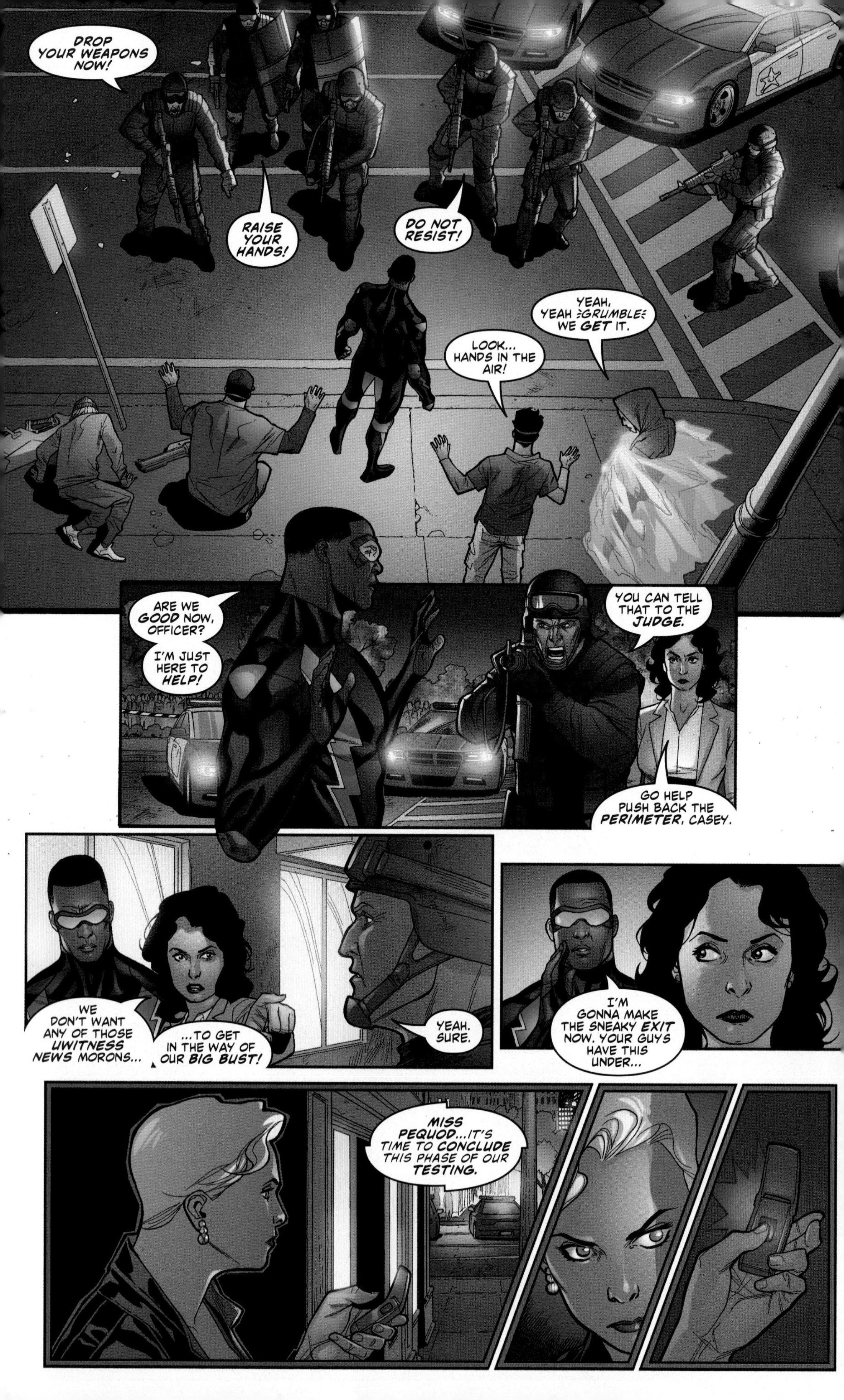
DROP YOUR WEAPONS NOW!
RAISE YOUR HANDS!
DO NOT RESIST!
LOOK... HANDS IN THE AIR!
YEAH, YEAH ≋GRUMBLE≋ WE GET IT.
ARE WE GOOD NOW, OFFICER?
I'M JUST HERE TO HELP!
YOU CAN TELL THAT TO THE JUDGE.
GO HELP PUSH BACK THE PERIMETER, CASEY.
WE DON'T WANT ANY OF THOSE UWITNESS NEWS MORONS...
...TO GET IN THE WAY OF OUR BIG BUST!
YEAH. SURE.
I'M GONNA MAKE THE SNEAKY EXIT NOW. YOUR GUYS HAVE THIS UNDER...
MISS PEQUOD...IT'S TIME TO CONCLUDE THIS PHASE OF OUR TESTING.

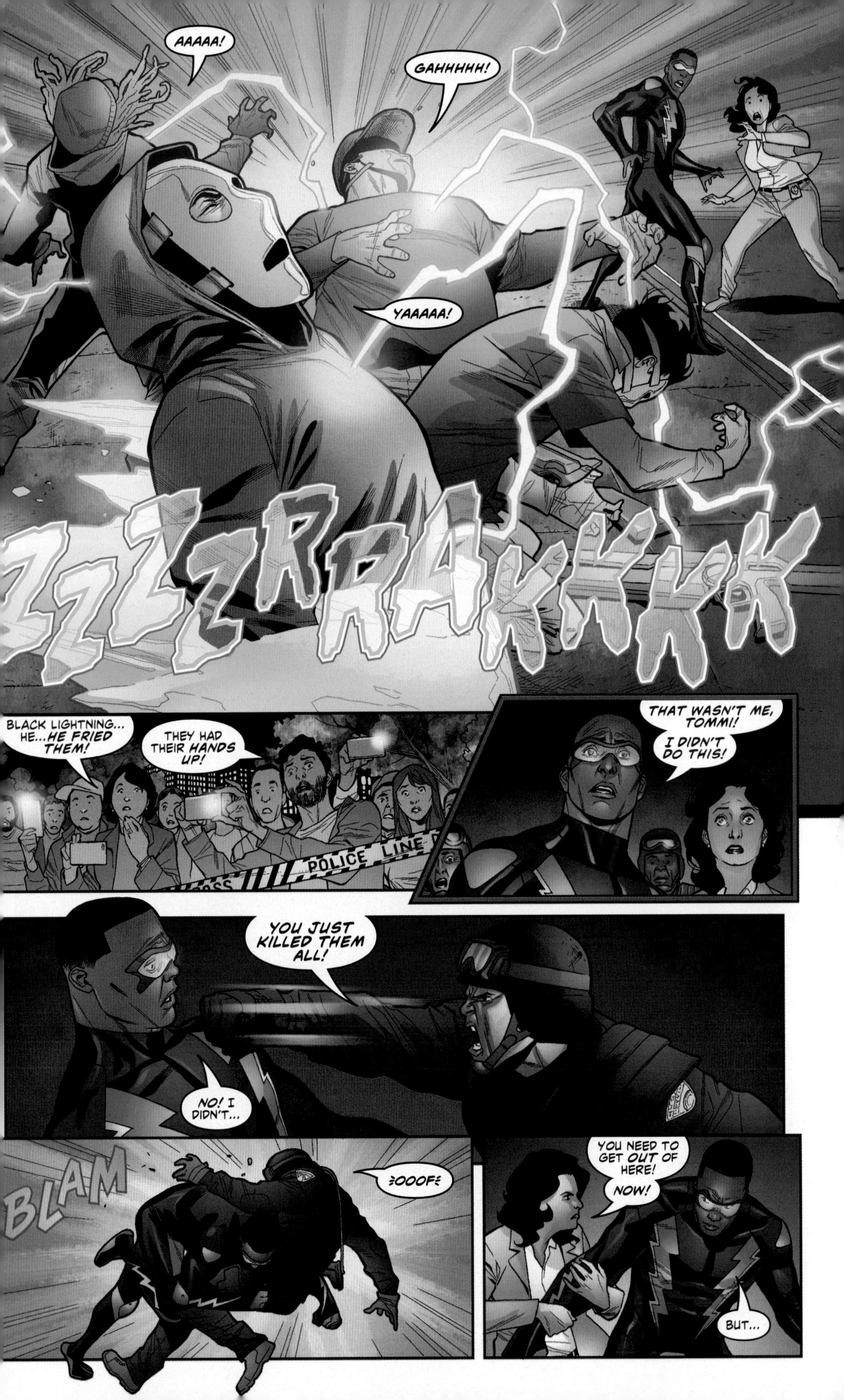
AAAAA!
GAHHHHH!
YAAAAA!
ZZZZRRRAKKKKK
BLACK LIGHTNING... HE...HE FRIED THEM!
THEY HAD THEIR HANDS UP!
POLICE LINE
THAT WASN'T ME, TOMMI!
I DIDN'T DO THIS!
YOU JUST KILLED THEM ALL!
NO! I DIDN'T...
BLAM
OOOF
YOU NEED TO GET OUT OF HERE!
NOW!
BUT...

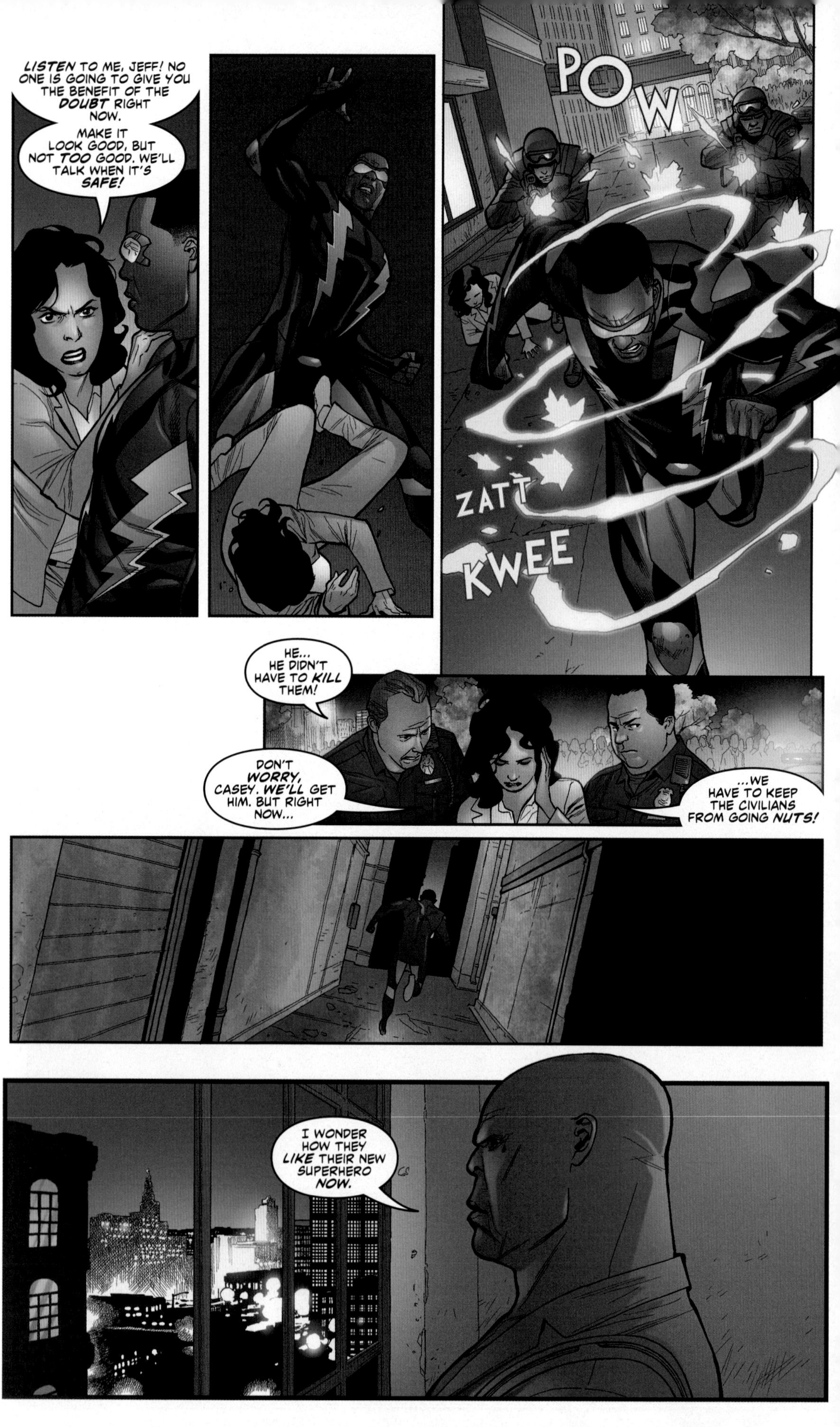

LISTEN TO ME, JEFF! NO ONE IS GOING TO GIVE YOU THE BENEFIT OF THE DOUBT RIGHT NOW.
MAKE IT LOOK GOOD, BUT NOT TOO GOOD. WE'LL TALK WHEN IT'S SAFE!
POW
ZATT
KWEE
HE... HE DIDN'T HAVE TO KILL THEM!
DON'T WORRY, CASEY. WE'LL GET HIM. BUT RIGHT NOW...
...WE HAVE TO KEEP THE CIVILIANS FROM GOING NUTS!
I WONDER HOW THEY LIKE THEIR NEW SUPERHERO NOW.

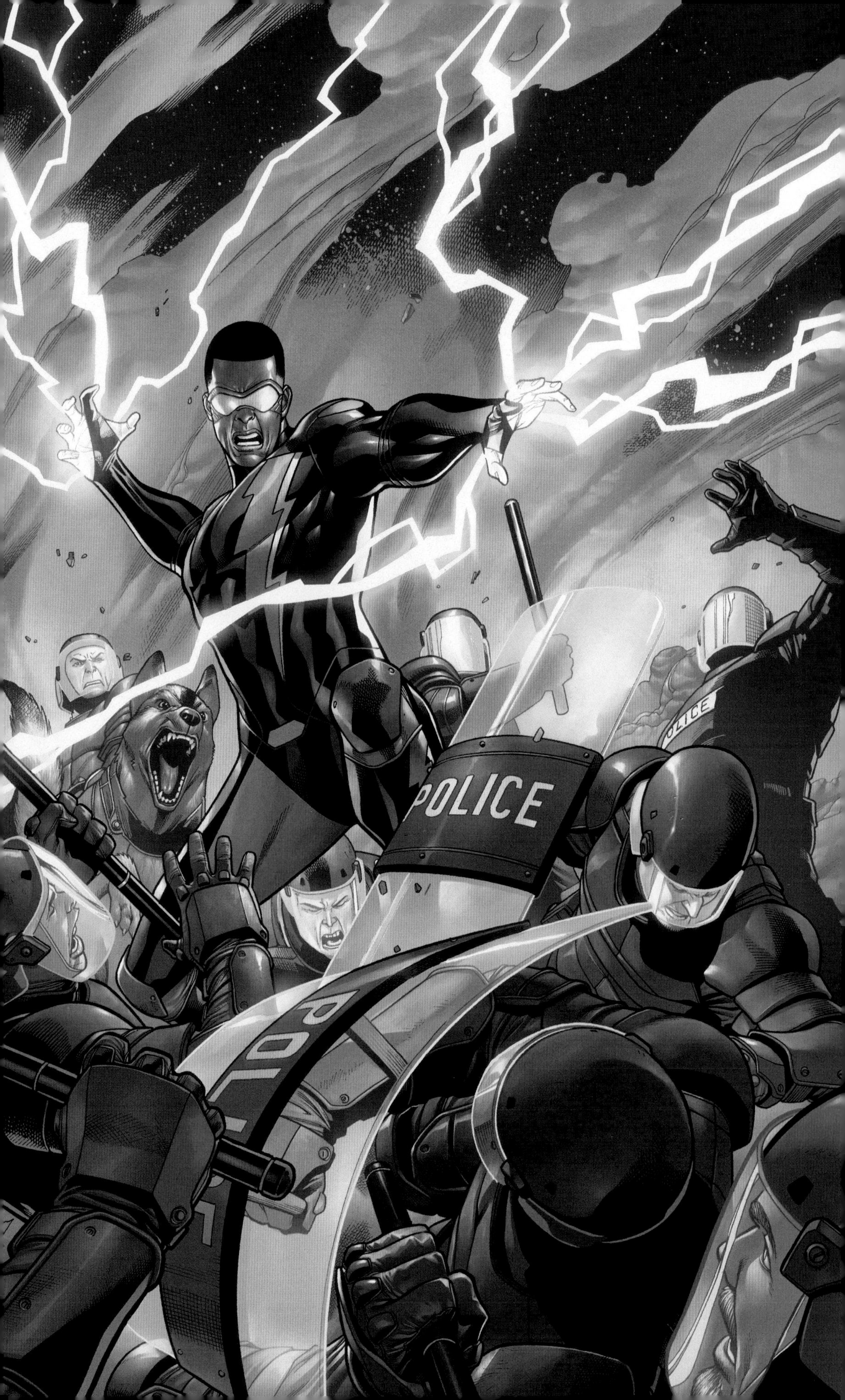
POLICE

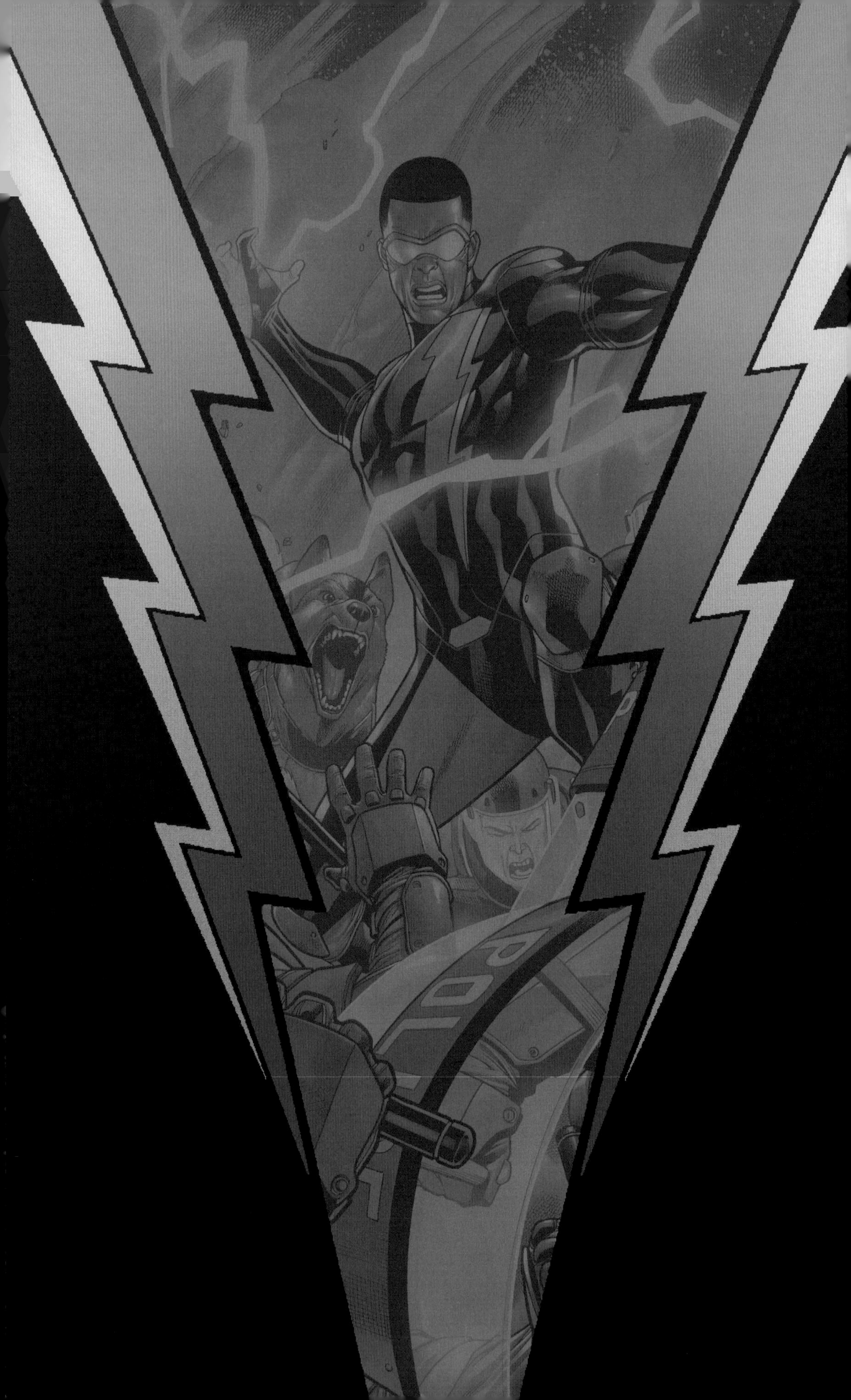

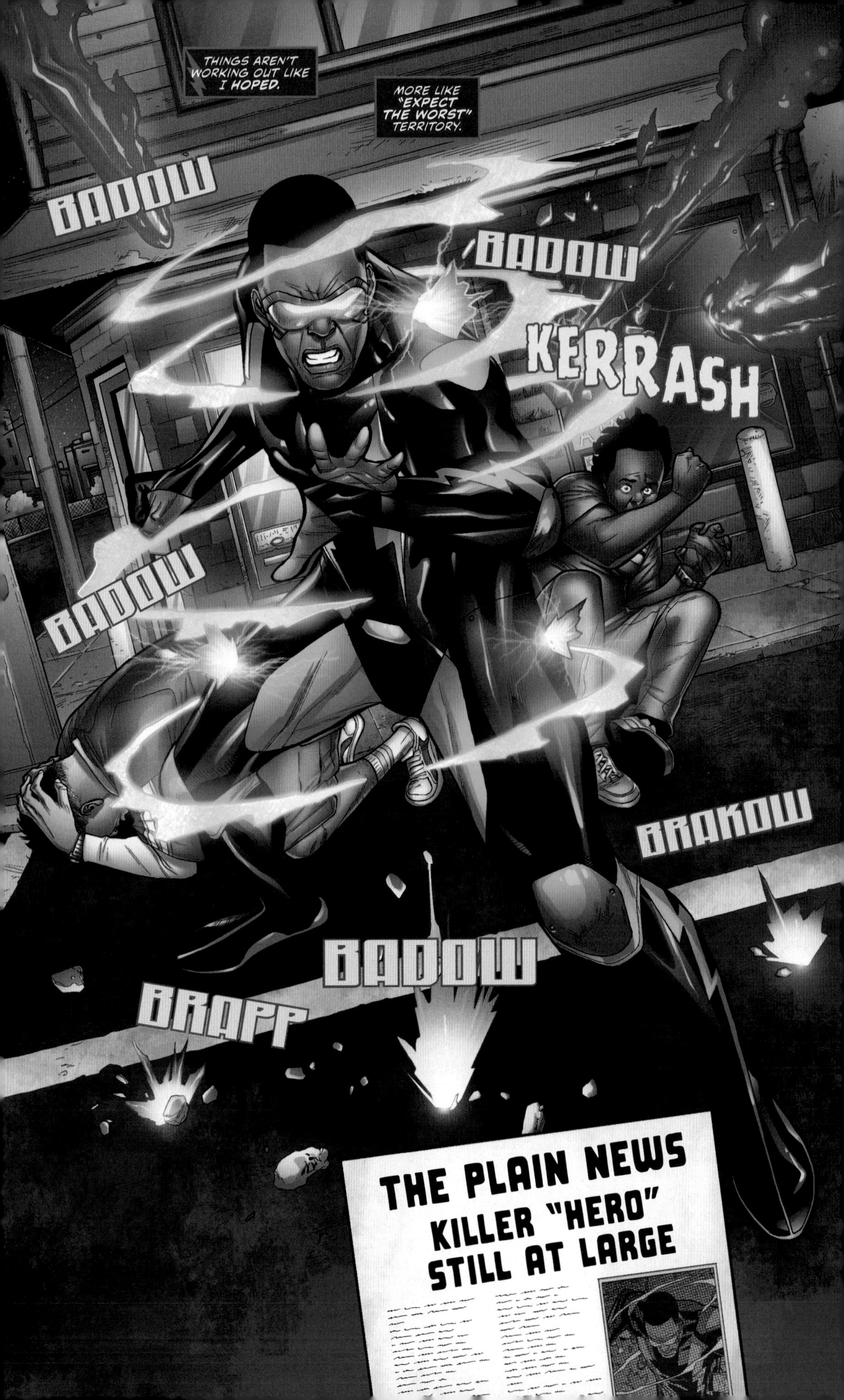
THINGS AREN'T WORKING OUT LIKE I HOPED.
MORE LIKE "EXPECT THE WORST" TERRITORY.
BADOW
BADOW
KERRASH
BADOW
BRAKOW
BADOW
BRAPP
THE PLAIN NEWS
KILLER "HERO" STILL AT LARGE

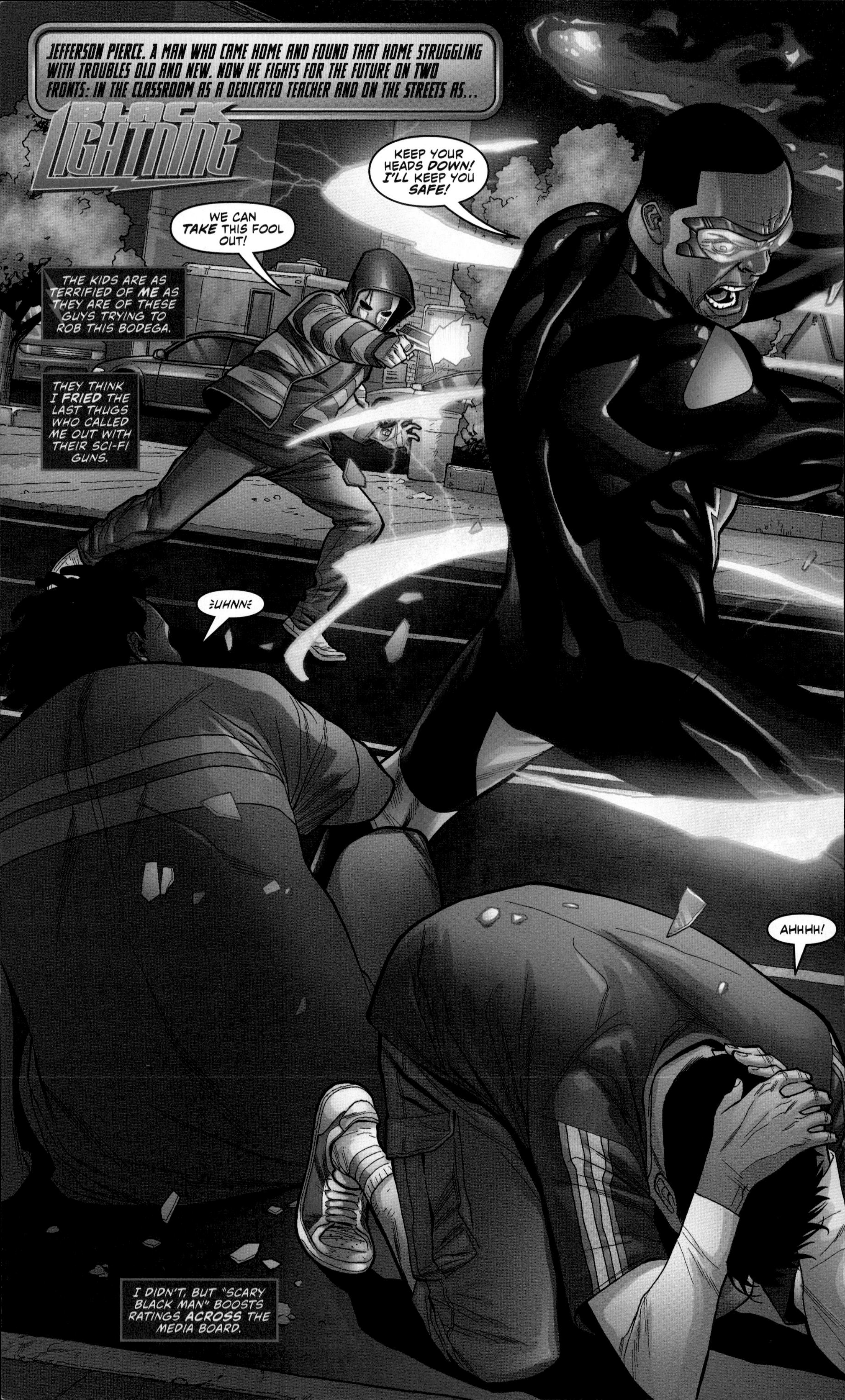
JEFFERSON PIERCE. A MAN WHO CAME HOME AND FOUND THAT HOME STRUGGLING WITH TROUBLES OLD AND NEW. NOW HE FIGHTS FOR THE FUTURE ON TWO FRONTS: IN THE CLASSROOM AS A DEDICATED TEACHER AND ON THE STREETS AS...
BLACK LIGHTNING
KEEP YOUR HEADS DOWN! I'LL KEEP YOU SAFE!
WE CAN TAKE THIS FOOL OUT!
THE KIDS ARE AS TERRIFIED OF ME AS THEY ARE OF THESE GUYS TRYING TO ROB THIS BODEGA.
THEY THINK I FRIED THE LAST THUGS WHO CALLED ME OUT WITH THEIR SCI-FI GUNS.
UHNN
AHHHH!
I DIDN'T, BUT "SCARY BLACK MAN" BOOSTS RATINGS ACROSS THE MEDIA BOARD.

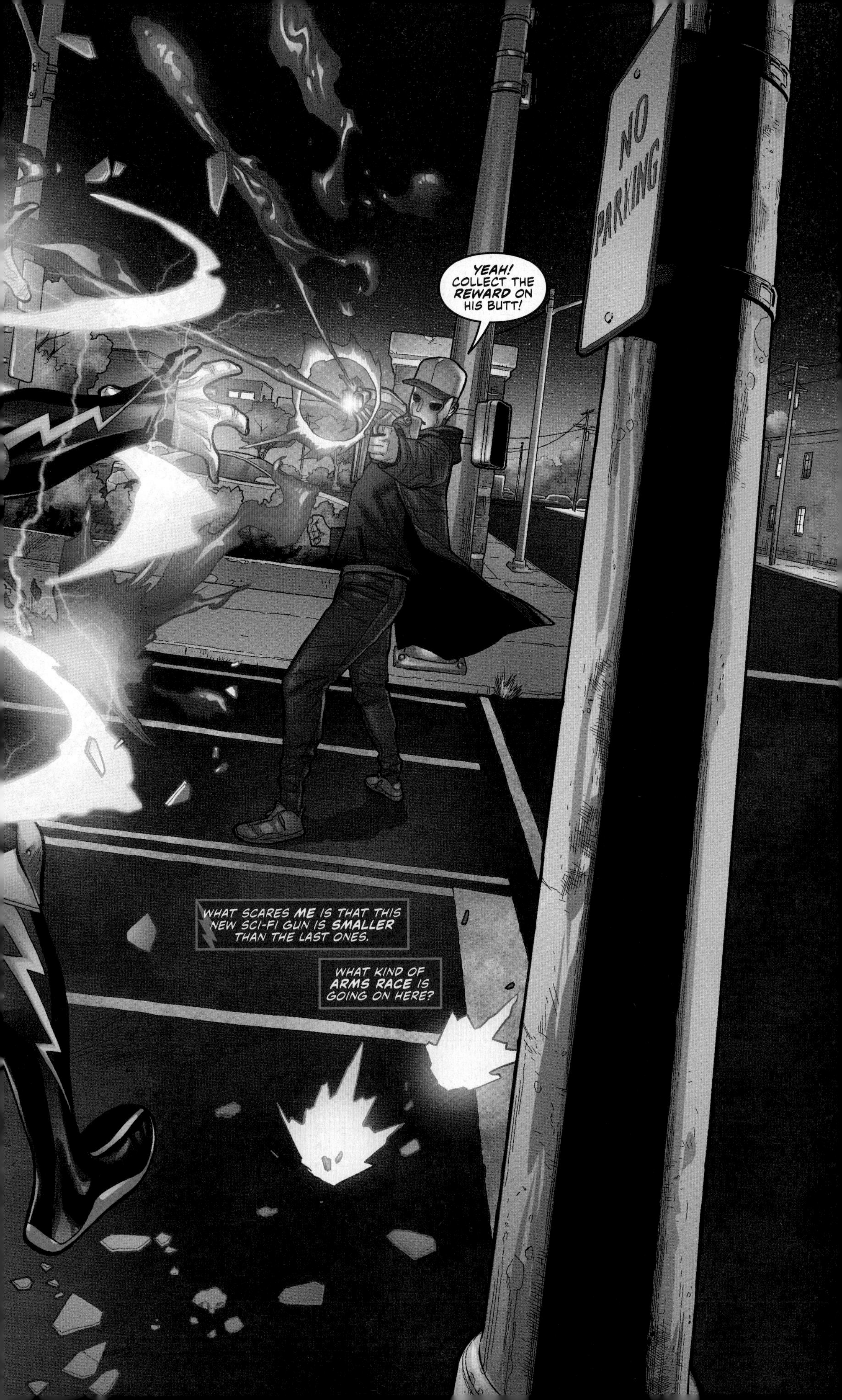
NO PARKING
YEAH! COLLECT THE REWARD ON HIS BUTT!
WHAT SCARES ME IS THAT THIS NEW SCI-FI GUN IS SMALLER THAN THE LAST ONES.
WHAT KIND OF ARMS RACE IS GOING ON HERE?

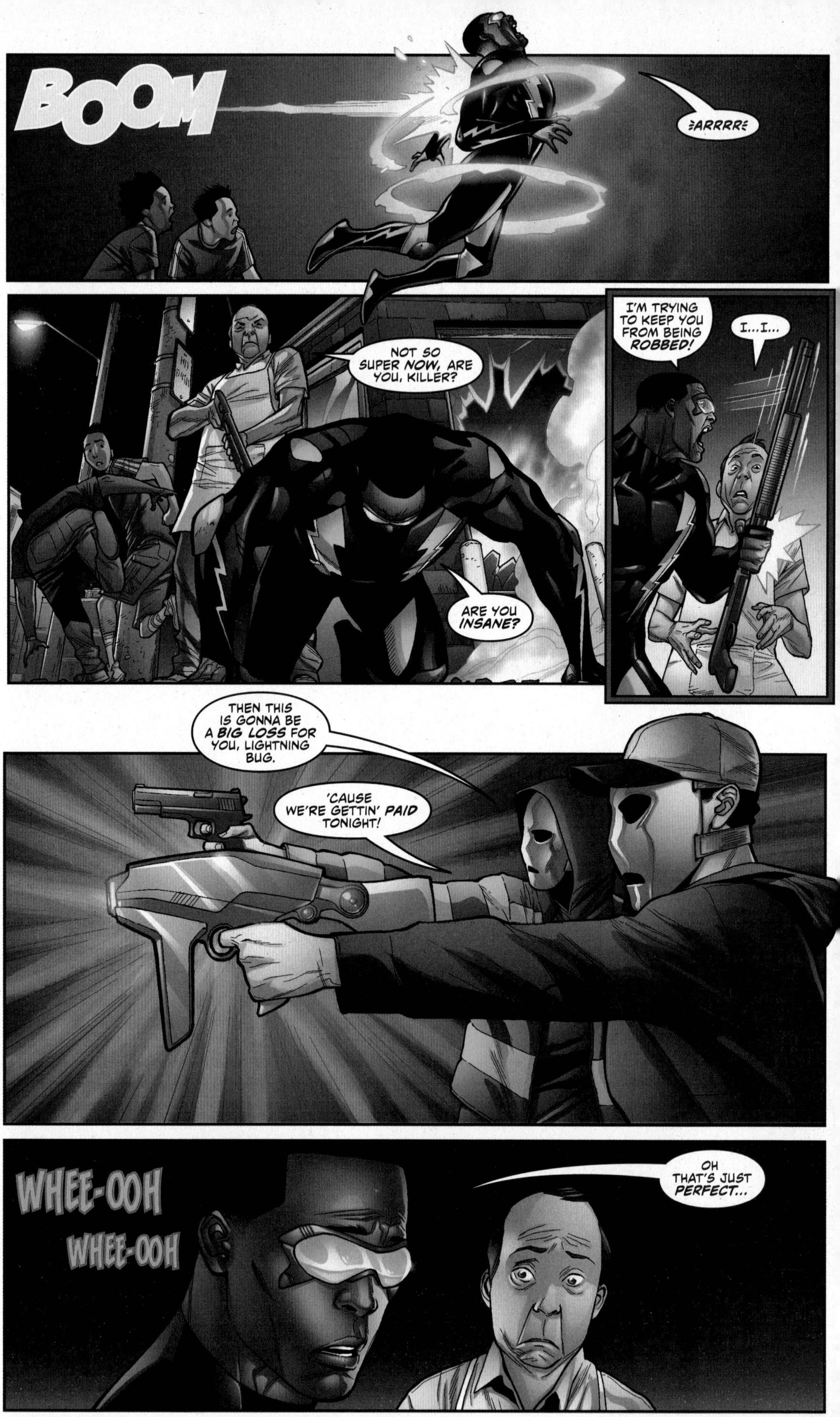
BOOM
ARRRR
NOT SO SUPER NOW, ARE YOU, KILLER?
ARE YOU INSANE?
I'M TRYING TO KEEP YOU FROM BEING ROBBED!
I...I...
THEN THIS IS GONNA BE A BIG LOSS FOR YOU, LIGHTNING BUG.
'CAUSE WE'RE GETTIN' PAID TONIGHT!
WHEE-OOH
WHEE-OOH
OH THAT'S JUST PERFECT...

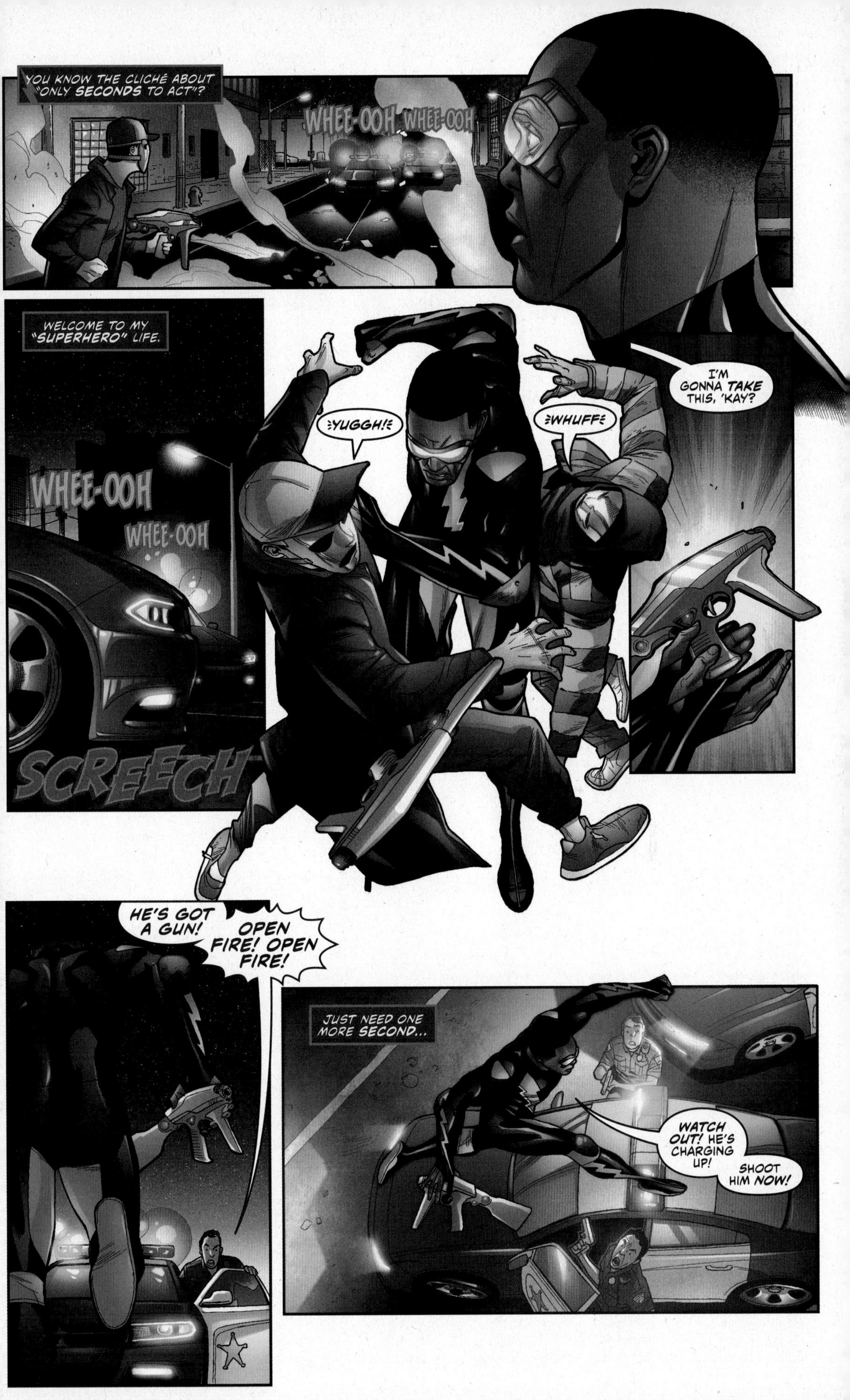

YOU KNOW THE CLICHÉ ABOUT "ONLY SECONDS TO ACT"?
WHEE-OOH WHEE-OOH
WELCOME TO MY "SUPERHERO" LIFE.
WHEE-OOH
WHEE-OOH
SCREECH
YUGGH!
WHUFF
I'M GONNA TAKE THIS, 'KAY?
HE'S GOT A GUN!
OPEN FIRE! OPEN FIRE!
JUST NEED ONE MORE SECOND...
WATCH OUT! HE'S CHARGING UP!
SHOOT HIM NOW!

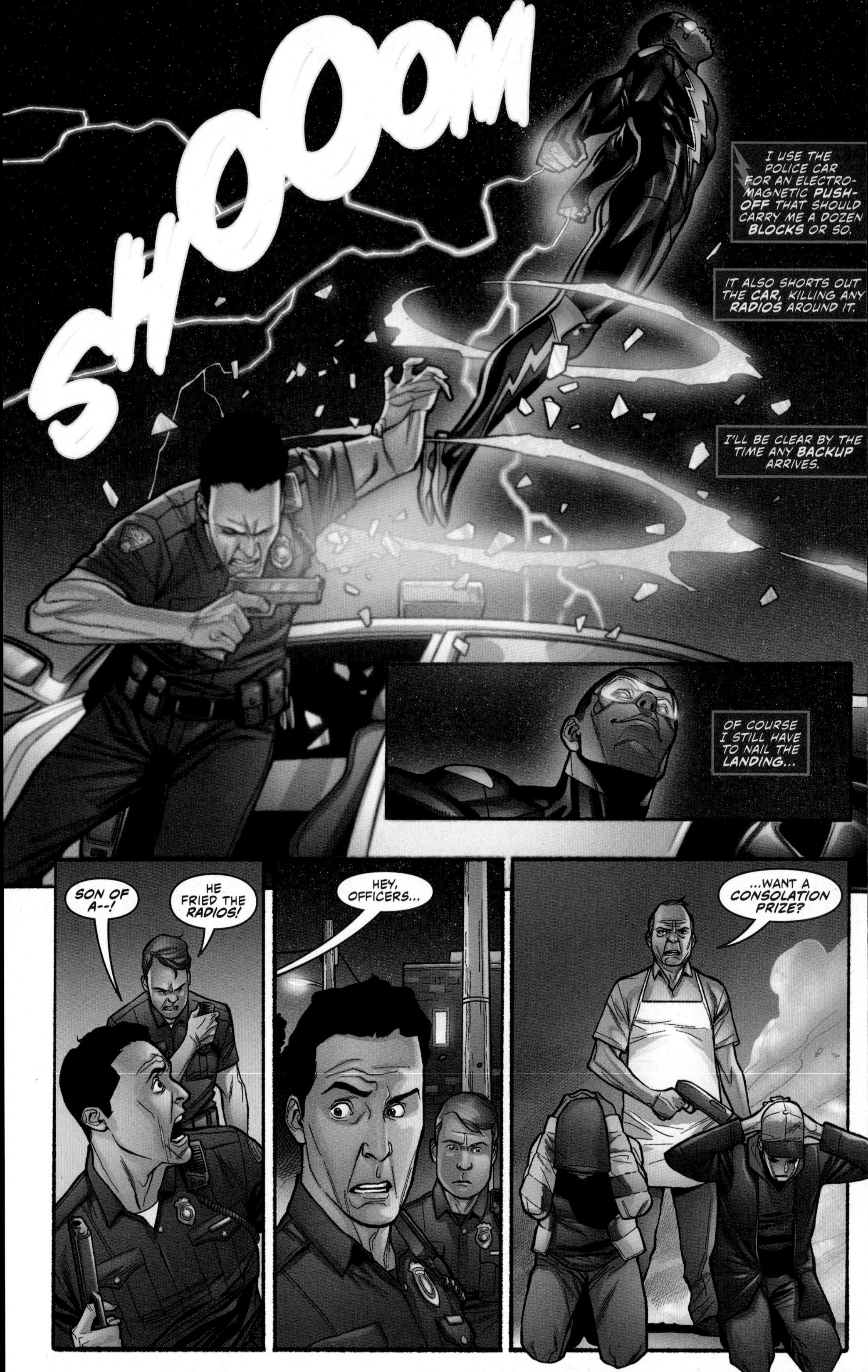
SHOOOM
I USE THE POLICE CAR FOR AN ELECTRO-MAGNETIC PUSH-OFF THAT SHOULD CARRY ME A DOZEN BLOCKS OR SO.
IT ALSO SHORTS OUT THE CAR, KILLING ANY RADIOS AROUND IT.
I'LL BE CLEAR BY THE TIME ANY BACKUP ARRIVES.
OF COURSE I STILL HAVE TO NAIL THE LANDING...
SON OF A--!
HE FRIED THE RADIOS!
HEY, OFFICERS...
...WANT A CONSOLATION PRIZE?

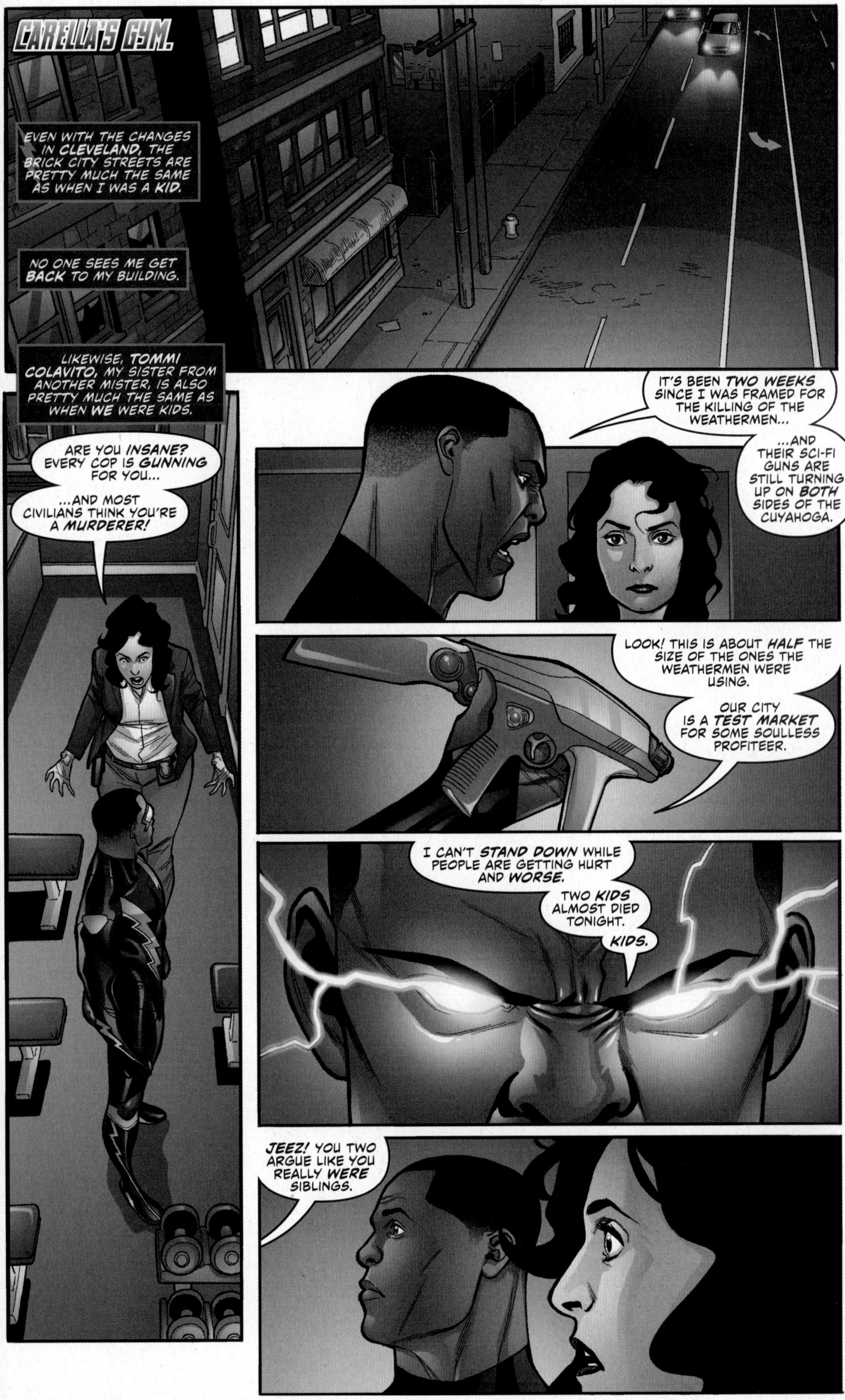
CARELLA'S GYM.
EVEN WITH THE CHANGES IN CLEVELAND, THE BRICK CITY STREETS ARE PRETTY MUCH THE SAME AS WHEN I WAS A KID.
NO ONE SEES ME GET BACK TO MY BUILDING.
LIKEWISE, TOMMI COLAVITO, MY SISTER FROM ANOTHER MISTER, IS ALSO PRETTY MUCH THE SAME AS WHEN WE WERE KIDS.
ARE YOU INSANE? EVERY COP IS GUNNING FOR YOU...
...AND MOST CIVILIANS THINK YOU'RE A MURDERER!
IT'S BEEN TWO WEEKS SINCE I WAS FRAMED FOR THE KILLING OF THE WEATHERMEN...
...AND THEIR SCI-FI GUNS ARE STILL TURNING UP ON BOTH SIDES OF THE CUYAHOGA.
LOOK! THIS IS ABOUT HALF THE SIZE OF THE ONES THE WEATHERMEN WERE USING.
OUR CITY IS A TEST MARKET FOR SOME SOULLESS PROFITEER.
I CAN'T STAND DOWN WHILE PEOPLE ARE GETTING HURT AND WORSE.
TWO KIDS ALMOST DIED TONIGHT.
KIDS.
JEEZ! YOU TWO ARGUE LIKE YOU REALLY WERE SIBLINGS.

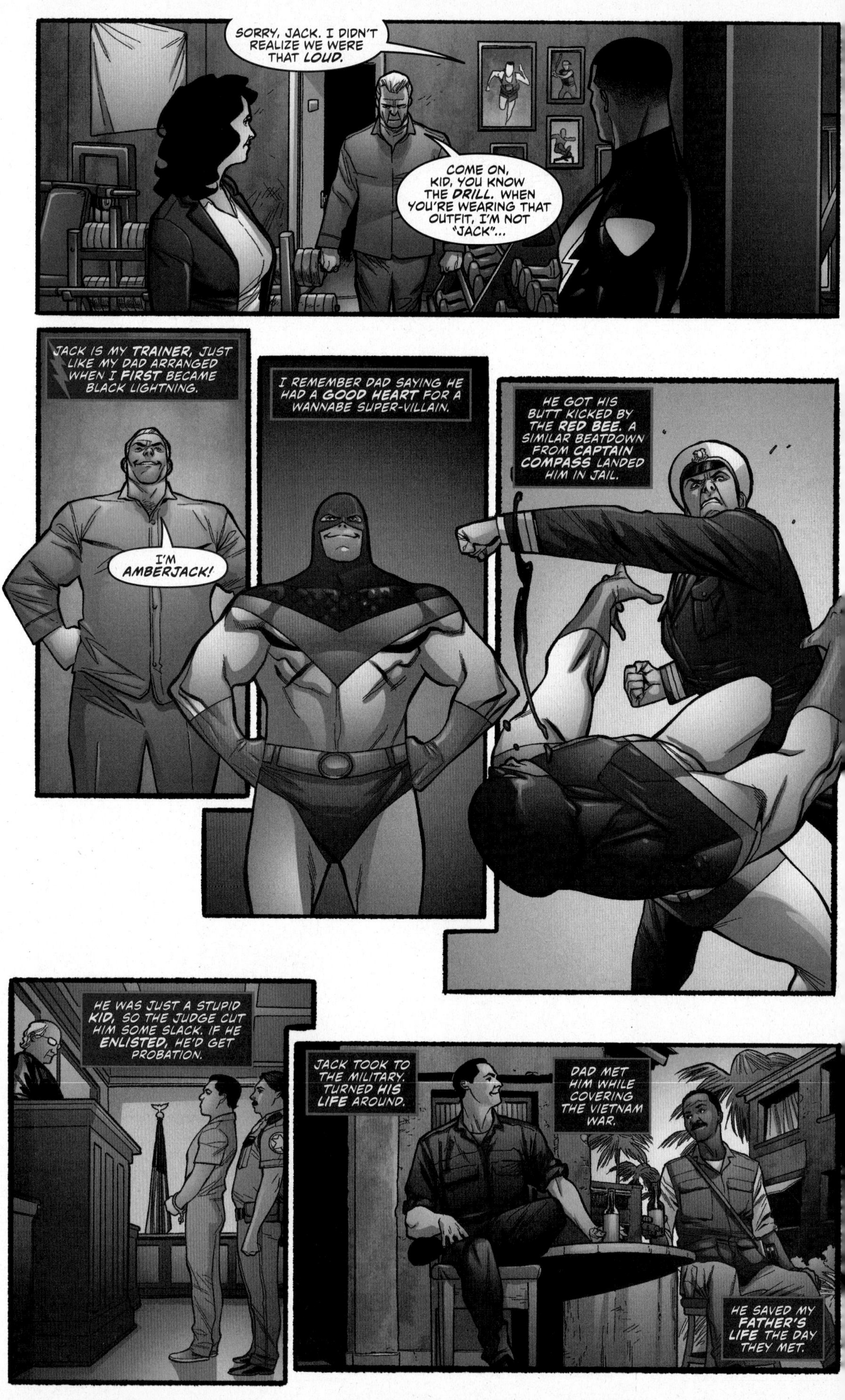

SORRY, JACK. I DIDN'T REALIZE WE WERE THAT LOUD.
COME ON, KID, YOU KNOW THE DRILL. WHEN YOU'RE WEARING THAT OUTFIT, I'M NOT "JACK"...
JACK IS MY TRAINER, JUST LIKE MY DAD ARRANGED WHEN I FIRST BECAME BLACK LIGHTNING.
I'M AMBERJACK!
I REMEMBER DAD SAYING HE HAD A GOOD HEART FOR A WANNABE SUPER-VILLAIN.
HE GOT HIS BUTT KICKED BY THE RED BEE. A SIMILAR BEATDOWN FROM CAPTAIN COMPASS LANDED HIM IN JAIL.
HE WAS JUST A STUPID KID, SO THE JUDGE CUT HIM SOME SLACK. IF HE ENLISTED, HE'D GET PROBATION.
JACK TOOK TO THE MILITARY. TURNED HIS LIFE AROUND.
DAD MET HIM WHILE COVERING THE VIETNAM WAR.
HE SAVED MY FATHER'S LIFE THE DAY THEY MET.

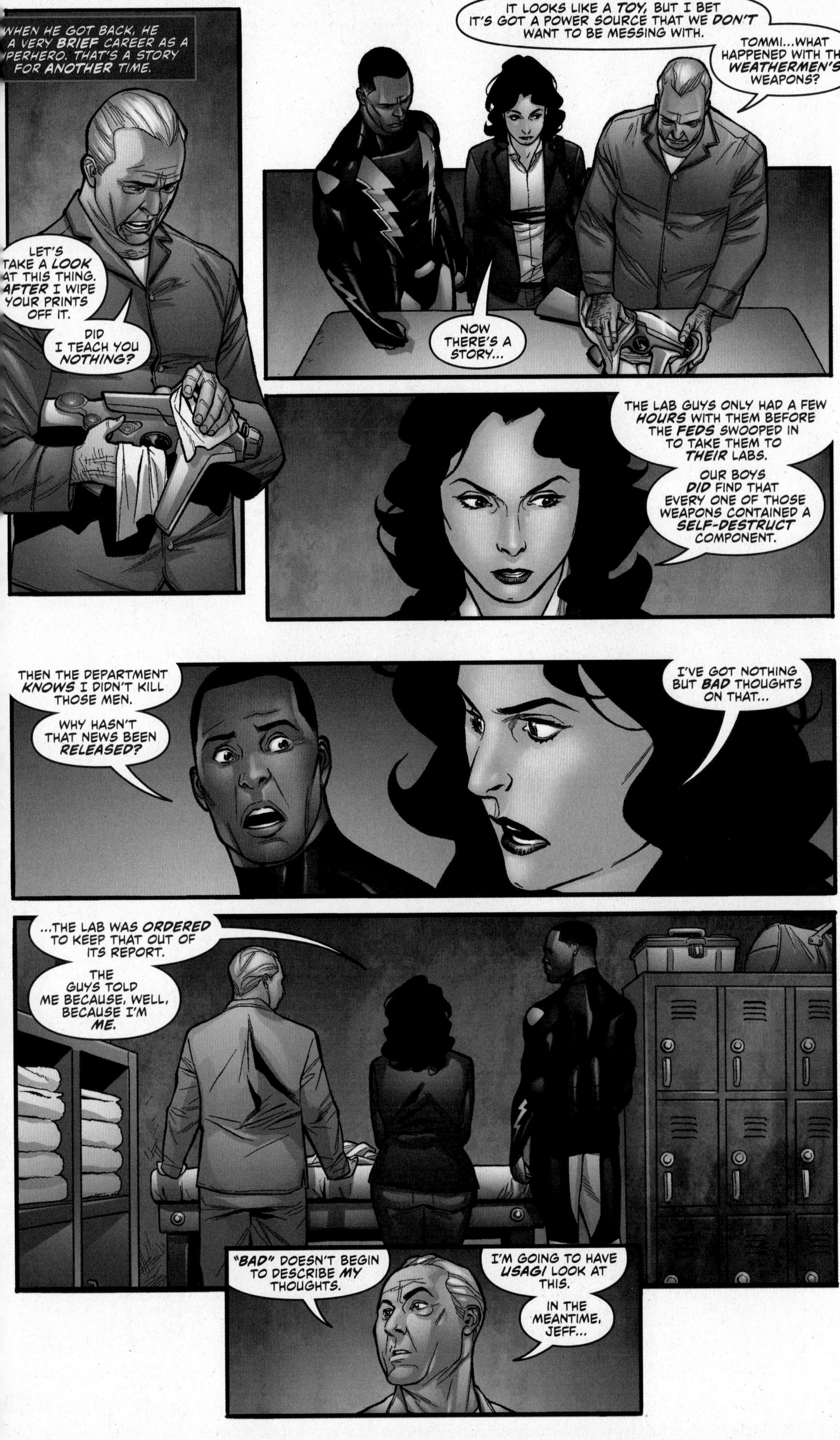
WHEN HE GOT BACK, HE A VERY BRIEF CAREER AS A PERHERO. THAT'S A STORY FOR ANOTHER TIME.
LET'S TAKE A LOOK AT THIS THING. AFTER I WIPE YOUR PRINTS OFF IT.
DID I TEACH YOU NOTHING?
IT LOOKS LIKE A TOY, BUT I BET IT'S GOT A POWER SOURCE THAT WE DON'T WANT TO BE MESSING WITH.
TOMMI...WHAT HAPPENED WITH THE WEATHERMEN'S WEAPONS?
NOW THERE'S A STORY...
THE LAB GUYS ONLY HAD A FEW HOURS WITH THEM BEFORE THE FEDS SWOOPED IN TO TAKE THEM TO THEIR LABS.
OUR BOYS DID FIND THAT EVERY ONE OF THOSE WEAPONS CONTAINED A SELF-DESTRUCT COMPONENT.
THEN THE DEPARTMENT KNOWS I DIDN'T KILL THOSE MEN.
WHY HASN'T THAT NEWS BEEN RELEASED?
I'VE GOT NOTHING BUT BAD THOUGHTS ON THAT...
...THE LAB WAS ORDERED TO KEEP THAT OUT OF ITS REPORT.
THE GUYS TOLD ME BECAUSE, WELL, BECAUSE I'M ME.
"BAD" DOESN'T BEGIN TO DESCRIBE MY THOUGHTS.
I'M GOING TO HAVE USAGI LOOK AT THIS.
IN THE MEANTIME, JEFF...

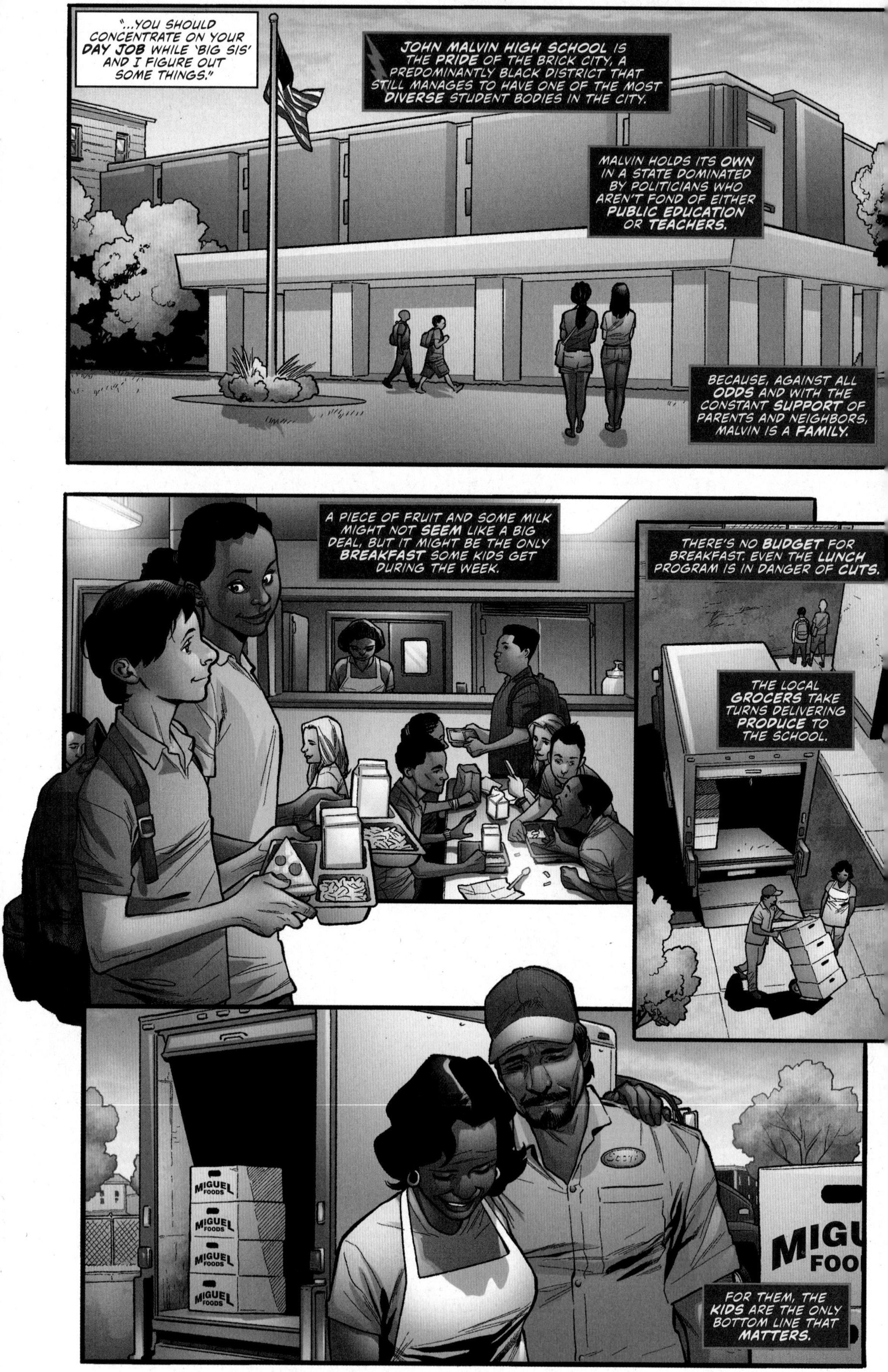
"...YOU SHOULD CONCENTRATE ON YOUR DAY JOB WHILE 'BIG SIS' AND I FIGURE OUT SOME THINGS."
JOHN MALVIN HIGH SCHOOL IS THE PRIDE OF THE BRICK CITY, A PREDOMINANTLY BLACK DISTRICT THAT STILL MANAGES TO HAVE ONE OF THE MOST DIVERSE STUDENT BODIES IN THE CITY.
MALVIN HOLDS ITS OWN IN A STATE DOMINATED BY POLITICIANS WHO AREN'T FOND OF EITHER PUBLIC EDUCATION OR TEACHERS.
BECAUSE, AGAINST ALL ODDS AND WITH THE CONSTANT SUPPORT OF PARENTS AND NEIGHBORS, MALVIN IS A FAMILY.
A PIECE OF FRUIT AND SOME MILK MIGHT NOT SEEM LIKE A BIG DEAL, BUT IT MIGHT BE THE ONLY BREAKFAST SOME KIDS GET DURING THE WEEK.
THERE'S NO BUDGET FOR BREAKFAST. EVEN THE LUNCH PROGRAM IS IN DANGER OF CUTS.
THE LOCAL GROCERS TAKE TURNS DELIVERING PRODUCE TO THE SCHOOL.
MIGUEL FOODS
FOR THEM, THE KIDS ARE THE ONLY BOTTOM LINE THAT MATTERS.

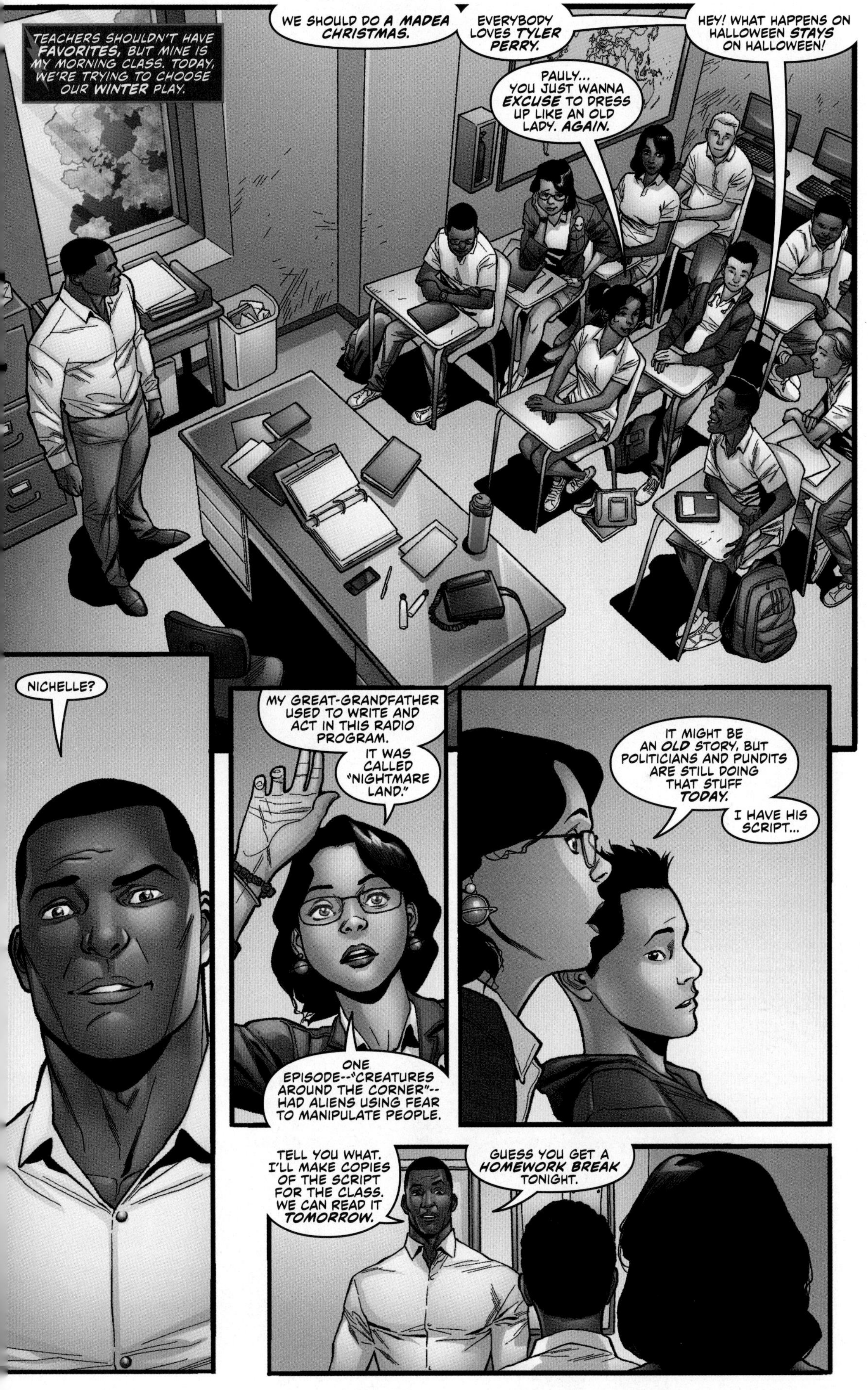
TEACHERS SHOULDN'T HAVE FAVORITES, BUT MINE IS MY MORNING CLASS. TODAY, WE'RE TRYING TO CHOOSE OUR WINTER PLAY.
WE SHOULD DO A MADEA CHRISTMAS.
EVERYBODY LOVES TYLER PERRY.
PAULY... YOU JUST WANNA EXCUSE TO DRESS UP LIKE AN OLD LADY. AGAIN.
HEY! WHAT HAPPENS ON HALLOWEEN STAYS ON HALLOWEEN!
NICHELLE?
MY GREAT-GRANDFATHER USED TO WRITE AND ACT IN THIS RADIO PROGRAM.
IT WAS CALLED "NIGHTMARE LAND."
ONE EPISODE--"CREATURES AROUND THE CORNER"--HAD ALIENS USING FEAR TO MANIPULATE PEOPLE.
IT MIGHT BE AN OLD STORY, BUT POLITICIANS AND PUNDITS ARE STILL DOING THAT STUFF TODAY.
I HAVE HIS SCRIPT...
TELL YOU WHAT. I'LL MAKE COPIES OF THE SCRIPT FOR THE CLASS. WE CAN READ IT TOMORROW.
GUESS YOU GET A HOMEWORK BREAK TONIGHT.

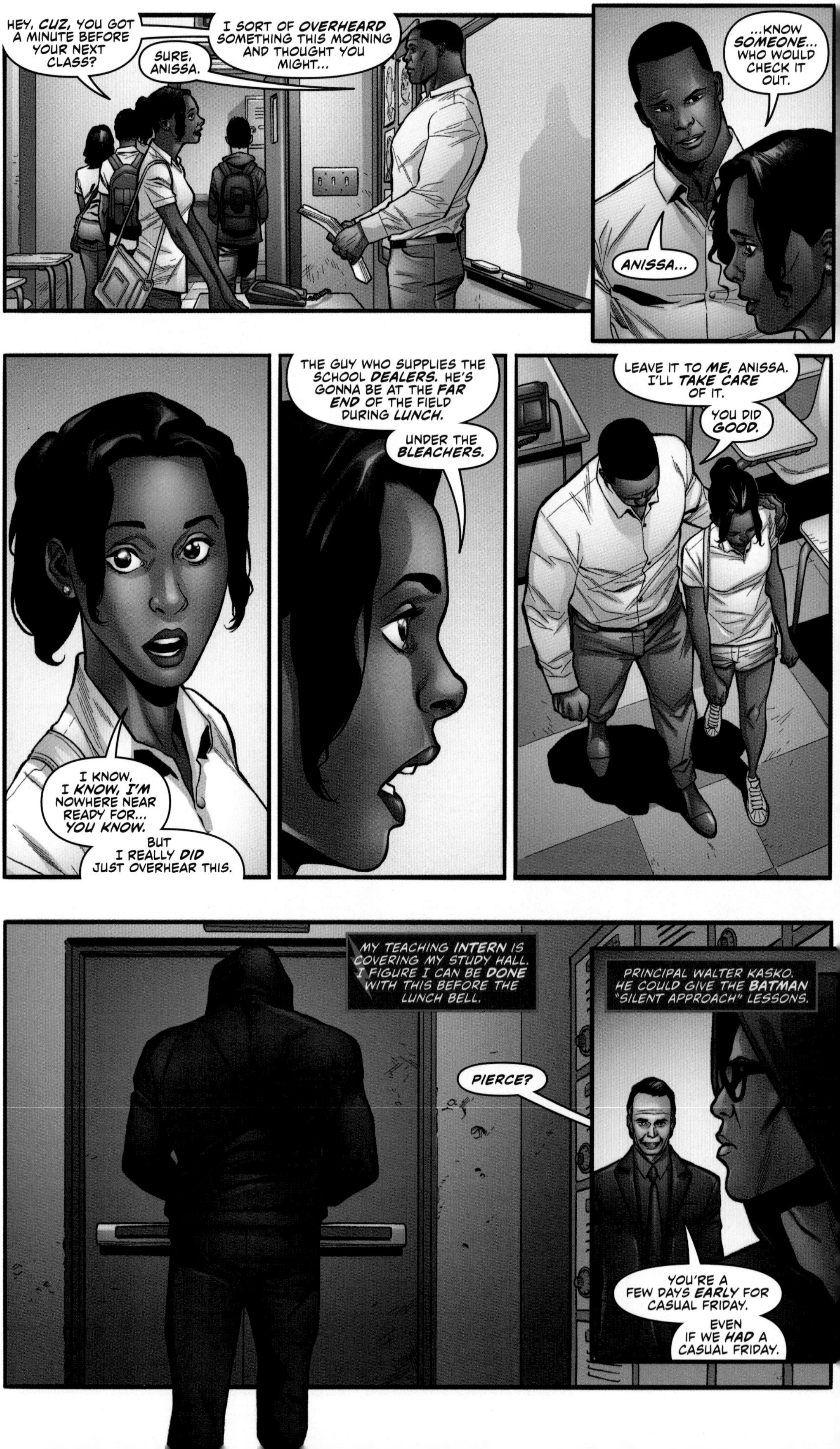
HEY, CUZ, YOU GOT A MINUTE BEFORE YOUR NEXT CLASS?
SURE, ANISSA.
I SORT OF OVERHEARD SOMETHING THIS MORNING AND THOUGHT YOU MIGHT...
...KNOW SOMEONE... WHO WOULD CHECK IT OUT.
ANISSA...
I KNOW, I KNOW, I'M NOWHERE NEAR READY FOR... YOU KNOW.
BUT I REALLY DID JUST OVERHEAR THIS.
THE GUY WHO SUPPLIES THE SCHOOL DEALERS. HE'S GONNA BE AT THE FAR END OF THE FIELD DURING LUNCH.
UNDER THE BLEACHERS.
LEAVE IT TO ME, ANISSA. I'LL TAKE CARE OF IT.
YOU DID GOOD.
MY TEACHING INTERN IS COVERING MY STUDY HALL. I FIGURE I CAN BE DONE WITH THIS BEFORE THE LUNCH BELL.
PRINCIPAL WALTER KASKO. HE COULD GIVE THE BATMAN "SILENT APPROACH" LESSONS.
PIERCE?
YOU'RE A FEW DAYS EARLY FOR CASUAL FRIDAY.
EVEN IF WE HAD A CASUAL FRIDAY.

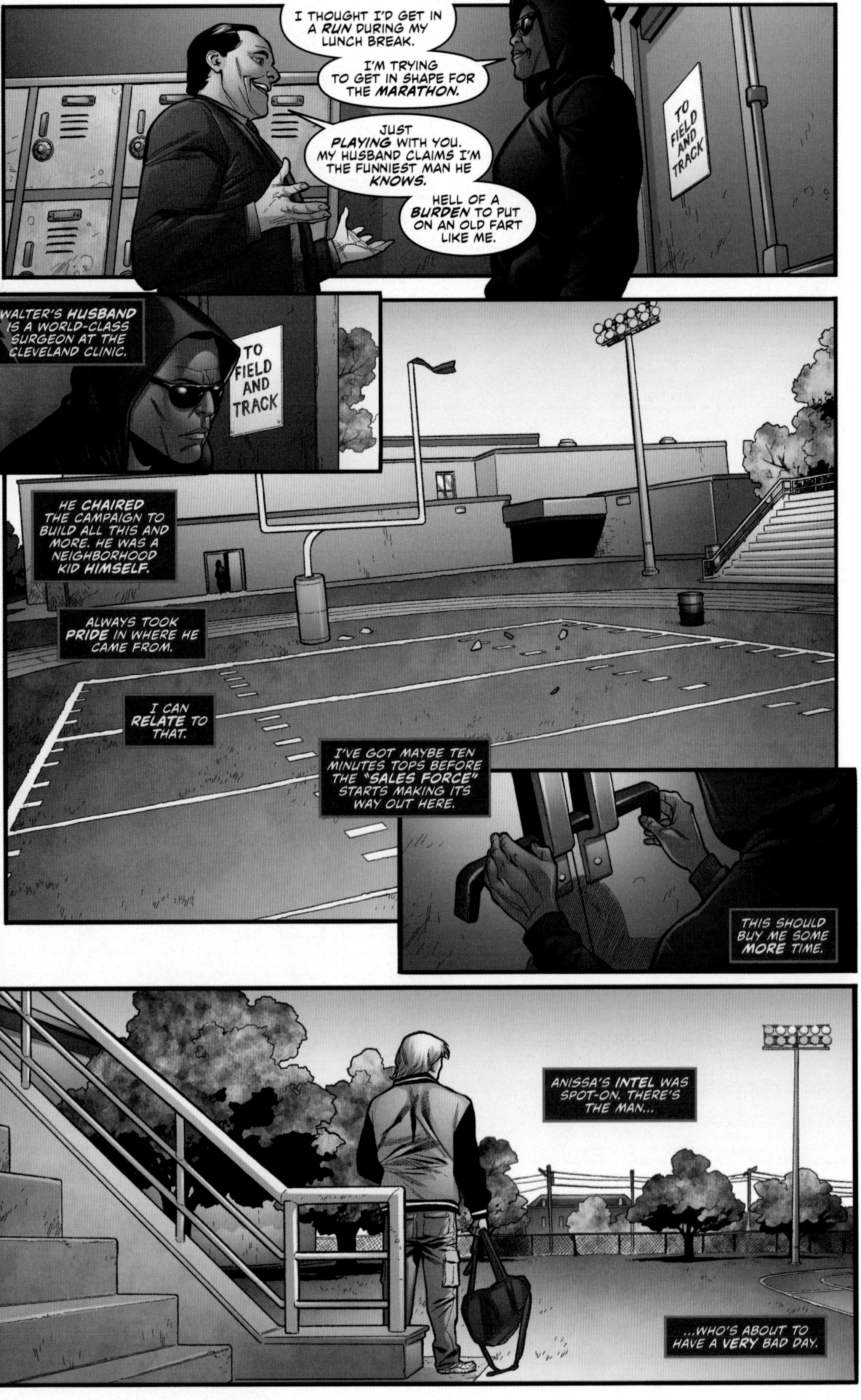
I THOUGHT I'D GET IN A RUN DURING MY LUNCH BREAK.
I'M TRYING TO GET IN SHAPE FOR THE MARATHON.
JUST PLAYING WITH YOU. MY HUSBAND CLAIMS I'M THE FUNNIEST MAN HE KNOWS.
HELL OF A BURDEN TO PUT ON AN OLD FART LIKE ME.
TO FIELD AND TRACK
WALTER'S HUSBAND IS A WORLD-CLASS SURGEON AT THE CLEVELAND CLINIC.
TO FIELD AND TRACK
HE CHAIRED THE CAMPAIGN TO BUILD ALL THIS AND MORE. HE WAS A NEIGHBORHOOD KID HIMSELF.
ALWAYS TOOK PRIDE IN WHERE HE CAME FROM.
I CAN RELATE TO THAT.
I'VE GOT MAYBE TEN MINUTES TOPS BEFORE THE "SALES FORCE" STARTS MAKING ITS WAY OUT HERE.
THIS SHOULD BUY ME SOME MORE TIME.
ANISSA'S INTEL WAS SPOT-ON. THERE'S THE MAN...
...WHO'S ABOUT TO HAVE A VERY BAD DAY.

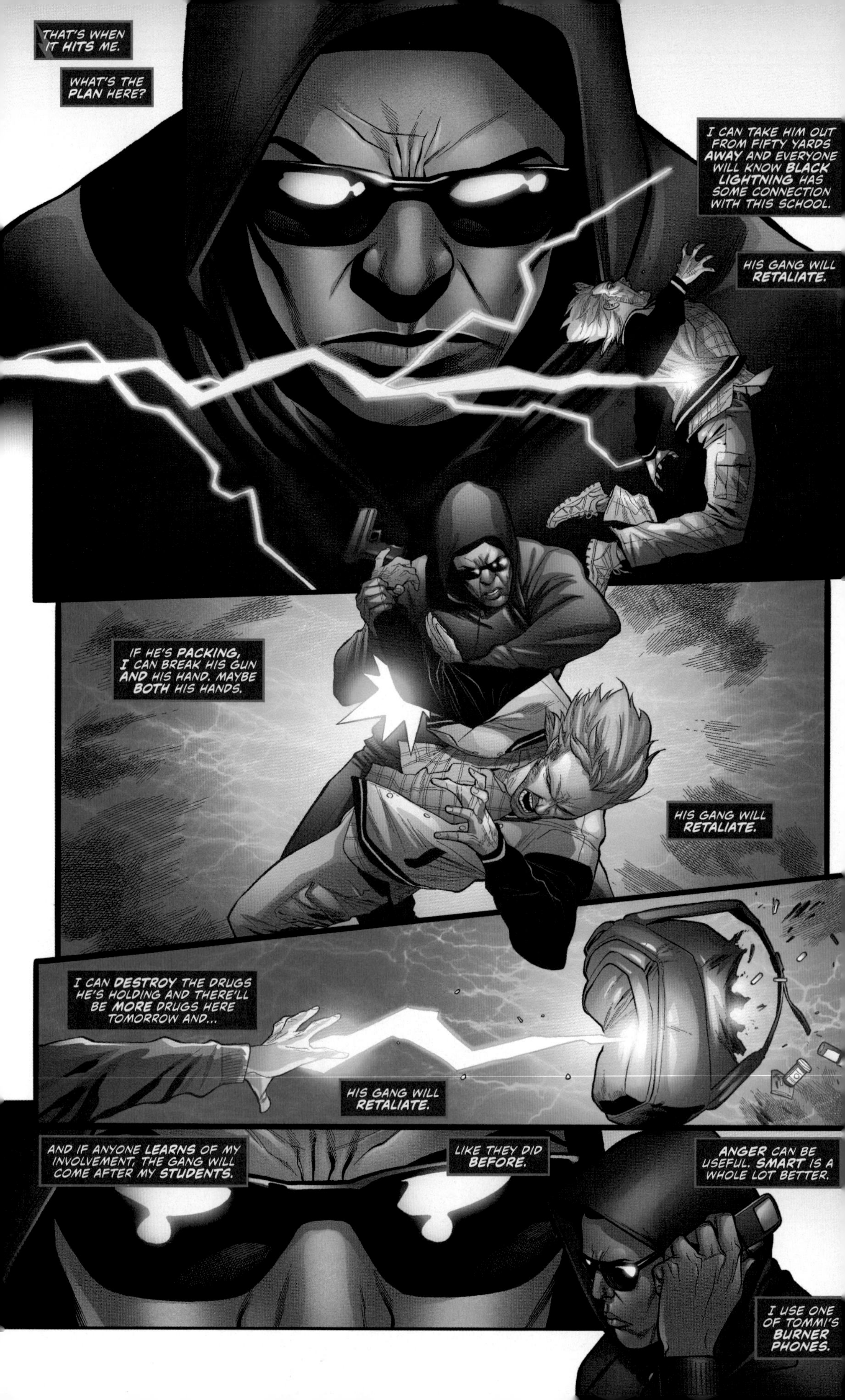
THAT'S WHEN IT HITS ME.
WHAT'S THE PLAN HERE?
I CAN TAKE HIM OUT FROM FIFTY YARDS AWAY AND EVERYONE WILL KNOW BLACK LIGHTNING HAS SOME CONNECTION WITH THIS SCHOOL.
HIS GANG WILL RETALIATE.
IF HE'S PACKING, I CAN BREAK HIS GUN AND HIS HAND. MAYBE BOTH HIS HANDS.
HIS GANG WILL RETALIATE.
I CAN DESTROY THE DRUGS HE'S HOLDING AND THERE'LL BE MORE DRUGS HERE TOMORROW AND...
HIS GANG WILL RETALIATE.
AND IF ANYONE LEARNS OF MY INVOLVEMENT, THE GANG WILL COME AFTER MY STUDENTS.
LIKE THEY DID BEFORE.
ANGER CAN BE USEFUL. SMART IS A WHOLE LOT BETTER.
I USE ONE OF TOMMI'S BURNER PHONES.

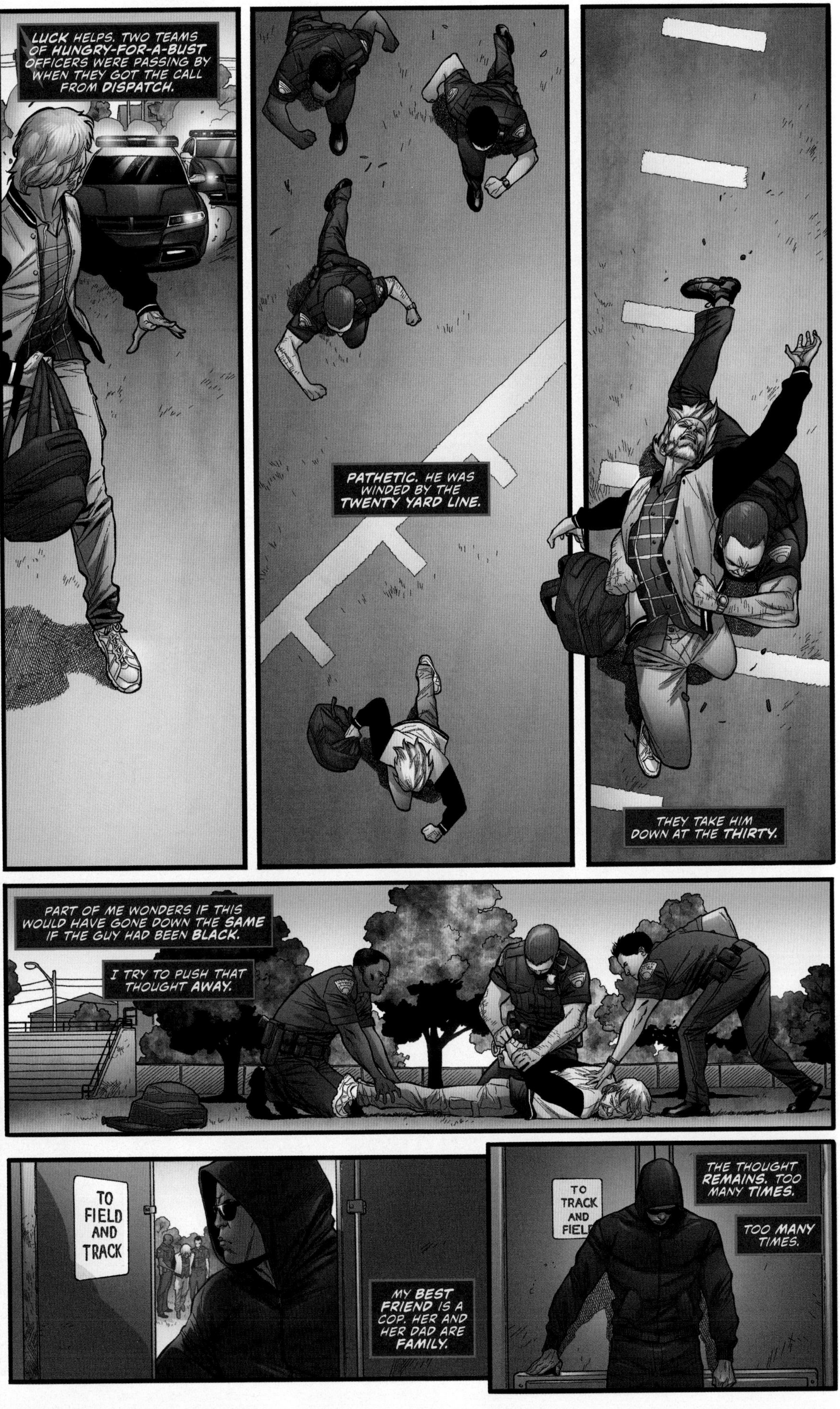
LUCK HELPS. TWO TEAMS OF HUNGRY-FOR-A-BUST OFFICERS WERE PASSING BY WHEN THEY GOT THE CALL FROM DISPATCH.
PATHETIC. HE WAS WINDED BY THE TWENTY YARD LINE.
THEY TAKE HIM DOWN AT THE THIRTY.
PART OF ME WONDERS IF THIS WOULD HAVE GONE DOWN THE SAME IF THE GUY HAD BEEN BLACK.
I TRY TO PUSH THAT THOUGHT AWAY.
TO FIELD AND TRACK
MY BEST FRIEND IS A COP. HER AND HER DAD ARE FAMILY.
TO TRACK AND FIEL
THE THOUGHT REMAINS. TOO MANY TIMES.
TOO MANY TIMES.

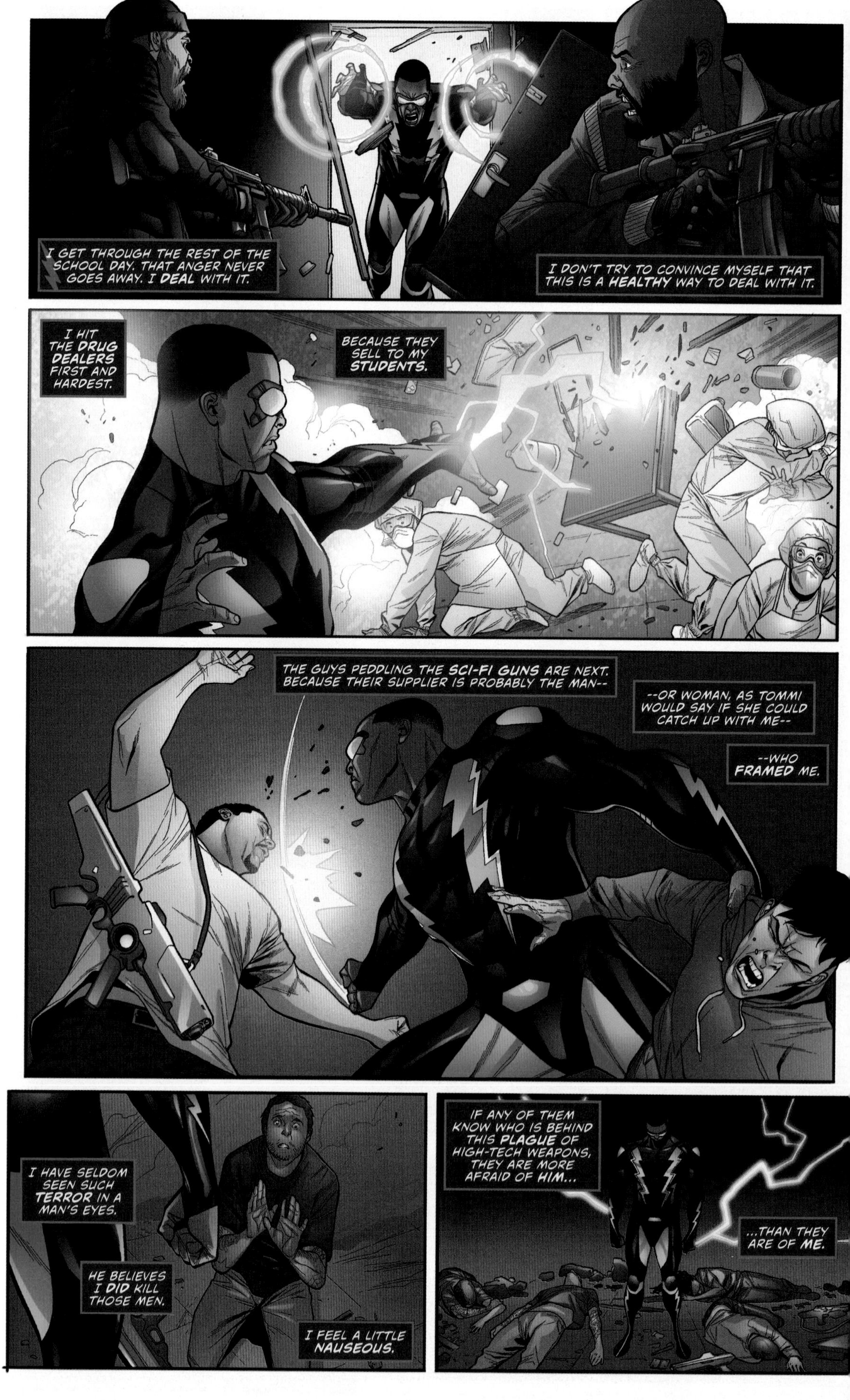
I GET THROUGH THE REST OF THE SCHOOL DAY. THAT ANGER NEVER GOES AWAY. I DEAL WITH IT.
I DON'T TRY TO CONVINCE MYSELF THAT THIS IS A HEALTHY WAY TO DEAL WITH IT.
I HIT THE DRUG DEALERS FIRST AND HARDEST.
BECAUSE THEY SELL TO MY STUDENTS.
THE GUYS PEDDLING THE SCI-FI GUNS ARE NEXT. BECAUSE THEIR SUPPLIER IS PROBABLY THE MAN--
--OR WOMAN, AS TOMMI WOULD SAY IF SHE COULD CATCH UP WITH ME--
--WHO FRAMED ME.
I HAVE SELDOM SEEN SUCH TERROR IN A MAN'S EYES.
HE BELIEVES I DID KILL THOSE MEN.
I FEEL A LITTLE NAUSEOUS.
IF ANY OF THEM KNOW WHO IS BEHIND THIS PLAGUE OF HIGH-TECH WEAPONS, THEY ARE MORE AFRAID OF HIM...
...THAN THEY ARE OF ME.

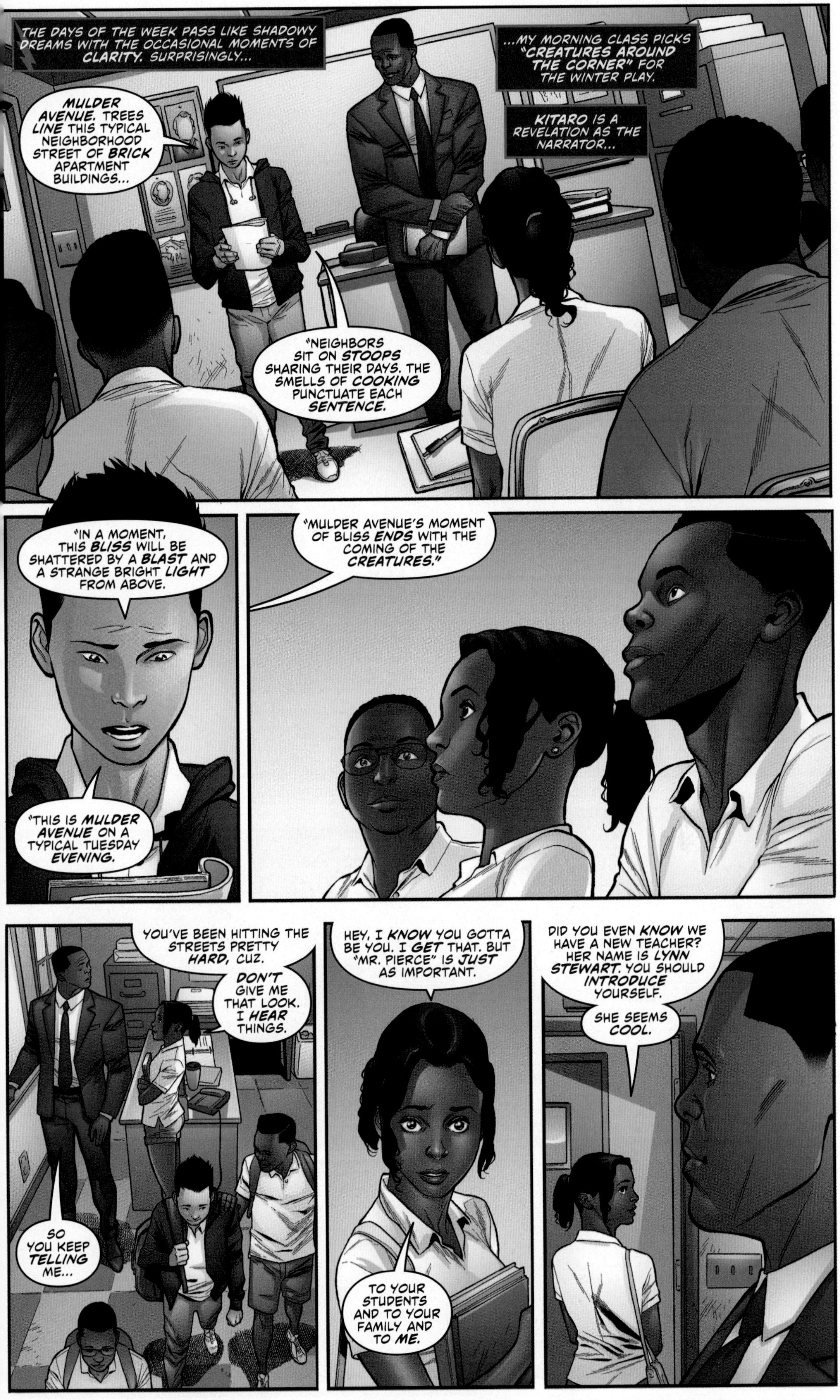
THE DAYS OF THE WEEK PASS LIKE SHADOWY DREAMS WITH THE OCCASIONAL MOMENTS OF CLARITY. SURPRISINGLY...
...MY MORNING CLASS PICKS "CREATURES AROUND THE CORNER" FOR THE WINTER PLAY.
KITARO IS A REVELATION AS THE NARRATOR...
MULDER AVENUE. TREES LINE THIS TYPICAL NEIGHBORHOOD STREET OF BRICK APARTMENT BUILDINGS...
"NEIGHBORS SIT ON STOOPS SHARING THEIR DAYS. THE SMELLS OF COOKING PUNCTUATE EACH SENTENCE.
"IN A MOMENT, THIS BLISS WILL BE SHATTERED BY A BLAST AND A STRANGE BRIGHT LIGHT FROM ABOVE.
"THIS IS MULDER AVENUE ON A TYPICAL TUESDAY EVENING.
"MULDER AVENUE'S MOMENT OF BLISS ENDS WITH THE COMING OF THE CREATURES."
YOU'VE BEEN HITTING THE STREETS PRETTY HARD, CUZ.
DON'T GIVE ME THAT LOOK. I HEAR THINGS.
SO YOU KEEP TELLING ME...
HEY, I KNOW YOU GOTTA BE YOU. I GET THAT. BUT "MR. PIERCE" IS JUST AS IMPORTANT.
TO YOUR STUDENTS AND TO YOUR FAMILY AND TO ME.
DID YOU EVEN KNOW WE HAVE A NEW TEACHER? HER NAME IS LYNN STEWART. YOU SHOULD INTRODUCE YOURSELF.
SHE SEEMS COOL.

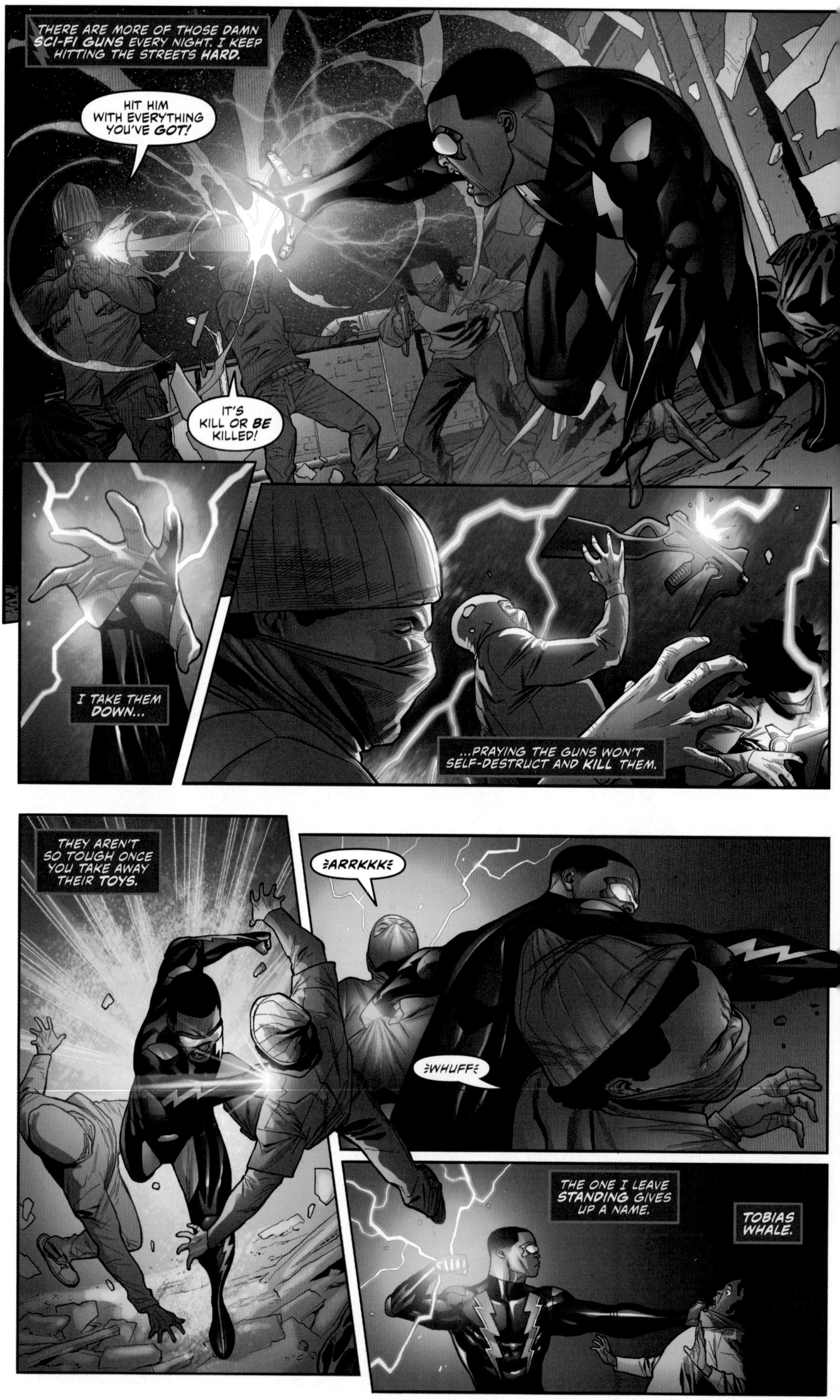
THERE ARE MORE OF THOSE DAMN SCI-FI GUNS EVERY NIGHT. I KEEP HITTING THE STREETS HARD.
HIT HIM WITH EVERYTHING YOU'VE GOT!
IT'S KILL OR BE KILLED!
I TAKE THEM DOWN...
...PRAYING THE GUNS WON'T SELF-DESTRUCT AND KILL THEM.
THEY AREN'T SO TOUGH ONCE YOU TAKE AWAY THEIR TOYS.
ARRKKK
WHUFF
THE ONE I LEAVE STANDING GIVES UP A NAME.
TOBIAS WHALE.

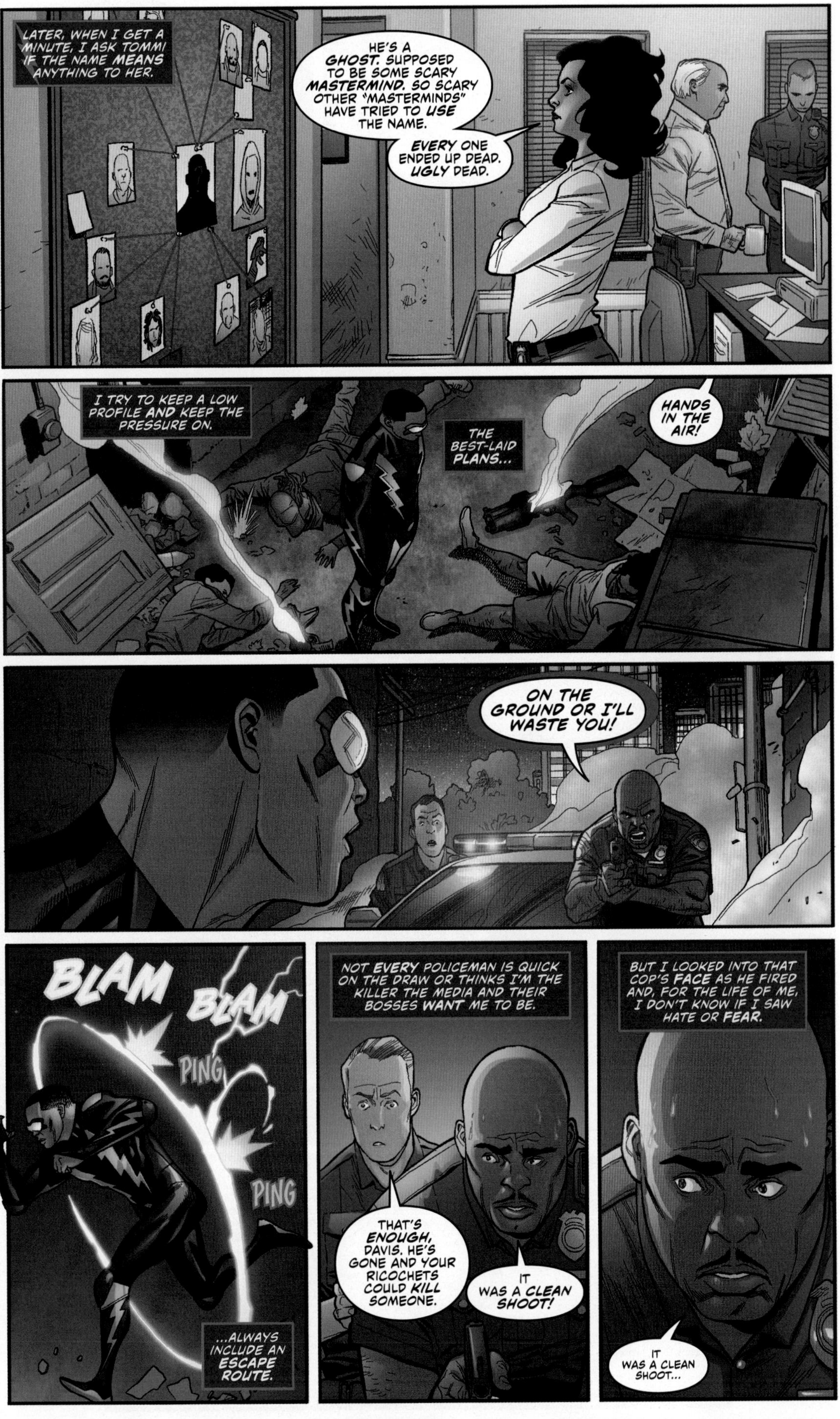
LATER, WHEN I GET A MINUTE, I ASK TOMMI IF THE NAME MEANS ANYTHING TO HER.
HE'S A GHOST. SUPPOSED TO BE SOME SCARY MASTERMIND. SO SCARY OTHER "MASTERMINDS" HAVE TRIED TO USE THE NAME.
EVERY ONE ENDED UP DEAD. UGLY DEAD.
I TRY TO KEEP A LOW PROFILE AND KEEP THE PRESSURE ON.
THE BEST-LAID PLANS...
HANDS IN THE AIR!
ON THE GROUND OR I'LL WASTE YOU!
BLAM
BLAM
PING
PING
...ALWAYS INCLUDE AN ESCAPE ROUTE.
NOT EVERY POLICEMAN IS QUICK ON THE DRAW OR THINKS I'M THE KILLER THE MEDIA AND THEIR BOSSES WANT ME TO BE.
THAT'S ENOUGH, DAVIS. HE'S GONE AND YOUR RICOCHETS COULD KILL SOMEONE.
IT WAS A CLEAN SHOOT!
BUT I LOOKED INTO THAT COP'S FACE AS HE FIRED AND, FOR THE LIFE OF ME, I DON'T KNOW IF I SAW HATE OR FEAR.
IT WAS A CLEAN SHOOT...

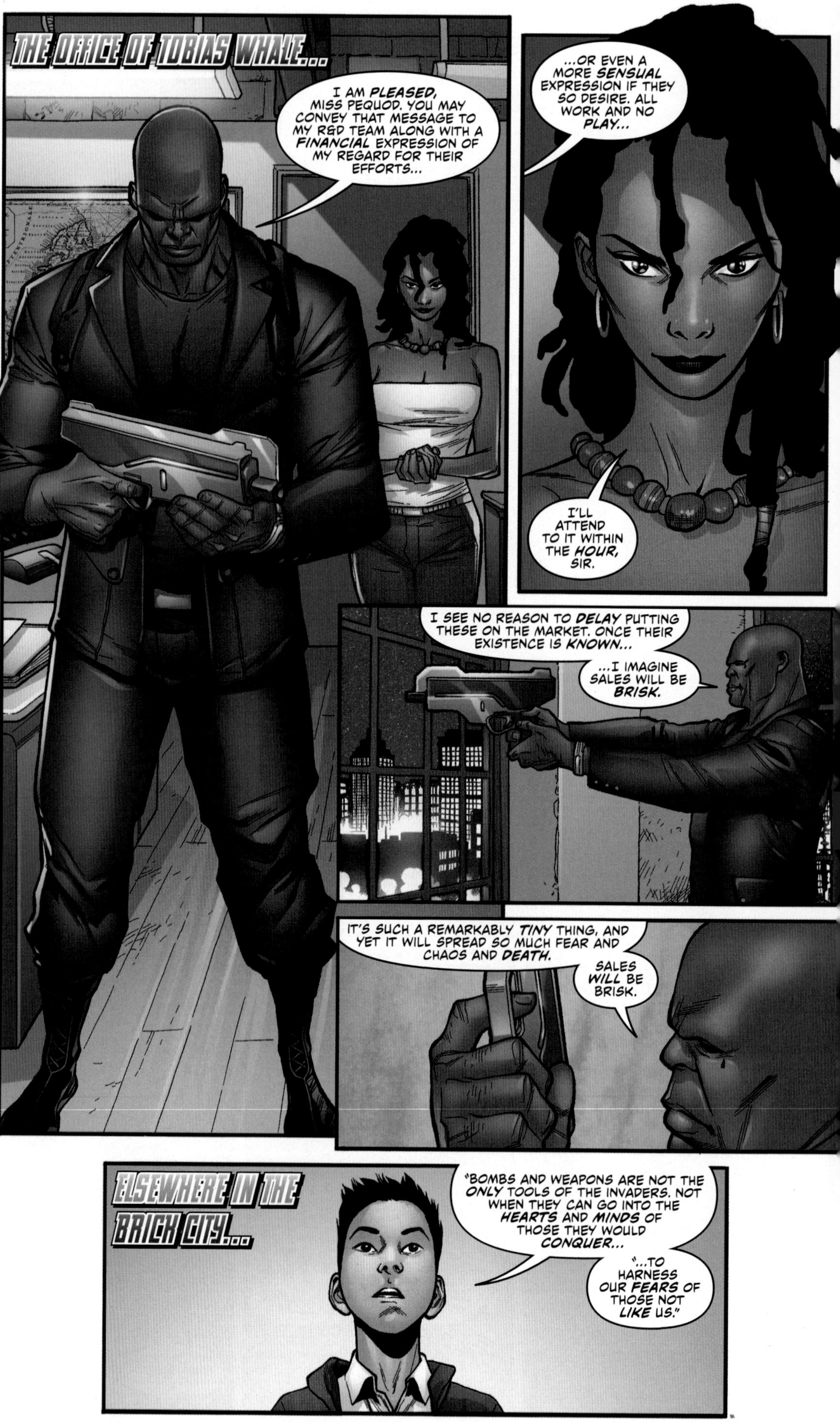
THE OFFICE OF TOBIAS WHALE...
I AM PLEASED, MISS PEQUOD. YOU MAY CONVEY THAT MESSAGE TO MY R&D TEAM ALONG WITH A FINANCIAL EXPRESSION OF MY REGARD FOR THEIR EFFORTS...
...OR EVEN A MORE SENSUAL EXPRESSION IF THEY SO DESIRE. ALL WORK AND NO PLAY...
I'LL ATTEND TO IT WITHIN THE HOUR, SIR.
I SEE NO REASON TO DELAY PUTTING THESE ON THE MARKET. ONCE THEIR EXISTENCE IS KNOWN...
...I IMAGINE SALES WILL BE BRISK.
IT'S SUCH A REMARKABLY TINY THING, AND YET IT WILL SPREAD SO MUCH FEAR AND CHAOS AND DEATH.
SALES WILL BE BRISK.
ELSEWHERE IN THE BRICK CITY...
"BOMBS AND WEAPONS ARE NOT THE ONLY TOOLS OF THE INVADERS. NOT WHEN THEY CAN GO INTO THE HEARTS AND MINDS OF THOSE THEY WOULD CONQUER...
"...TO HARNESS OUR FEARS OF THOSE NOT LIKE US."

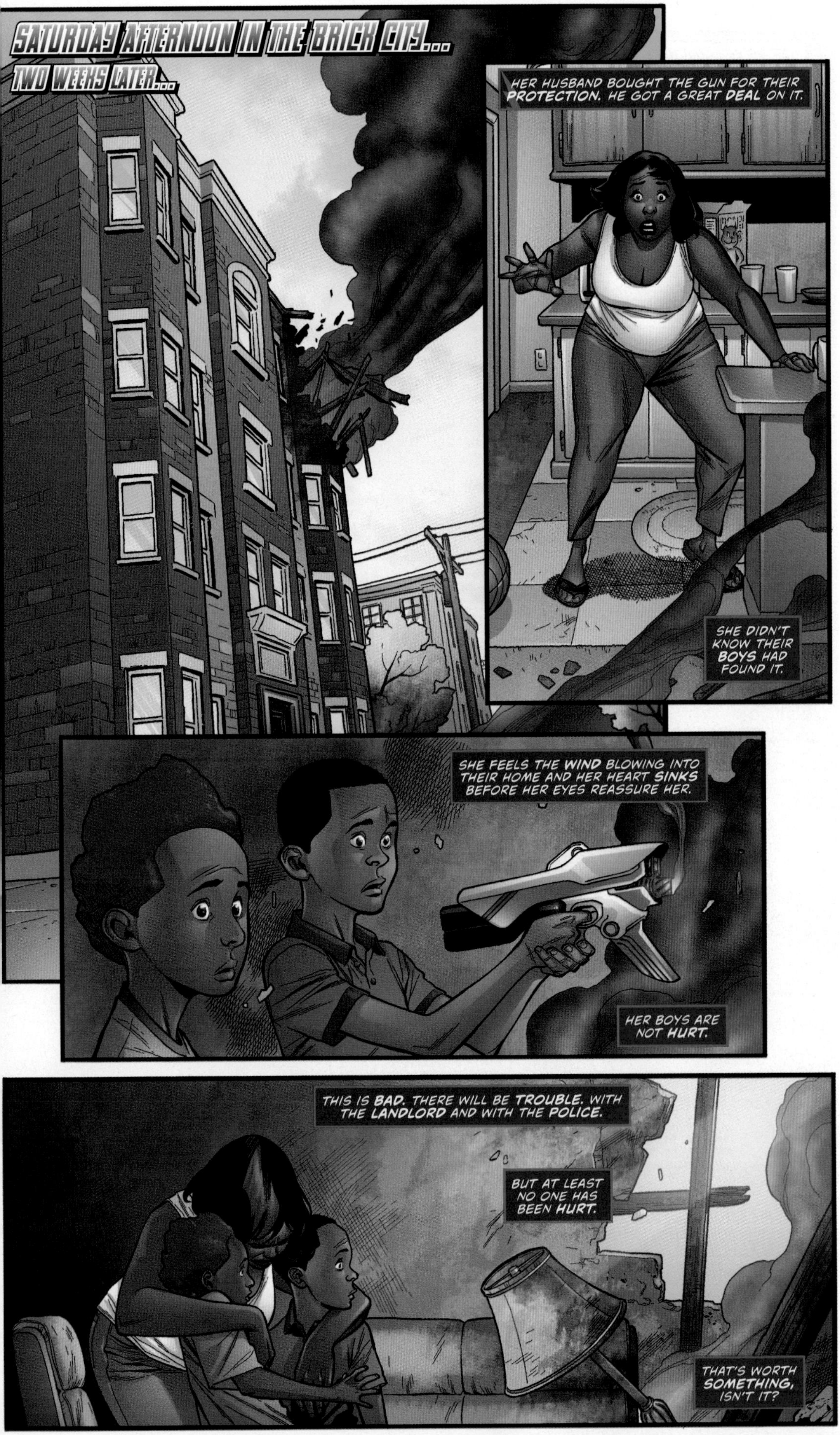

SATURDAY AFTERNOON IN THE BRICK CITY...
TWO WEEKS LATER...
HER HUSBAND BOUGHT THE GUN FOR THEIR PROTECTION. HE GOT A GREAT DEAL ON IT.
SHE DIDN'T KNOW THEIR BOYS HAD FOUND IT.
SHE FEELS THE WIND BLOWING INTO THEIR HOME AND HER HEART SINKS BEFORE HER EYES REASSURE HER.
HER BOYS ARE NOT HURT.
THIS IS BAD. THERE WILL BE TROUBLE. WITH THE LANDLORD AND WITH THE POLICE.
BUT AT LEAST NO ONE HAS BEEN HURT.
THAT'S WORTH SOMETHING, ISN'T IT?

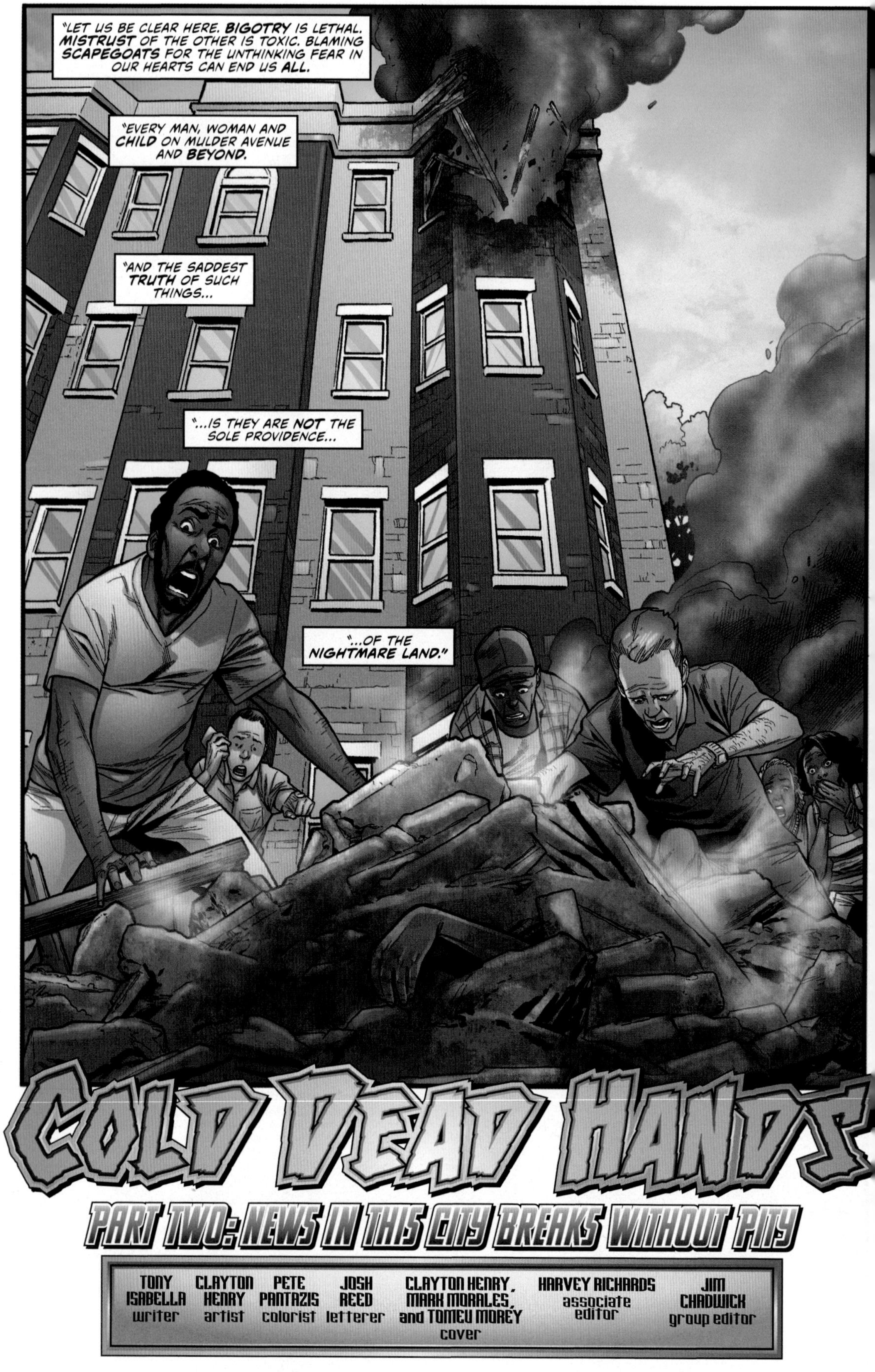
"LET US BE CLEAR HERE. BIGOTRY IS LETHAL. MISTRUST OF THE OTHER IS TOXIC. BLAMING SCAPEGOATS FOR THE UNTHINKING FEAR IN OUR HEARTS CAN END US ALL.
"EVERY MAN, WOMAN AND CHILD ON MULDER AVENUE AND BEYOND.
"AND THE SADDEST TRUTH OF SUCH THINGS...
"...IS THEY ARE NOT THE SOLE PROVIDENCE...
"...OF THE NIGHTMARE LAND."

COLD DEAD HANDS

PART TWO: NEWS IN THIS CITY BREAKS WITHOUT PITY

TONY ISABELLA writer
CLAYTON HENRY artist
PETE PANTAZIS colorist
JOSH REED letterer
CLAYTON HENRY, MARK MORALES, and TOMEU MOREY cover
HARVEY RICHARDS associate editor
JIM CHADWICK group editor

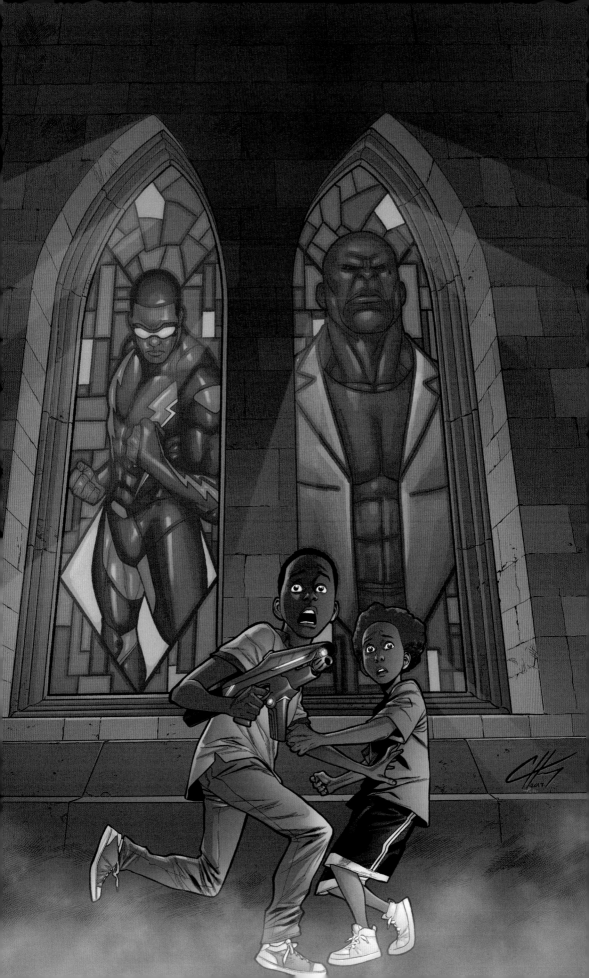

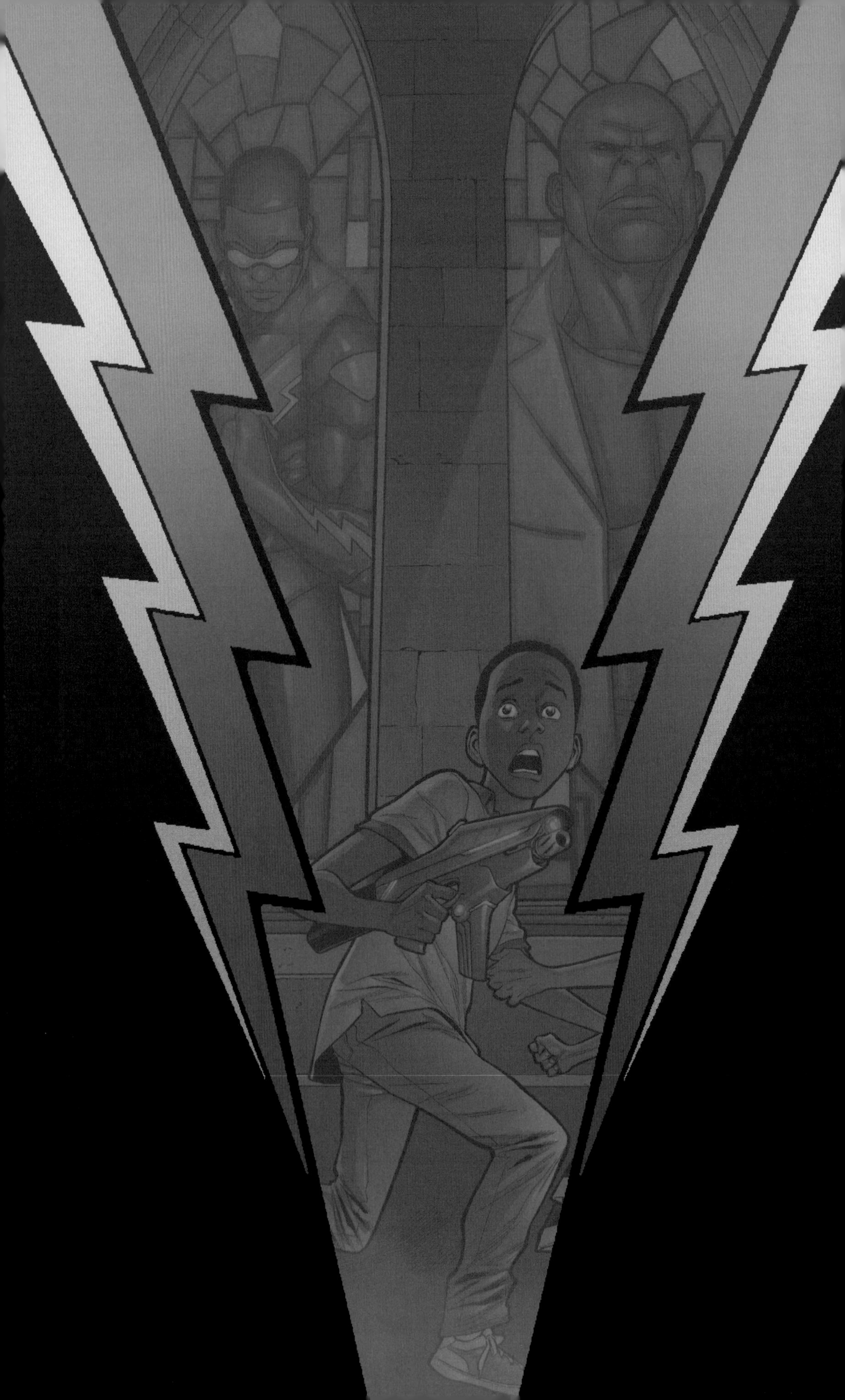

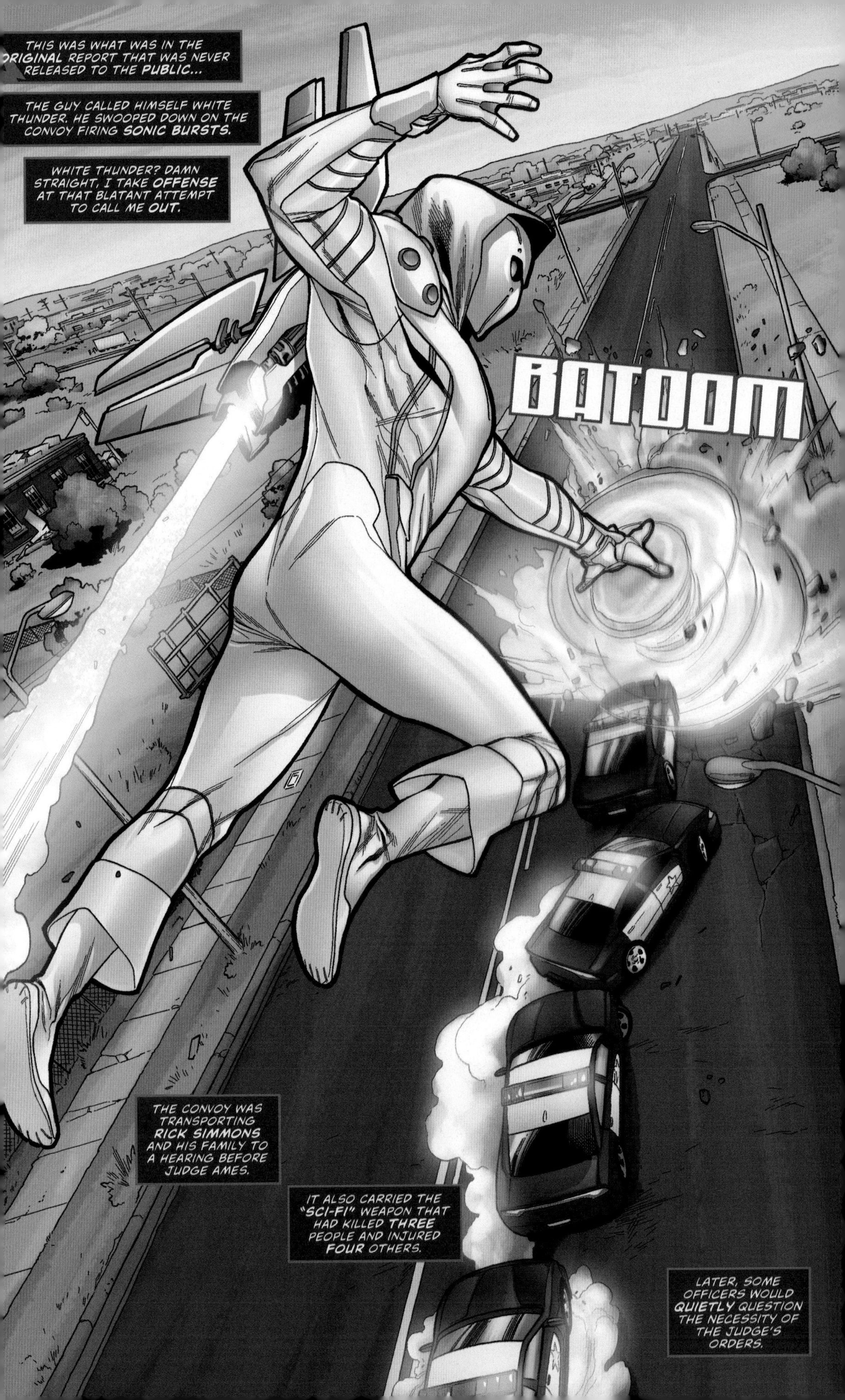
THIS WAS WHAT WAS IN THE ORIGINAL REPORT THAT WAS NEVER RELEASED TO THE PUBLIC...
THE GUY CALLED HIMSELF WHITE THUNDER. HE SWOOPED DOWN ON THE CONVOY FIRING SONIC BURSTS.
WHITE THUNDER? DAMN STRAIGHT, I TAKE OFFENSE AT THAT BLATANT ATTEMPT TO CALL ME OUT.
BATOOM
THE CONVOY WAS TRANSPORTING RICK SIMMONS AND HIS FAMILY TO A HEARING BEFORE JUDGE AMES.
IT ALSO CARRIED THE "SCI-FI" WEAPON THAT HAD KILLED THREE PEOPLE AND INJURED FOUR OTHERS.
LATER, SOME OFFICERS WOULD QUIETLY QUESTION THE NECESSITY OF THE JUDGE'S ORDERS.

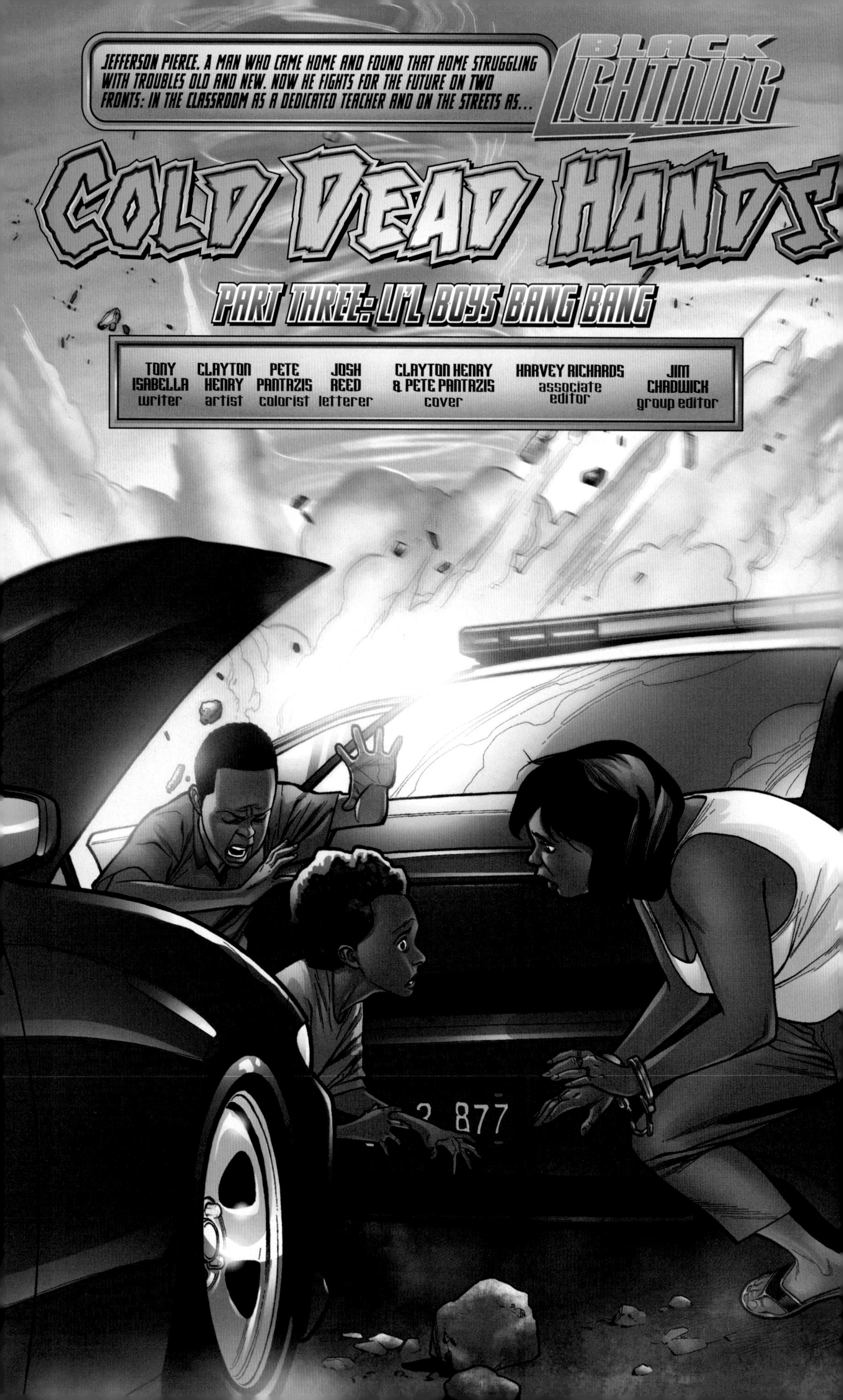
JEFFERSON PIERCE. A MAN WHO CAME HOME AND FOUND THAT HOME STRUGGLING WITH TROUBLES OLD AND NEW. NOW HE FIGHTS FOR THE FUTURE ON TWO FRONTS: IN THE CLASSROOM AS A DEDICATED TEACHER AND ON THE STREETS AS...
BLACK LIGHTNING
COLD DEAD HANDS
PART THREE: LI'L BOYS BANG BANG
TONY ISABELLA writer
CLAYTON HENRY artist
PETE PANTAZIS colorist
JOSH REED letterer
CLAYTON HENRY & PETE PANTAZIS cover
HARVEY RICHARDS associate editor
JIM CHADWICK group editor

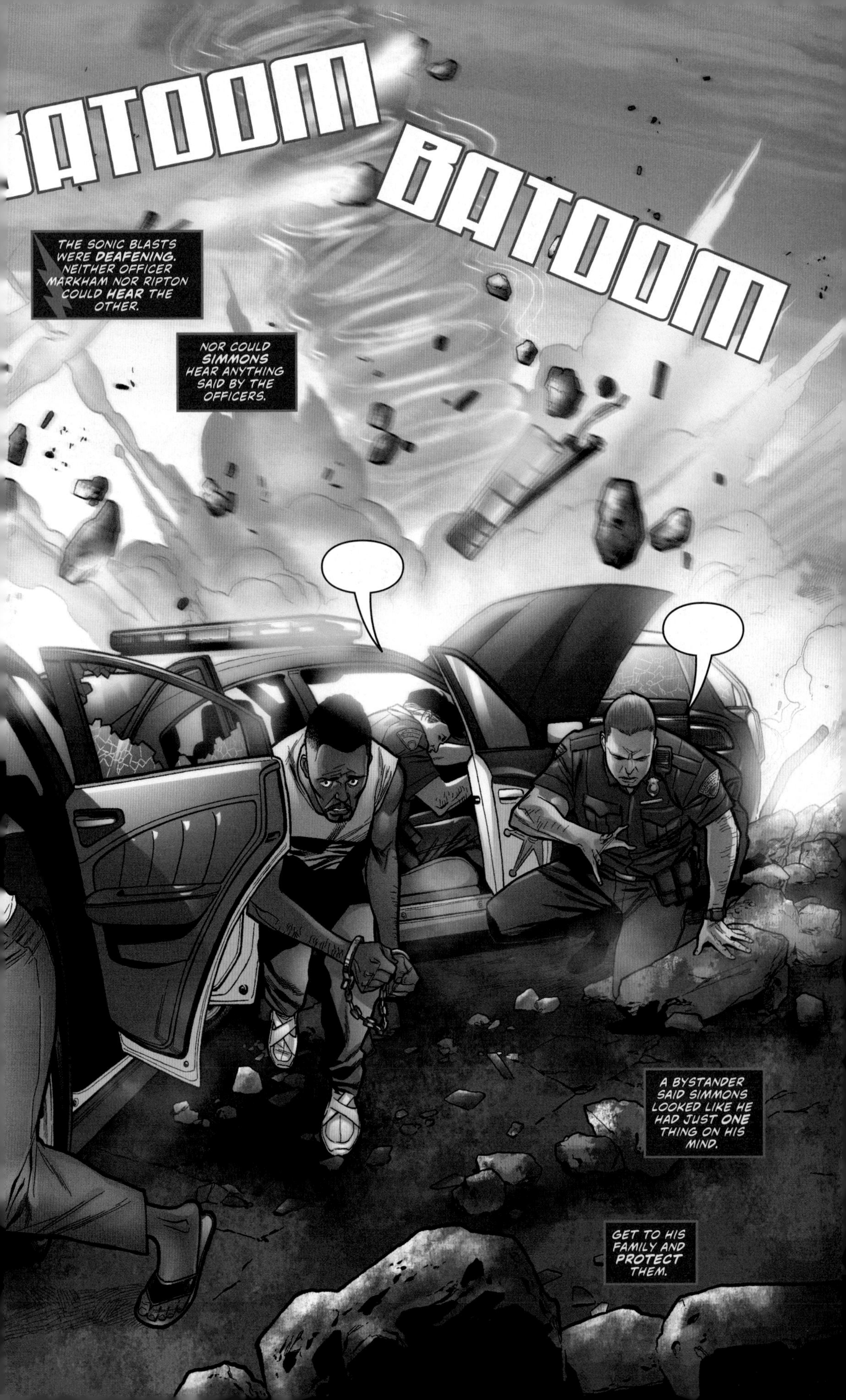
BATOOM
BATOOM
THE SONIC BLASTS WERE DEAFENING. NEITHER OFFICER MARKHAM NOR RIPTON COULD HEAR THE OTHER.
NOR COULD SIMMONS HEAR ANYTHING SAID BY THE OFFICERS.
A BYSTANDER SAID SIMMONS LOOKED LIKE HE HAD JUST ONE THING ON HIS MIND.
GET TO HIS FAMILY AND PROTECT THEM.

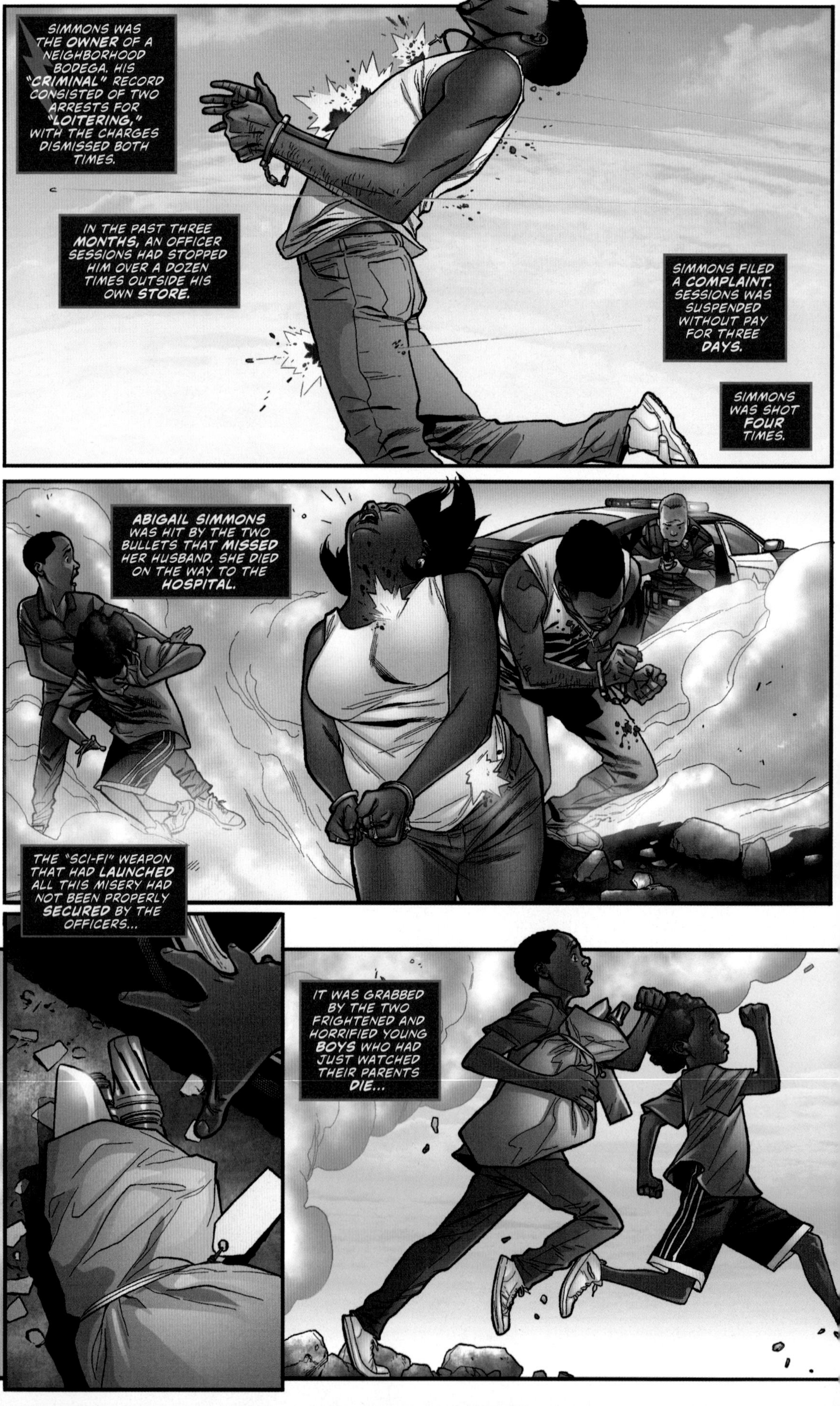
SIMMONS WAS THE OWNER OF A NEIGHBORHOOD BODEGA. HIS "CRIMINAL" RECORD CONSISTED OF TWO ARRESTS FOR "LOITERING," WITH THE CHARGES DISMISSED BOTH TIMES.
IN THE PAST THREE MONTHS, AN OFFICER SESSIONS HAD STOPPED HIM OVER A DOZEN TIMES OUTSIDE HIS OWN STORE.
SIMMONS FILED A COMPLAINT. SESSIONS WAS SUSPENDED WITHOUT PAY FOR THREE DAYS.
SIMMONS WAS SHOT FOUR TIMES.
ABIGAIL SIMMONS WAS HIT BY THE TWO BULLETS THAT MISSED HER HUSBAND. SHE DIED ON THE WAY TO THE HOSPITAL.
THE "SCI-FI" WEAPON THAT HAD LAUNCHED ALL THIS MISERY HAD NOT BEEN PROPERLY SECURED BY THE OFFICERS...
IT WAS GRABBED BY THE TWO FRIGHTENED AND HORRIFIED YOUNG BOYS WHO HAD JUST WATCHED THEIR PARENTS DIE...

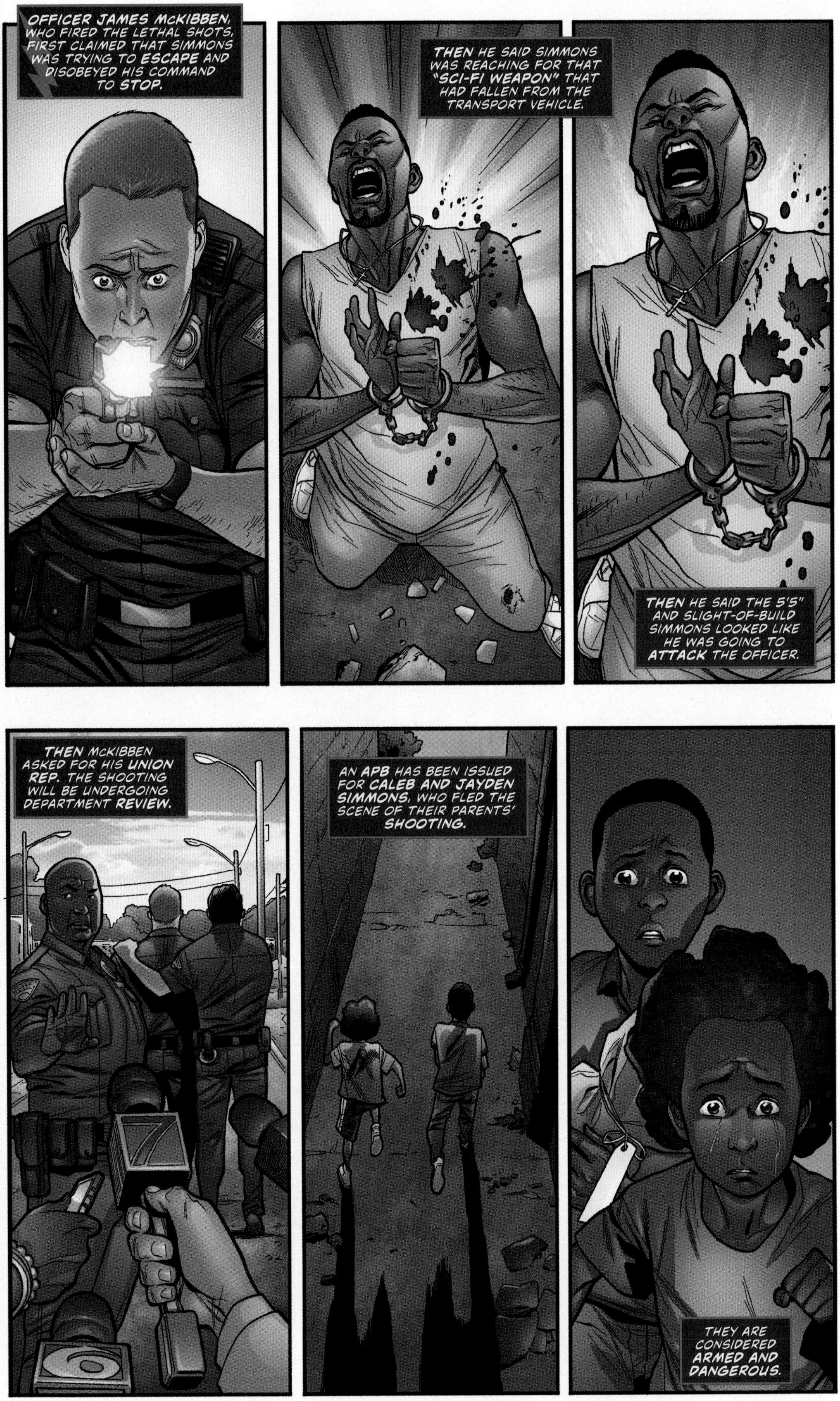
OFFICER JAMES McKIBBEN, WHO FIRED THE LETHAL SHOTS, FIRST CLAIMED THAT SIMMONS WAS TRYING TO ESCAPE AND DISOBEYED HIS COMMAND TO STOP.
THEN HE SAID SIMMONS WAS REACHING FOR THAT "SCI-FI WEAPON" THAT HAD FALLEN FROM THE TRANSPORT VEHICLE.
THEN HE SAID THE 5'5" AND SLIGHT-OF-BUILD SIMMONS LOOKED LIKE HE WAS GOING TO ATTACK THE OFFICER.
THEN McKIBBEN ASKED FOR HIS UNION REP. THE SHOOTING WILL BE UNDERGOING DEPARTMENT REVIEW.
7
AN APB HAS BEEN ISSUED FOR CALEB AND JAYDEN SIMMONS, WHO FLED THE SCENE OF THEIR PARENTS' SHOOTING.
THEY ARE CONSIDERED ARMED AND DANGEROUS.

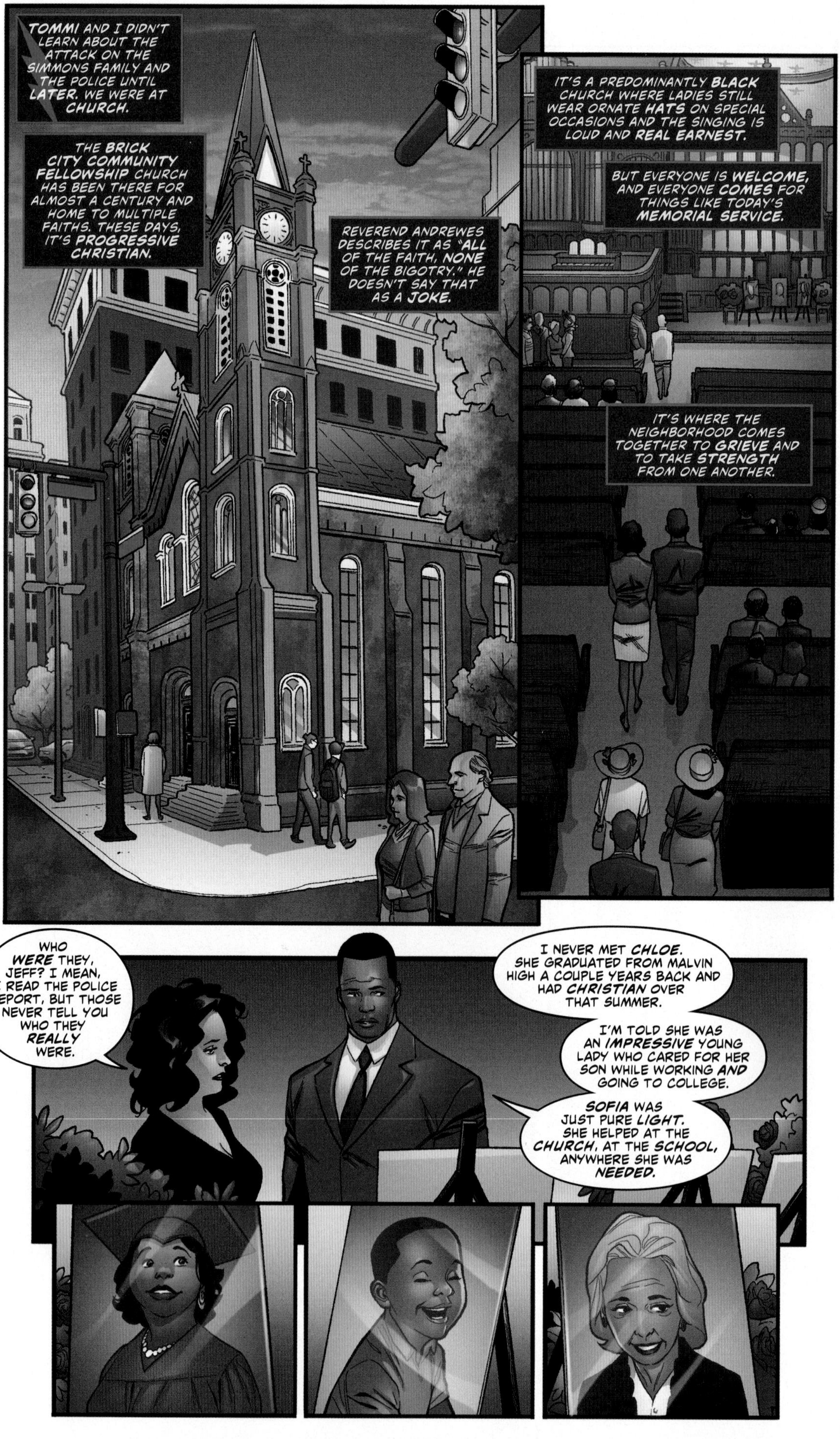
TOMMI AND I DIDN'T LEARN ABOUT THE ATTACK ON THE SIMMONS FAMILY AND THE POLICE UNTIL LATER. WE WERE AT CHURCH.
THE BRICK CITY COMMUNITY FELLOWSHIP CHURCH HAS BEEN THERE FOR ALMOST A CENTURY AND HOME TO MULTIPLE FAITHS. THESE DAYS, IT'S PROGRESSIVE CHRISTIAN.
REVEREND ANDREWES DESCRIBES IT AS "ALL OF THE FAITH, NONE OF THE BIGOTRY." HE DOESN'T SAY THAT AS A JOKE.
IT'S A PREDOMINANTLY BLACK CHURCH WHERE LADIES STILL WEAR ORNATE HATS ON SPECIAL OCCASIONS AND THE SINGING IS LOUD AND REAL EARNEST.
BUT EVERYONE IS WELCOME, AND EVERYONE COMES FOR THINGS LIKE TODAY'S MEMORIAL SERVICE.
IT'S WHERE THE NEIGHBORHOOD COMES TOGETHER TO GRIEVE AND TO TAKE STRENGTH FROM ONE ANOTHER.
WHO WERE THEY, JEFF? I MEAN, I READ THE POLICE REPORT, BUT THOSE NEVER TELL YOU WHO THEY REALLY WERE.
I NEVER MET CHLOE. SHE GRADUATED FROM MALVIN HIGH A COUPLE YEARS BACK AND HAD CHRISTIAN OVER THAT SUMMER.
I'M TOLD SHE WAS AN IMPRESSIVE YOUNG LADY WHO CARED FOR HER SON WHILE WORKING AND GOING TO COLLEGE.
SOFIA WAS JUST PURE LIGHT. SHE HELPED AT THE CHURCH, AT THE SCHOOL, ANYWHERE SHE WAS NEEDED.

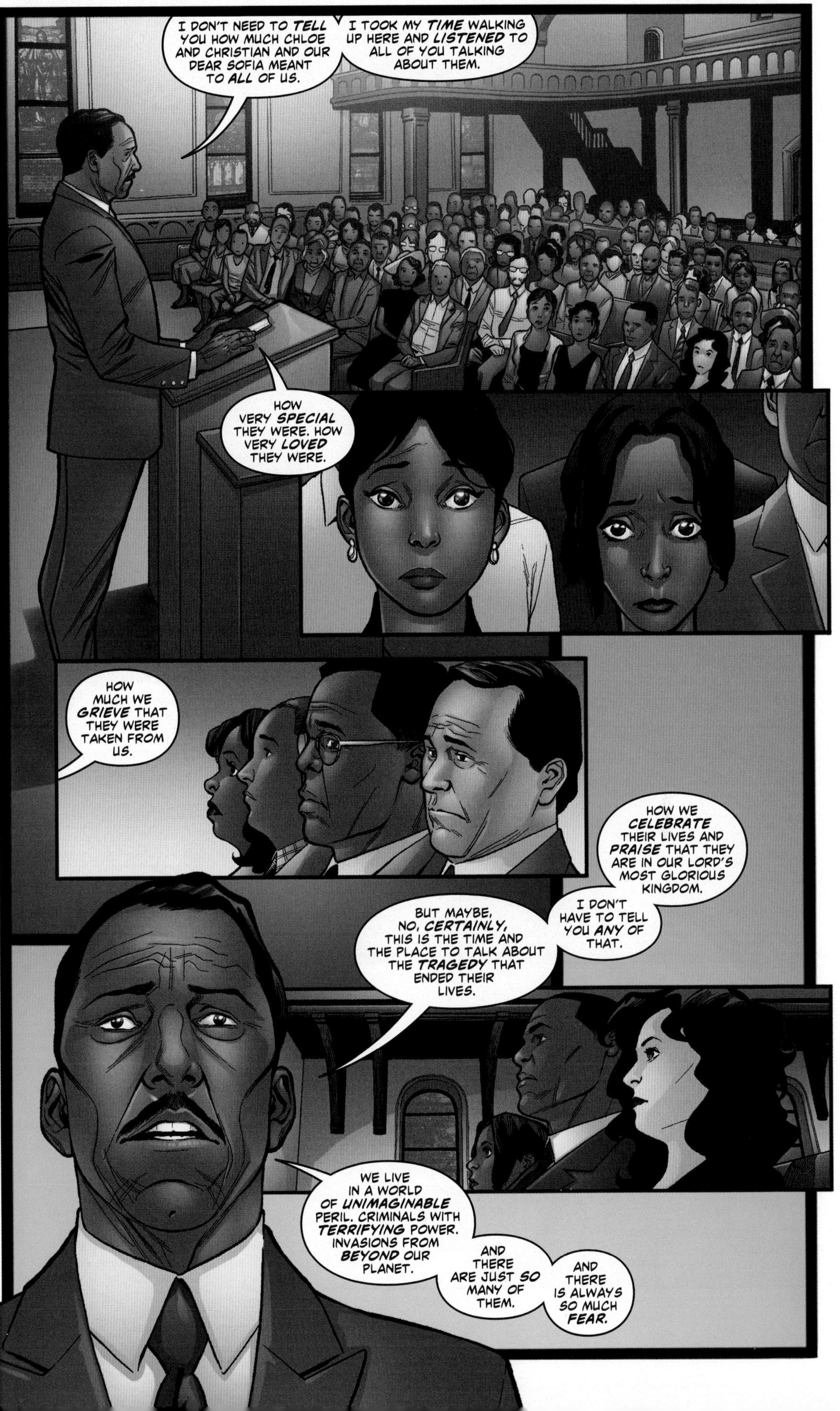
I DON'T NEED TO TELL YOU HOW MUCH CHLOE AND CHRISTIAN AND OUR DEAR SOFIA MEANT TO ALL OF US.
I TOOK MY TIME WALKING UP HERE AND LISTENED TO ALL OF YOU TALKING ABOUT THEM.
HOW VERY SPECIAL THEY WERE. HOW VERY LOVED THEY WERE.
HOW MUCH WE GRIEVE THAT THEY WERE TAKEN FROM US.
HOW WE CELEBRATE THEIR LIVES AND PRAISE THAT THEY ARE IN OUR LORD'S MOST GLORIOUS KINGDOM.
I DON'T HAVE TO TELL YOU ANY OF THAT.
BUT MAYBE, NO, CERTAINLY, THIS IS THE TIME AND THE PLACE TO TALK ABOUT THE TRAGEDY THAT ENDED THEIR LIVES.
WE LIVE IN A WORLD OF UNIMAGINABLE PERIL. CRIMINALS WITH TERRIFYING POWER. INVASIONS FROM BEYOND OUR PLANET.
AND THERE ARE JUST SO MANY OF THEM.
AND THERE IS ALWAYS SO MUCH FEAR.

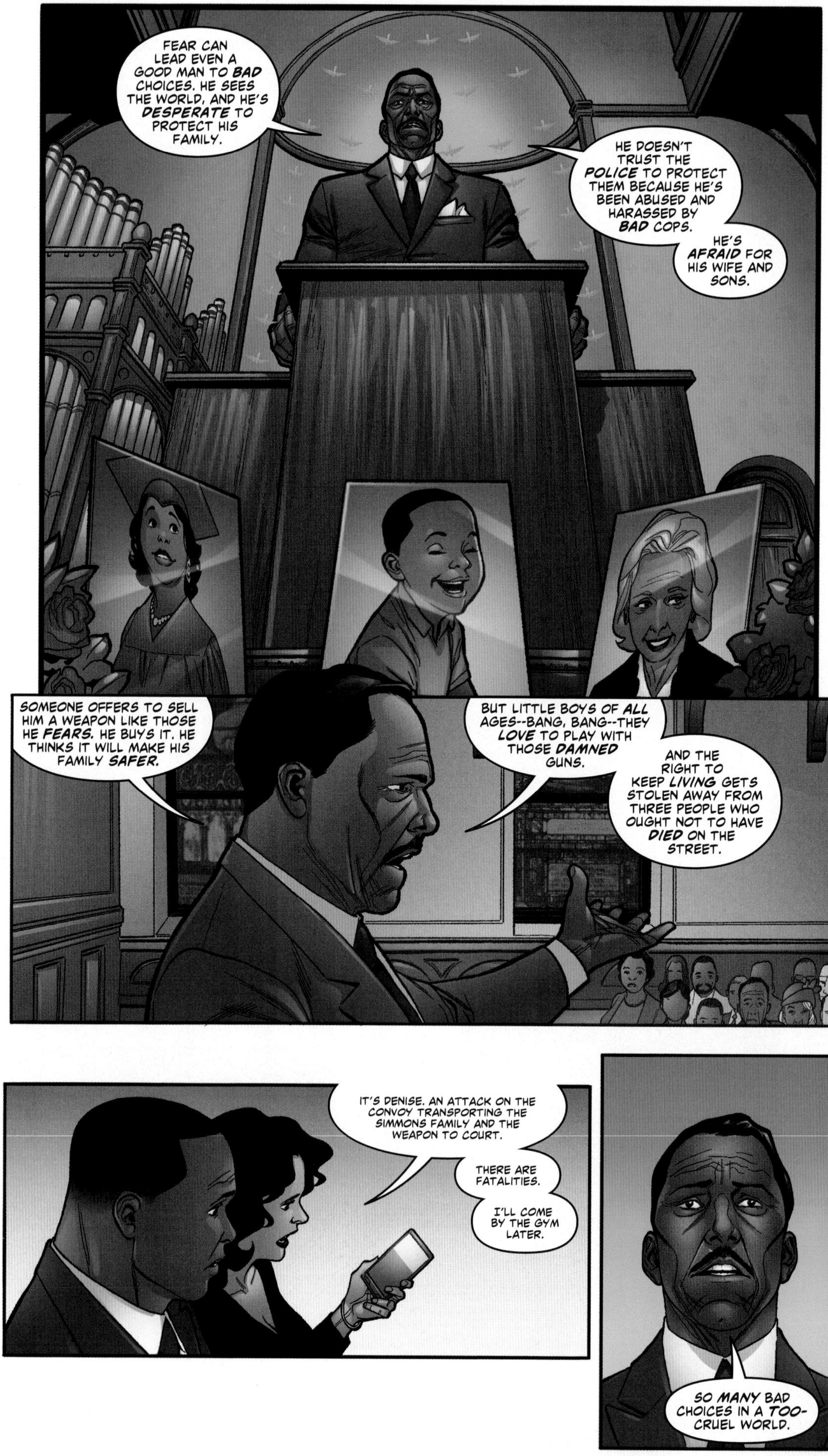
FEAR CAN LEAD EVEN A GOOD MAN TO BAD CHOICES. HE SEES THE WORLD, AND HE'S DESPERATE TO PROTECT HIS FAMILY.
HE DOESN'T TRUST THE POLICE TO PROTECT THEM BECAUSE HE'S BEEN ABUSED AND HARASSED BY BAD COPS.
HE'S AFRAID FOR HIS WIFE AND SONS.
SOMEONE OFFERS TO SELL HIM A WEAPON LIKE THOSE HE FEARS. HE BUYS IT. HE THINKS IT WILL MAKE HIS FAMILY SAFER.
BUT LITTLE BOYS OF ALL AGES--BANG, BANG--THEY LOVE TO PLAY WITH THOSE DAMNED GUNS.
AND THE RIGHT TO KEEP LIVING GETS STOLEN AWAY FROM THREE PEOPLE WHO OUGHT NOT TO HAVE DIED ON THE STREET.
IT'S DENISE. AN ATTACK ON THE CONVOY TRANSPORTING THE SIMMONS FAMILY AND THE WEAPON TO COURT.
THERE ARE FATALITIES.
I'LL COME BY THE GYM LATER.
SO MANY BAD CHOICES IN A TOO-CRUEL WORLD.

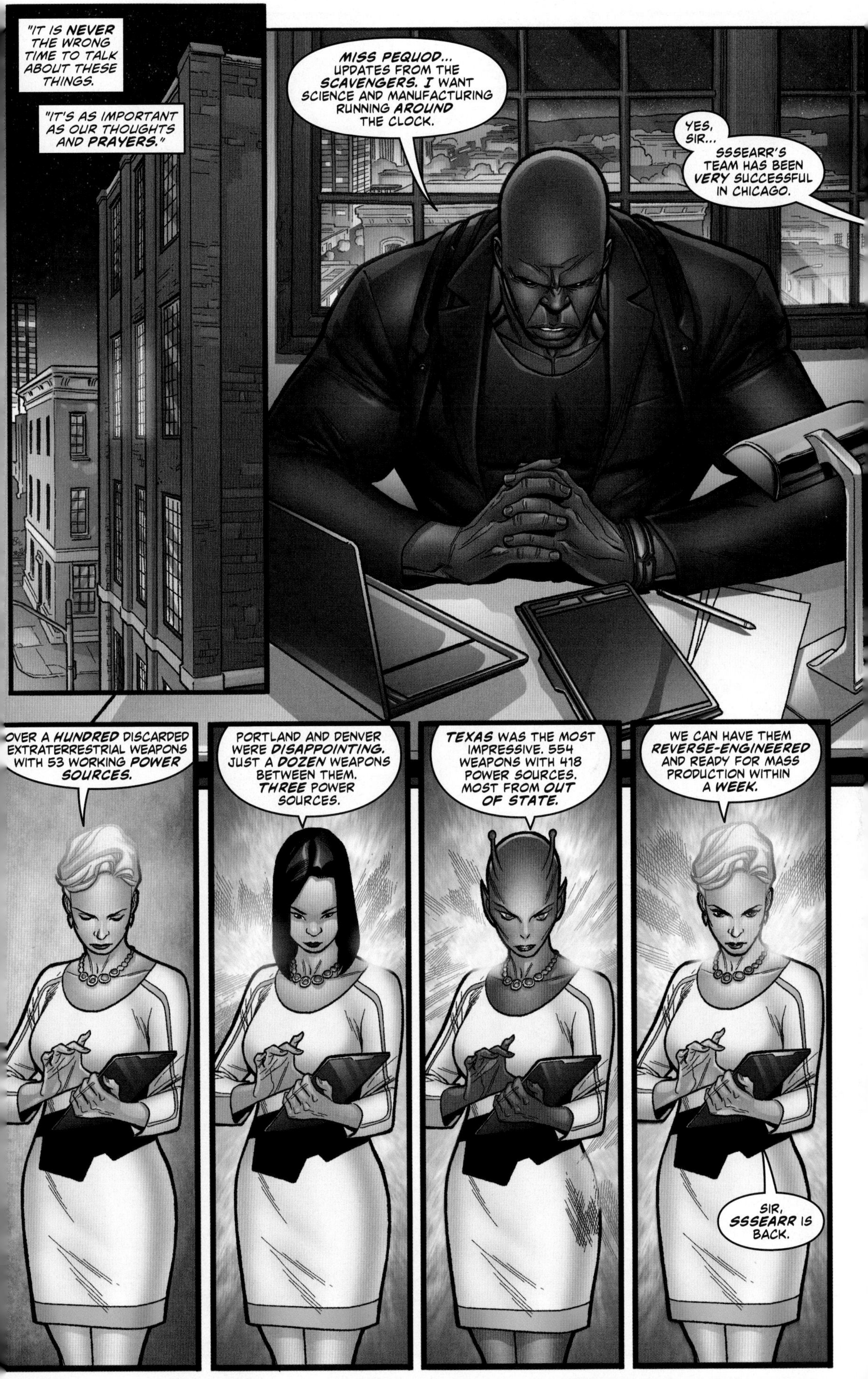
"IT IS NEVER THE WRONG TIME TO TALK ABOUT THESE THINGS.
"IT'S AS IMPORTANT AS OUR THOUGHTS AND PRAYERS."
MISS PEQUOD... UPDATES FROM THE SCAVENGERS. I WANT SCIENCE AND MANUFACTURING RUNNING AROUND THE CLOCK.
YES, SIR...
SSSEARR'S TEAM HAS BEEN VERY SUCCESSFUL IN CHICAGO.
OVER A HUNDRED DISCARDED EXTRATERRESTRIAL WEAPONS WITH 53 WORKING POWER SOURCES.
PORTLAND AND DENVER WERE DISAPPOINTING. JUST A DOZEN WEAPONS BETWEEN THEM. THREE POWER SOURCES.
TEXAS WAS THE MOST IMPRESSIVE. 554 WEAPONS WITH 418 POWER SOURCES. MOST FROM OUT OF STATE.
WE CAN HAVE THEM REVERSE-ENGINEERED AND READY FOR MASS PRODUCTION WITHIN A WEEK.
SIR, SSSEARR IS BACK.

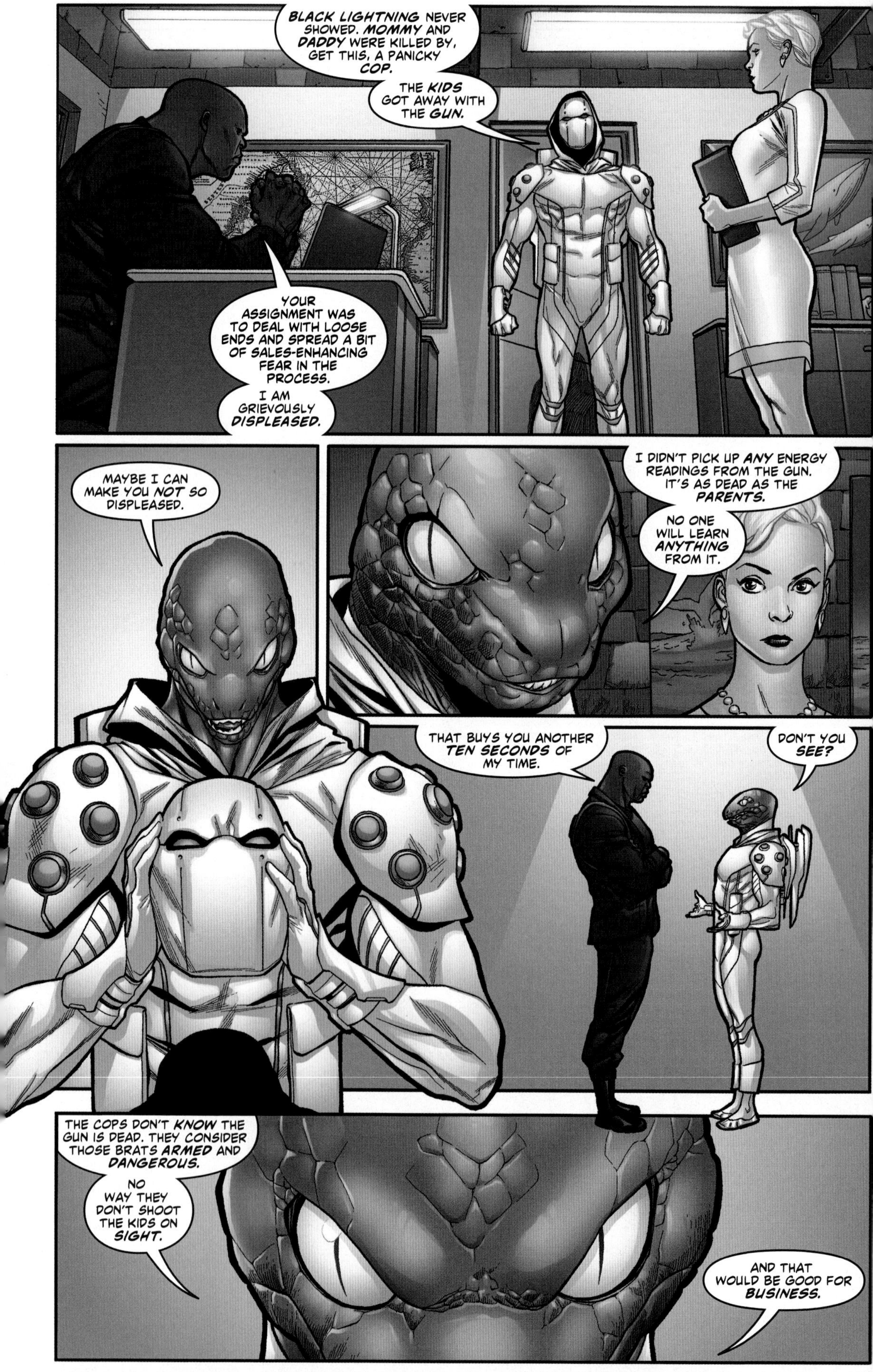
BLACK LIGHTNING NEVER SHOWED. MOMMY AND DADDY WERE KILLED BY, GET THIS, A PANICKY COP.
THE KIDS GOT AWAY WITH THE GUN.
YOUR ASSIGNMENT WAS TO DEAL WITH LOOSE ENDS AND SPREAD A BIT OF SALES-ENHANCING FEAR IN THE PROCESS.
I AM GRIEVOUSLY DISPLEASED.
MAYBE I CAN MAKE YOU NOT SO DISPLEASED.
I DIDN'T PICK UP ANY ENERGY READINGS FROM THE GUN. IT'S AS DEAD AS THE PARENTS.
NO ONE WILL LEARN ANYTHING FROM IT.
THAT BUYS YOU ANOTHER TEN SECONDS OF MY TIME.
DON'T YOU SEE?
THE COPS DON'T KNOW THE GUN IS DEAD. THEY CONSIDER THOSE BRATS ARMED AND DANGEROUS.
NO WAY THEY DON'T SHOOT THE KIDS ON SIGHT.
AND THAT WOULD BE GOOD FOR BUSINESS.

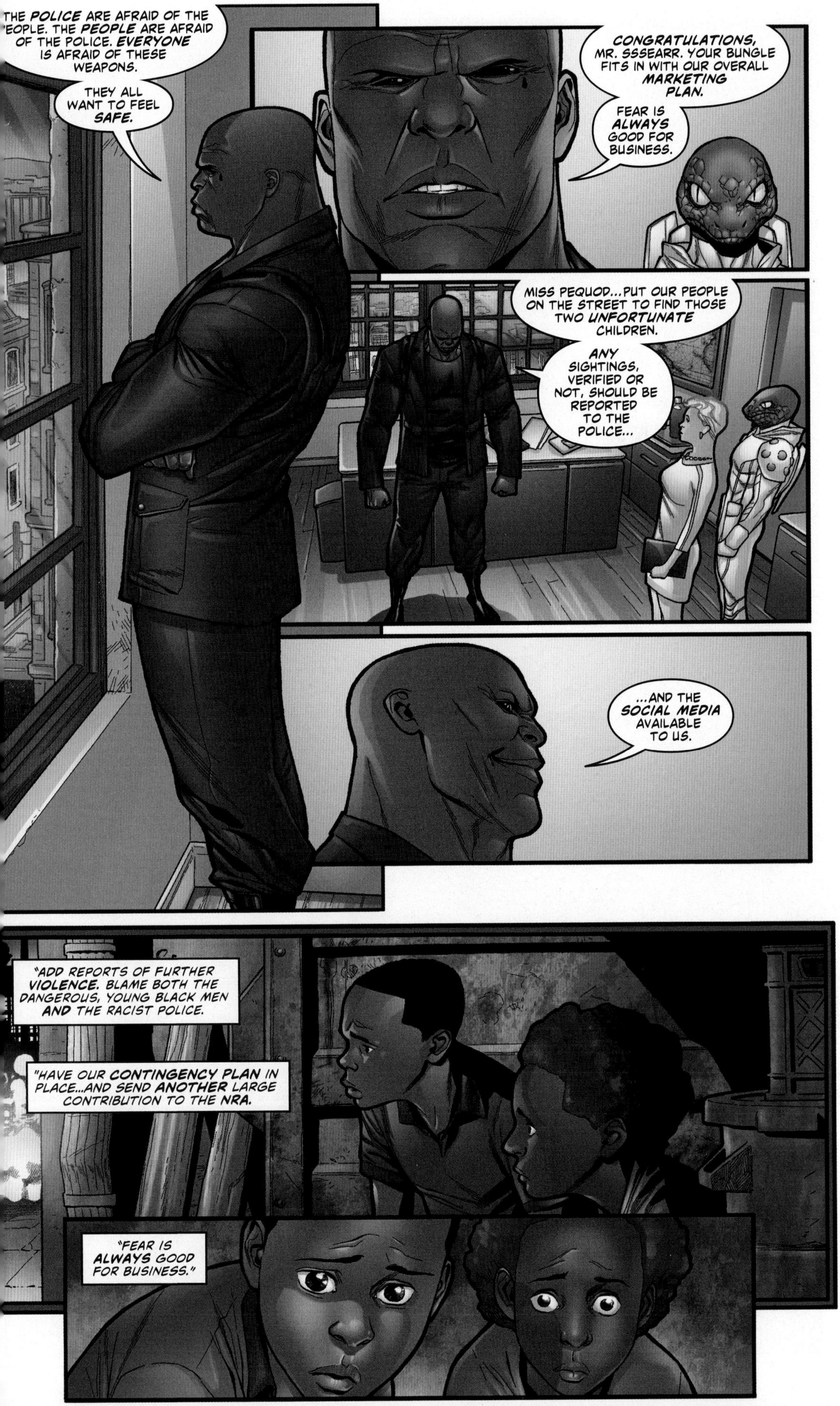
THE POLICE ARE AFRAID OF THE PEOPLE. THE PEOPLE ARE AFRAID OF THE POLICE. EVERYONE IS AFRAID OF THESE WEAPONS.
THEY ALL WANT TO FEEL SAFE.
CONGRATULATIONS, MR. SSSEARR. YOUR BUNGLE FITS IN WITH OUR OVERALL MARKETING PLAN.
FEAR IS ALWAYS GOOD FOR BUSINESS.
MISS PEQUOD...PUT OUR PEOPLE ON THE STREET TO FIND THOSE TWO UNFORTUNATE CHILDREN.
ANY SIGHTINGS, VERIFIED OR NOT, SHOULD BE REPORTED TO THE POLICE...
...AND THE SOCIAL MEDIA AVAILABLE TO US.
"ADD REPORTS OF FURTHER VIOLENCE. BLAME BOTH THE DANGEROUS, YOUNG BLACK MEN AND THE RACIST POLICE.
"HAVE OUR CONTINGENCY PLAN IN PLACE...AND SEND ANOTHER LARGE CONTRIBUTION TO THE NRA.
"FEAR IS ALWAYS GOOD FOR BUSINESS."

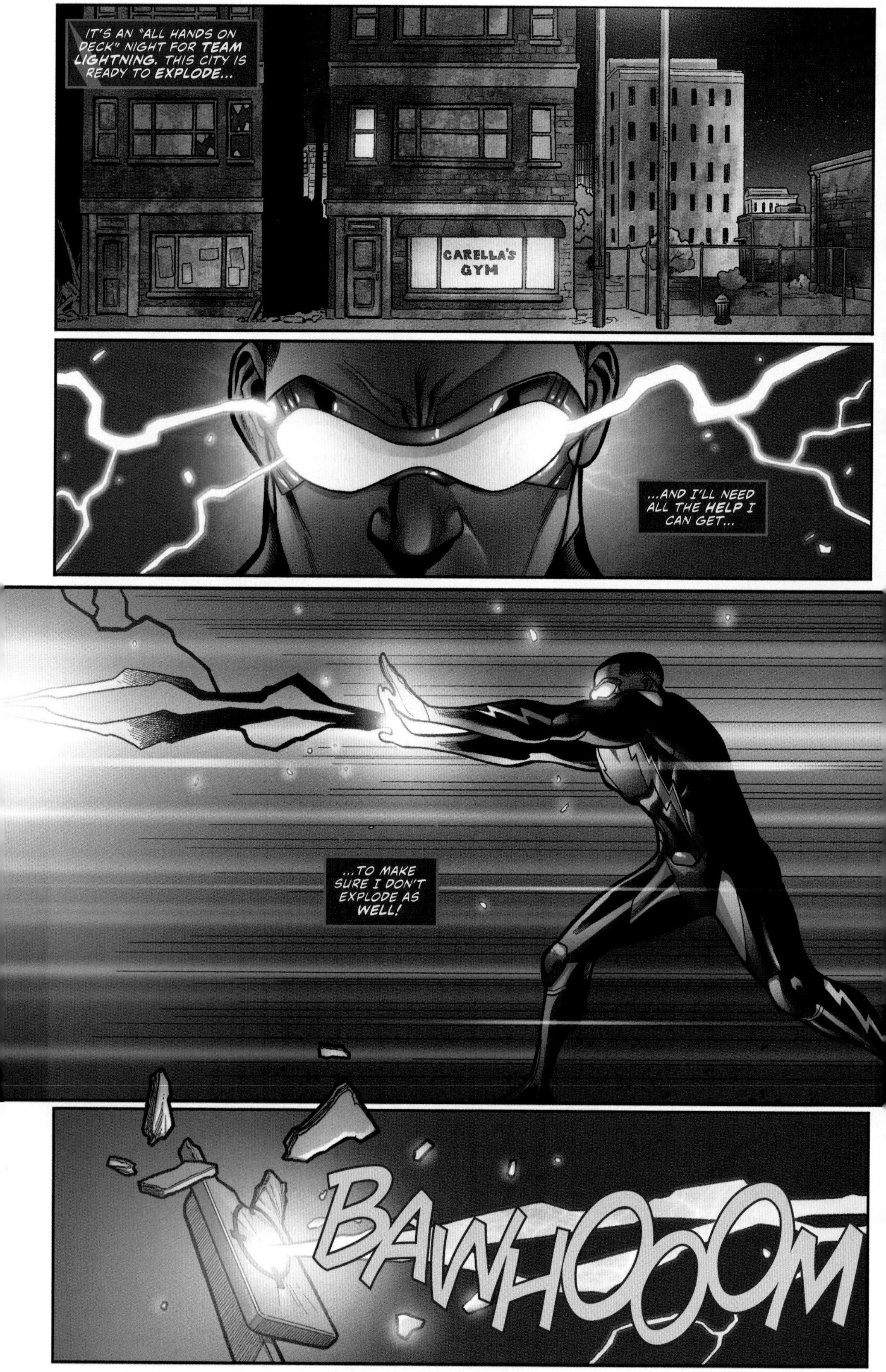
IT'S AN "ALL HANDS ON DECK" NIGHT FOR TEAM LIGHTNING. THIS CITY IS READY TO EXPLODE...
CARELLA'S GYM
...AND I'LL NEED ALL THE HELP I CAN GET...
...TO MAKE SURE I DON'T EXPLODE AS WELL!
BAWHOOOOM

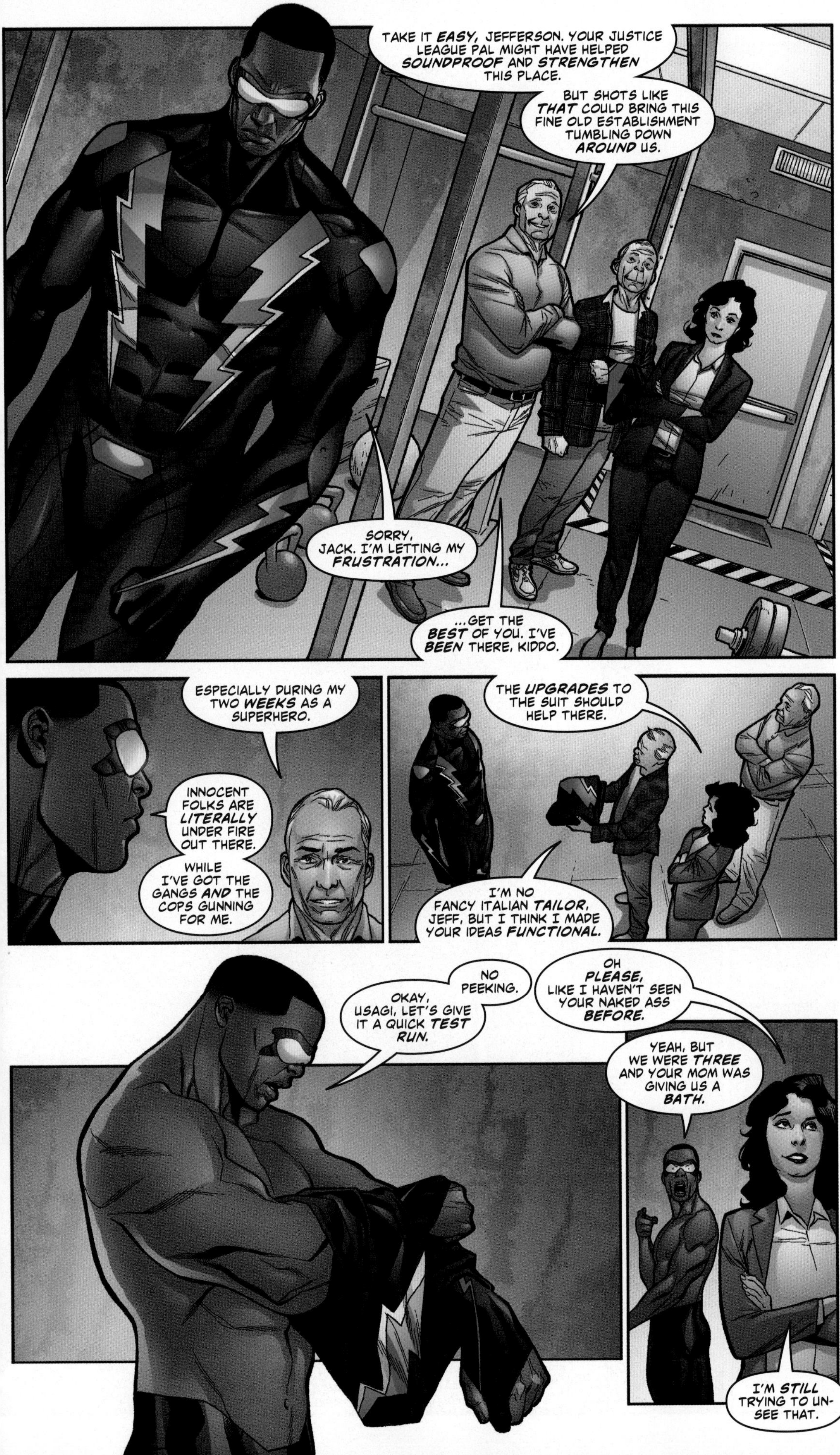
TAKE IT EASY, JEFFERSON. YOUR JUSTICE LEAGUE PAL MIGHT HAVE HELPED SOUNDPROOF AND STRENGTHEN THIS PLACE.
BUT SHOTS LIKE THAT COULD BRING THIS FINE OLD ESTABLISHMENT TUMBLING DOWN AROUND US.
SORRY, JACK. I'M LETTING MY FRUSTRATION...
...GET THE BEST OF YOU. I'VE BEEN THERE, KIDDO.
ESPECIALLY DURING MY TWO WEEKS AS A SUPERHERO.
INNOCENT FOLKS ARE LITERALLY UNDER FIRE OUT THERE.
WHILE I'VE GOT THE GANGS AND THE COPS GUNNING FOR ME.
THE UPGRADES TO THE SUIT SHOULD HELP THERE.
I'M NO FANCY ITALIAN TAILOR, JEFF, BUT I THINK I MADE YOUR IDEAS FUNCTIONAL.
OKAY, USAGI, LET'S GIVE IT A QUICK TEST RUN.
NO PEEKING.
OH PLEASE, LIKE I HAVEN'T SEEN YOUR NAKED ASS BEFORE.
YEAH, BUT WE WERE THREE AND YOUR MOM WAS GIVING US A BATH.
I'M STILL TRYING TO UN-SEE THAT.

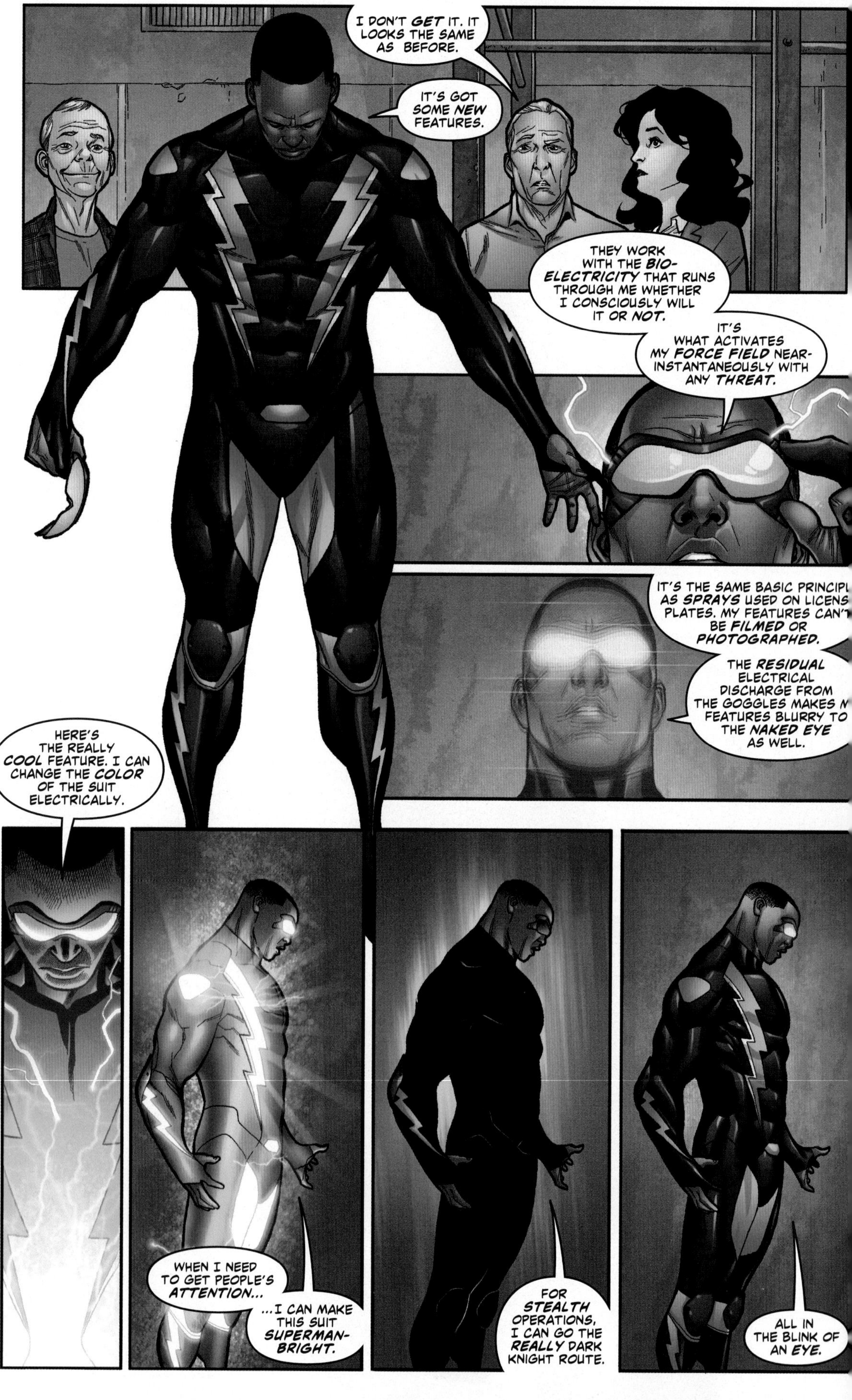

I DON'T GET IT. IT LOOKS THE SAME AS BEFORE.
IT'S GOT SOME NEW FEATURES.
THEY WORK WITH THE BIO-ELECTRICITY THAT RUNS THROUGH ME WHETHER I CONSCIOUSLY WILL IT OR NOT.
IT'S WHAT ACTIVATES MY FORCE FIELD NEAR-INSTANTANEOUSLY WITH ANY THREAT.
IT'S THE SAME BASIC PRINCIPL AS SPRAYS USED ON LICENS PLATES. MY FEATURES CAN'T BE FILMED OR PHOTOGRAPHED.
THE RESIDUAL ELECTRICAL DISCHARGE FROM THE GOGGLES MAKES M FEATURES BLURRY TO THE NAKED EYE AS WELL.
HERE'S THE REALLY COOL FEATURE. I CAN CHANGE THE COLOR OF THE SUIT ELECTRICALLY.
WHEN I NEED TO GET PEOPLE'S ATTENTION...
...I CAN MAKE THIS SUIT SUPERMAN-BRIGHT.
FOR STEALTH OPERATIONS, I CAN GO THE REALLY DARK KNIGHT ROUTE.
ALL IN THE BLINK OF AN EYE.

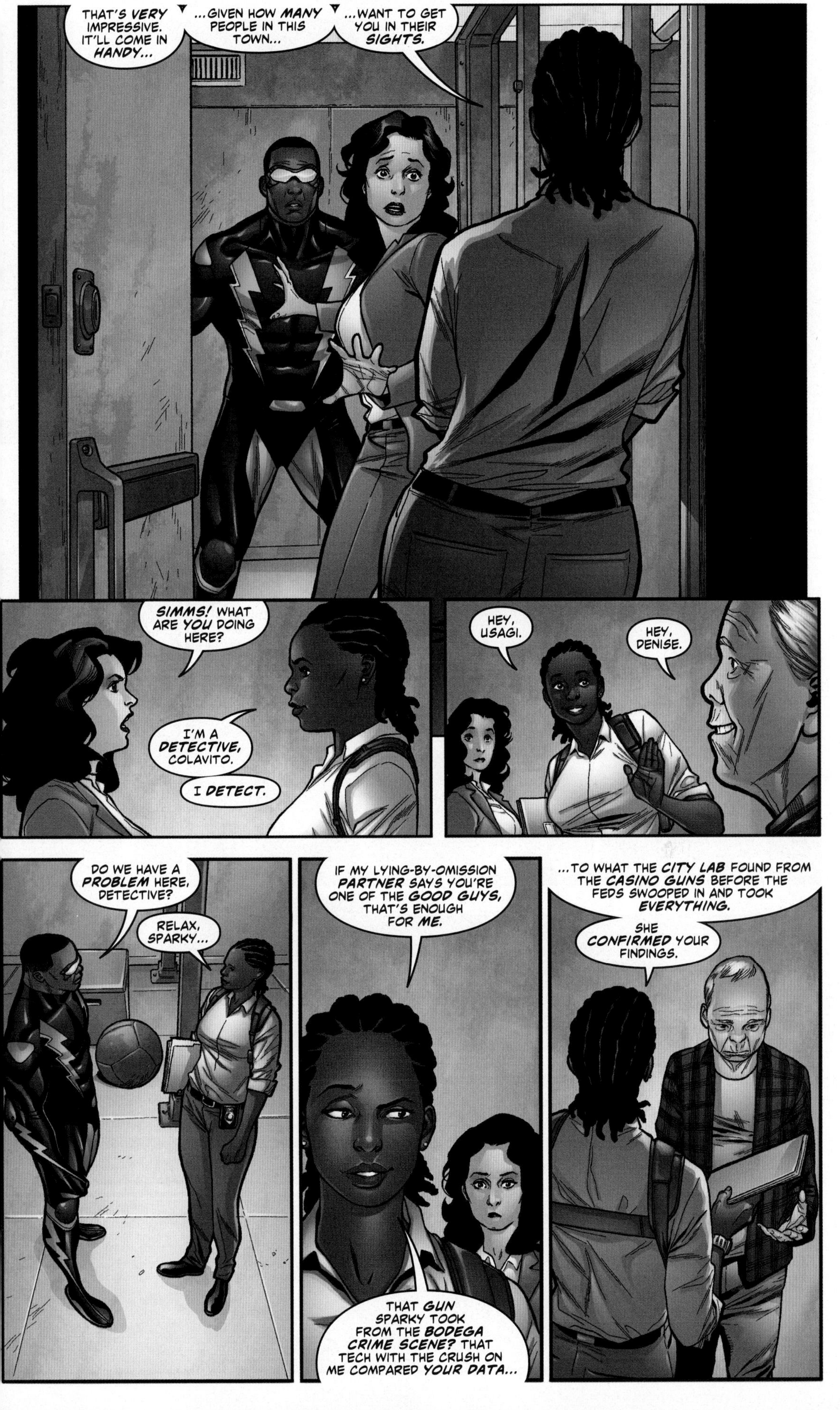
THAT'S VERY IMPRESSIVE. IT'LL COME IN HANDY...
...GIVEN HOW MANY PEOPLE IN THIS TOWN...
...WANT TO GET YOU IN THEIR SIGHTS.
SIMMS! WHAT ARE YOU DOING HERE?
I'M A DETECTIVE, COLAVITO.
I DETECT.
HEY, USAGI.
HEY, DENISE.
DO WE HAVE A PROBLEM HERE, DETECTIVE?
RELAX, SPARKY...
IF MY LYING-BY-OMISSION PARTNER SAYS YOU'RE ONE OF THE GOOD GUYS, THAT'S ENOUGH FOR ME.
THAT GUN SPARKY TOOK FROM THE BODEGA CRIME SCENE? THAT TECH WITH THE CRUSH ON ME COMPARED YOUR DATA...
...TO WHAT THE CITY LAB FOUND FROM THE CASINO GUNS BEFORE THE FEDS SWOOPED IN AND TOOK EVERYTHING.
SHE CONFIRMED YOUR FINDINGS.

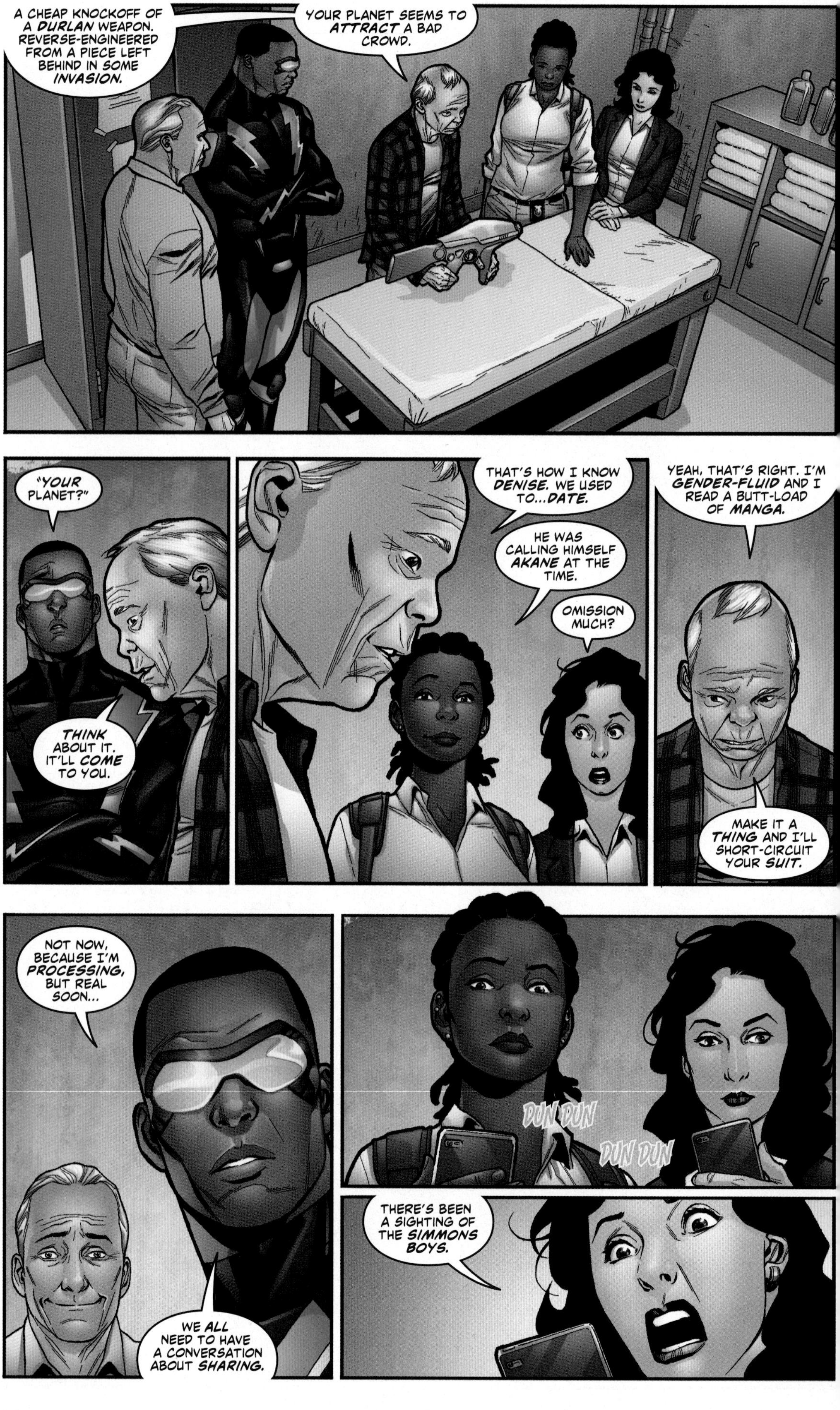
A CHEAP KNOCKOFF OF A DURLAN WEAPON. REVERSE-ENGINEERED FROM A PIECE LEFT BEHIND IN SOME INVASION.
YOUR PLANET SEEMS TO ATTRACT A BAD CROWD.
"YOUR PLANET?"
THINK ABOUT IT. IT'LL COME TO YOU.
THAT'S HOW I KNOW DENISE. WE USED TO...DATE.
HE WAS CALLING HIMSELF AKANE AT THE TIME.
OMISSION MUCH?
YEAH, THAT'S RIGHT. I'M GENDER-FLUID AND I READ A BUTT-LOAD OF MANGA.
MAKE IT A THING AND I'LL SHORT-CIRCUIT YOUR SUIT.
NOT NOW, BECAUSE I'M PROCESSING, BUT REAL SOON...
WE ALL NEED TO HAVE A CONVERSATION ABOUT SHARING.
DUN DUN
DUN DUN
THERE'S BEEN A SIGHTING OF THE SIMMONS BOYS.

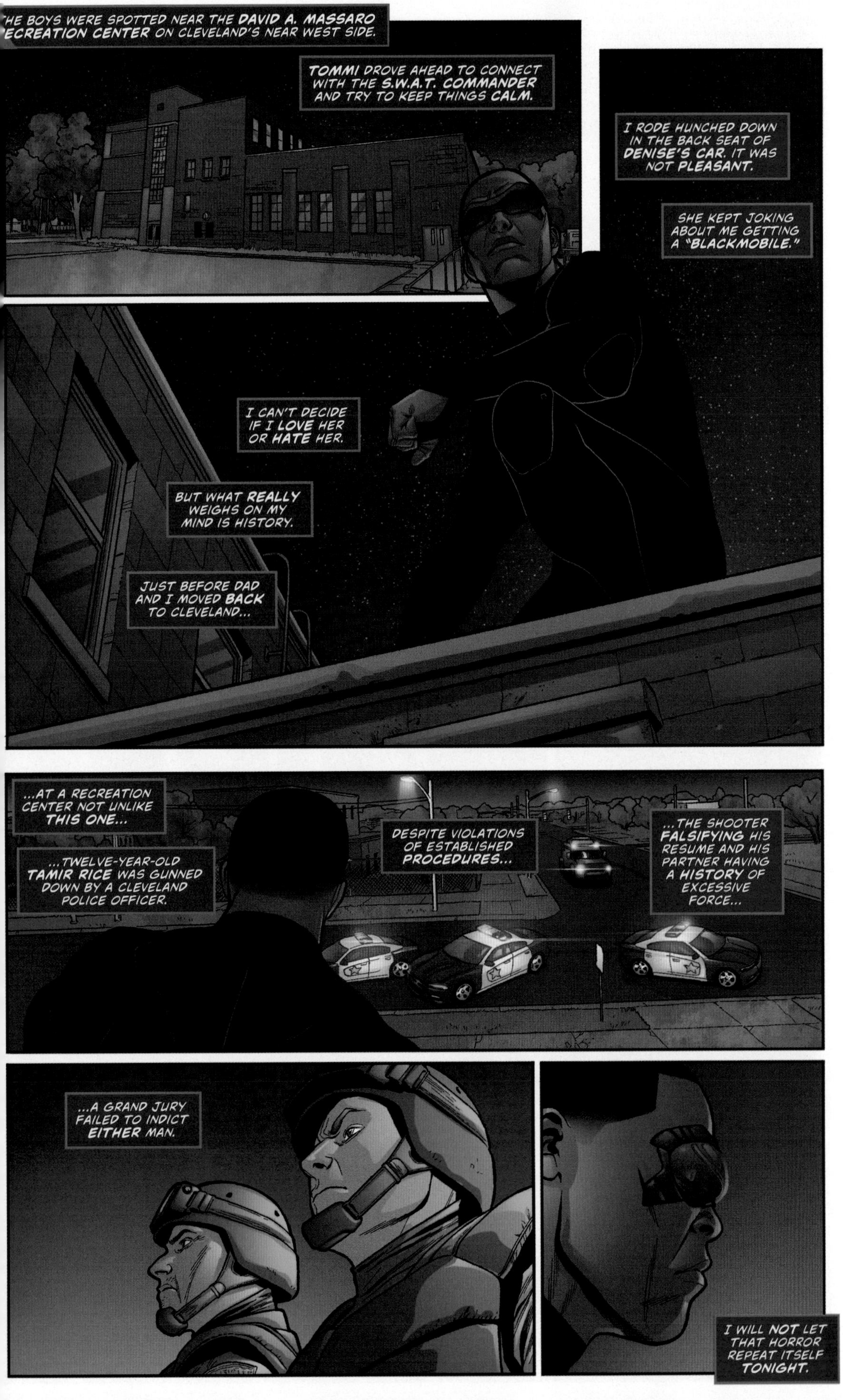
THE BOYS WERE SPOTTED NEAR THE DAVID A. MASSARO RECREATION CENTER ON CLEVELAND'S NEAR WEST SIDE.
TOMMI DROVE AHEAD TO CONNECT WITH THE S.W.A.T. COMMANDER AND TRY TO KEEP THINGS CALM.
I RODE HUNCHED DOWN IN THE BACK SEAT OF DENISE'S CAR. IT WAS NOT PLEASANT.
SHE KEPT JOKING ABOUT ME GETTING A "BLACKMOBILE."
I CAN'T DECIDE IF I LOVE HER OR HATE HER.
BUT WHAT REALLY WEIGHS ON MY MIND IS HISTORY.
JUST BEFORE DAD AND I MOVED BACK TO CLEVELAND...
...AT A RECREATION CENTER NOT UNLIKE THIS ONE...
...TWELVE-YEAR-OLD TAMIR RICE WAS GUNNED DOWN BY A CLEVELAND POLICE OFFICER.
DESPITE VIOLATIONS OF ESTABLISHED PROCEDURES...
...THE SHOOTER FALSIFYING HIS RESUME AND HIS PARTNER HAVING A HISTORY OF EXCESSIVE FORCE...
...A GRAND JURY FAILED TO INDICT EITHER MAN.
I WILL NOT LET THAT HORROR REPEAT ITSELF TONIGHT.

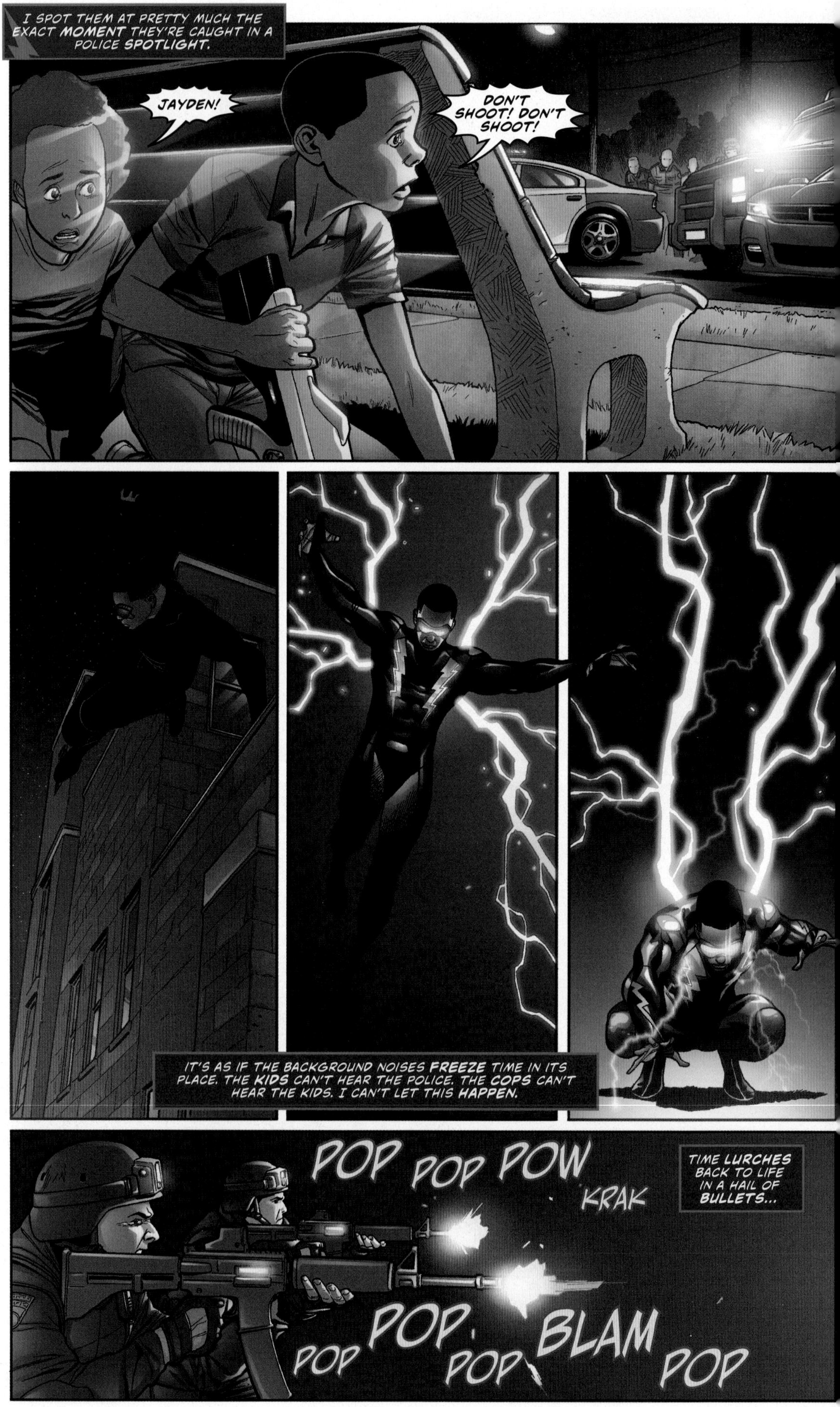
I SPOT THEM AT PRETTY MUCH THE EXACT MOMENT THEY'RE CAUGHT IN A POLICE SPOTLIGHT.
JAYDEN!
DON'T SHOOT! DON'T SHOOT!
IT'S AS IF THE BACKGROUND NOISES FREEZE TIME IN ITS PLACE. THE KIDS CAN'T HEAR THE POLICE. THE COPS CAN'T HEAR THE KIDS. I CAN'T LET THIS HAPPEN.
POP POP POW
KRAK
TIME LURCHES BACK TO LIFE IN A HAIL OF BULLETS...
POP POP POP BLAM POP

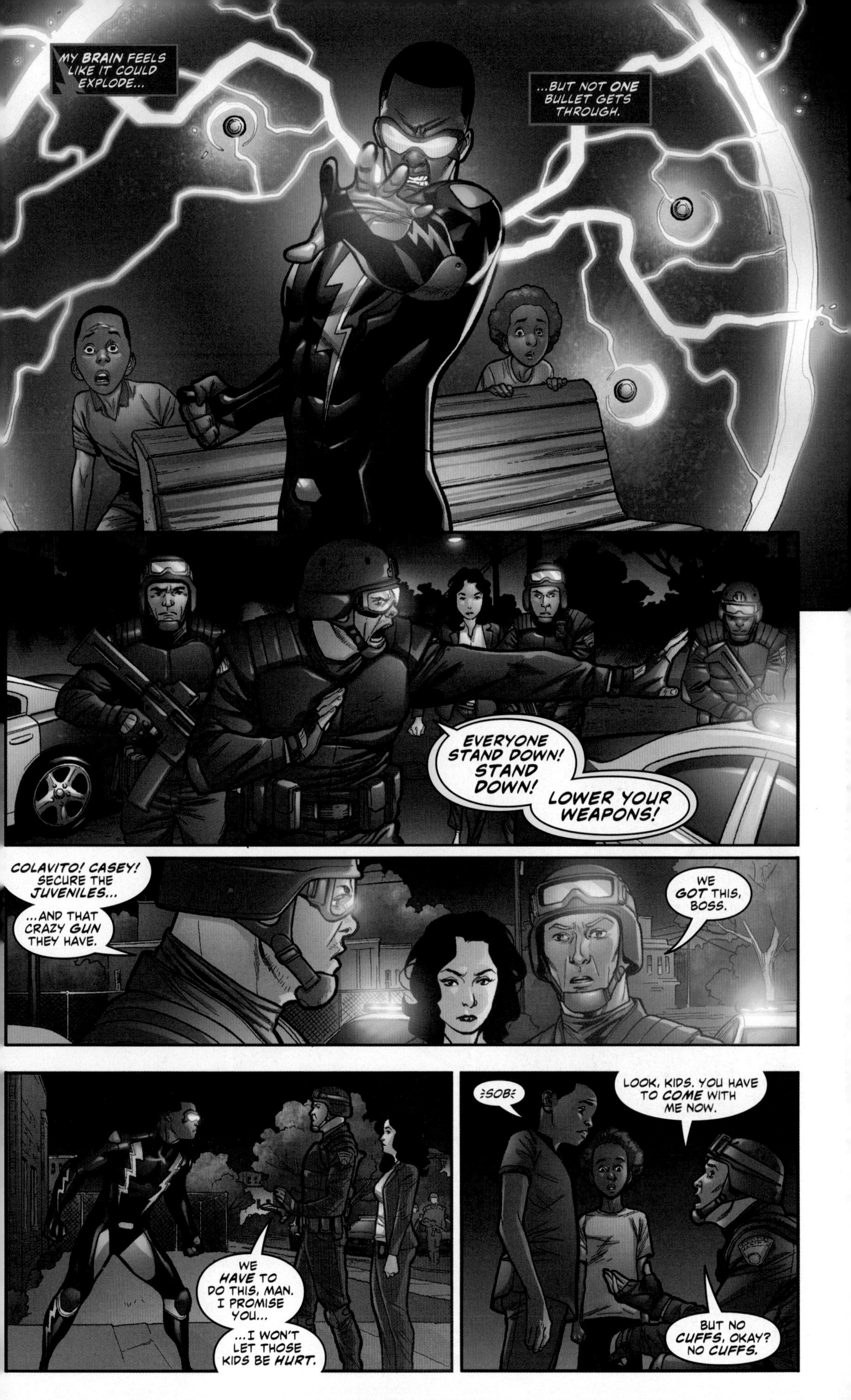

MY BRAIN FEELS LIKE IT COULD EXPLODE...
...BUT NOT ONE BULLET GETS THROUGH.
EVERYONE STAND DOWN! STAND DOWN!
LOWER YOUR WEAPONS!
COLAVITO! CASEY! SECURE THE JUVENILES...
...AND THAT CRAZY GUN THEY HAVE.
WE GOT THIS, BOSS.
WE HAVE TO DO THIS, MAN. I PROMISE YOU...
...I WON'T LET THOSE KIDS BE HURT.
SOB
LOOK, KIDS. YOU HAVE TO COME WITH ME NOW.
BUT NO CUFFS, OKAY? NO CUFFS.

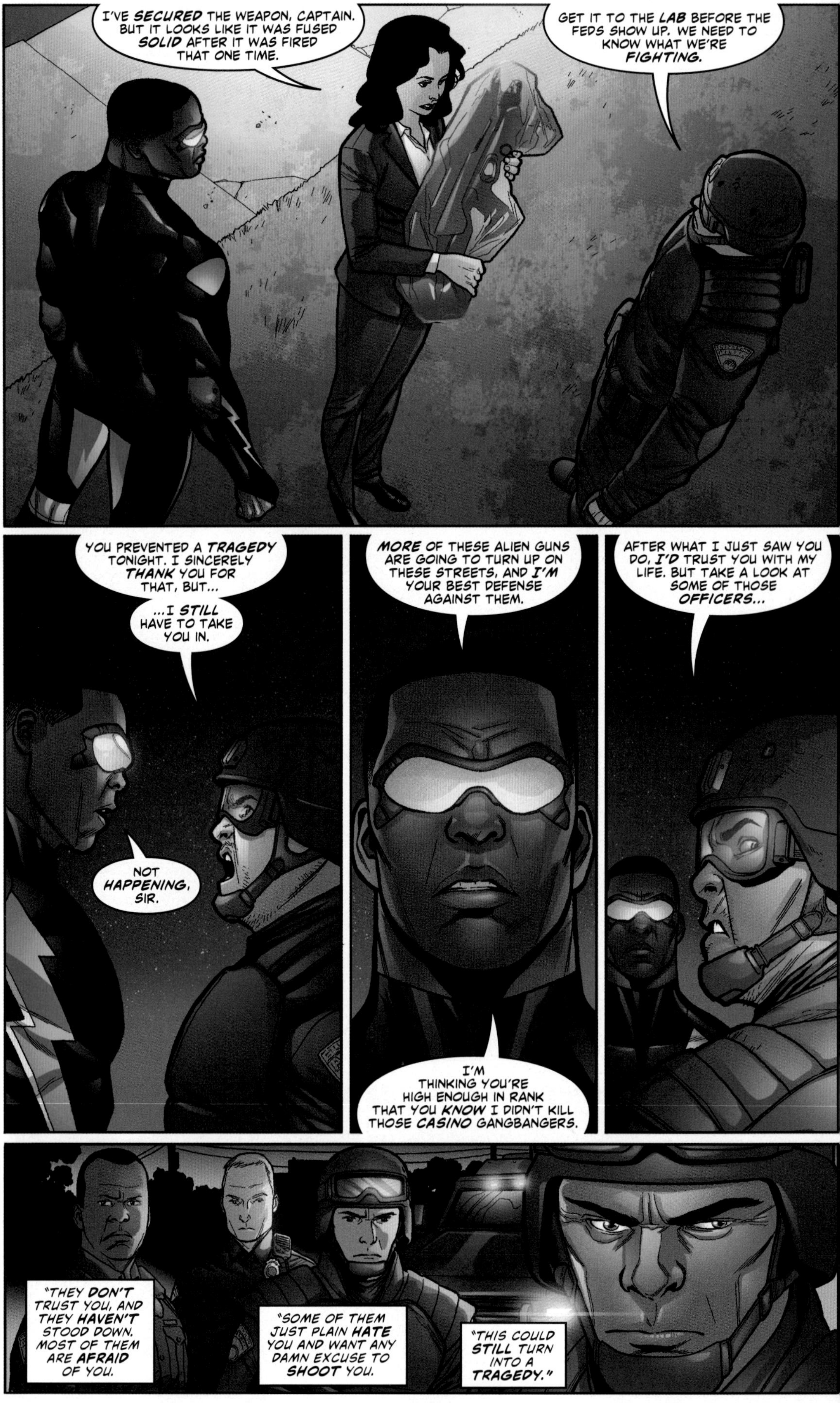
I'VE **SECURED** THE WEAPON, CAPTAIN. BUT IT LOOKS LIKE IT WAS FUSED **SOLID** AFTER IT WAS FIRED THAT ONE TIME.
GET IT TO THE **LAB** BEFORE THE FEDS SHOW UP. WE NEED TO KNOW WHAT WE'RE **FIGHTING.**
YOU PREVENTED A **TRAGEDY** TONIGHT. I SINCERELY **THANK** YOU FOR THAT, BUT...
...I **STILL** HAVE TO TAKE YOU IN.
NOT **HAPPENING,** SIR.
MORE OF THESE ALIEN GUNS ARE GOING TO TURN UP ON THESE STREETS, AND **I'M** YOUR BEST DEFENSE AGAINST THEM.
I'M THINKING YOU'RE HIGH ENOUGH IN RANK THAT YOU **KNOW** I DIDN'T KILL THOSE **CASINO** GANGBANGERS.
AFTER WHAT I JUST SAW YOU DO, **I'D** TRUST YOU WITH MY LIFE. BUT TAKE A LOOK AT SOME OF THOSE **OFFICERS...**
"THEY **DON'T** TRUST YOU, AND THEY **HAVEN'T** STOOD DOWN. MOST OF THEM ARE **AFRAID** OF YOU.
"SOME OF THEM JUST PLAIN **HATE** YOU AND WANT ANY DAMN EXCUSE TO **SHOOT** YOU.
"THIS COULD **STILL** TURN INTO A **TRAGEDY.**"

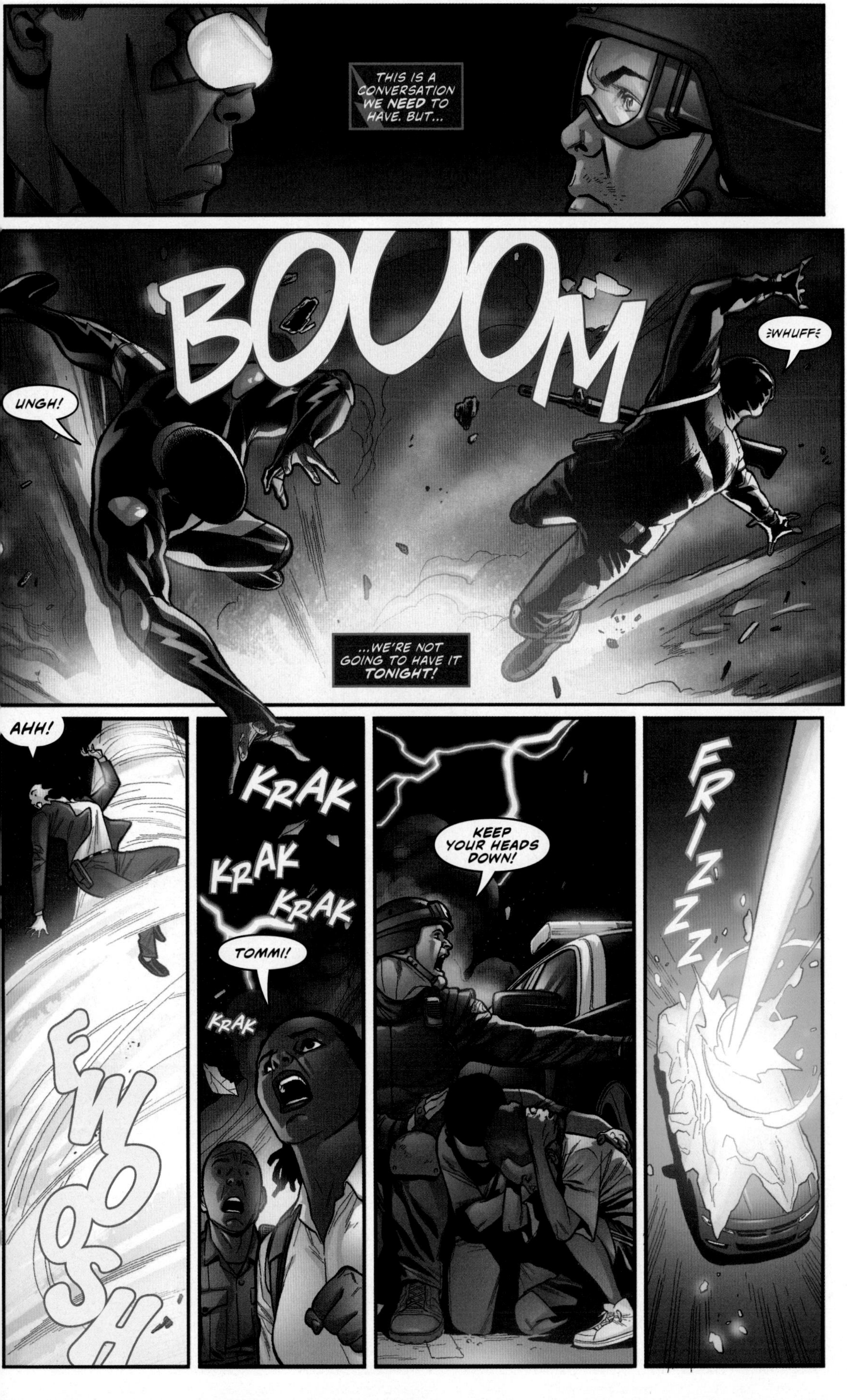
THIS IS A CONVERSATION WE NEED TO HAVE. BUT...
BOUOM
UNGH!
WHUFF
...WE'RE NOT GOING TO HAVE IT TONIGHT!
AHH!
FWOOSH
KRAK
KRAK
KRAK
TOMMI!
KRAK
KEEP YOUR HEADS DOWN!
FRIZZZ

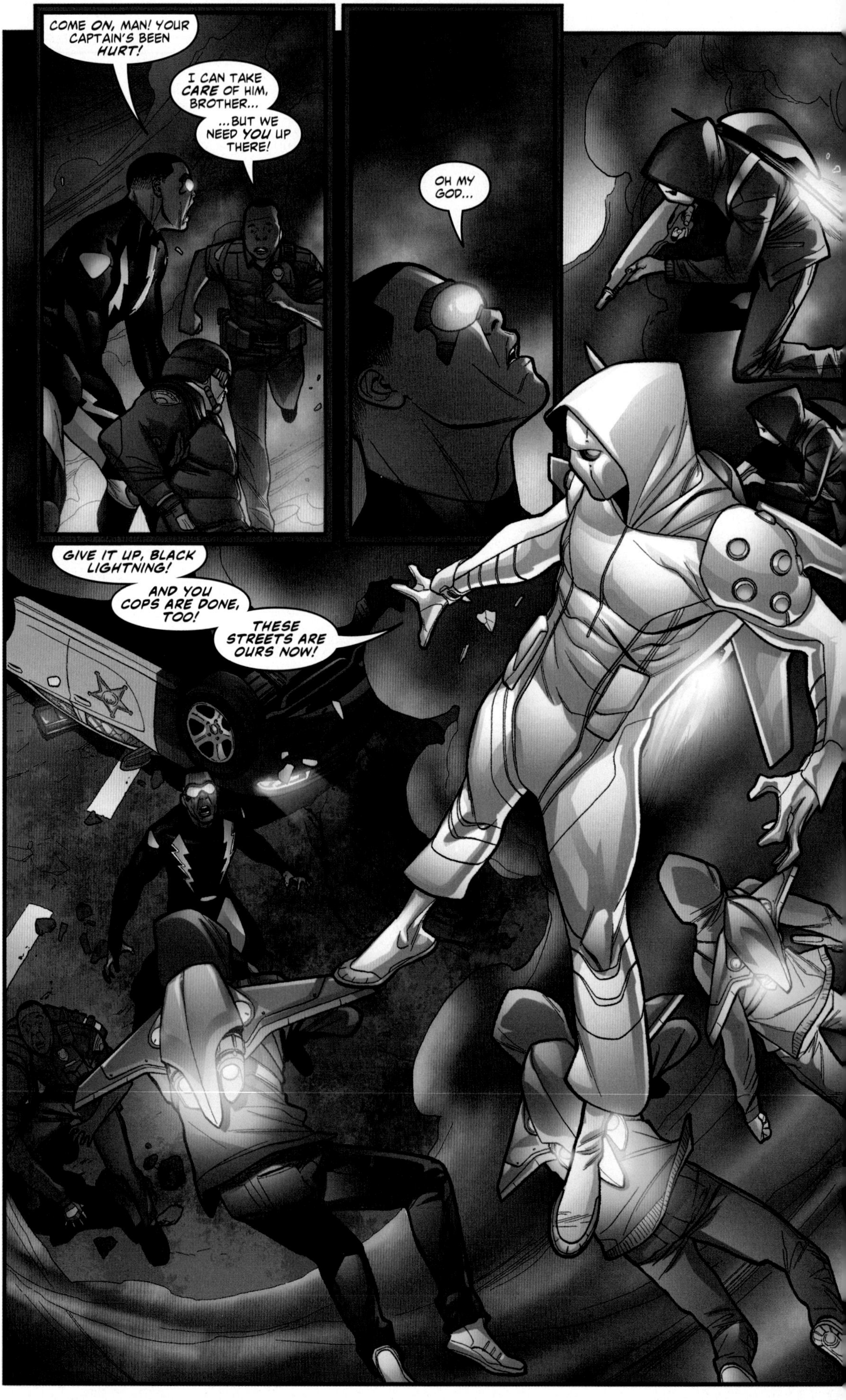
COME ON, MAN! YOUR CAPTAIN'S BEEN HURT!
I CAN TAKE CARE OF HIM, BROTHER...
...BUT WE NEED YOU UP THERE!
OH MY GOD...
GIVE IT UP, BLACK LIGHTNING!
AND YOU COPS ARE DONE, TOO!
THESE STREETS ARE OURS NOW!

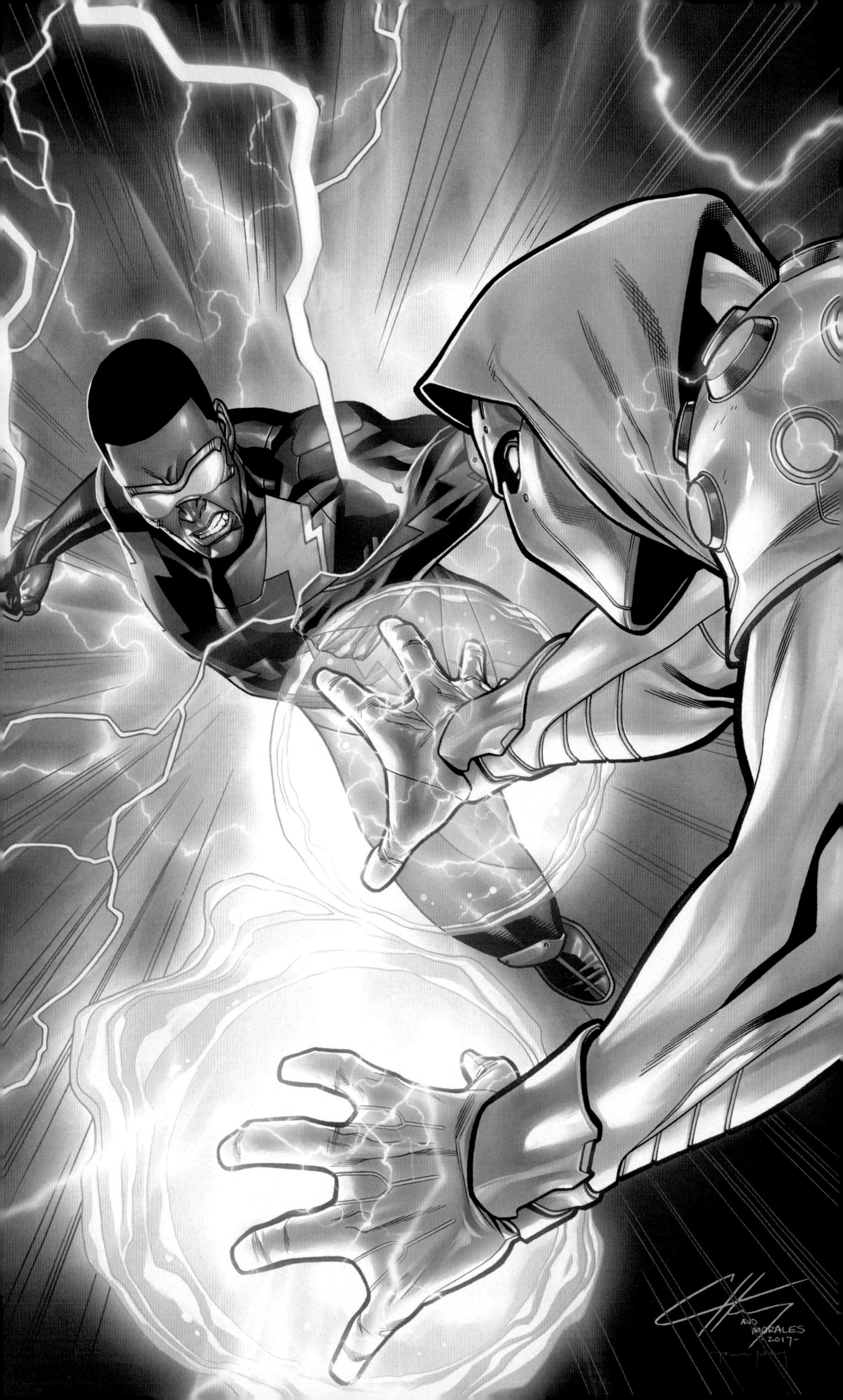
AND MORALES
-2017-

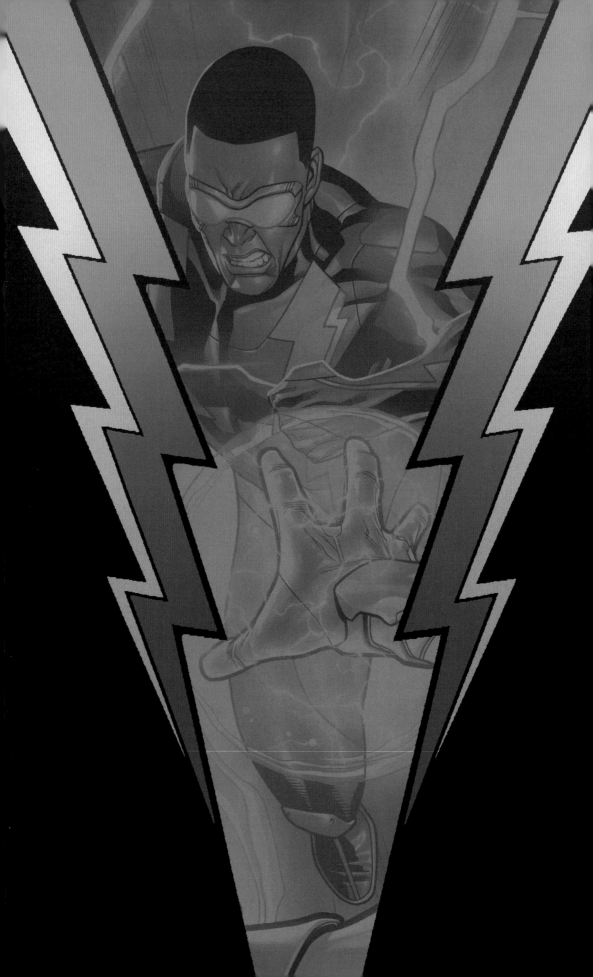

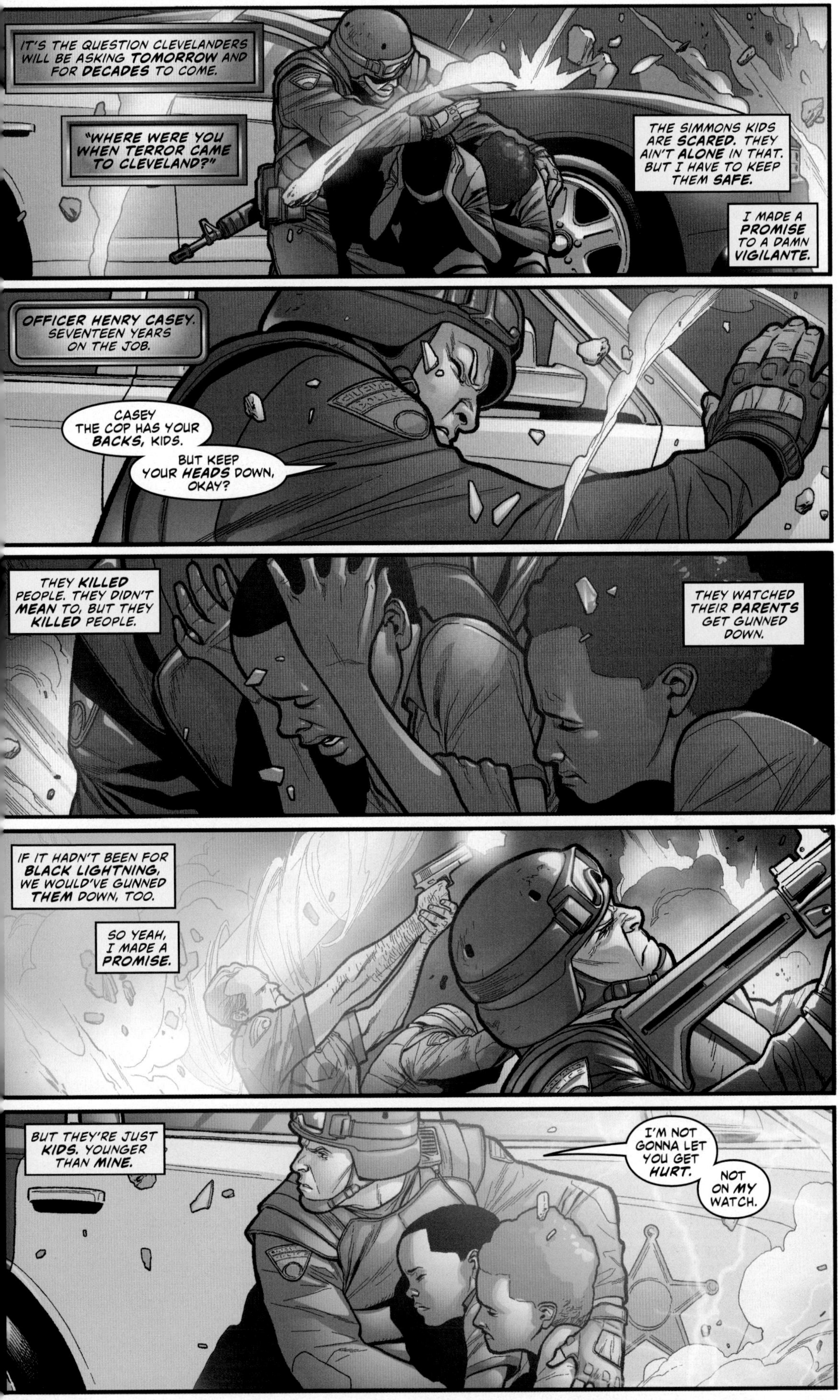
IT'S THE QUESTION CLEVELANDERS WILL BE ASKING TOMORROW AND FOR DECADES TO COME.
"WHERE WERE YOU WHEN TERROR CAME TO CLEVELAND?"
THE SIMMONS KIDS ARE SCARED. THEY AIN'T ALONE IN THAT. BUT I HAVE TO KEEP THEM SAFE.
I MADE A PROMISE TO A DAMN VIGILANTE.
OFFICER HENRY CASEY. SEVENTEEN YEARS ON THE JOB.
CASEY THE COP HAS YOUR BACKS, KIDS.
BUT KEEP YOUR HEADS DOWN, OKAY?
THEY KILLED PEOPLE. THEY DIDN'T MEAN TO, BUT THEY KILLED PEOPLE.
THEY WATCHED THEIR PARENTS GET GUNNED DOWN.
IF IT HADN'T BEEN FOR BLACK LIGHTNING, WE WOULD'VE GUNNED THEM DOWN, TOO.
SO YEAH, I MADE A PROMISE.
BUT THEY'RE JUST KIDS. YOUNGER THAN MINE.
I'M NOT GONNA LET YOU GET HURT.
NOT ON MY WATCH.

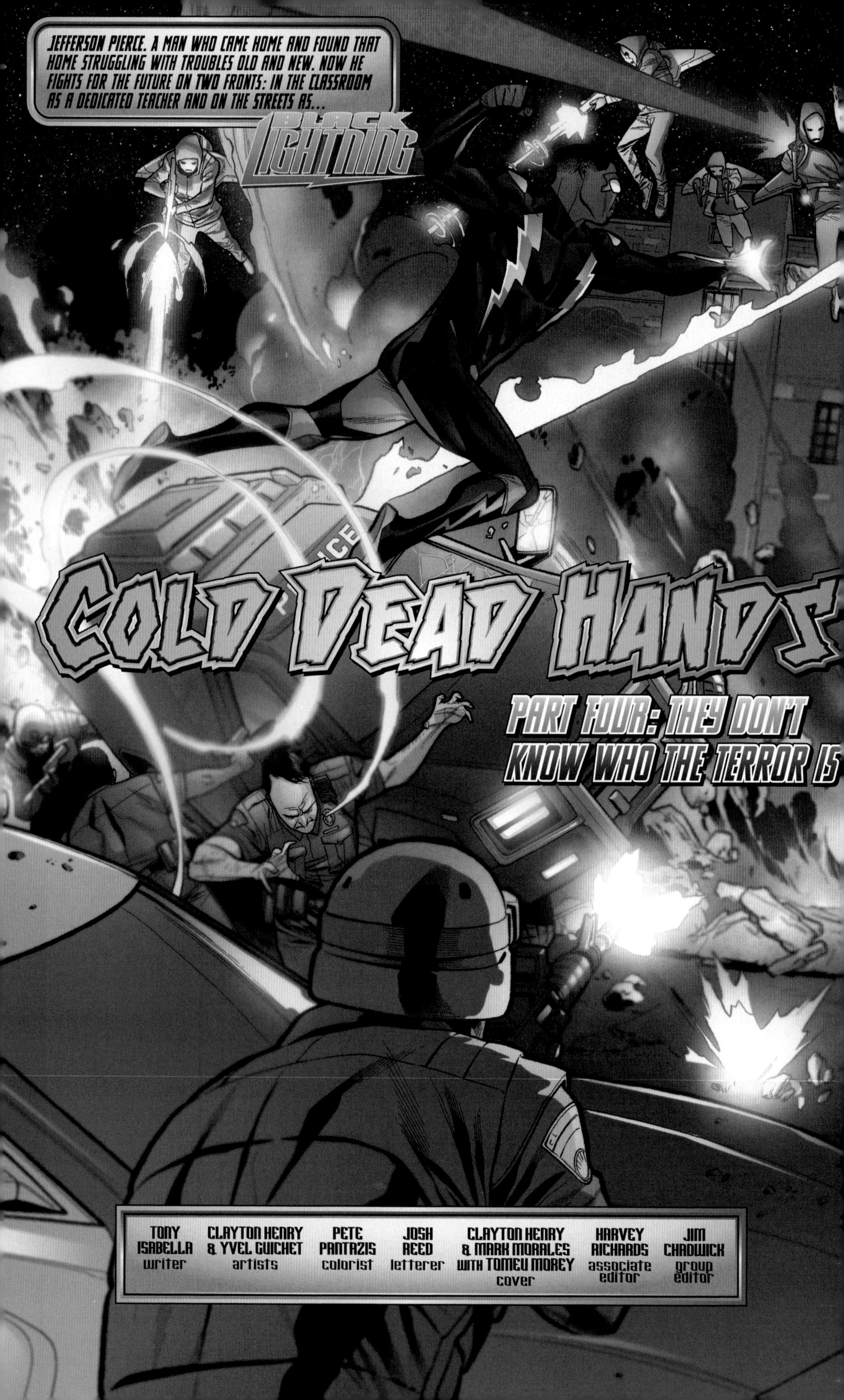
JEFFERSON PIERCE. A MAN WHO CAME HOME AND FOUND THAT HOME STRUGGLING WITH TROUBLES OLD AND NEW. NOW HE FIGHTS FOR THE FUTURE ON TWO FRONTS: IN THE CLASSROOM AS A DEDICATED TEACHER AND ON THE STREETS AS...
BLACK LIGHTNING
COLD DEAD HANDS
PART FOUR: THEY DON'T KNOW WHO THE TERROR IS
TONY ISABELLA writer
CLAYTON HENRY & YVEL GUICHET artists
PETE PANTAZIS colorist
JOSH REED letterer
CLAYTON HENRY & MARK MORALES WITH TOMEU MOREY cover
HARVEY RICHARDS associate editor
JIM CHADWICK group editor

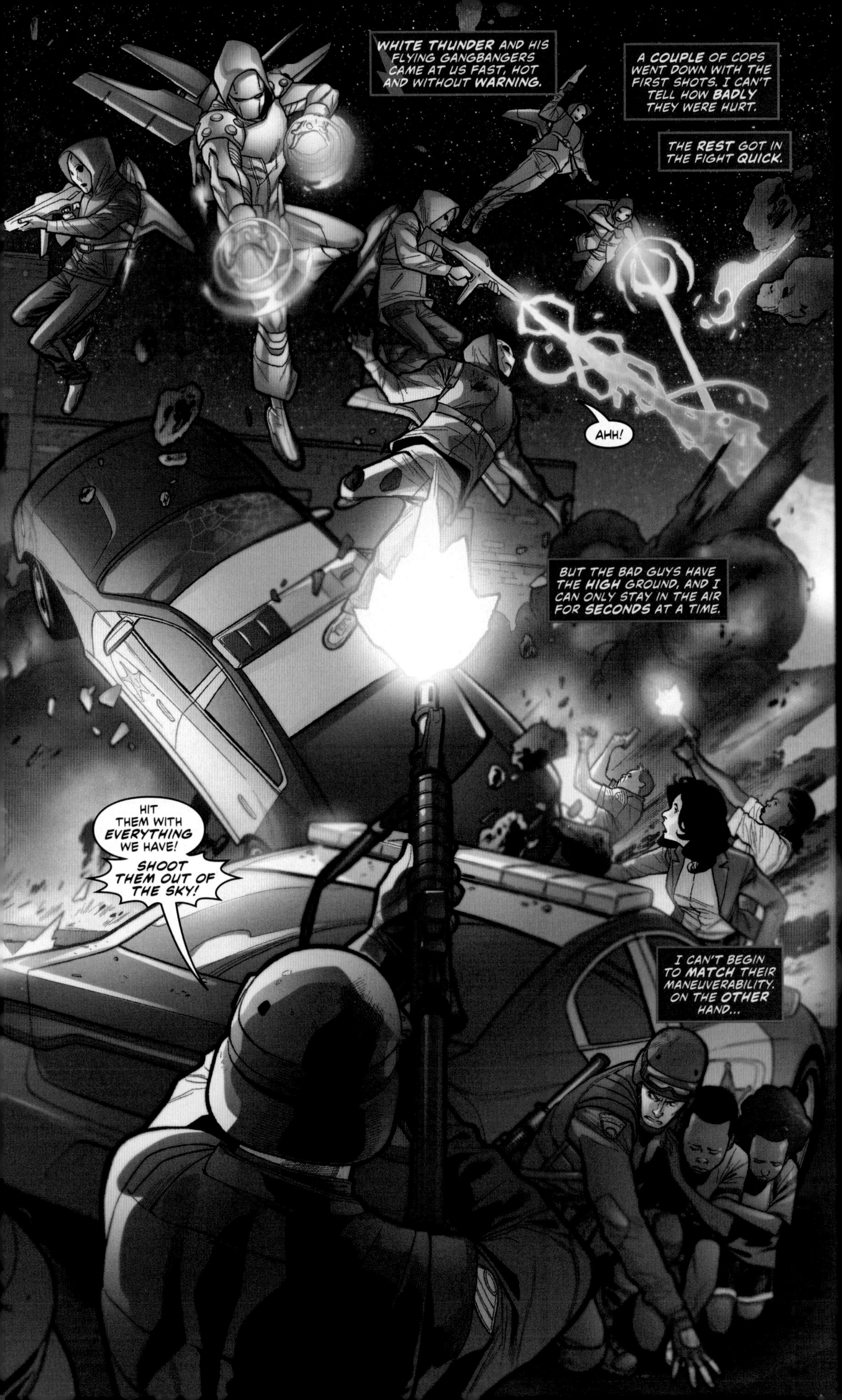
WHITE THUNDER AND HIS FLYING GANGBANGERS CAME AT US FAST, HOT AND WITHOUT WARNING.
A COUPLE OF COPS WENT DOWN WITH THE FIRST SHOTS. I CAN'T TELL HOW BADLY THEY WERE HURT.
THE REST GOT IN THE FIGHT QUICK.
AHH!
BUT THE BAD GUYS HAVE THE HIGH GROUND, AND I CAN ONLY STAY IN THE AIR FOR SECONDS AT A TIME.
HIT THEM WITH EVERYTHING WE HAVE!
SHOOT THEM OUT OF THE SKY!
I CAN'T BEGIN TO MATCH THEIR MANEUVERABILITY. ON THE OTHER HAND...

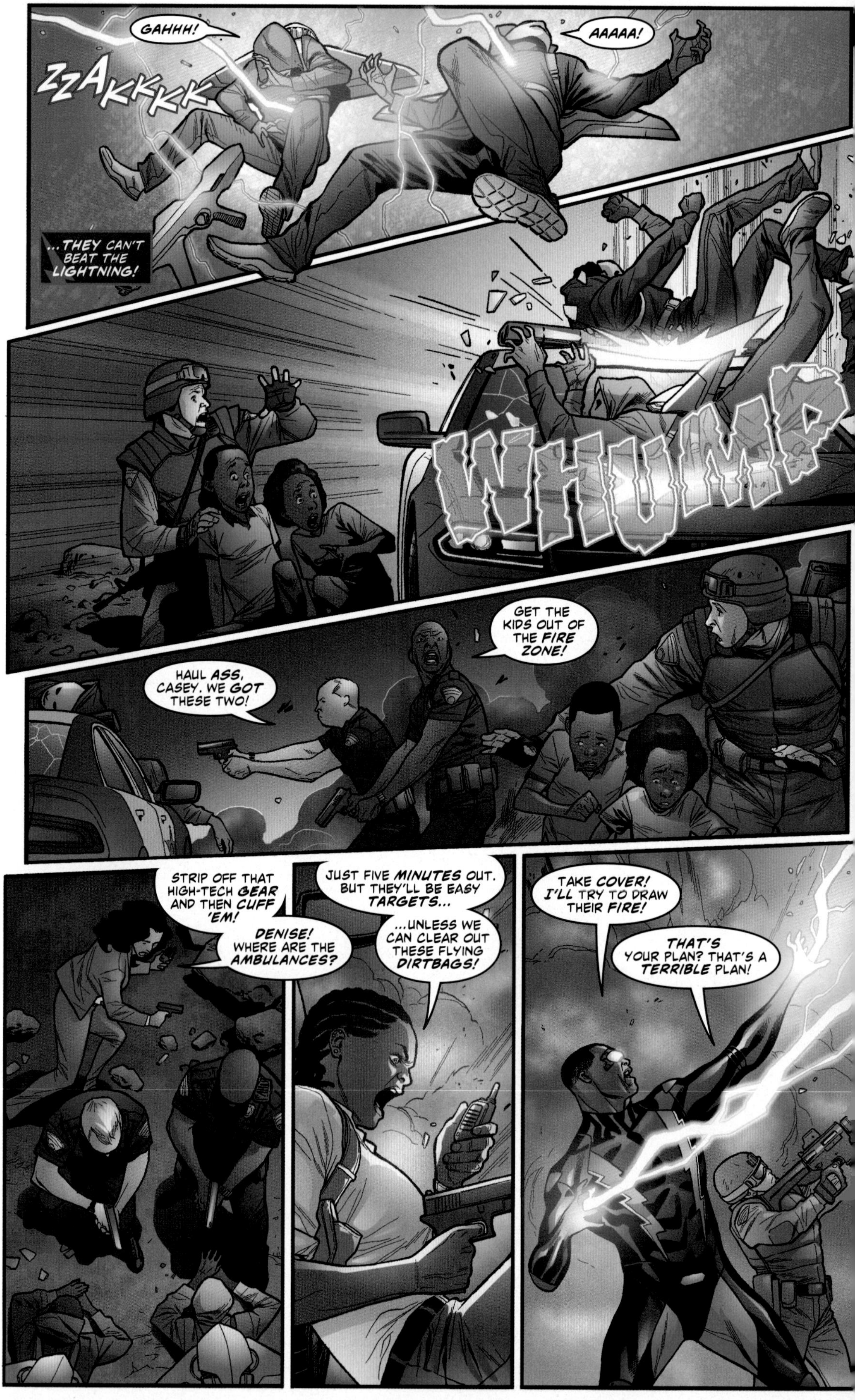
GAHHH!
AAAAA!
ZZAKKKK
...THEY CAN'T BEAT THE LIGHTNING!
WHUMP
GET THE KIDS OUT OF THE FIRE ZONE!
HAUL ASS, CASEY. WE GOT THESE TWO!
STRIP OFF THAT HIGH-TECH GEAR AND THEN CUFF 'EM!
DENISE! WHERE ARE THE AMBULANCES?
JUST FIVE MINUTES OUT. BUT THEY'LL BE EASY TARGETS...
...UNLESS WE CAN CLEAR OUT THESE FLYING DIRTBAGS!
TAKE COVER! I'LL TRY TO DRAW THEIR FIRE!
THAT'S YOUR PLAN? THAT'S A TERRIBLE PLAN!

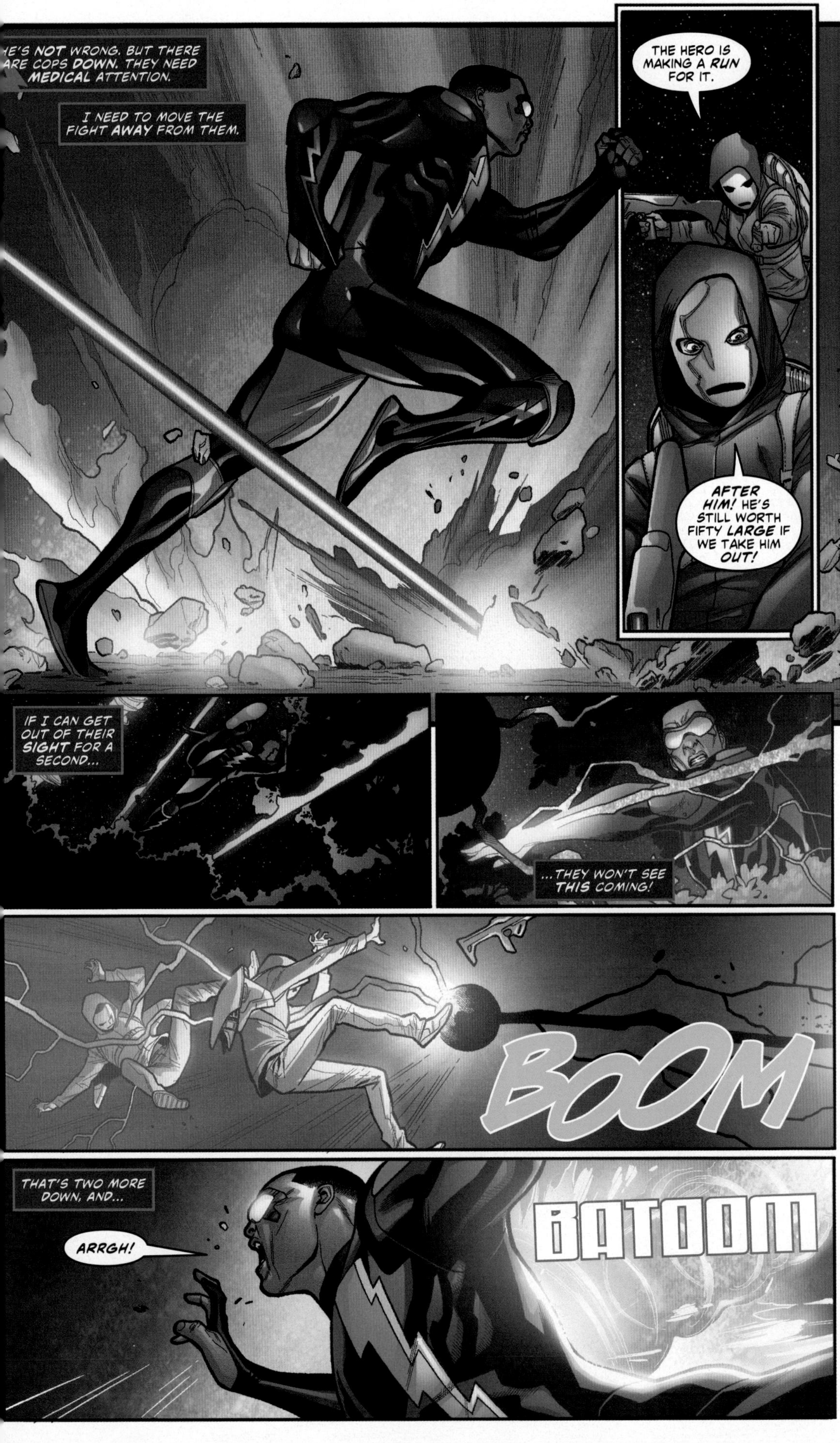
HE'S NOT WRONG. BUT THERE ARE COPS DOWN. THEY NEED MEDICAL ATTENTION.
I NEED TO MOVE THE FIGHT AWAY FROM THEM.
THE HERO IS MAKING A RUN FOR IT.
AFTER HIM! HE'S STILL WORTH FIFTY LARGE IF WE TAKE HIM OUT!
IF I CAN GET OUT OF THEIR SIGHT FOR A SECOND...
...THEY WON'T SEE THIS COMING!
BOOM
THAT'S TWO MORE DOWN, AND...
BATOOM
ARRGH!

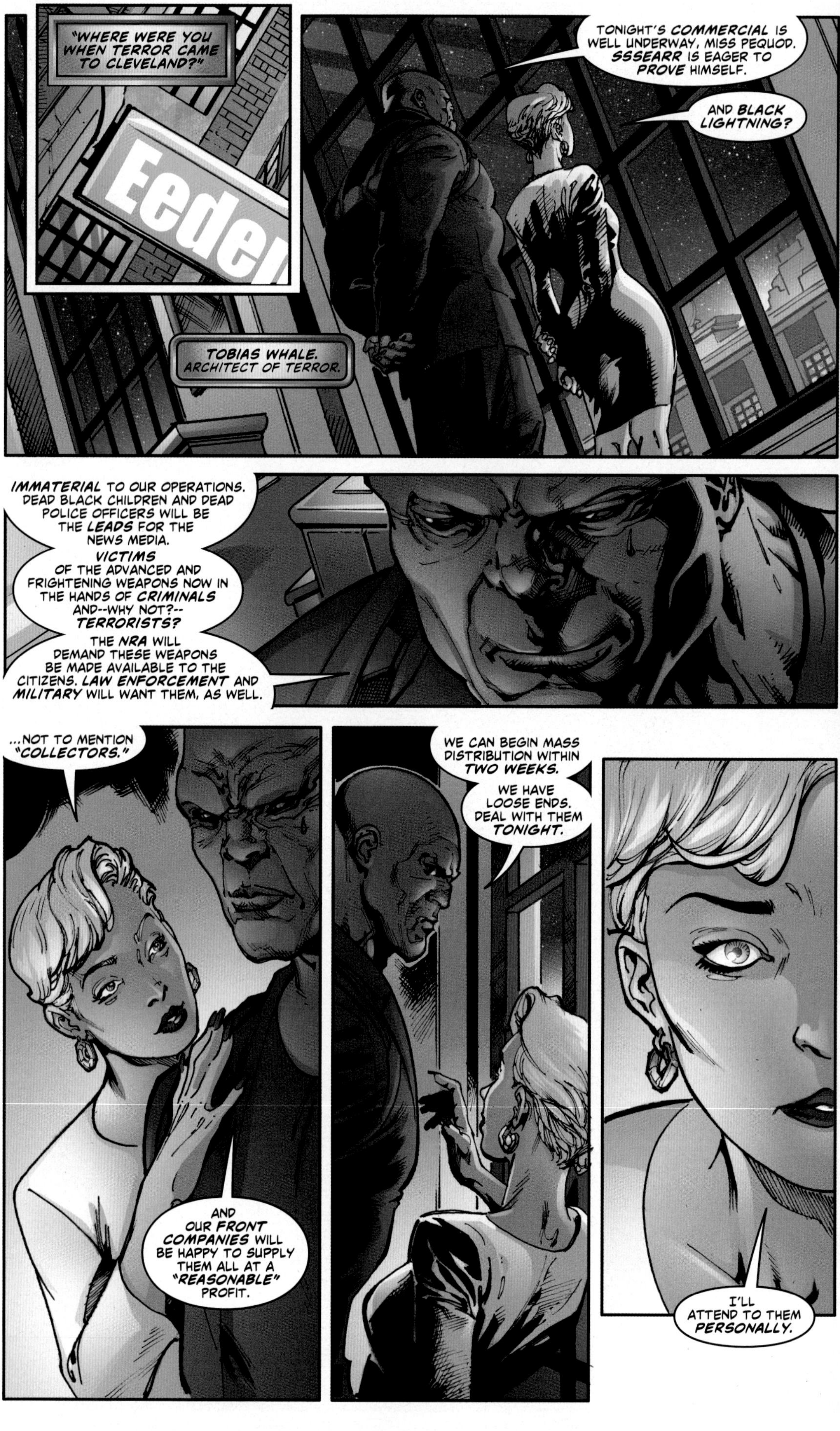
"WHERE WERE YOU WHEN TERROR CAME TO CLEVELAND?"
Eeden
TONIGHT'S COMMERCIAL IS WELL UNDERWAY, MISS PEQUOD. SSSEARR IS EAGER TO PROVE HIMSELF.
AND BLACK LIGHTNING?
TOBIAS WHALE. ARCHITECT OF TERROR.
IMMATERIAL TO OUR OPERATIONS. DEAD BLACK CHILDREN AND DEAD POLICE OFFICERS WILL BE THE LEADS FOR THE NEWS MEDIA.
VICTIMS OF THE ADVANCED AND FRIGHTENING WEAPONS NOW IN THE HANDS OF CRIMINALS AND--WHY NOT?--TERRORISTS?
THE NRA WILL DEMAND THESE WEAPONS BE MADE AVAILABLE TO THE CITIZENS. LAW ENFORCEMENT AND MILITARY WILL WANT THEM, AS WELL.
...NOT TO MENTION "COLLECTORS."
AND OUR FRONT COMPANIES WILL BE HAPPY TO SUPPLY THEM ALL AT A "REASONABLE" PROFIT.
WE CAN BEGIN MASS DISTRIBUTION WITHIN TWO WEEKS.
WE HAVE LOOSE ENDS. DEAL WITH THEM TONIGHT.
I'LL ATTEND TO THEM PERSONALLY.

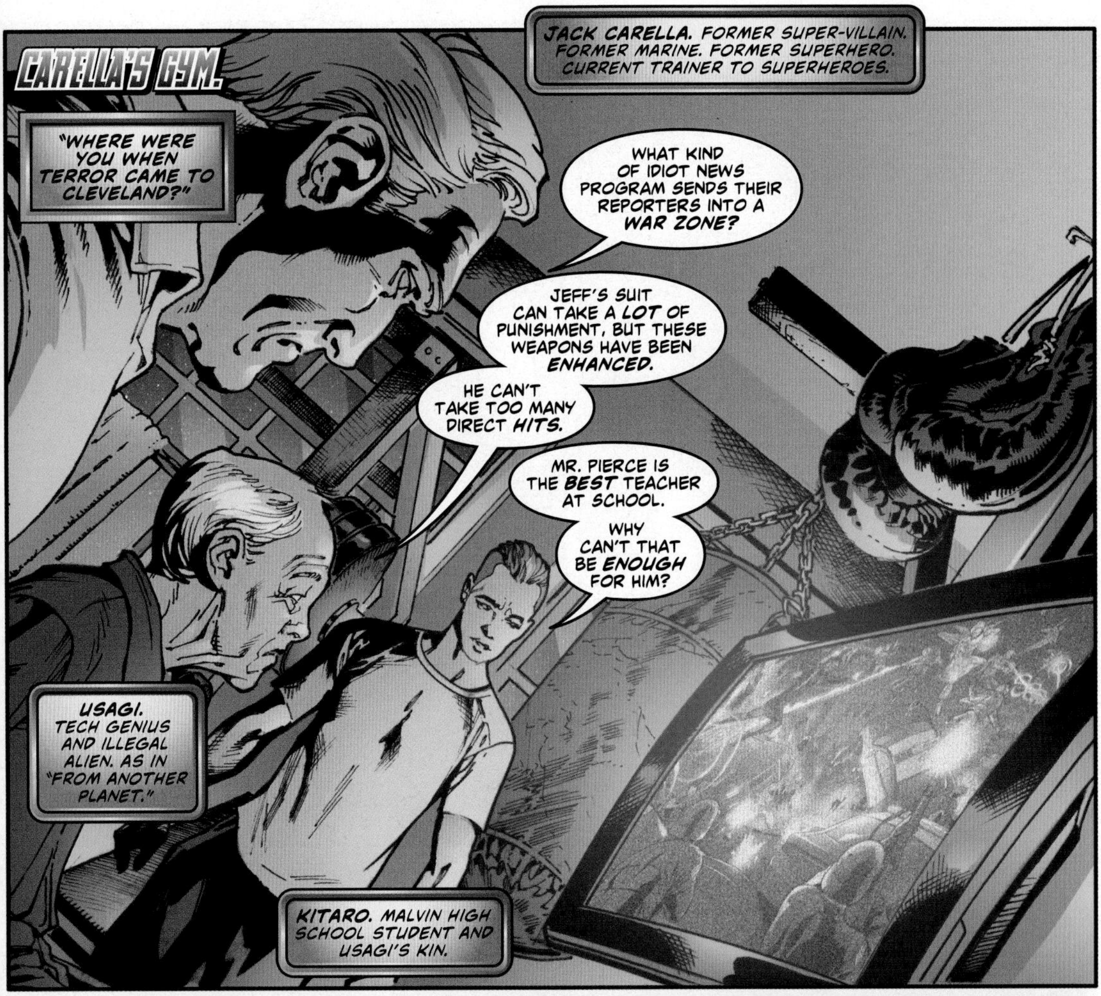
CARELLA'S GYM.
JACK CARELLA. FORMER SUPER-VILLAIN. FORMER MARINE. FORMER SUPERHERO. CURRENT TRAINER TO SUPERHEROES.
"WHERE WERE YOU WHEN TERROR CAME TO CLEVELAND?"
WHAT KIND OF IDIOT NEWS PROGRAM SENDS THEIR REPORTERS INTO A WAR ZONE?
JEFF'S SUIT CAN TAKE A LOT OF PUNISHMENT, BUT THESE WEAPONS HAVE BEEN ENHANCED.
HE CAN'T TAKE TOO MANY DIRECT HITS.
MR. PIERCE IS THE BEST TEACHER AT SCHOOL.
WHY CAN'T THAT BE ENOUGH FOR HIM?
USAGI. TECH GENIUS AND ILLEGAL ALIEN. AS IN "FROM ANOTHER PLANET."
KITARO. MALVIN HIGH SCHOOL STUDENT AND USAGI'S KIN.

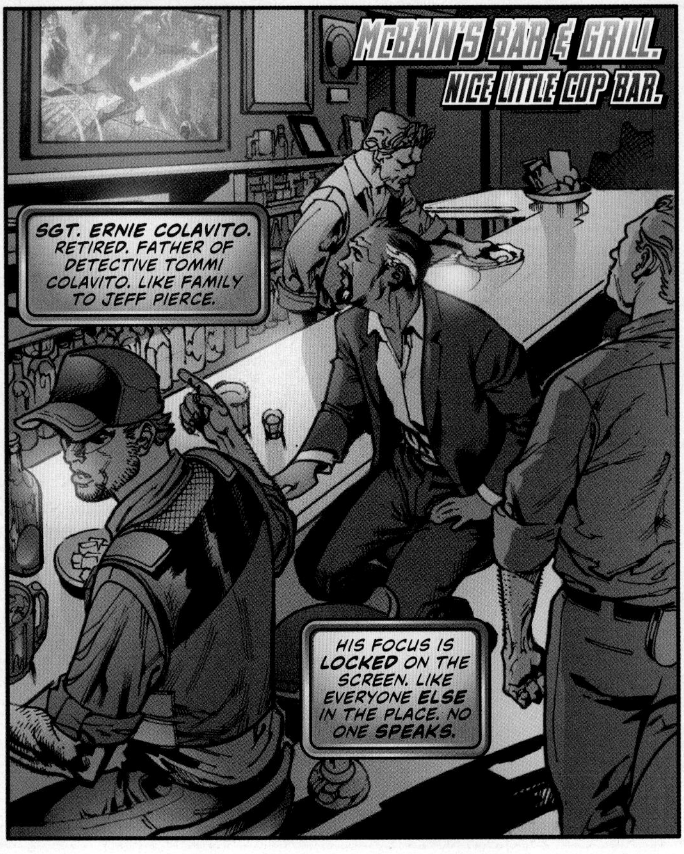
McBAIN'S BAR & GRILL.
NICE LITTLE COP BAR.
SGT. ERNIE COLAVITO. RETIRED. FATHER OF DETECTIVE TOMMI COLAVITO. LIKE FAMILY TO JEFF PIERCE.
HIS FOCUS IS LOCKED ON THE SCREEN. LIKE EVERYONE ELSE IN THE PLACE. NO ONE SPEAKS.

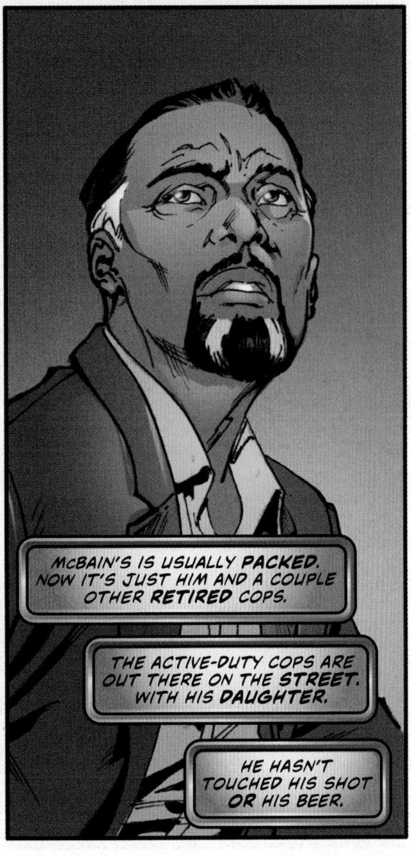
McBAIN'S IS USUALLY PACKED. NOW IT'S JUST HIM AND A COUPLE OTHER RETIRED COPS.
THE ACTIVE-DUTY COPS ARE OUT THERE ON THE STREET. WITH HIS DAUGHTER.
HE HASN'T TOUCHED HIS SHOT OR HIS BEER.

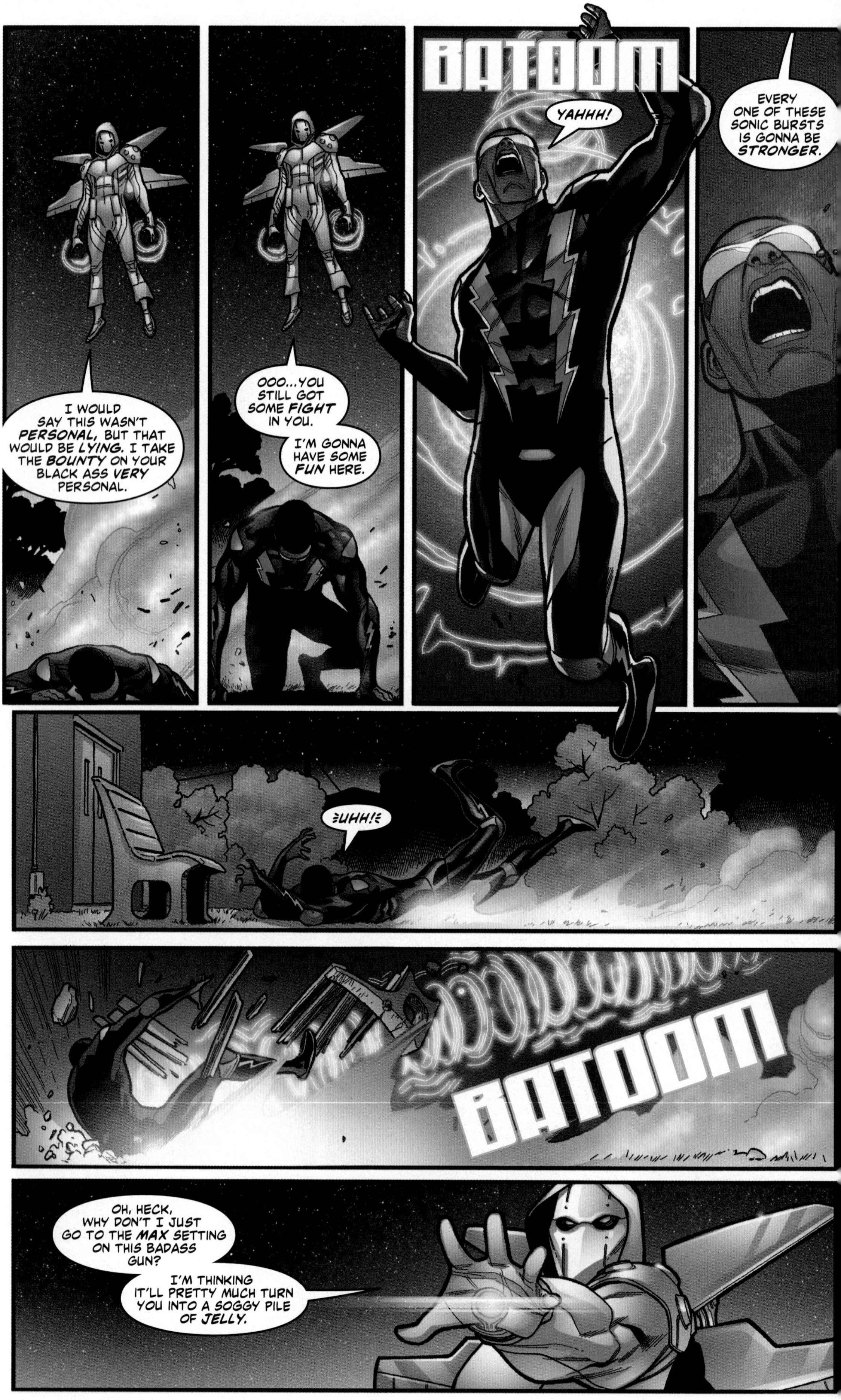
I WOULD SAY THIS WASN'T PERSONAL, BUT THAT WOULD BE LYING. I TAKE THE BOUNTY ON YOUR BLACK ASS VERY PERSONAL.
OOO...YOU STILL GOT SOME FIGHT IN YOU.
I'M GONNA HAVE SOME FUN HERE.
BATOOM
YAHHH!
EVERY ONE OF THESE SONIC BURSTS IS GONNA BE STRONGER.
UHH!
BATOOM
OH, HECK, WHY DON'T I JUST GO TO THE MAX SETTING ON THIS BADASS GUN?
I'M THINKING IT'LL PRETTY MUCH TURN YOU INTO A SOGGY PILE OF JELLY.

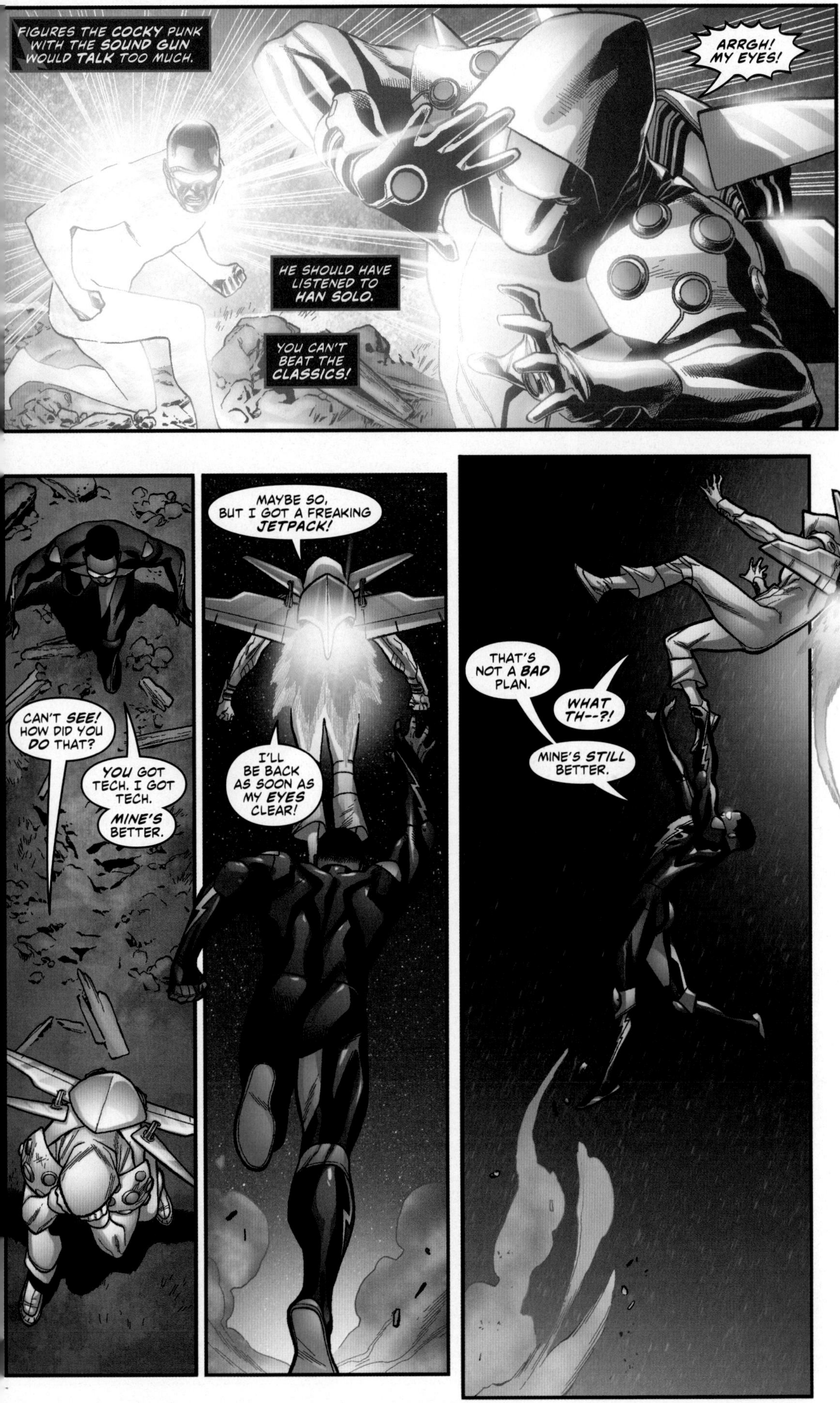
FIGURES THE COCKY PUNK WITH THE SOUND GUN WOULD TALK TOO MUCH.
ARRGH! MY EYES!
HE SHOULD HAVE LISTENED TO HAN SOLO.
YOU CAN'T BEAT THE CLASSICS!
CAN'T SEE! HOW DID YOU DO THAT?
YOU GOT TECH. I GOT TECH. MINE'S BETTER.
MAYBE SO, BUT I GOT A FREAKING JETPACK!
I'LL BE BACK AS SOON AS MY EYES CLEAR!
THAT'S NOT A BAD PLAN.
WHAT TH--?!
MINE'S STILL BETTER.

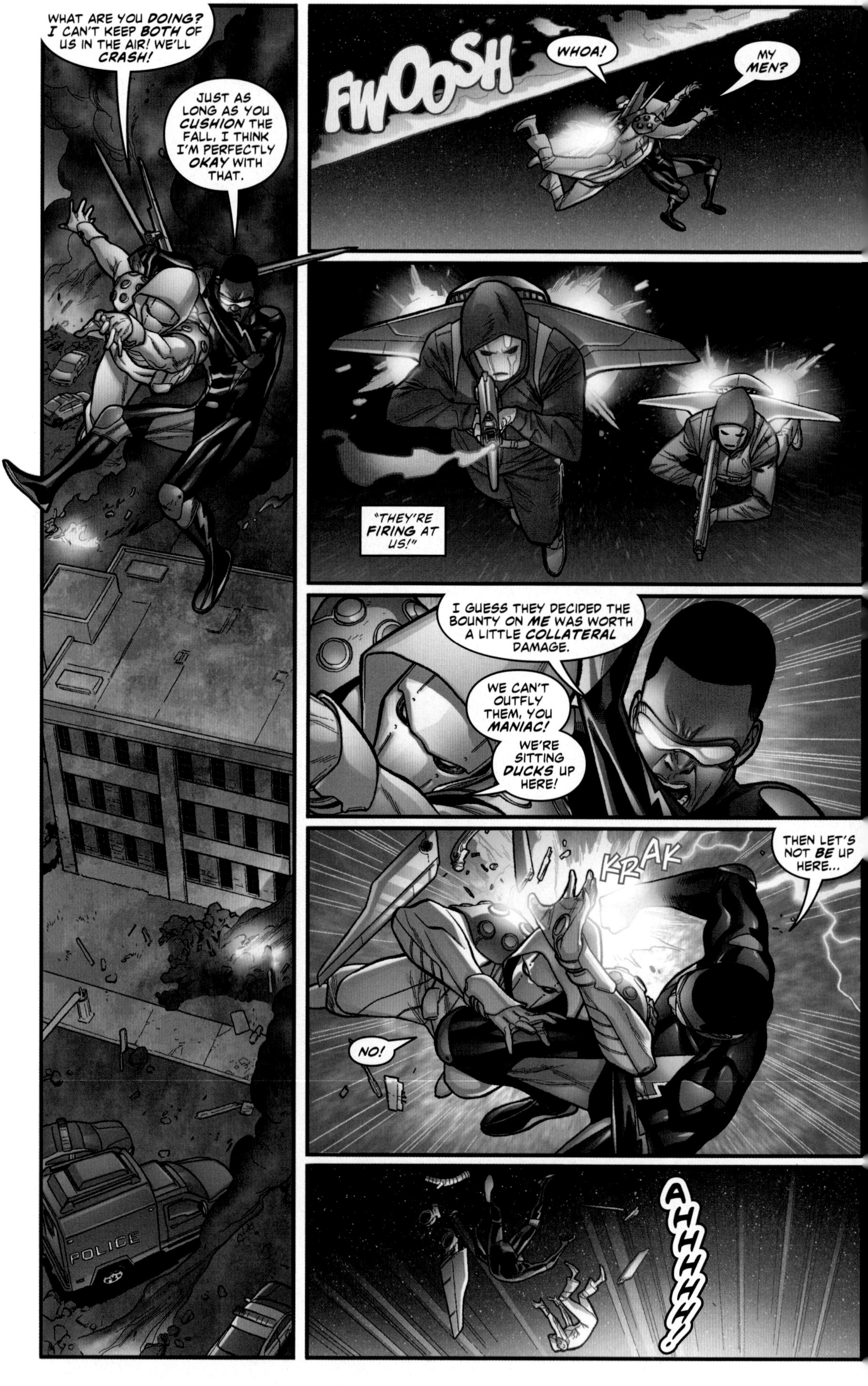

WHAT ARE YOU DOING? I CAN'T KEEP BOTH OF US IN THE AIR! WE'LL CRASH!
JUST AS LONG AS YOU CUSHION THE FALL, I THINK I'M PERFECTLY OKAY WITH THAT.
FWOOSH
WHOA!
MY MEN?
"THEY'RE FIRING AT US!"
I GUESS THEY DECIDED THE BOUNTY ON ME WAS WORTH A LITTLE COLLATERAL DAMAGE.
WE CAN'T OUTFLY THEM, YOU MANIAC!
WE'RE SITTING DUCKS UP HERE!
THEN LET'S NOT BE UP HERE...
KRAK
NO!
AHHHHH!
POLICE

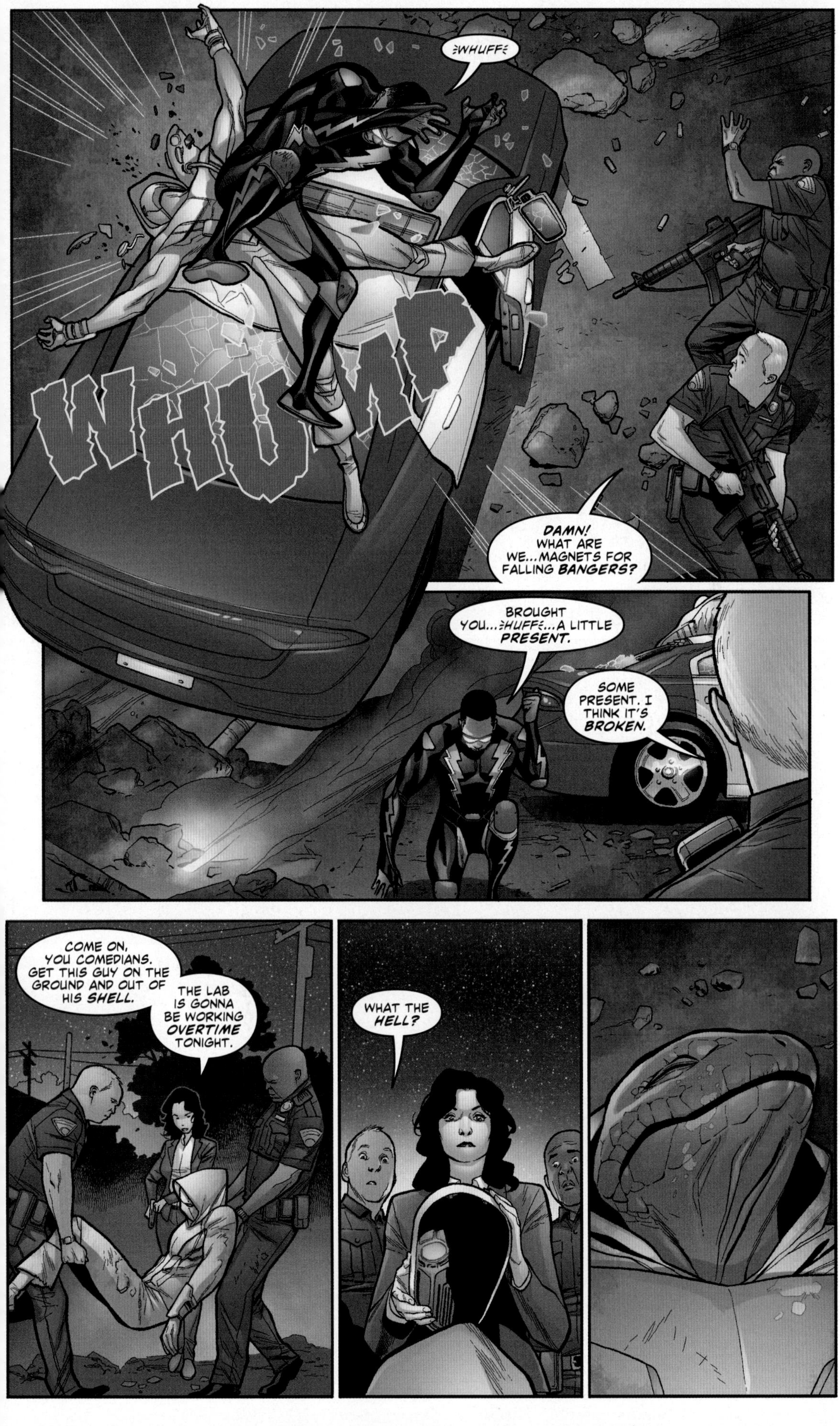

WHUFF
WHUMP
DAMN! WHAT ARE WE...MAGNETS FOR FALLING BANGERS?
BROUGHT YOU...HUFF...A LITTLE PRESENT.
SOME PRESENT. I THINK IT'S BROKEN.
COME ON, YOU COMEDIANS. GET THIS GUY ON THE GROUND AND OUT OF HIS SHELL.
THE LAB IS GONNA BE WORKING OVERTIME TONIGHT.
WHAT THE HELL?

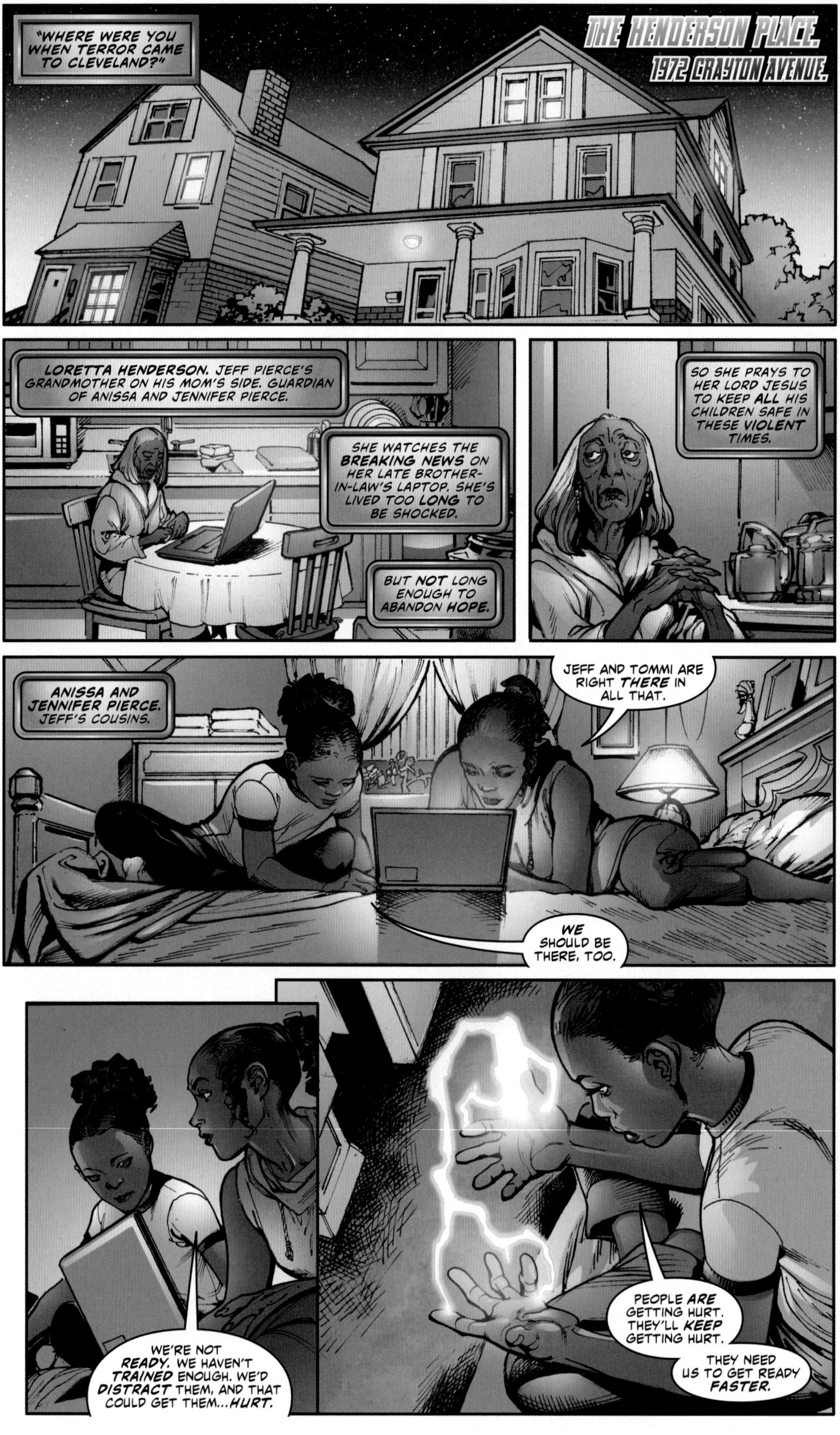
"WHERE WERE YOU WHEN TERROR CAME TO CLEVELAND?"
THE HENDERSON PLACE. 1972 CRAYTON AVENUE.
LORETTA HENDERSON. JEFF PIERCE'S GRANDMOTHER ON HIS MOM'S SIDE. GUARDIAN OF ANISSA AND JENNIFER PIERCE.
SHE WATCHES THE BREAKING NEWS ON HER LATE BROTHER-IN-LAW'S LAPTOP. SHE'S LIVED TOO LONG TO BE SHOCKED.
BUT NOT LONG ENOUGH TO ABANDON HOPE.
SO SHE PRAYS TO HER LORD JESUS TO KEEP ALL HIS CHILDREN SAFE IN THESE VIOLENT TIMES.
ANISSA AND JENNIFER PIERCE. JEFF'S COUSINS.
JEFF AND TOMMI ARE RIGHT THERE IN ALL THAT.
WE SHOULD BE THERE, TOO.
WE'RE NOT READY. WE HAVEN'T TRAINED ENOUGH. WE'D DISTRACT THEM, AND THAT COULD GET THEM...HURT.
PEOPLE ARE GETTING HURT. THEY'LL KEEP GETTING HURT.
THEY NEED US TO GET READY FASTER.

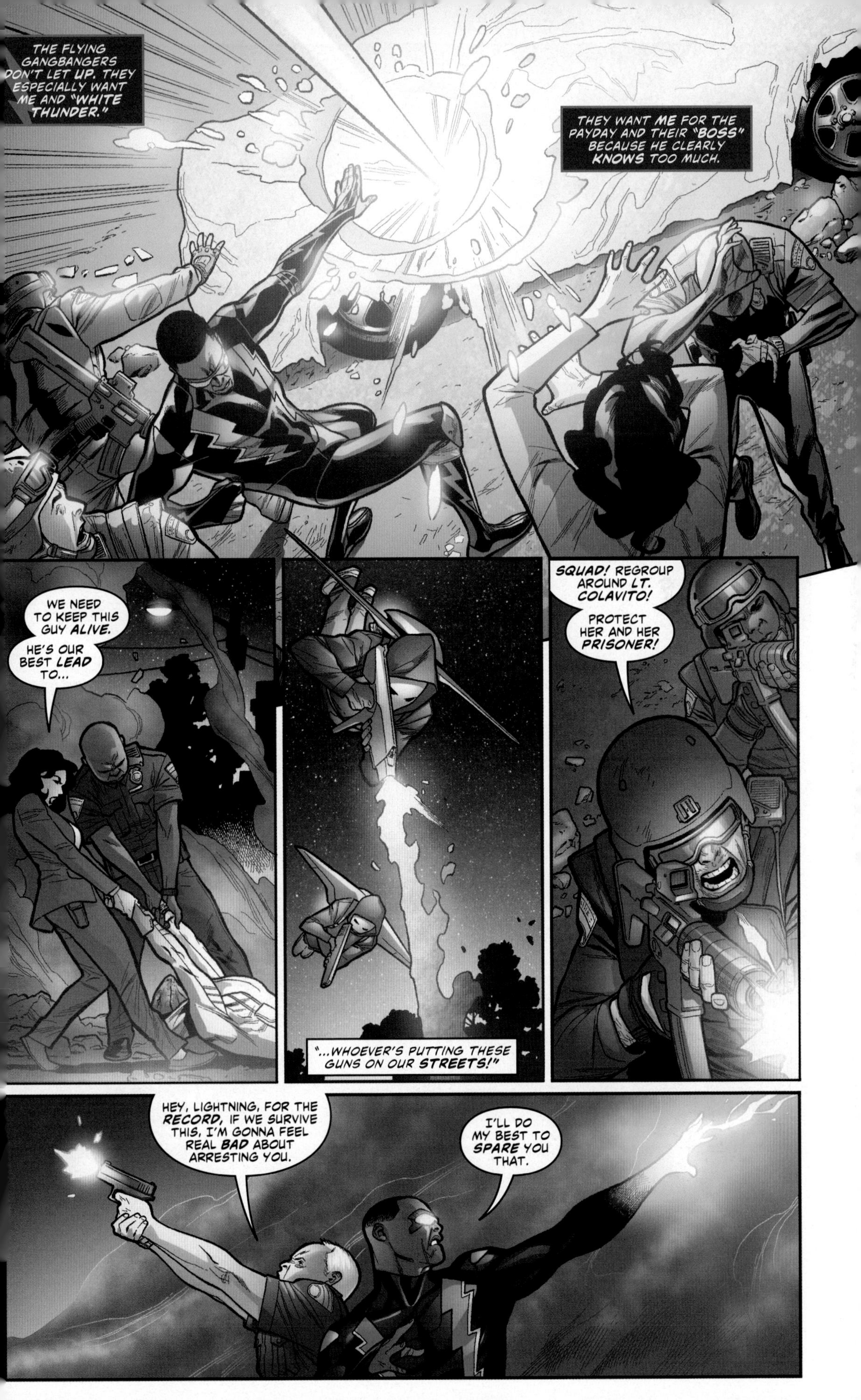
THE FLYING GANGBANGERS DON'T LET UP. THEY ESPECIALLY WANT ME AND "WHITE THUNDER."
THEY WANT ME FOR THE PAYDAY AND THEIR "BOSS" BECAUSE HE CLEARLY KNOWS TOO MUCH.
WE NEED TO KEEP THIS GUY ALIVE.
HE'S OUR BEST LEAD TO...
"...WHOEVER'S PUTTING THESE GUNS ON OUR STREETS!"
SQUAD! REGROUP AROUND LT. COLAVITO!
PROTECT HER AND HER PRISONER!
HEY, LIGHTNING, FOR THE RECORD, IF WE SURVIVE THIS, I'M GONNA FEEL REAL BAD ABOUT ARRESTING YOU.
I'LL DO MY BEST TO SPARE YOU THAT.

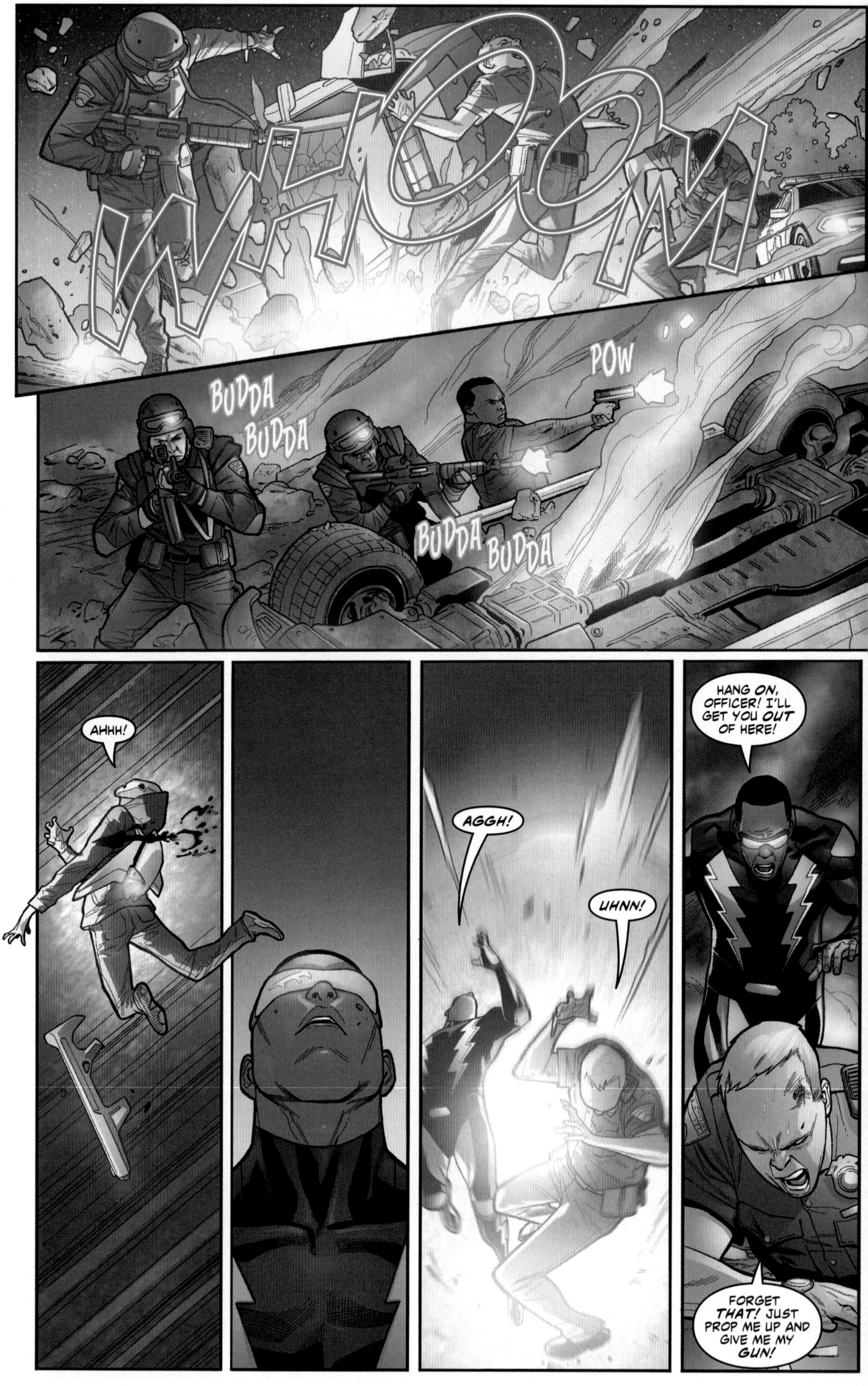
WHOOOM
BUDDA
BUDDA
POW
BUDDA
BUDDA
AHHH!
AGGH!
UHNN!
HANG ON, OFFICER! I'LL GET YOU OUT OF HERE!
FORGET THAT! JUST PROP ME UP AND GIVE ME MY GUN!

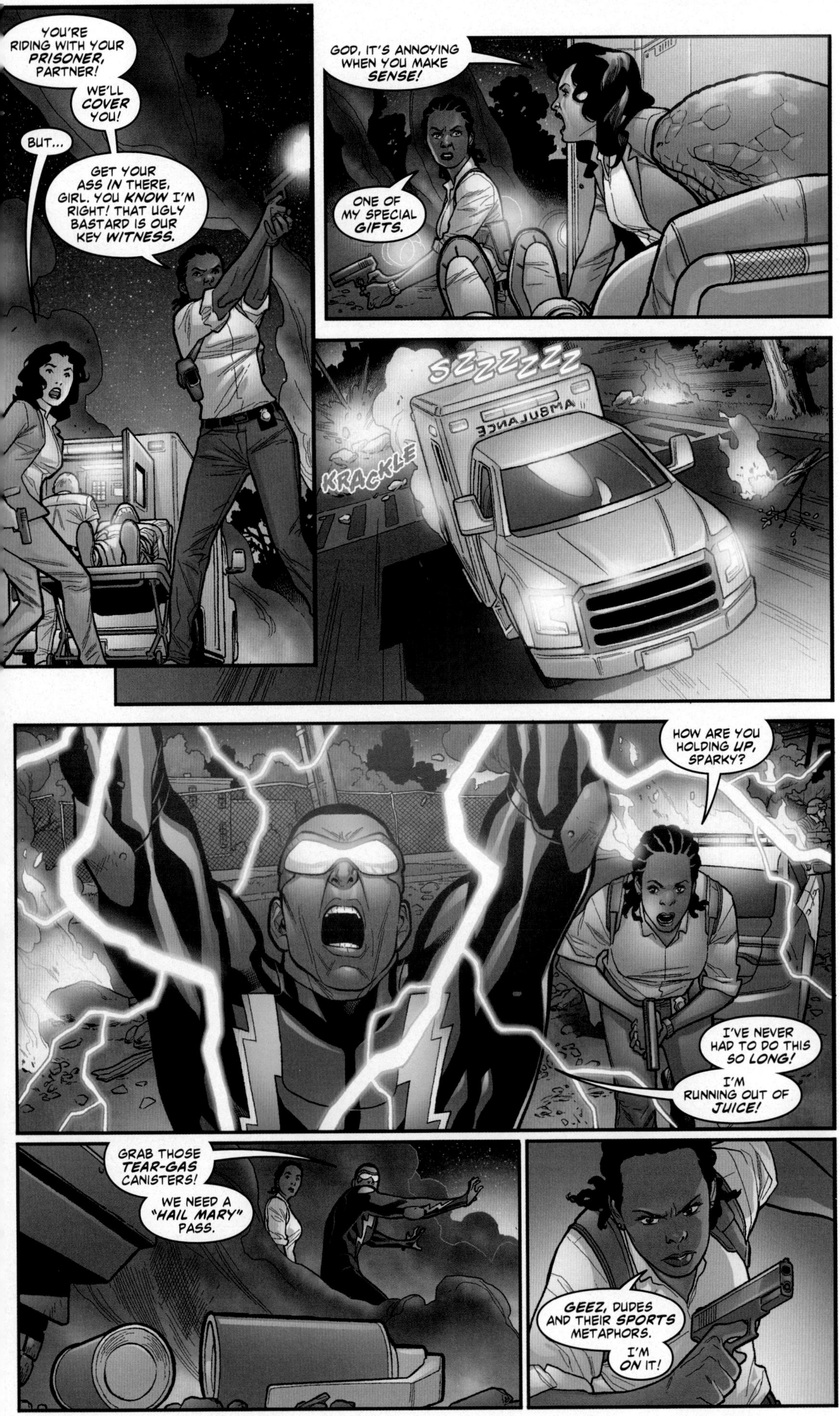

YOU'RE RIDING WITH YOUR PRISONER, PARTNER!
WE'LL COVER YOU!
BUT...
GET YOUR ASS IN THERE, GIRL. YOU KNOW I'M RIGHT! THAT UGLY BASTARD IS OUR KEY WITNESS.
GOD, IT'S ANNOYING WHEN YOU MAKE SENSE!
ONE OF MY SPECIAL GIFTS.
SZZZZZZ
AMBULANCE
KRACKLE
HOW ARE YOU HOLDING UP, SPARKY?
I'VE NEVER HAD TO DO THIS SO LONG!
I'M RUNNING OUT OF JUICE!
GRAB THOSE TEAR-GAS CANISTERS!
WE NEED A "HAIL MARY" PASS.
GEEZ, DUDES AND THEIR SPORTS METAPHORS.
I'M ON IT!

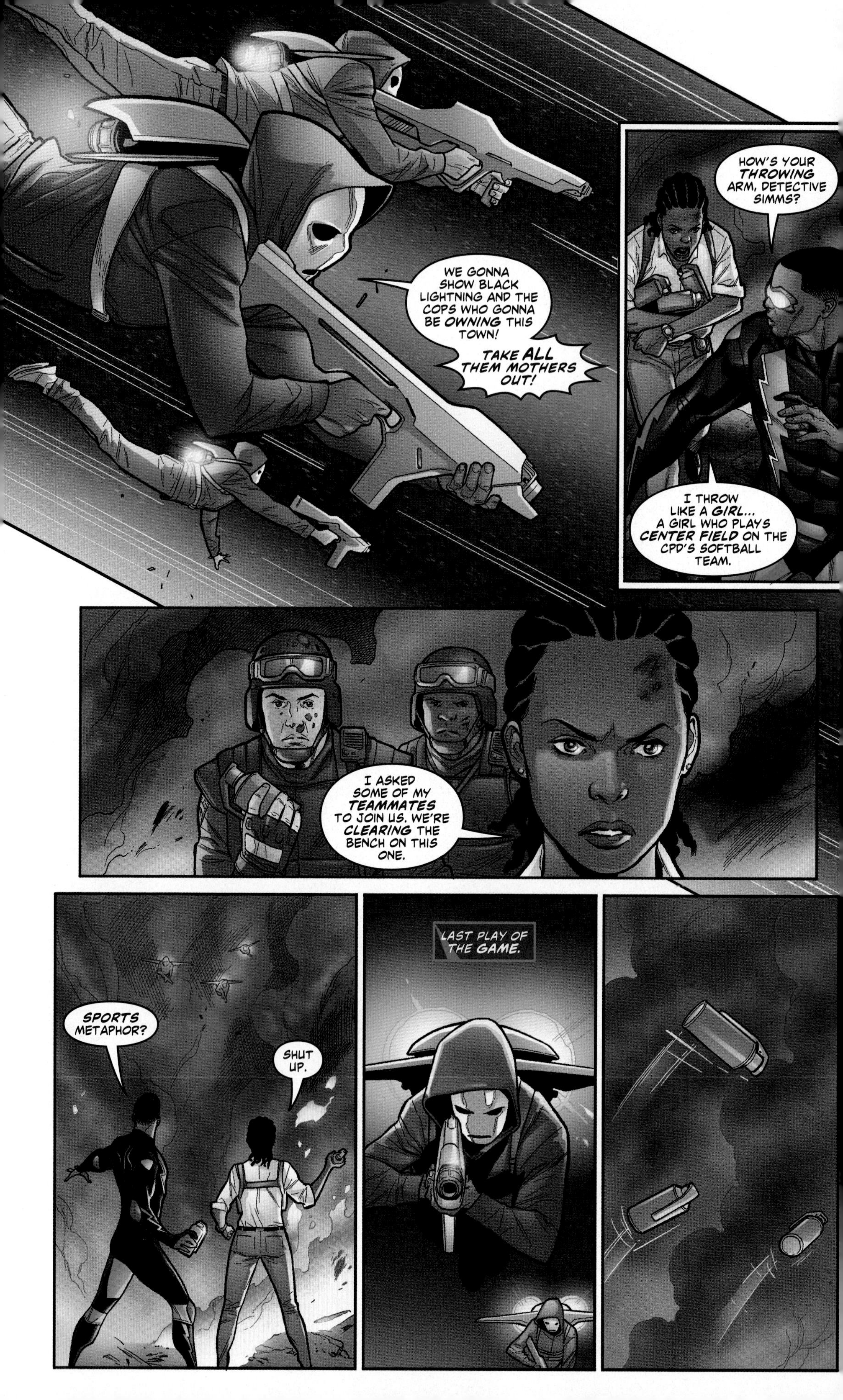
WE GONNA SHOW BLACK LIGHTNING AND THE COPS WHO GONNA BE OWNING THIS TOWN!
TAKE ALL THEM MOTHERS OUT!
HOW'S YOUR THROWING ARM, DETECTIVE SIMMS?
I THROW LIKE A GIRL... A GIRL WHO PLAYS CENTER FIELD ON THE CPD'S SOFTBALL TEAM.
I ASKED SOME OF MY TEAMMATES TO JOIN US. WE'RE CLEARING THE BENCH ON THIS ONE.
SPORTS METAPHOR?
SHUT UP.
LAST PLAY OF THE GAME.

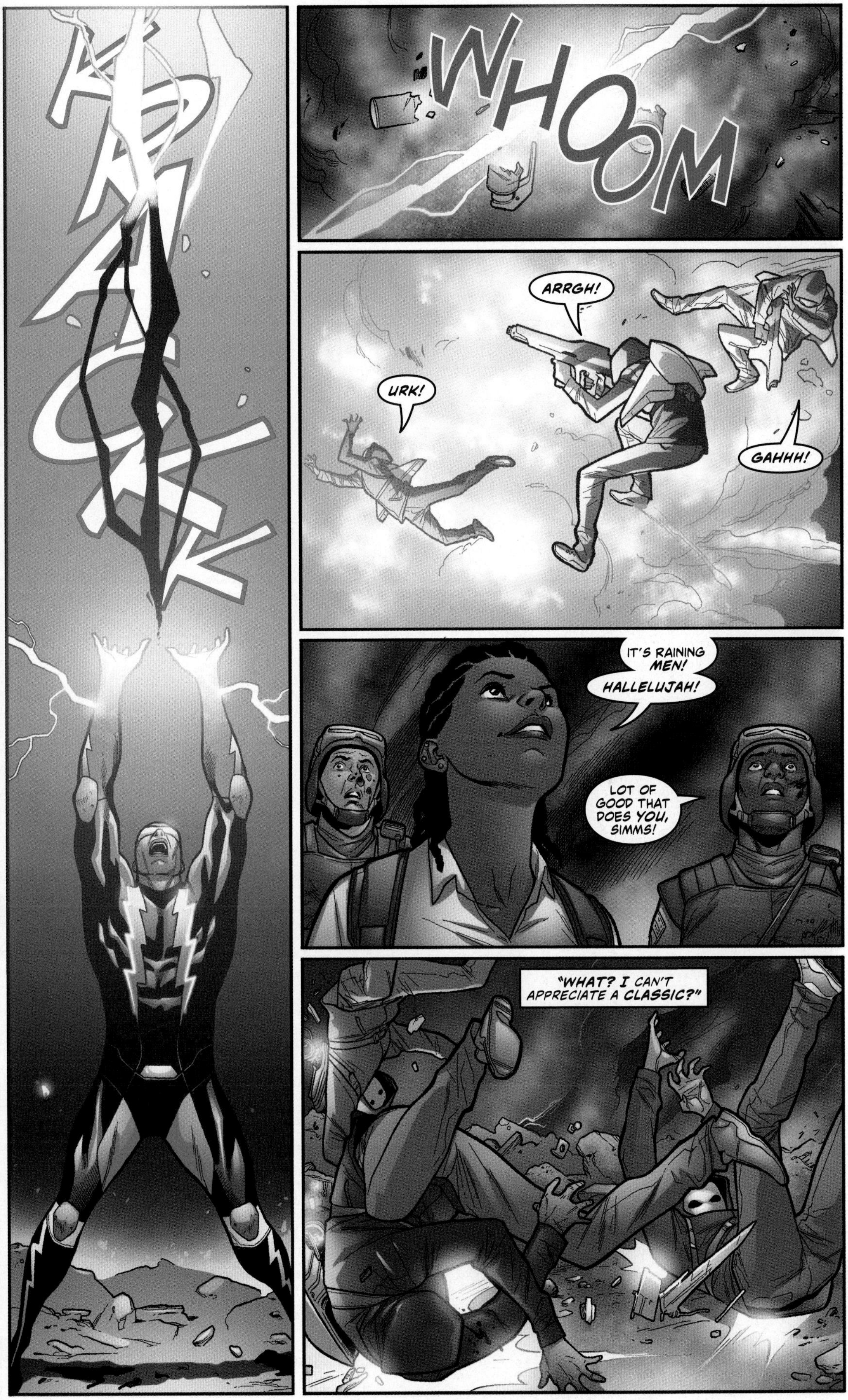
KRAKACK
WHOOM
ARRGH!
URK!
GAHHH!
IT'S RAINING MEN!
HALLELUJAH!
LOT OF GOOD THAT DOES YOU, SIMMS!
"WHAT? I CAN'T APPRECIATE A CLASSIC?"

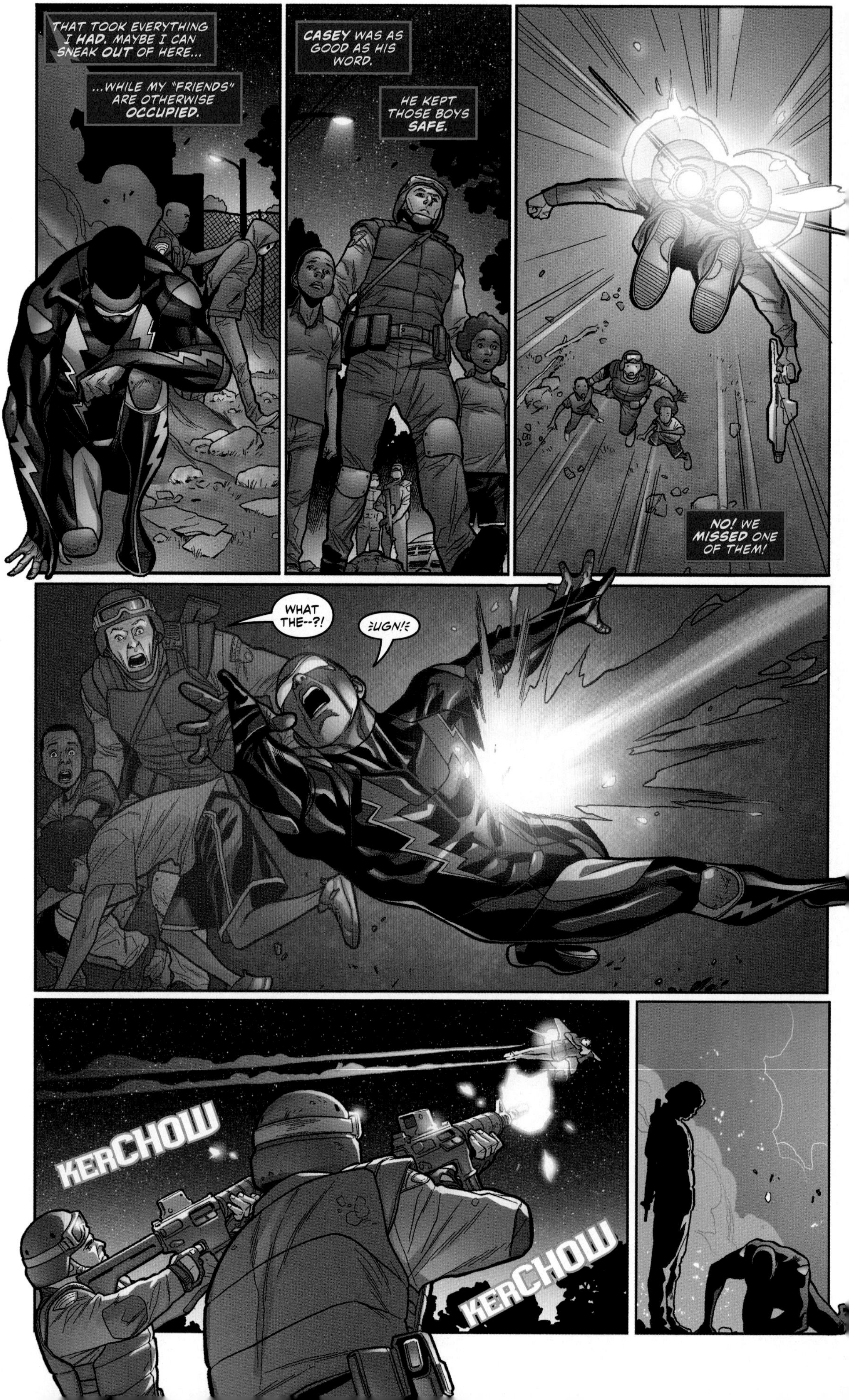
THAT TOOK EVERYTHING I HAD. MAYBE I CAN SNEAK OUT OF HERE...
...WHILE MY "FRIENDS" ARE OTHERWISE OCCUPIED.
CASEY WAS AS GOOD AS HIS WORD.
HE KEPT THOSE BOYS SAFE.
NO! WE MISSED ONE OF THEM!
WHAT THE--?!
UGN!
KERCHOW
KERCHOW

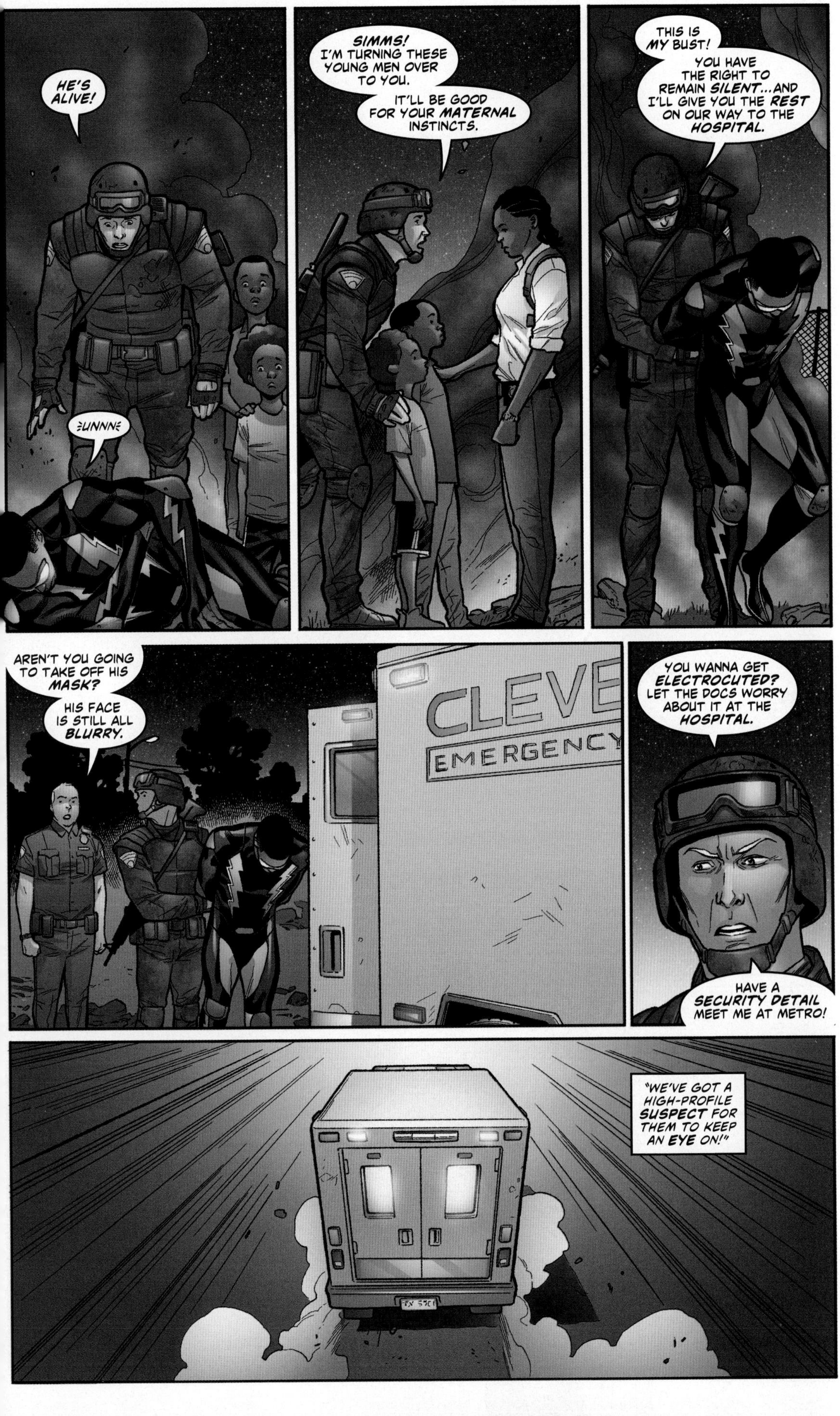
HE'S ALIVE!
UNNN
SIMMS! I'M TURNING THESE YOUNG MEN OVER TO YOU.
IT'LL BE GOOD FOR YOUR MATERNAL INSTINCTS.
THIS IS MY BUST!
YOU HAVE THE RIGHT TO REMAIN SILENT...AND I'LL GIVE YOU THE REST ON OUR WAY TO THE HOSPITAL.
AREN'T YOU GOING TO TAKE OFF HIS MASK?
HIS FACE IS STILL ALL BLURRY.
CLEVE
EMERGENCY
YOU WANNA GET ELECTROCUTED? LET THE DOCS WORRY ABOUT IT AT THE HOSPITAL.
HAVE A SECURITY DETAIL MEET ME AT METRO!
"WE'VE GOT A HIGH-PROFILE SUSPECT FOR THEM TO KEEP AN EYE ON!"

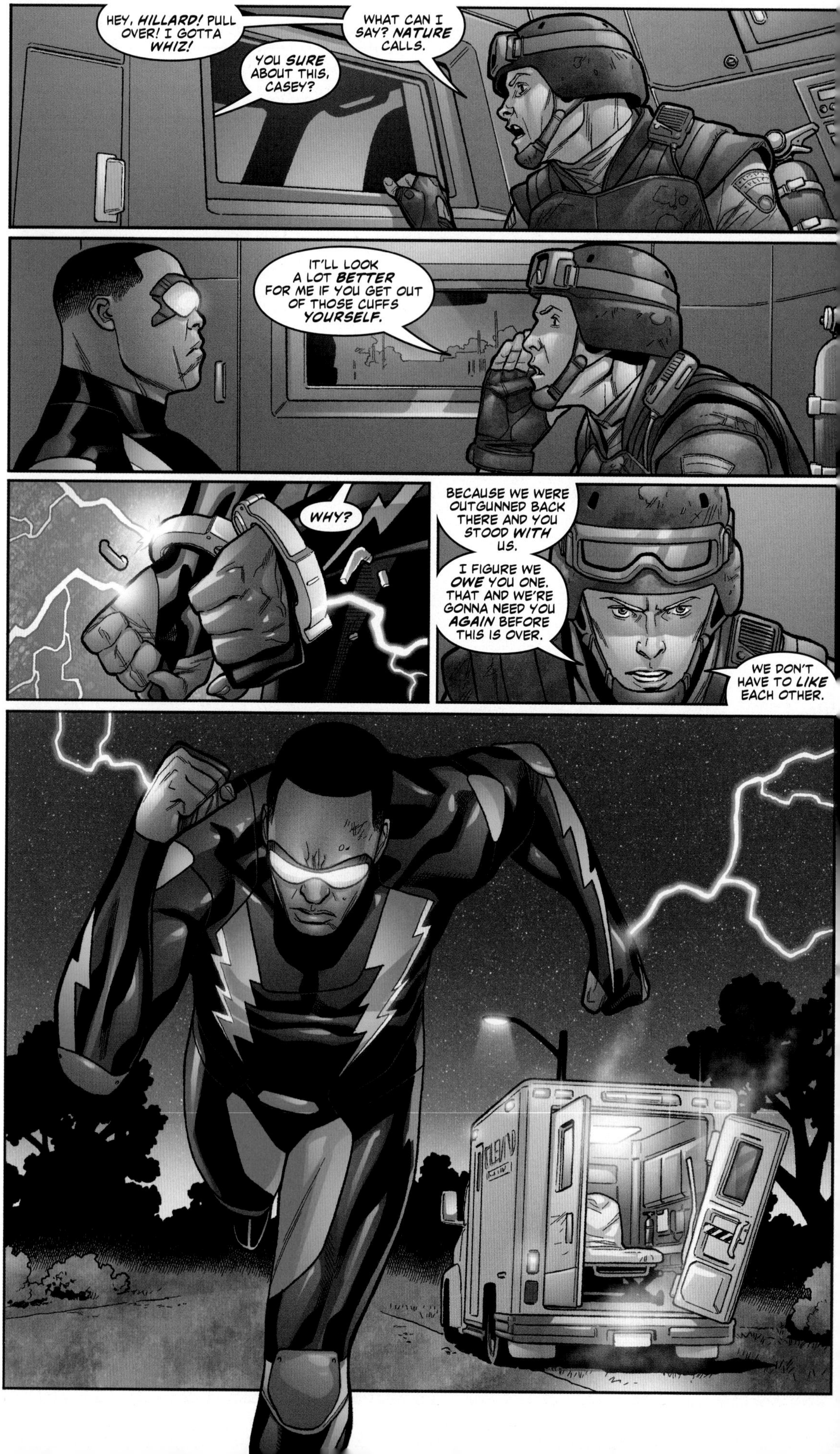
HEY, HILLARD! PULL OVER! I GOTTA WHIZ!
WHAT CAN I SAY? NATURE CALLS.
YOU SURE ABOUT THIS, CASEY?
IT'LL LOOK A LOT BETTER FOR ME IF YOU GET OUT OF THOSE CUFFS YOURSELF.
WHY?
BECAUSE WE WERE OUTGUNNED BACK THERE AND YOU STOOD WITH US.
I FIGURE WE OWE YOU ONE. THAT AND WE'RE GONNA NEED YOU AGAIN BEFORE THIS IS OVER.
WE DON'T HAVE TO LIKE EACH OTHER.

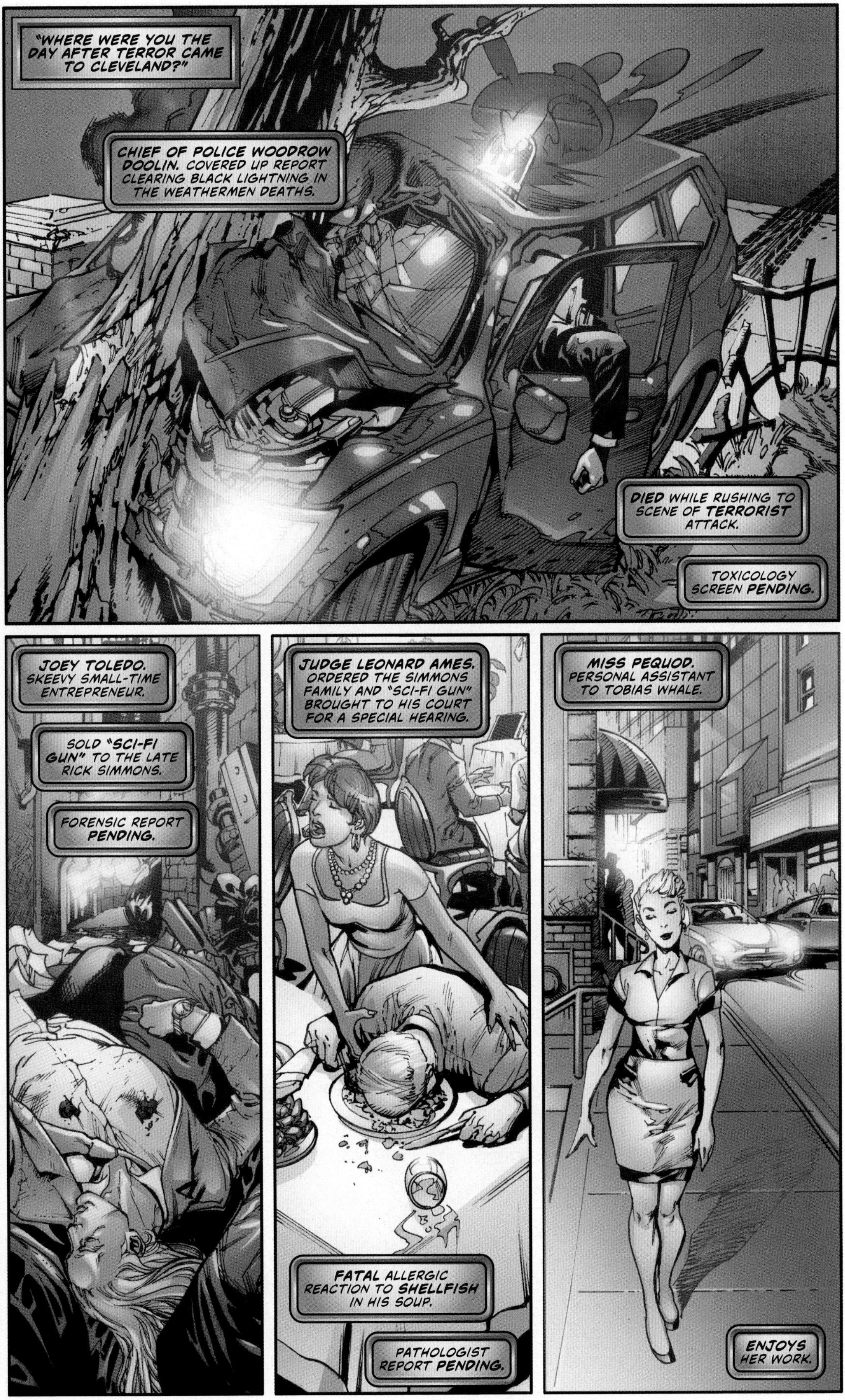
"WHERE WERE YOU THE DAY AFTER TERROR CAME TO CLEVELAND?"
CHIEF OF POLICE WOODROW DOOLIN. COVERED UP REPORT CLEARING BLACK LIGHTNING IN THE WEATHERMEN DEATHS.
DIED WHILE RUSHING TO SCENE OF TERRORIST ATTACK.
TOXICOLOGY SCREEN PENDING.
JOEY TOLEDO. SKEEVY SMALL-TIME ENTREPRENEUR.
SOLD "SCI-FI GUN" TO THE LATE RICK SIMMONS.
FORENSIC REPORT PENDING.
JUDGE LEONARD AMES. ORDERED THE SIMMONS FAMILY AND "SCI-FI GUN" BROUGHT TO HIS COURT FOR A SPECIAL HEARING.
FATAL ALLERGIC REACTION TO SHELLFISH IN HIS SOUP.
PATHOLOGIST REPORT PENDING.
MISS PEQUOD. PERSONAL ASSISTANT TO TOBIAS WHALE.
ENJOYS HER WORK.

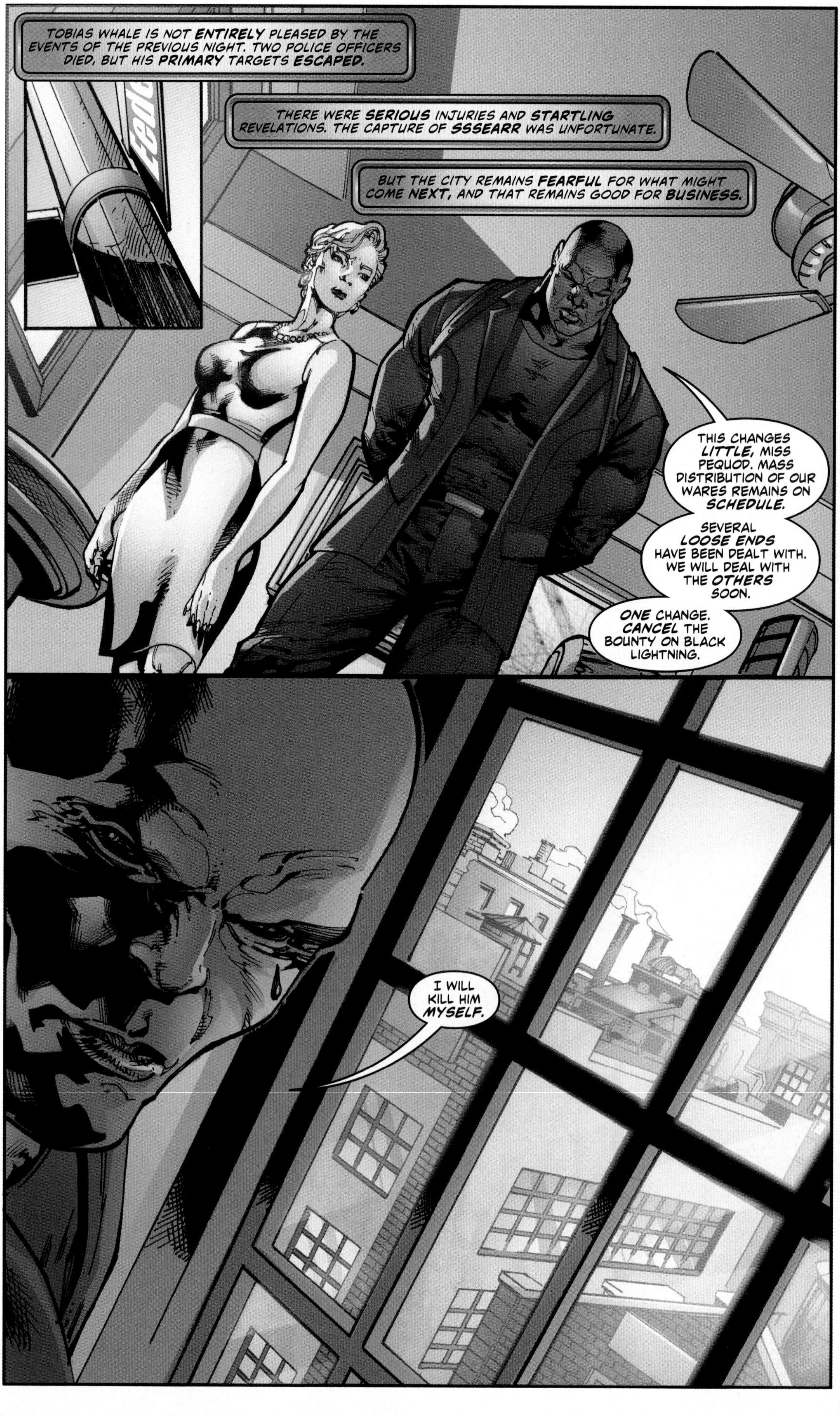
TOBIAS WHALE IS NOT ENTIRELY PLEASED BY THE EVENTS OF THE PREVIOUS NIGHT. TWO POLICE OFFICERS DIED, BUT HIS PRIMARY TARGETS ESCAPED.
THERE WERE SERIOUS INJURIES AND STARTLING REVELATIONS. THE CAPTURE OF SSSEARR WAS UNFORTUNATE.
BUT THE CITY REMAINS FEARFUL FOR WHAT MIGHT COME NEXT, AND THAT REMAINS GOOD FOR BUSINESS.
THIS CHANGES LITTLE, MISS PEQUOD. MASS DISTRIBUTION OF OUR WARES REMAINS ON SCHEDULE.
SEVERAL LOOSE ENDS HAVE BEEN DEALT WITH. WE WILL DEAL WITH THE OTHERS SOON.
ONE CHANGE. CANCEL THE BOUNTY ON BLACK LIGHTNING.
I WILL KILL HIM MYSELF.

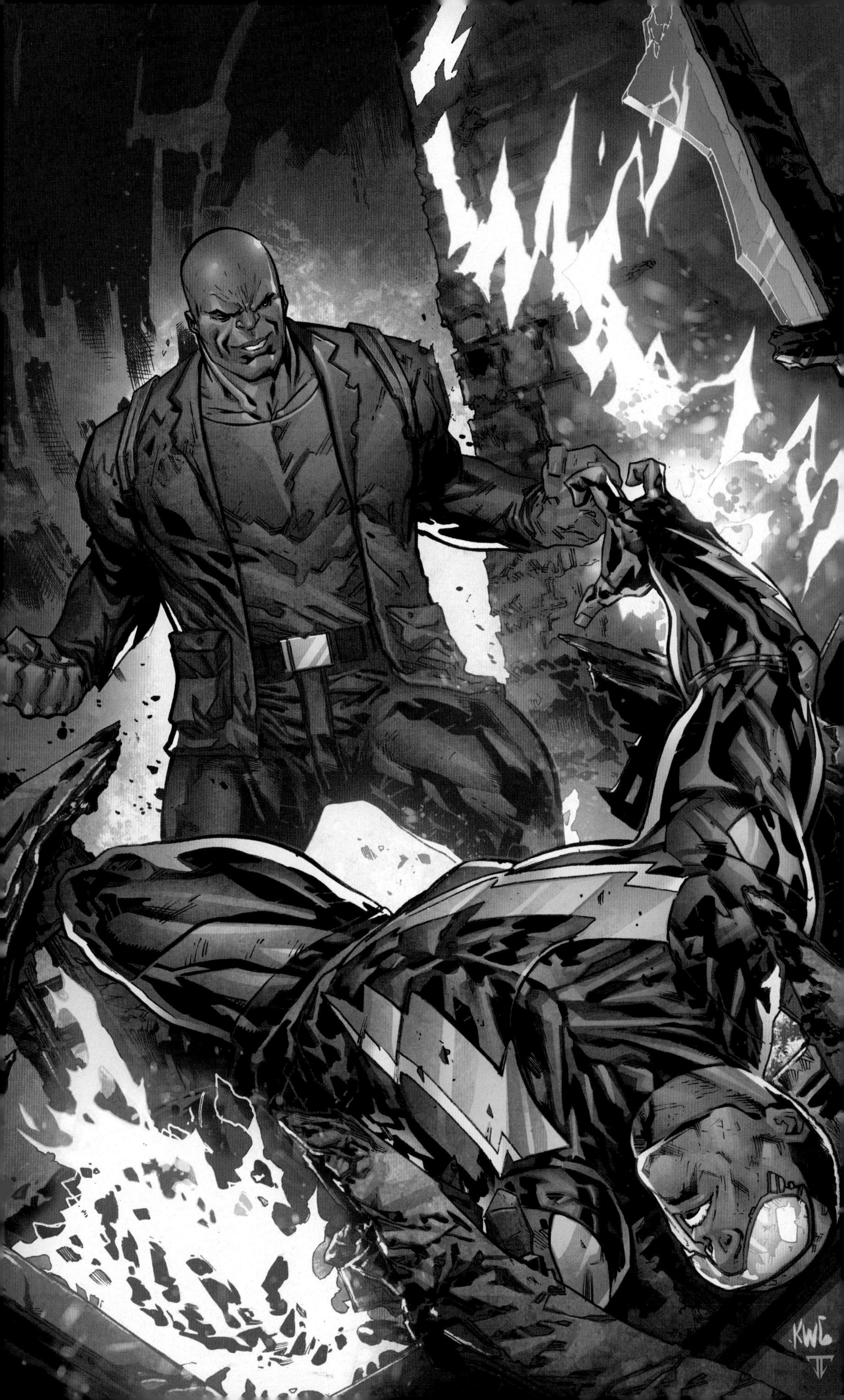

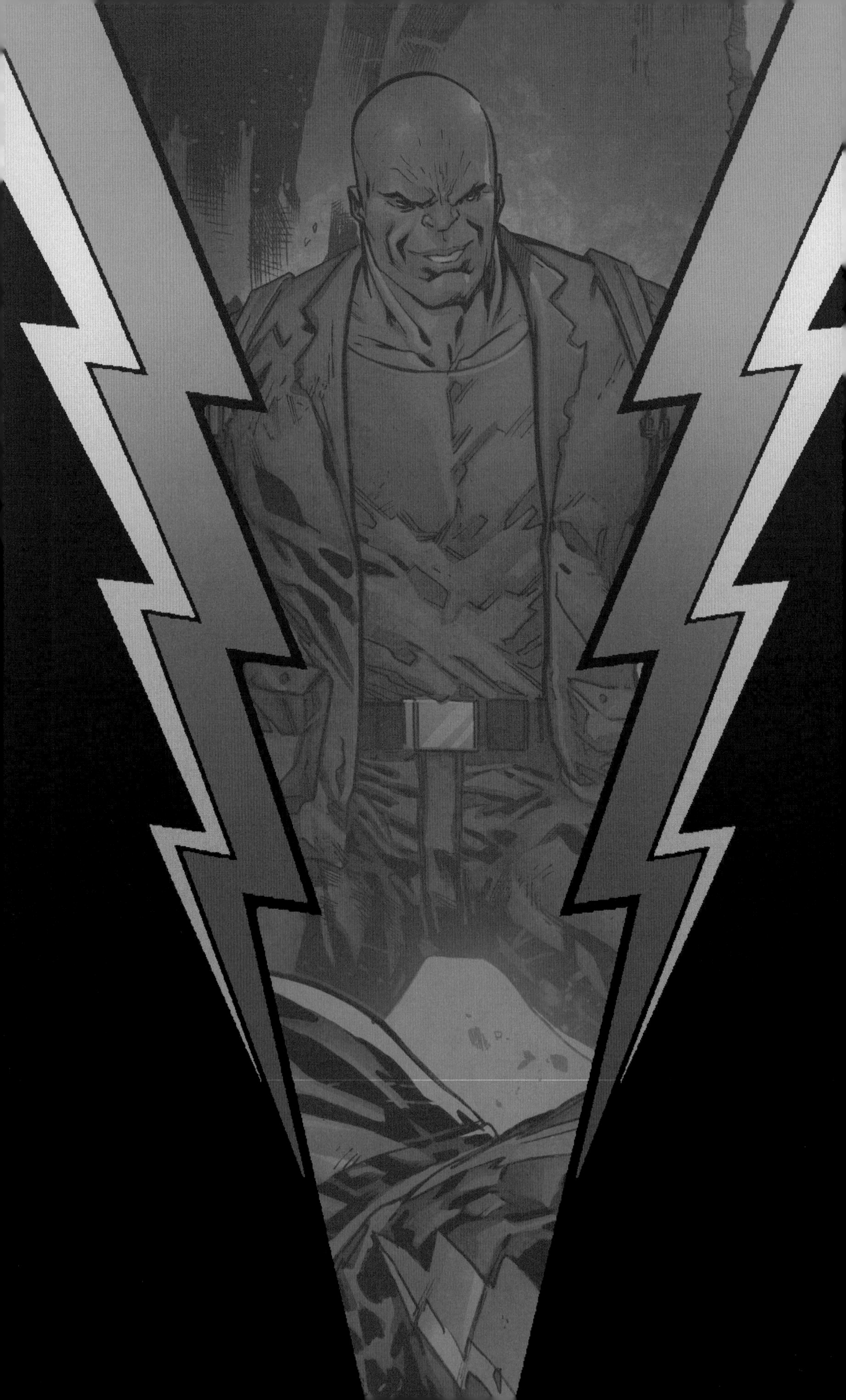

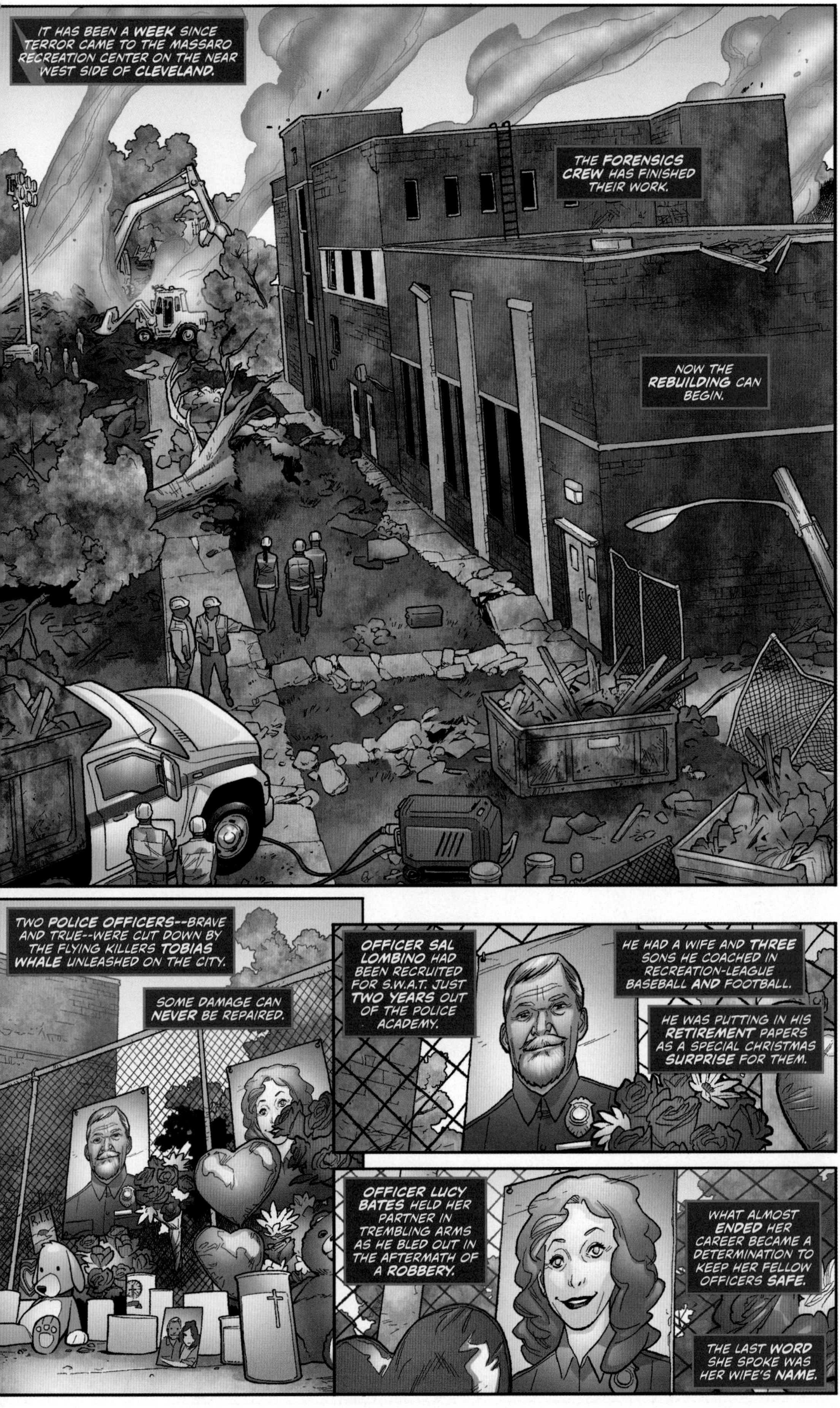
IT HAS BEEN A WEEK SINCE TERROR CAME TO THE MASSARO RECREATION CENTER ON THE NEAR WEST SIDE OF CLEVELAND.
THE FORENSICS CREW HAS FINISHED THEIR WORK.
NOW THE REBUILDING CAN BEGIN.
TWO POLICE OFFICERS--BRAVE AND TRUE--WERE CUT DOWN BY THE FLYING KILLERS TOBIAS WHALE UNLEASHED ON THE CITY.
SOME DAMAGE CAN NEVER BE REPAIRED.
OFFICER SAL LOMBINO HAD BEEN RECRUITED FOR S.W.A.T. JUST TWO YEARS OUT OF THE POLICE ACADEMY.
HE HAD A WIFE AND THREE SONS HE COACHED IN RECREATION-LEAGUE BASEBALL AND FOOTBALL.
HE WAS PUTTING IN HIS RETIREMENT PAPERS AS A SPECIAL CHRISTMAS SURPRISE FOR THEM.
OFFICER LUCY BATES HELD HER PARTNER IN TREMBLING ARMS AS HE BLED OUT IN THE AFTERMATH OF A ROBBERY.
WHAT ALMOST ENDED HER CAREER BECAME A DETERMINATION TO KEEP HER FELLOW OFFICERS SAFE.
THE LAST WORD SHE SPOKE WAS HER WIFE'S NAME.

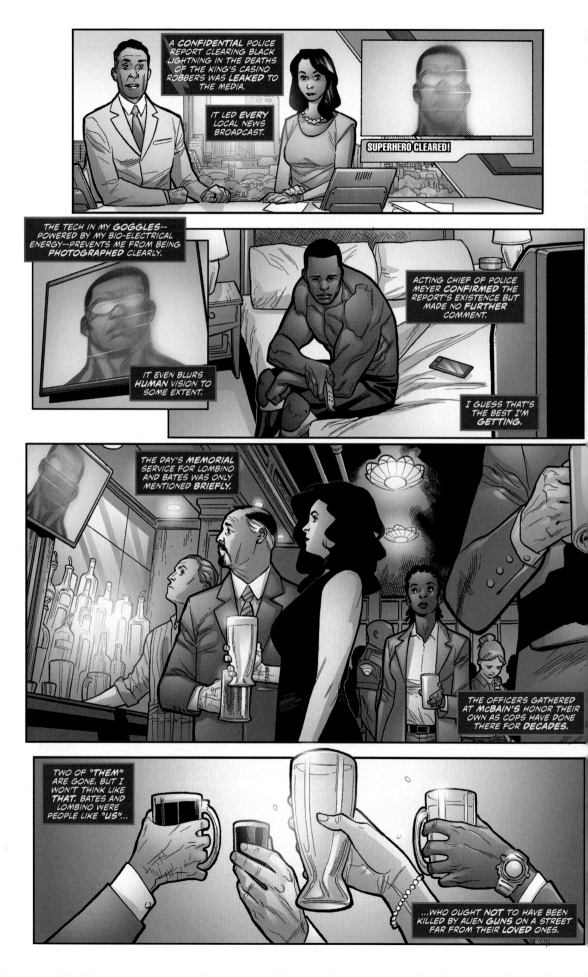

A *CONFIDENTIAL* POLICE REPORT CLEARING BLACK LIGHTNING IN THE DEATHS OF THE KING'S CASINO ROBBERS WAS *LEAKED* TO THE MEDIA.

IT LED *EVERY* LOCAL NEWS BROADCAST.

SUPERHERO CLEARED!

THE TECH IN MY *GOGGLES*-- POWERED BY MY BIO-ELECTRICAL ENERGY--PREVENTS ME FROM BEING *PHOTOGRAPHED* CLEARLY.

ACTING CHIEF OF POLICE MEYER *CONFIRMED* THE REPORT'S EXISTENCE BUT MADE NO *FURTHER* COMMENT.

IT EVEN BLURS *HUMAN* VISION TO SOME EXTENT.

I GUESS THAT'S THE BEST I'M *GETTING.*

THE DAY'S *MEMORIAL* SERVICE FOR LOMBINO AND BATES WAS ONLY MENTIONED *BRIEFLY.*

THE OFFICERS GATHERED AT McBAIN'S HONOR THEIR OWN AS COPS HAVE DONE THERE FOR *DECADES.*

TWO OF *"THEM"* ARE GONE, BUT I WON'T THINK LIKE *THAT.* BATES AND LOMBINO WERE PEOPLE LIKE *"US"*...

...WHO OUGHT *NOT* TO HAVE BEEN KILLED BY ALIEN *GUNS* ON A STREET FAR FROM THEIR *LOVED* ONES.

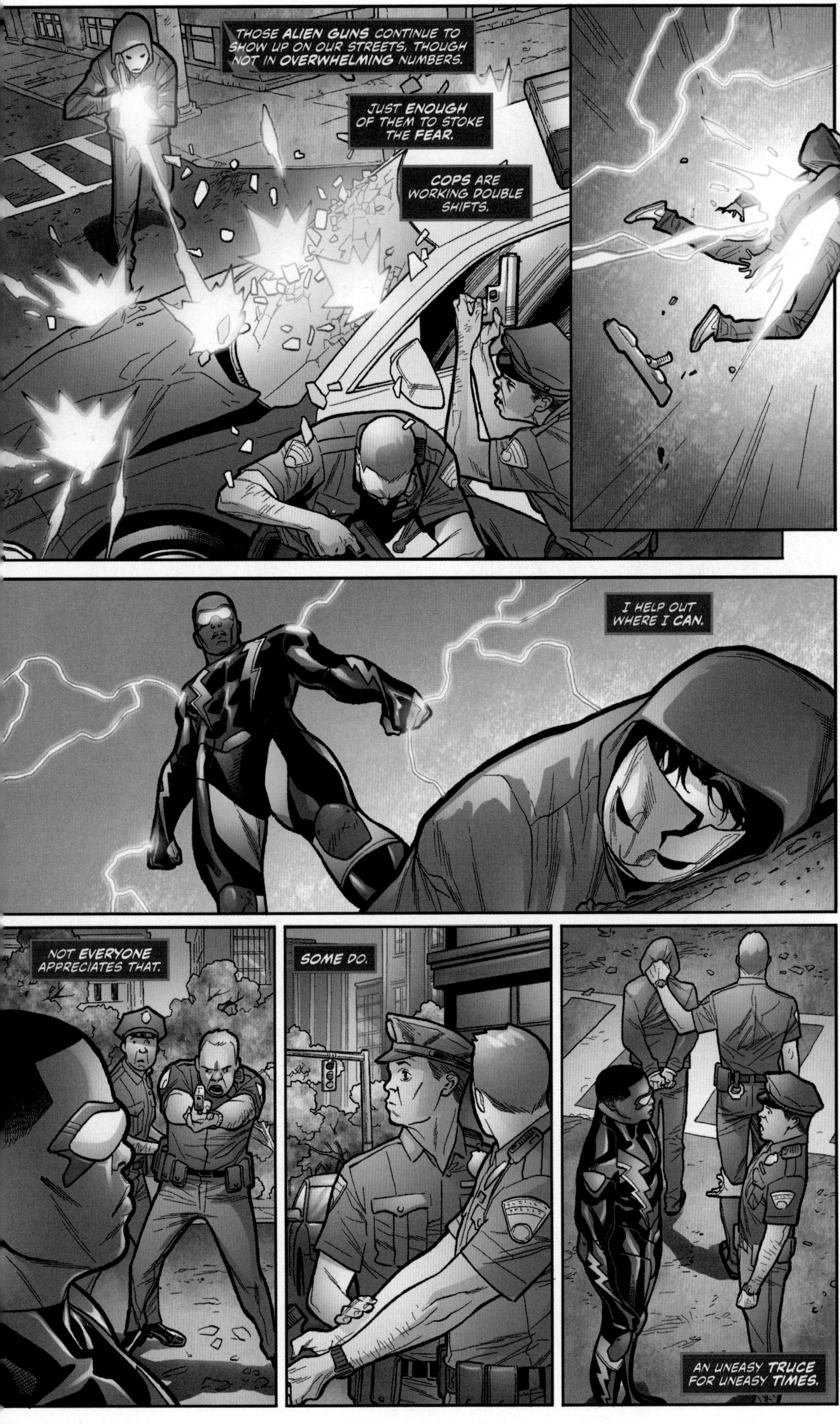
THOSE ALIEN GUNS CONTINUE TO SHOW UP ON OUR STREETS, THOUGH NOT IN OVERWHELMING NUMBERS.
JUST ENOUGH OF THEM TO STOKE THE FEAR.
COPS ARE WORKING DOUBLE SHIFTS.
I HELP OUT WHERE I CAN.
NOT EVERYONE APPRECIATES THAT.
SOME DO.
AN UNEASY TRUCE FOR UNEASY TIMES.

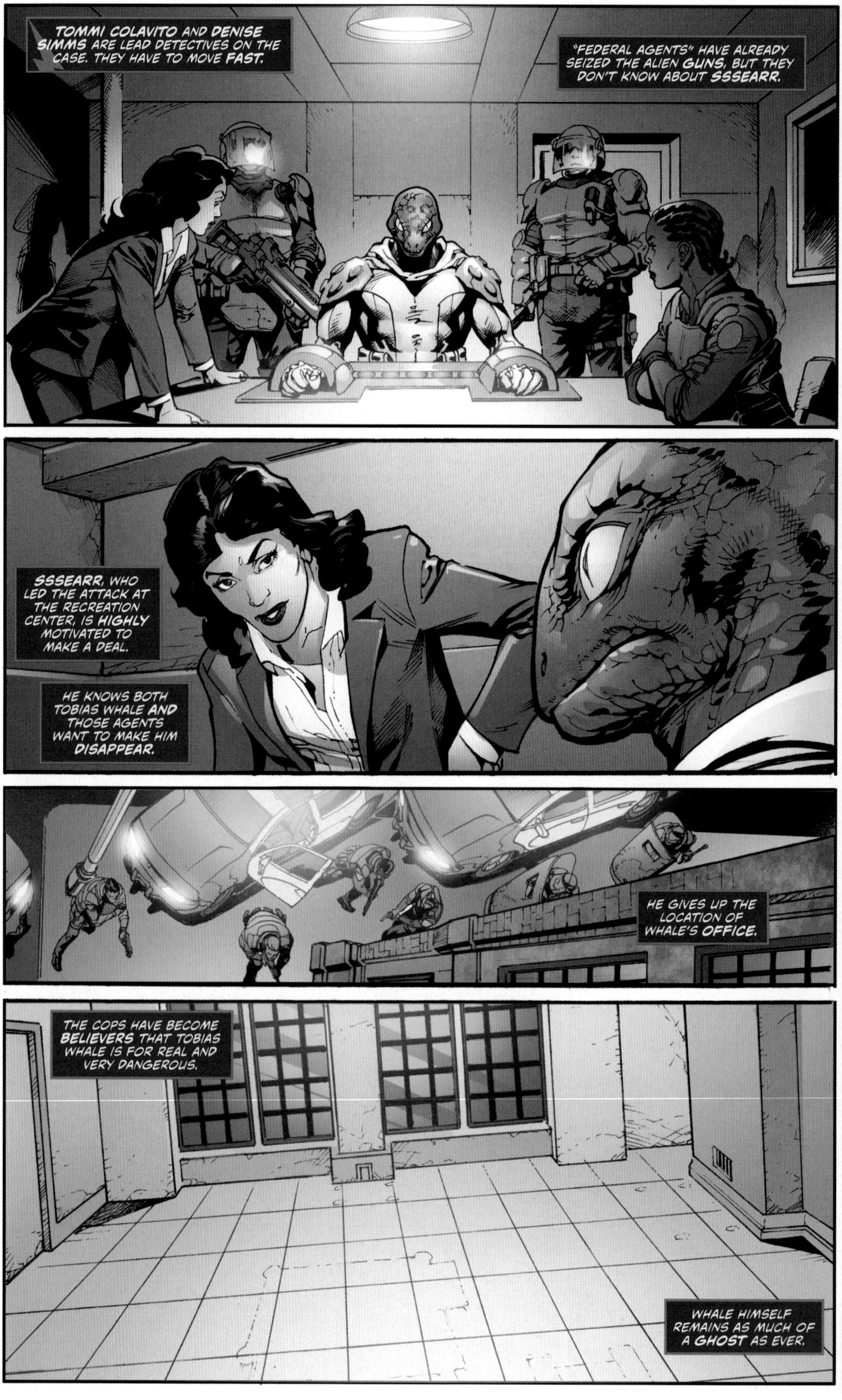
TOMMI COLAVITO AND DENISE SIMMS ARE LEAD DETECTIVES ON THE CASE. THEY HAVE TO MOVE FAST.
"FEDERAL AGENTS" HAVE ALREADY SEIZED THE ALIEN GUNS, BUT THEY DON'T KNOW ABOUT SSSEARR.
SSSEARR, WHO LED THE ATTACK AT THE RECREATION CENTER, IS HIGHLY MOTIVATED TO MAKE A DEAL.
HE KNOWS BOTH TOBIAS WHALE AND THOSE AGENTS WANT TO MAKE HIM DISAPPEAR.
HE GIVES UP THE LOCATION OF WHALE'S OFFICE.
THE COPS HAVE BECOME BELIEVERS THAT TOBIAS WHALE IS FOR REAL AND VERY DANGEROUS.
WHALE HIMSELF REMAINS AS MUCH OF A GHOST AS EVER.

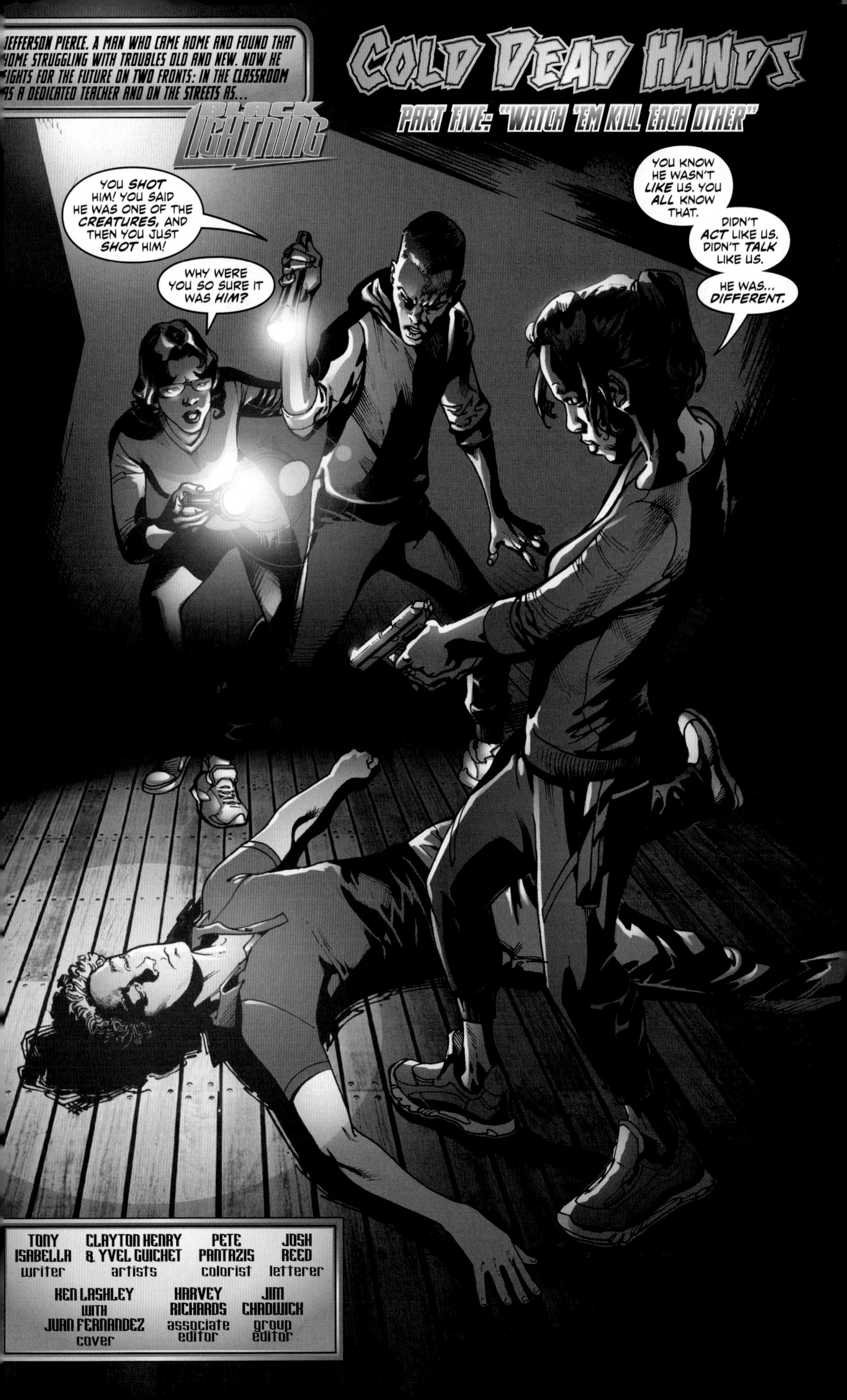
JEFFERSON PIERCE. A MAN WHO CAME HOME AND FOUND THAT HOME STRUGGLING WITH TROUBLES OLD AND NEW. NOW HE FIGHTS FOR THE FUTURE ON TWO FRONTS: IN THE CLASSROOM AS A DEDICATED TEACHER AND ON THE STREETS AS...
BLACK LIGHTNING
COLD DEAD HANDS
PART FIVE: "WATCH 'EM KILL EACH OTHER"
YOU SHOT HIM! YOU SAID HE WAS ONE OF THE CREATURES, AND THEN YOU JUST SHOT HIM!
WHY WERE YOU SO SURE IT WAS HIM?
YOU KNOW HE WASN'T LIKE US. YOU ALL KNOW THAT.
DIDN'T ACT LIKE US. DIDN'T TALK LIKE US.
HE WAS... DIFFERENT.
TONY ISABELLA writer
CLAYTON HENRY & YVEL GUICHET artists
PETE PANTAZIS colorist
JOSH REED letterer
KEN LASHLEY WITH JUAN FERNANDEZ cover
HARVEY RICHARDS associate editor
JIM CHADWICK group editor

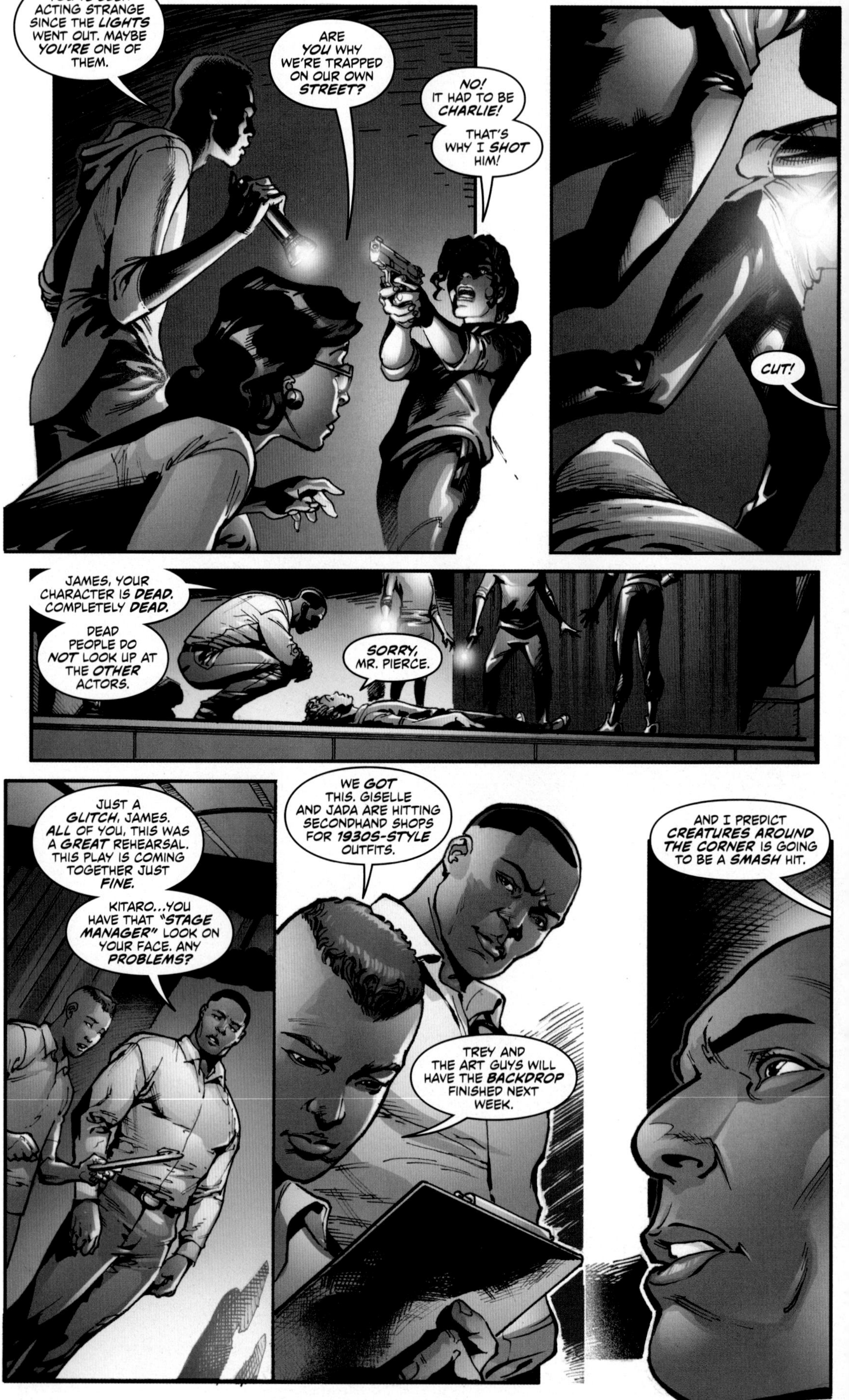

YOU'VE BEEN ACTING STRANGE SINCE THE LIGHTS WENT OUT. MAYBE YOU'RE ONE OF THEM.
ARE YOU WHY WE'RE TRAPPED ON OUR OWN STREET?
NO! IT HAD TO BE CHARLIE!
THAT'S WHY I SHOT HIM!
CUT!
JAMES, YOUR CHARACTER IS DEAD. COMPLETELY DEAD.
DEAD PEOPLE DO NOT LOOK UP AT THE OTHER ACTORS.
SORRY, MR. PIERCE.
JUST A GLITCH, JAMES. ALL OF YOU, THIS WAS A GREAT REHEARSAL. THIS PLAY IS COMING TOGETHER JUST FINE.
KITARO...YOU HAVE THAT "STAGE MANAGER" LOOK ON YOUR FACE. ANY PROBLEMS?
WE GOT THIS. GISELLE AND JADA ARE HITTING SECONDHAND SHOPS FOR 1930S-STYLE OUTFITS.
TREY AND THE ART GUYS WILL HAVE THE BACKDROP FINISHED NEXT WEEK.
AND I PREDICT CREATURES AROUND THE CORNER IS GOING TO BE A SMASH HIT.

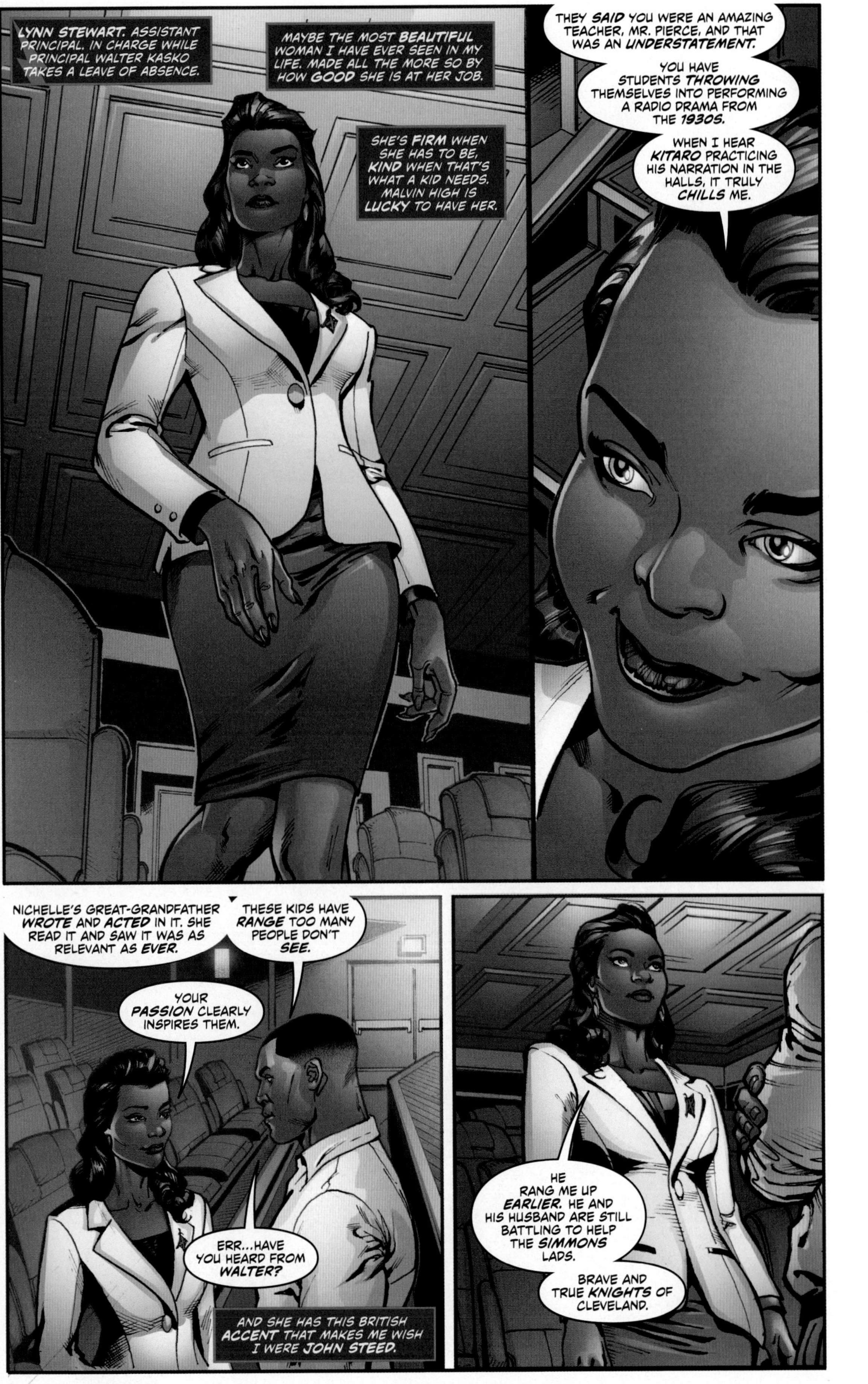
LYNN STEWART. ASSISTANT PRINCIPAL. IN CHARGE WHILE PRINCIPAL WALTER KASKO TAKES A LEAVE OF ABSENCE.
MAYBE THE MOST BEAUTIFUL WOMAN I HAVE EVER SEEN IN MY LIFE. MADE ALL THE MORE SO BY HOW GOOD SHE IS AT HER JOB.
SHE'S FIRM WHEN SHE HAS TO BE, KIND WHEN THAT'S WHAT A KID NEEDS. MALVIN HIGH IS LUCKY TO HAVE HER.
THEY SAID YOU WERE AN AMAZING TEACHER, MR. PIERCE, AND THAT WAS AN UNDERSTATEMENT.
YOU HAVE STUDENTS THROWING THEMSELVES INTO PERFORMING A RADIO DRAMA FROM THE 1930S.
WHEN I HEAR KITARO PRACTICING HIS NARRATION IN THE HALLS, IT TRULY CHILLS ME.
NICHELLE'S GREAT-GRANDFATHER WROTE AND ACTED IN IT. SHE READ IT AND SAW IT WAS AS RELEVANT AS EVER.
THESE KIDS HAVE RANGE TOO MANY PEOPLE DON'T SEE.
YOUR PASSION CLEARLY INSPIRES THEM.
ERR...HAVE YOU HEARD FROM WALTER?
AND SHE HAS THIS BRITISH ACCENT THAT MAKES ME WISH I WERE JOHN STEED.
HE RANG ME UP EARLIER. HE AND HIS HUSBAND ARE STILL BATTLING TO HELP THE SIMMONS LADS.
BRAVE AND TRUE KNIGHTS OF CLEVELAND.

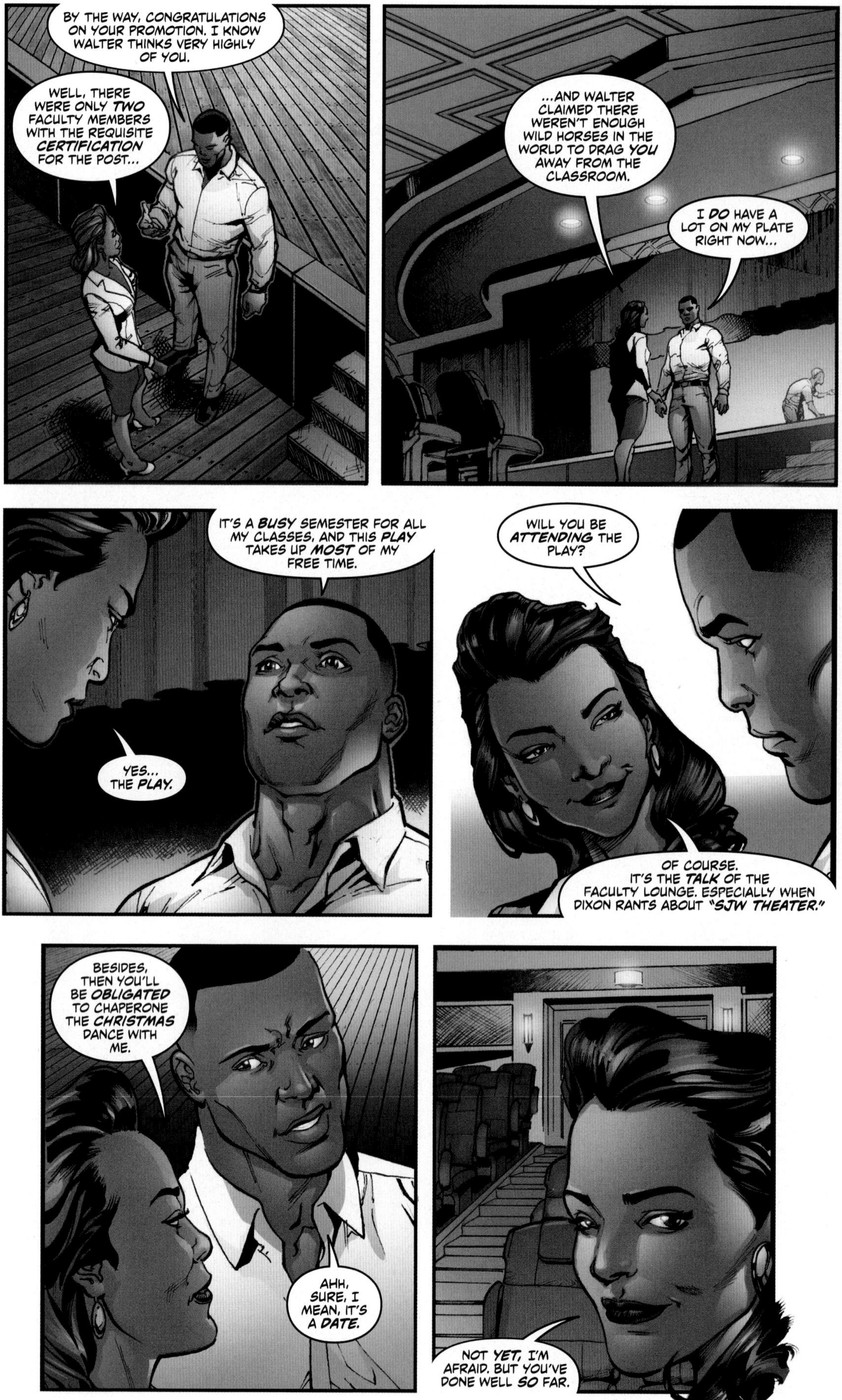
BY THE WAY, CONGRATULATIONS ON YOUR PROMOTION. I KNOW WALTER THINKS VERY HIGHLY OF YOU.
WELL, THERE WERE ONLY TWO FACULTY MEMBERS WITH THE REQUISITE CERTIFICATION FOR THE POST...
...AND WALTER CLAIMED THERE WEREN'T ENOUGH WILD HORSES IN THE WORLD TO DRAG YOU AWAY FROM THE CLASSROOM.
I DO HAVE A LOT ON MY PLATE RIGHT NOW...
IT'S A BUSY SEMESTER FOR ALL MY CLASSES, AND THIS PLAY TAKES UP MOST OF MY FREE TIME.
YES... THE PLAY.
WILL YOU BE ATTENDING THE PLAY?
OF COURSE. IT'S THE TALK OF THE FACULTY LOUNGE. ESPECIALLY WHEN DIXON RANTS ABOUT "SJW THEATER."
BESIDES, THEN YOU'LL BE OBLIGATED TO CHAPERONE THE CHRISTMAS DANCE WITH ME.
AHH, SURE, I MEAN, IT'S A DATE.
NOT YET, I'M AFRAID. BUT YOU'VE DONE WELL SO FAR.

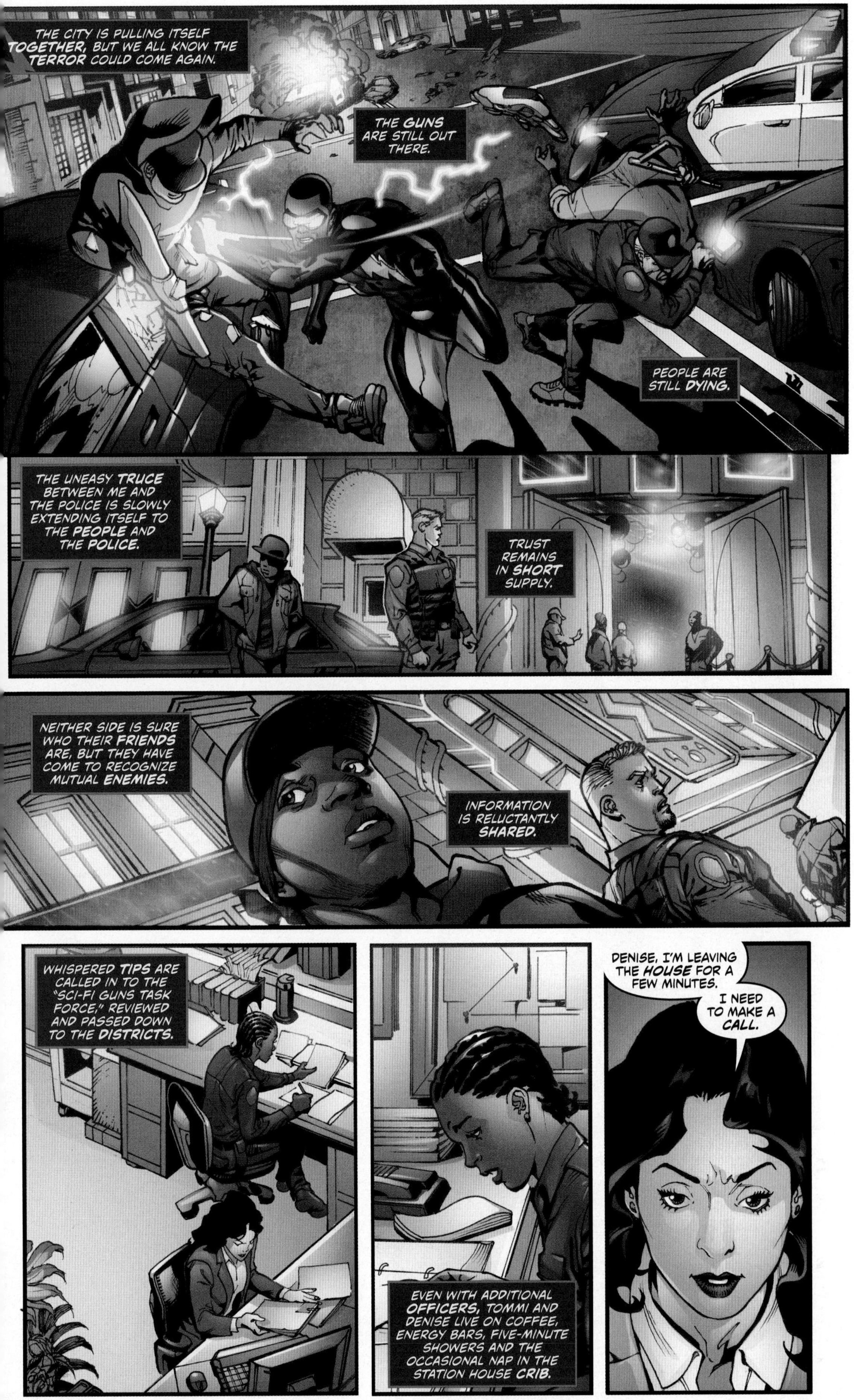

THE CITY IS PULLING ITSELF TOGETHER, BUT WE ALL KNOW THE TERROR COULD COME AGAIN.
THE GUNS ARE STILL OUT THERE.
PEOPLE ARE STILL DYING.
THE UNEASY TRUCE BETWEEN ME AND THE POLICE IS SLOWLY EXTENDING ITSELF TO THE PEOPLE AND THE POLICE.
TRUST REMAINS IN SHORT SUPPLY.
NEITHER SIDE IS SURE WHO THEIR FRIENDS ARE, BUT THEY HAVE COME TO RECOGNIZE MUTUAL ENEMIES.
INFORMATION IS RELUCTANTLY SHARED.
WHISPERED TIPS ARE CALLED IN TO THE "SCI-FI GUNS TASK FORCE," REVIEWED AND PASSED DOWN TO THE DISTRICTS.
EVEN WITH ADDITIONAL OFFICERS, TOMMI AND DENISE LIVE ON COFFEE, ENERGY BARS, FIVE-MINUTE SHOWERS AND THE OCCASIONAL NAP IN THE STATION HOUSE CRIB.
DENISE, I'M LEAVING THE HOUSE FOR A FEW MINUTES.
I NEED TO MAKE A CALL.

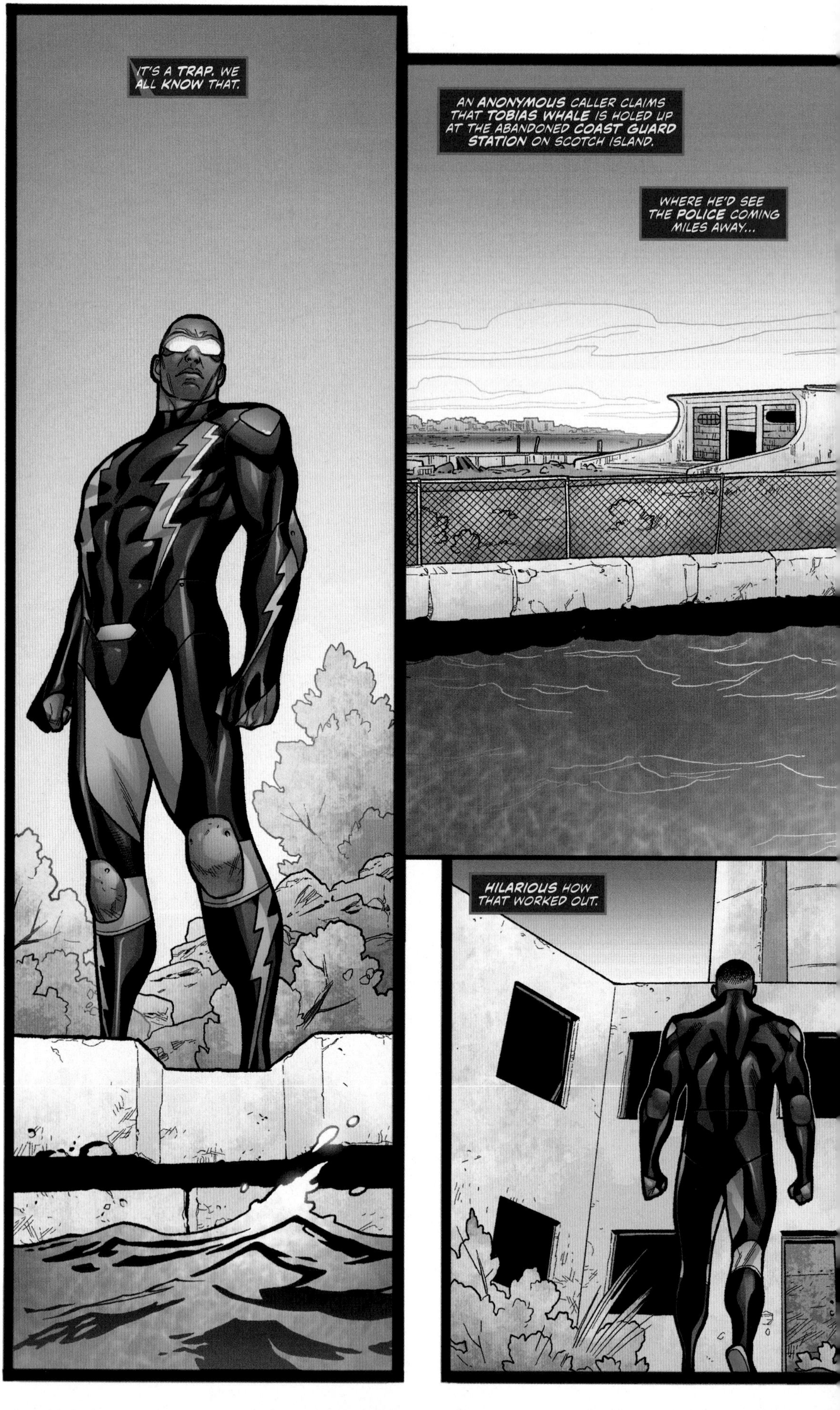
IT'S A TRAP. WE ALL KNOW THAT.
AN ANONYMOUS CALLER CLAIMS THAT TOBIAS WHALE IS HOLED UP AT THE ABANDONED COAST GUARD STATION ON SCOTCH ISLAND.
WHERE HE'D SEE THE POLICE COMING MILES AWAY...
HILARIOUS HOW THAT WORKED OUT.

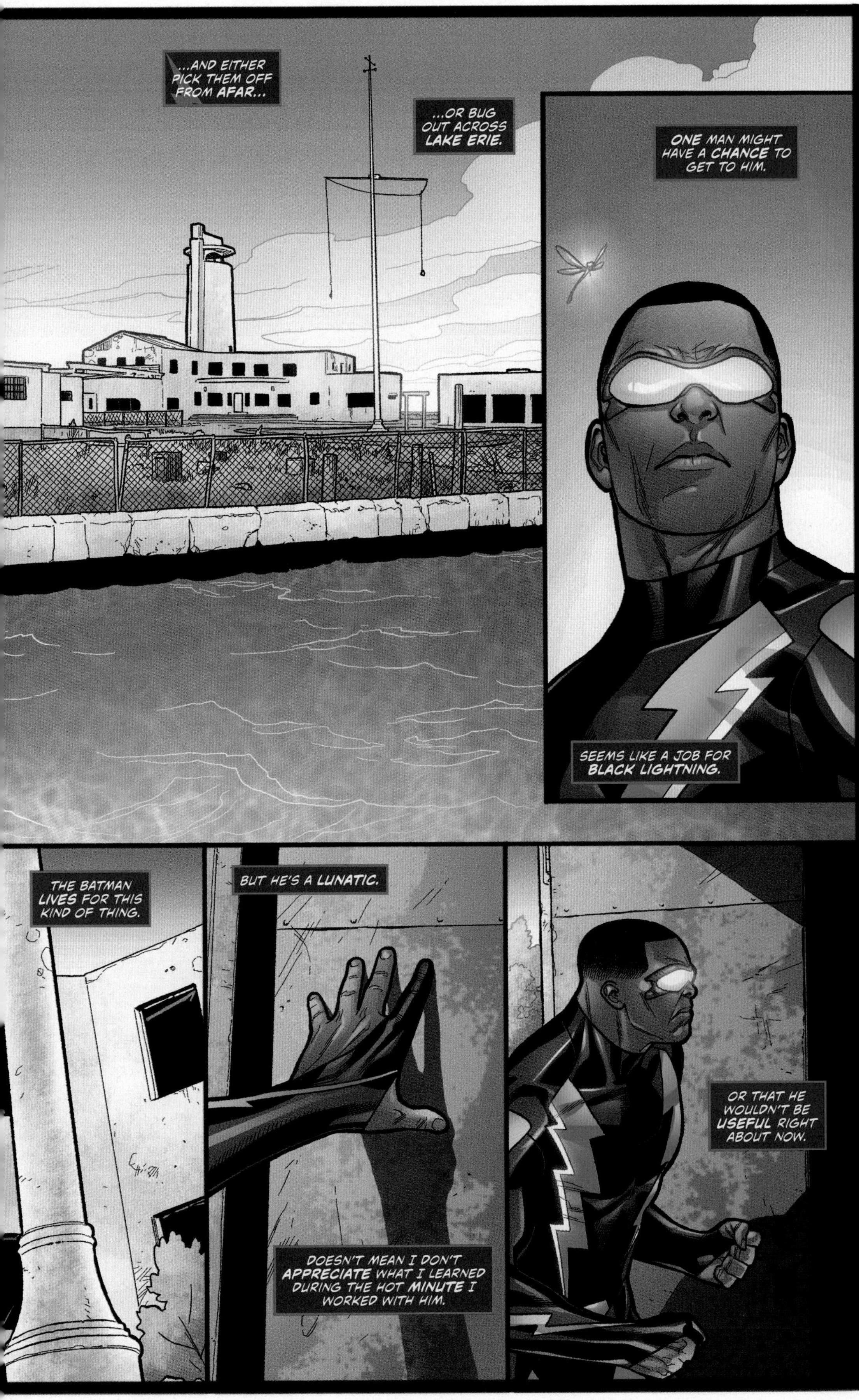
...AND EITHER PICK THEM OFF FROM AFAR...
...OR BUG OUT ACROSS LAKE ERIE.
ONE MAN MIGHT HAVE A CHANCE TO GET TO HIM.
SEEMS LIKE A JOB FOR BLACK LIGHTNING.
THE BATMAN LIVES FOR THIS KIND OF THING.
BUT HE'S A LUNATIC.
DOESN'T MEAN I DON'T APPRECIATE WHAT I LEARNED DURING THE HOT MINUTE I WORKED WITH HIM.
OR THAT HE WOULDN'T BE USEFUL RIGHT ABOUT NOW.

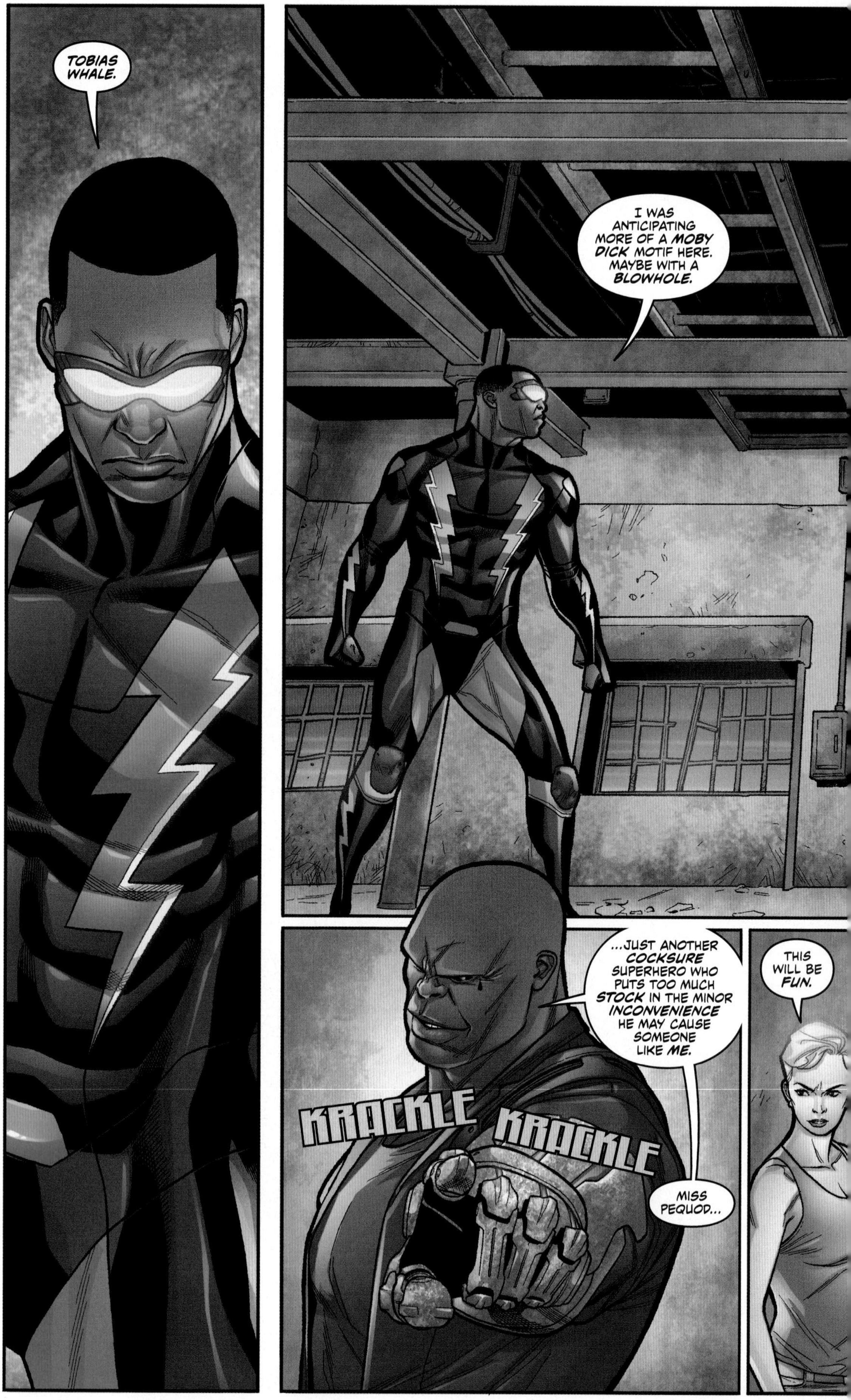
TOBIAS WHALE.
I WAS ANTICIPATING MORE OF A MOBY DICK MOTIF HERE. MAYBE WITH A BLOWHOLE.
...JUST ANOTHER COCKSURE SUPERHERO WHO PUTS TOO MUCH STOCK IN THE MINOR INCONVENIENCE HE MAY CAUSE SOMEONE LIKE ME.
KRACKLE KRACKLE
MISS PEQUOD...
THIS WILL BE FUN.

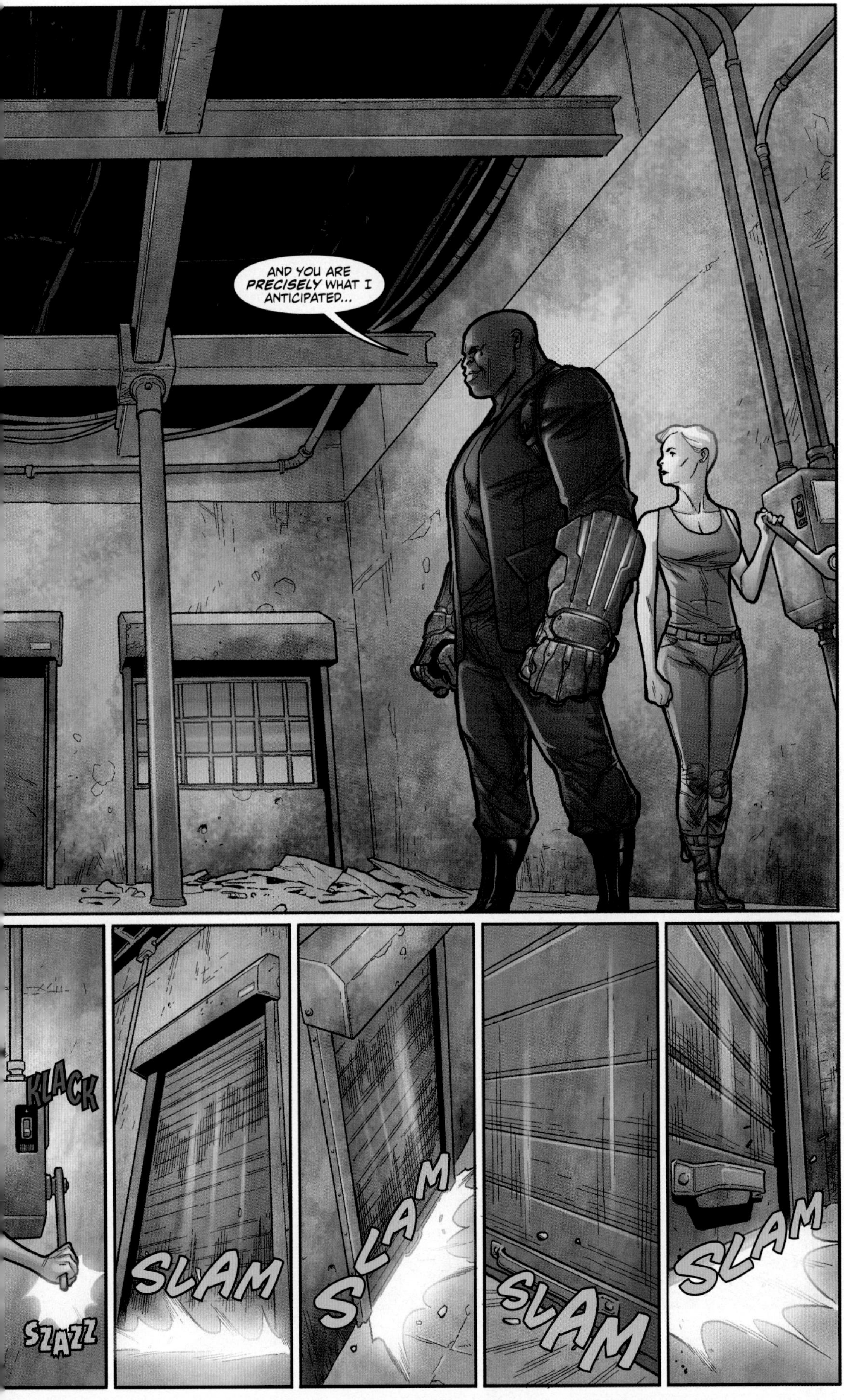
AND YOU ARE PRECISELY WHAT I ANTICIPATED...
KLACK
SZAZZ
SLAM
SLAM
SLAM
SLAM

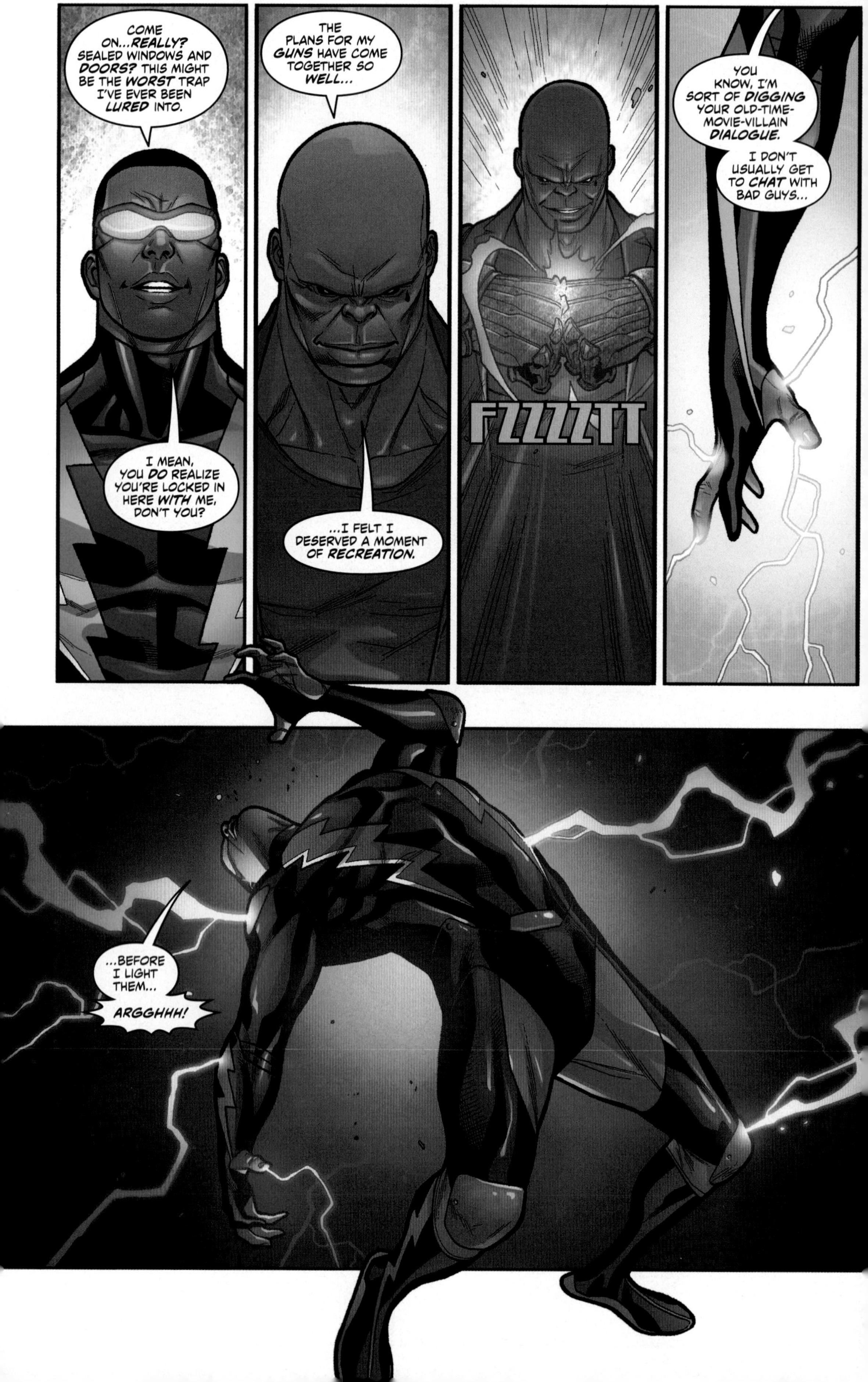
COME ON...REALLY? SEALED WINDOWS AND DOORS? THIS MIGHT BE THE WORST TRAP I'VE EVER BEEN LURED INTO.
I MEAN, YOU DO REALIZE YOU'RE LOCKED IN HERE WITH ME, DON'T YOU?
THE PLANS FOR MY GUNS HAVE COME TOGETHER SO WELL...
...I FELT I DESERVED A MOMENT OF RECREATION.
FZZZZZTT
YOU KNOW, I'M SORT OF DIGGING YOUR OLD-TIME-MOVIE-VILLAIN DIALOGUE.
I DON'T USUALLY GET TO CHAT WITH BAD GUYS...
...BEFORE I LIGHT THEM...
ARGGHHH!

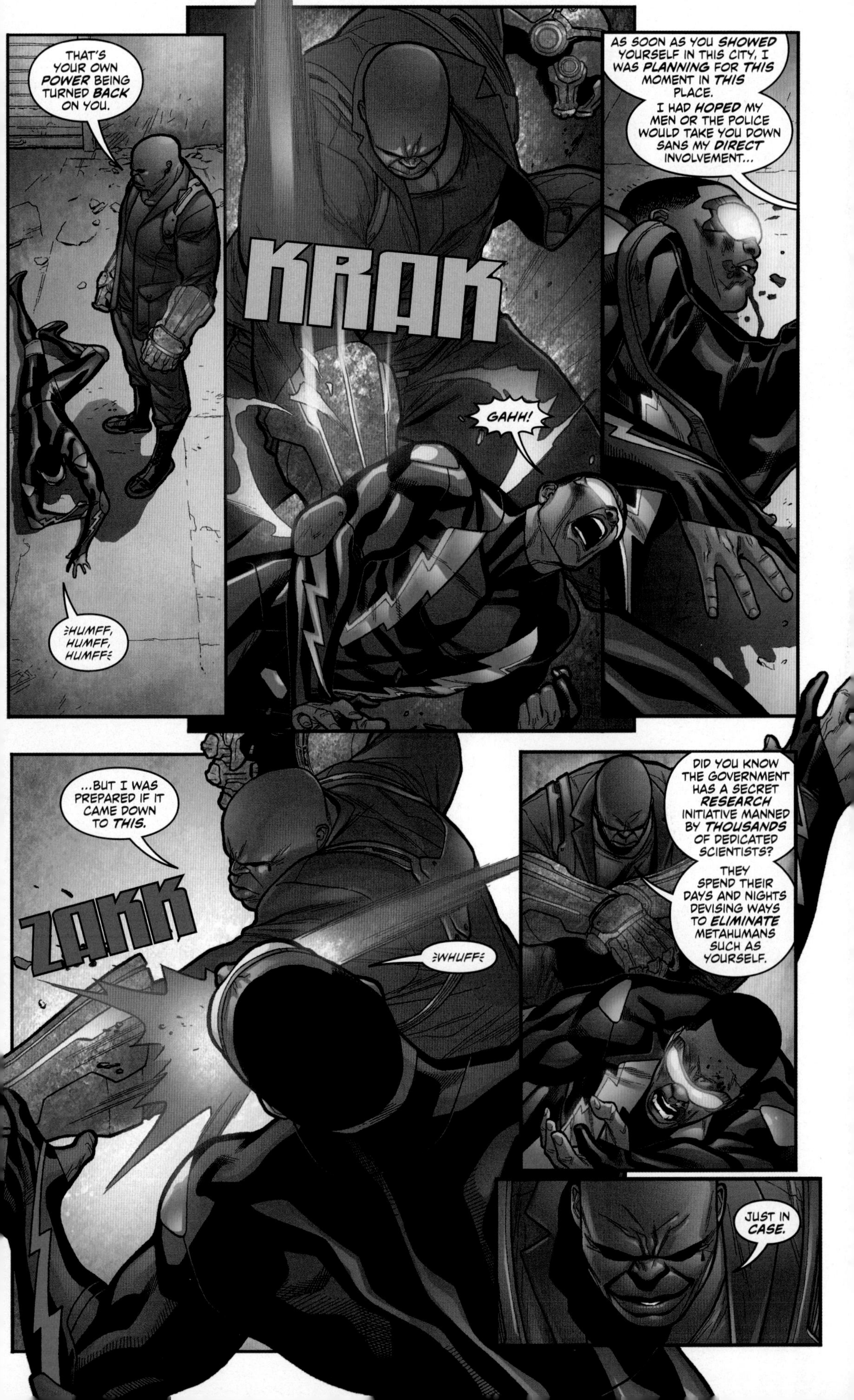

THAT'S YOUR OWN POWER BEING TURNED BACK ON YOU.
HUMFF, HUMFF, HUMFF
KRAK
GAHH!
AS SOON AS YOU SHOWED YOURSELF IN THIS CITY, I WAS PLANNING FOR THIS MOMENT IN THIS PLACE.
I HAD HOPED MY MEN OR THE POLICE WOULD TAKE YOU DOWN SANS MY DIRECT INVOLVEMENT...
...BUT I WAS PREPARED IF IT CAME DOWN TO THIS.
ZAKK
WHUFF
DID YOU KNOW THE GOVERNMENT HAS A SECRET RESEARCH INITIATIVE MANNED BY THOUSANDS OF DEDICATED SCIENTISTS?
THEY SPEND THEIR DAYS AND NIGHTS DEVISING WAYS TO ELIMINATE METAHUMANS SUCH AS YOURSELF.
JUST IN CASE.

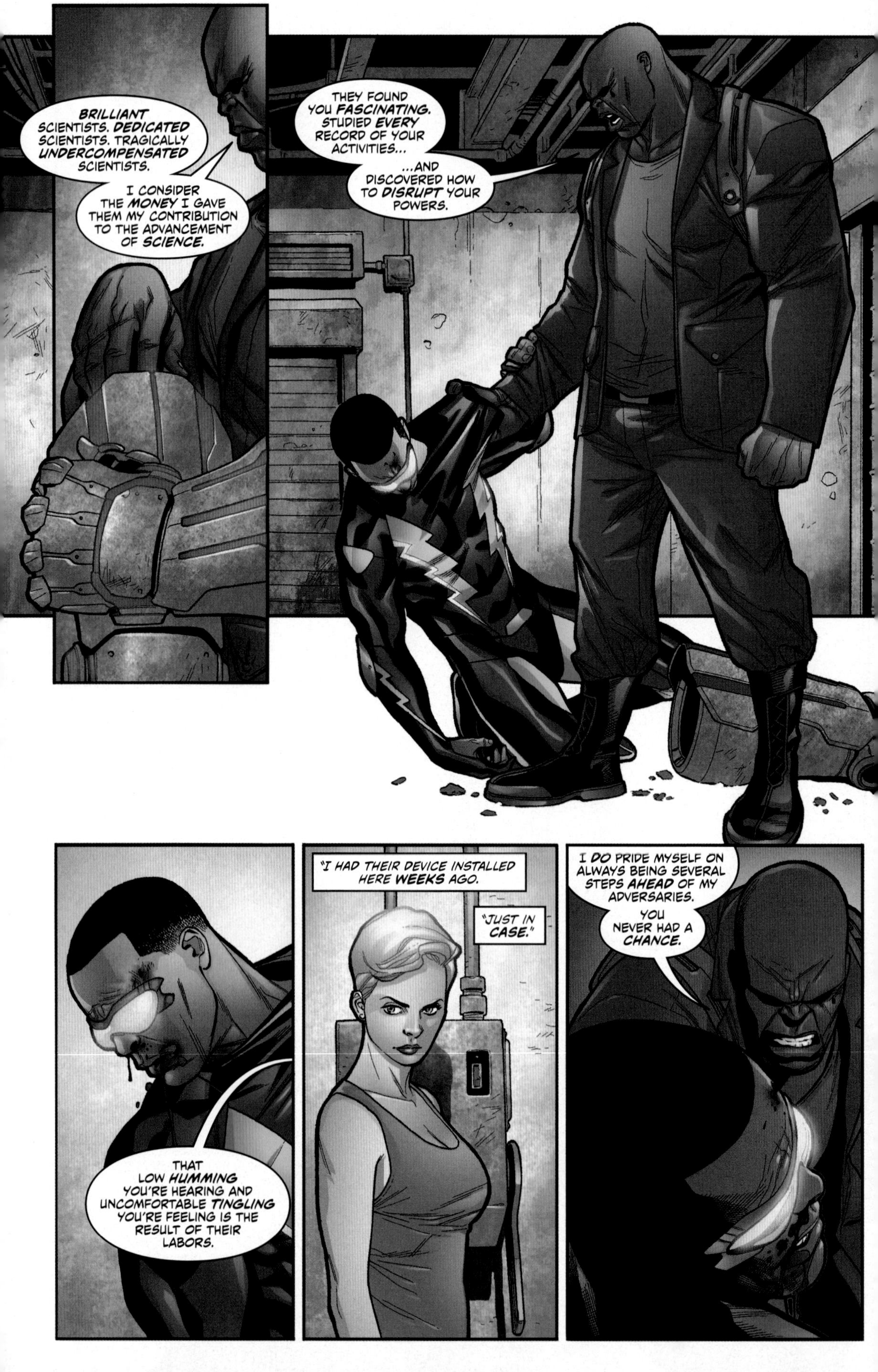
BRILLIANT SCIENTISTS. DEDICATED SCIENTISTS. TRAGICALLY UNDERCOMPENSATED SCIENTISTS.
I CONSIDER THE MONEY I GAVE THEM MY CONTRIBUTION TO THE ADVANCEMENT OF SCIENCE.
THEY FOUND YOU FASCINATING. STUDIED EVERY RECORD OF YOUR ACTIVITIES...
...AND DISCOVERED HOW TO DISRUPT YOUR POWERS.
THAT LOW HUMMING YOU'RE HEARING AND UNCOMFORTABLE TINGLING YOU'RE FEELING IS THE RESULT OF THEIR LABORS.
"I HAD THEIR DEVICE INSTALLED HERE WEEKS AGO.
"JUST IN CASE."
I DO PRIDE MYSELF ON ALWAYS BEING SEVERAL STEPS AHEAD OF MY ADVERSARIES.
YOU NEVER HAD A CHANCE.

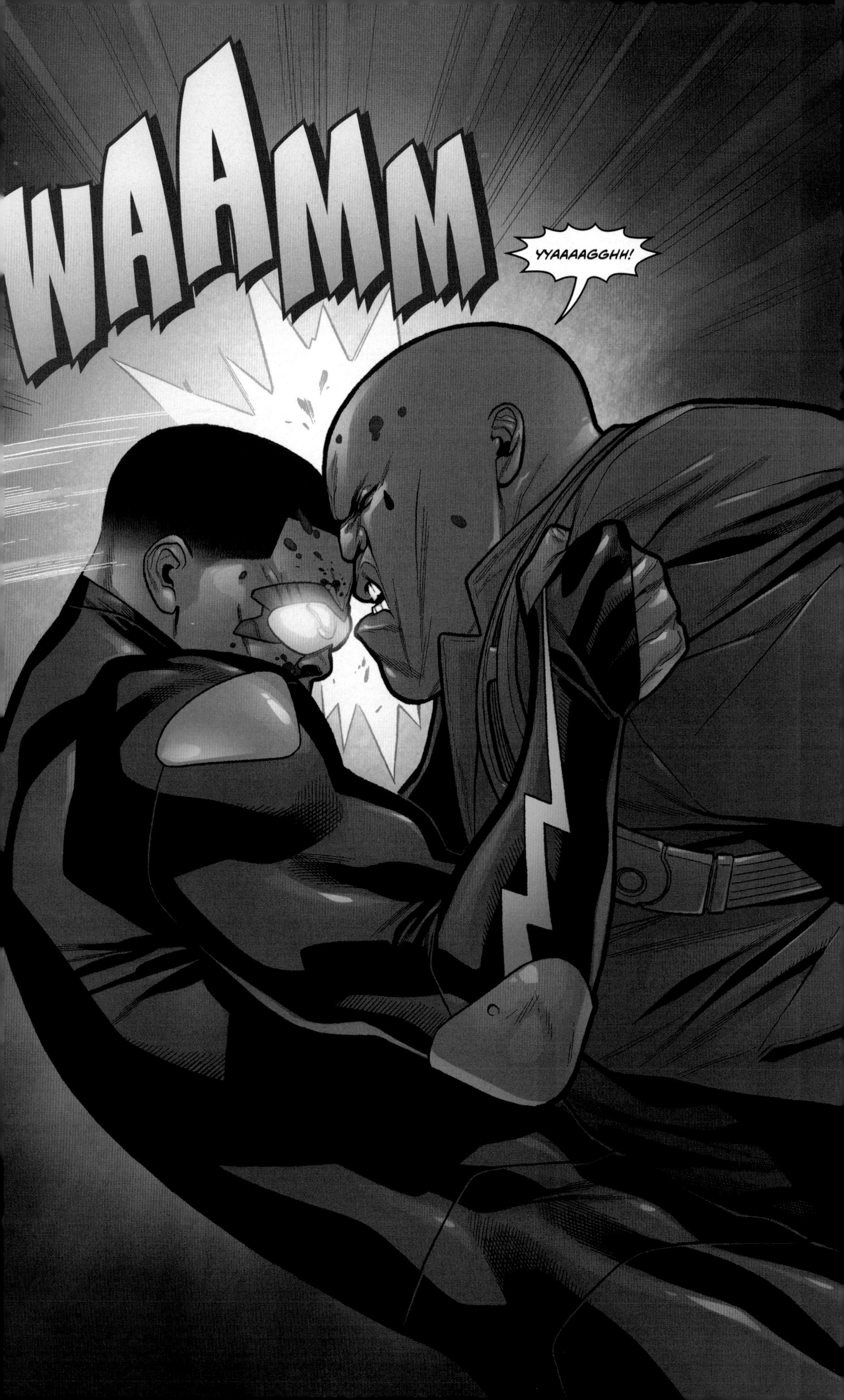
WAAMM
YYAAAAGGHH!

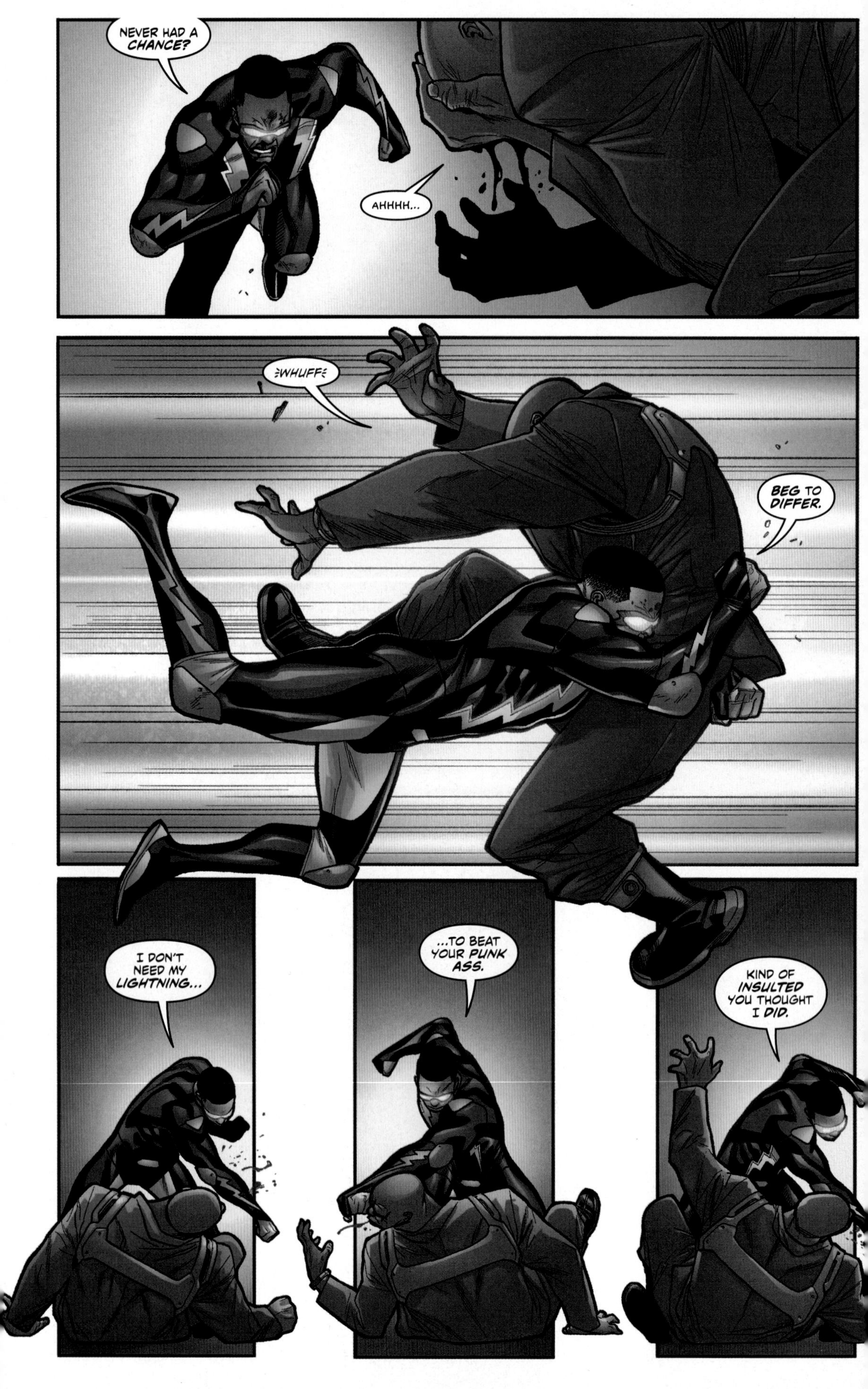
NEVER HAD A CHANCE?
AHHHH...
WHUFF
BEG TO DIFFER.
I DON'T NEED MY LIGHTNING...
...TO BEAT YOUR PUNK ASS.
KIND OF INSULTED YOU THOUGHT I DID.

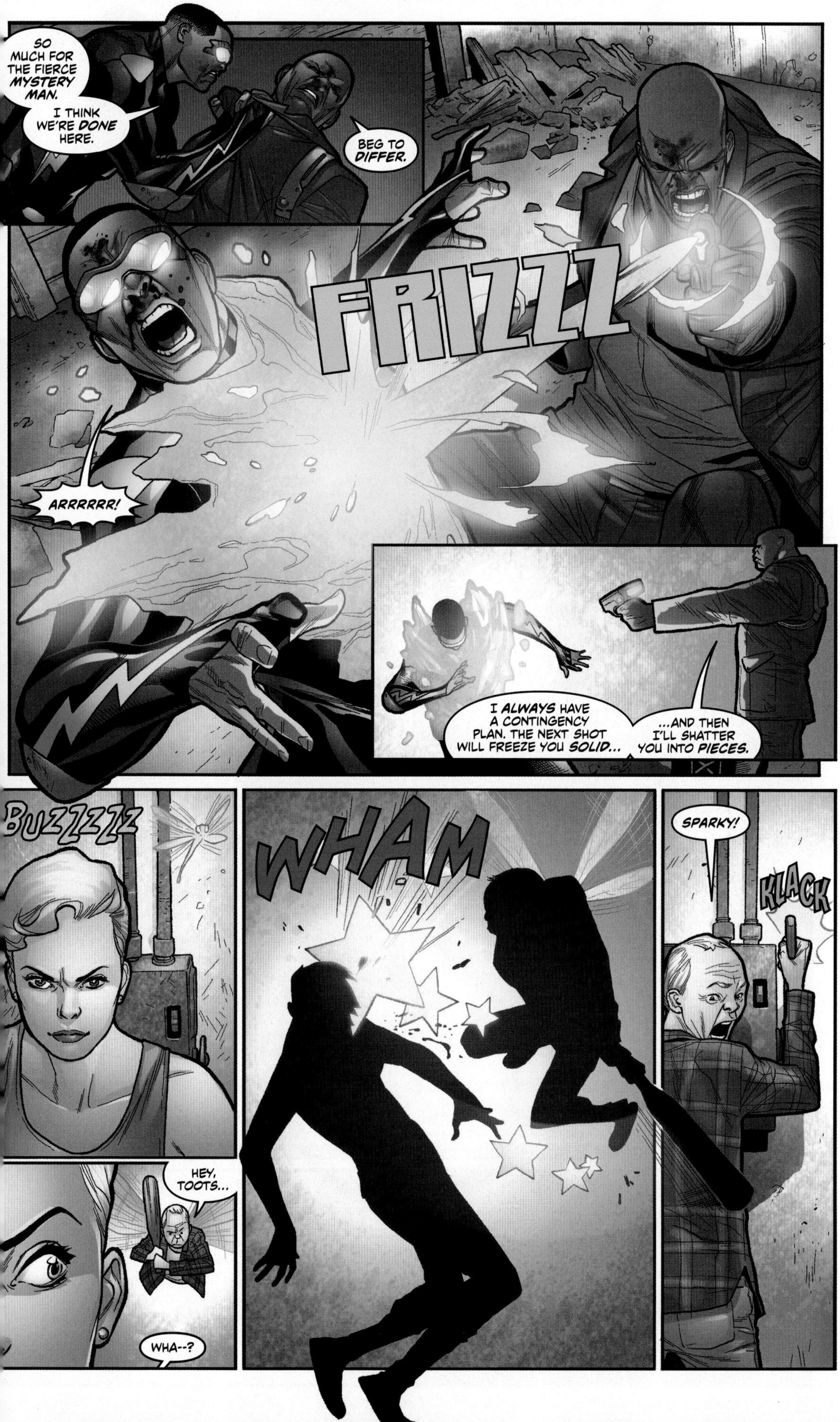
SO MUCH FOR THE FIERCE MYSTERY MAN.
I THINK WE'RE DONE HERE.
BEG TO DIFFER.
FRIZZZ
ARRRRRR!
I ALWAYS HAVE A CONTINGENCY PLAN. THE NEXT SHOT WILL FREEZE YOU SOLID...
...AND THEN I'LL SHATTER YOU INTO PIECES.
BUZZZZZ
HEY, TOOTS...
WHA--?
WHAM
SPARKY!
KLACK

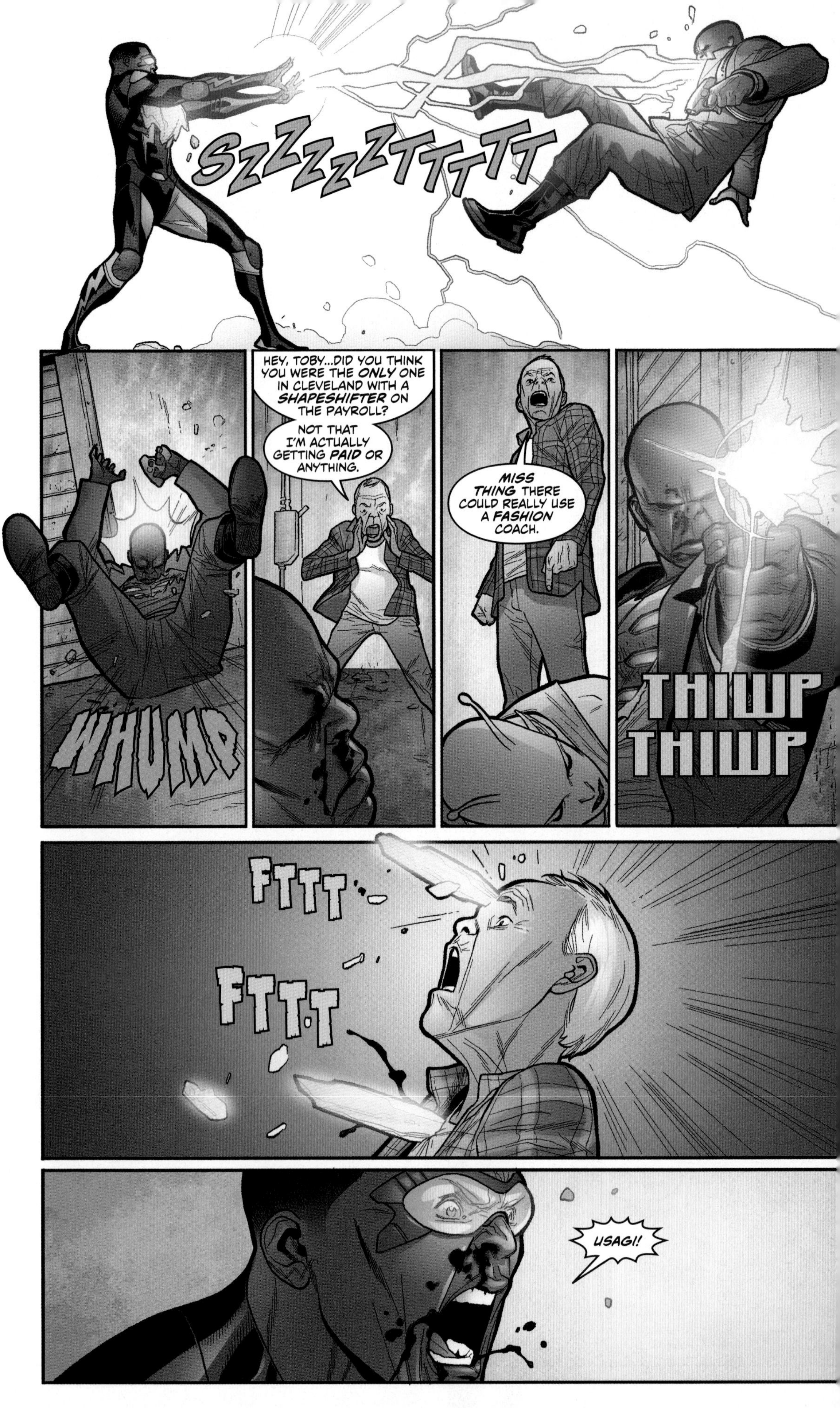
SZZZZZTTTTTT
WHUMP
HEY, TOBY...DID YOU THINK YOU WERE THE ONLY ONE IN CLEVELAND WITH A SHAPESHIFTER ON THE PAYROLL?
NOT THAT I'M ACTUALLY GETTING PAID OR ANYTHING.
MISS THING THERE COULD REALLY USE A FASHION COACH.
THIWP
THIWP
FTTT
FTTT
USAGI!

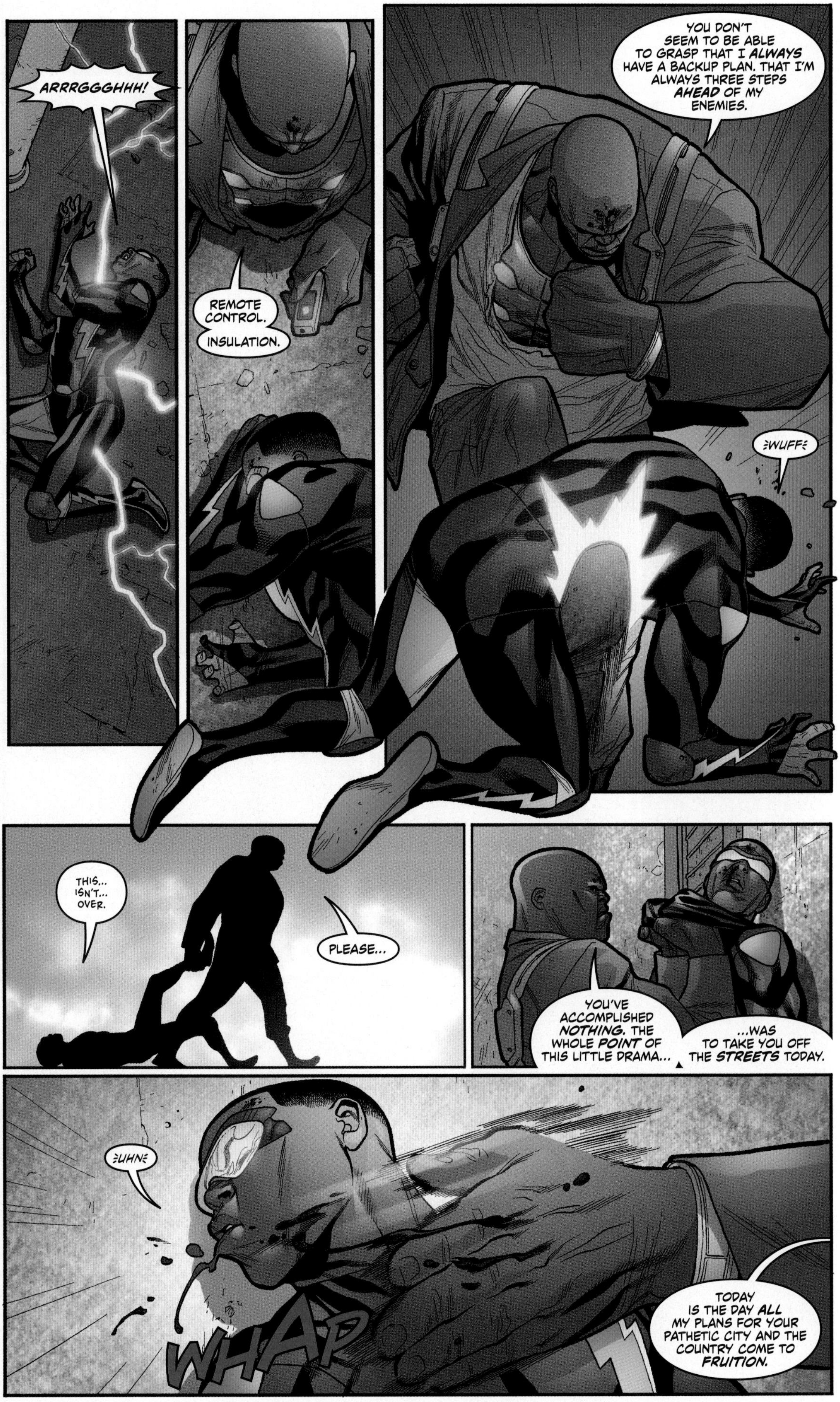
ARRRGGGHHH!
REMOTE CONTROL.
INSULATION.
YOU DON'T SEEM TO BE ABLE TO GRASP THAT I ALWAYS HAVE A BACKUP PLAN. THAT I'M ALWAYS THREE STEPS AHEAD OF MY ENEMIES.
WUFF
THIS... ISN'T... OVER.
PLEASE...
YOU'VE ACCOMPLISHED NOTHING. THE WHOLE POINT OF THIS LITTLE DRAMA...
...WAS TO TAKE YOU OFF THE STREETS TODAY.
UHN
TODAY IS THE DAY ALL MY PLANS FOR YOUR PATHETIC CITY AND THE COUNTRY COME TO FRUITION.
WHAP

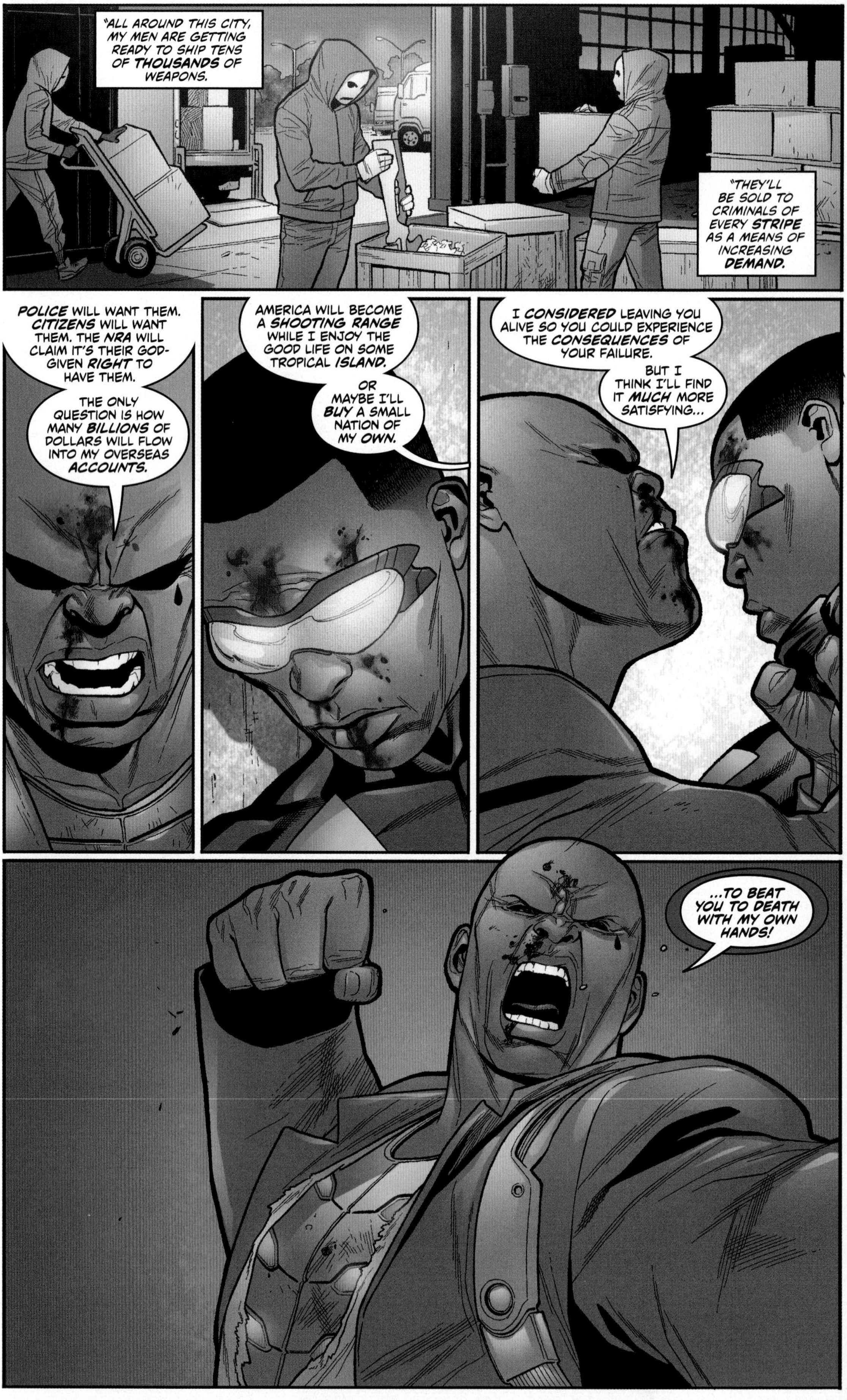
"ALL AROUND THIS CITY, MY MEN ARE GETTING READY TO SHIP TENS OF THOUSANDS OF WEAPONS.
"THEY'LL BE SOLD TO CRIMINALS OF EVERY STRIPE AS A MEANS OF INCREASING DEMAND.
POLICE WILL WANT THEM. CITIZENS WILL WANT THEM. THE NRA WILL CLAIM IT'S THEIR GOD-GIVEN RIGHT TO HAVE THEM.
THE ONLY QUESTION IS HOW MANY BILLIONS OF DOLLARS WILL FLOW INTO MY OVERSEAS ACCOUNTS.
AMERICA WILL BECOME A SHOOTING RANGE WHILE I ENJOY THE GOOD LIFE ON SOME TROPICAL ISLAND.
OR MAYBE I'LL BUY A SMALL NATION OF MY OWN.
I CONSIDERED LEAVING YOU ALIVE SO YOU COULD EXPERIENCE THE CONSEQUENCES OF YOUR FAILURE.
BUT I THINK I'LL FIND IT MUCH MORE SATISFYING...
...TO BEAT YOU TO DEATH WITH MY OWN HANDS!

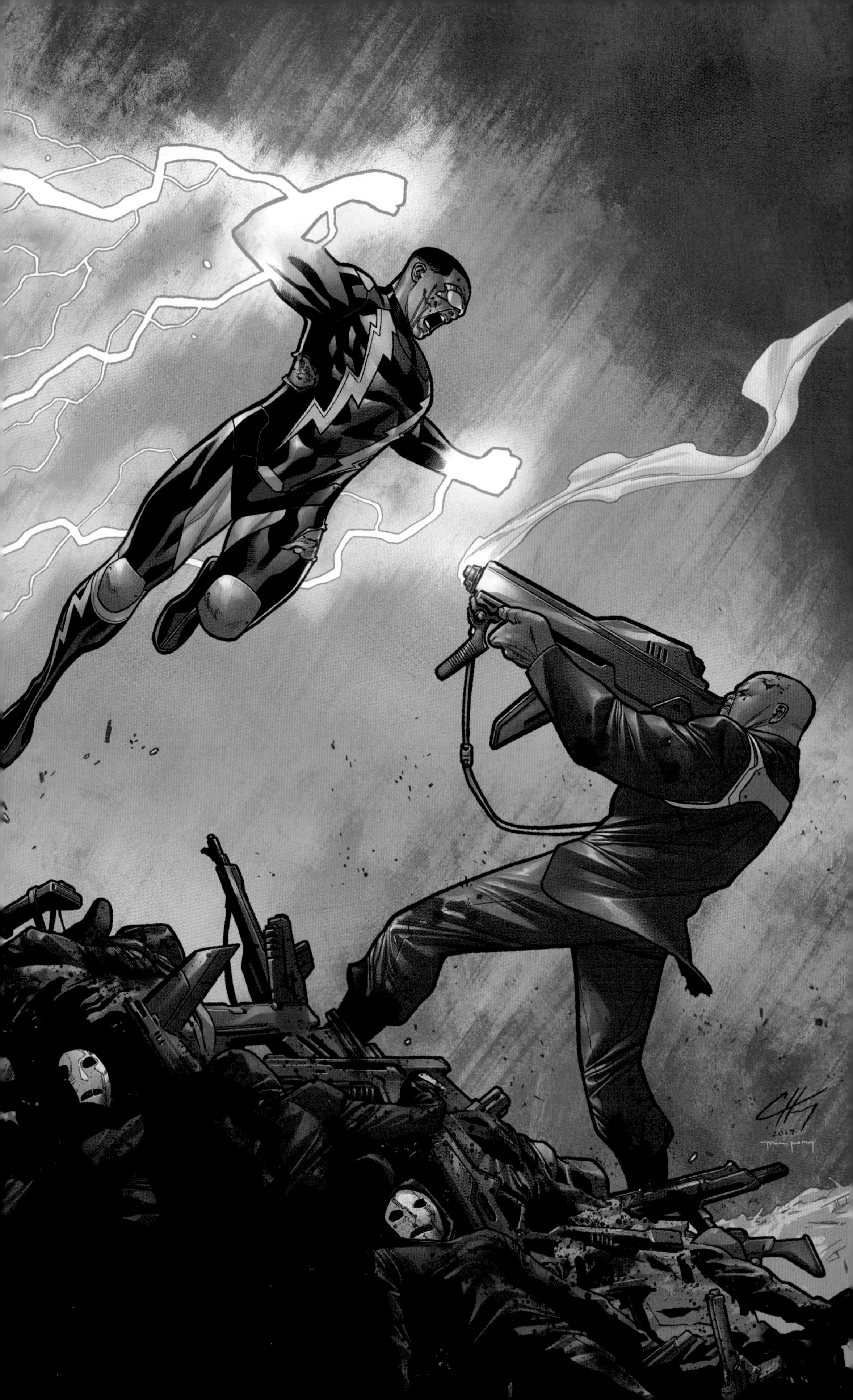

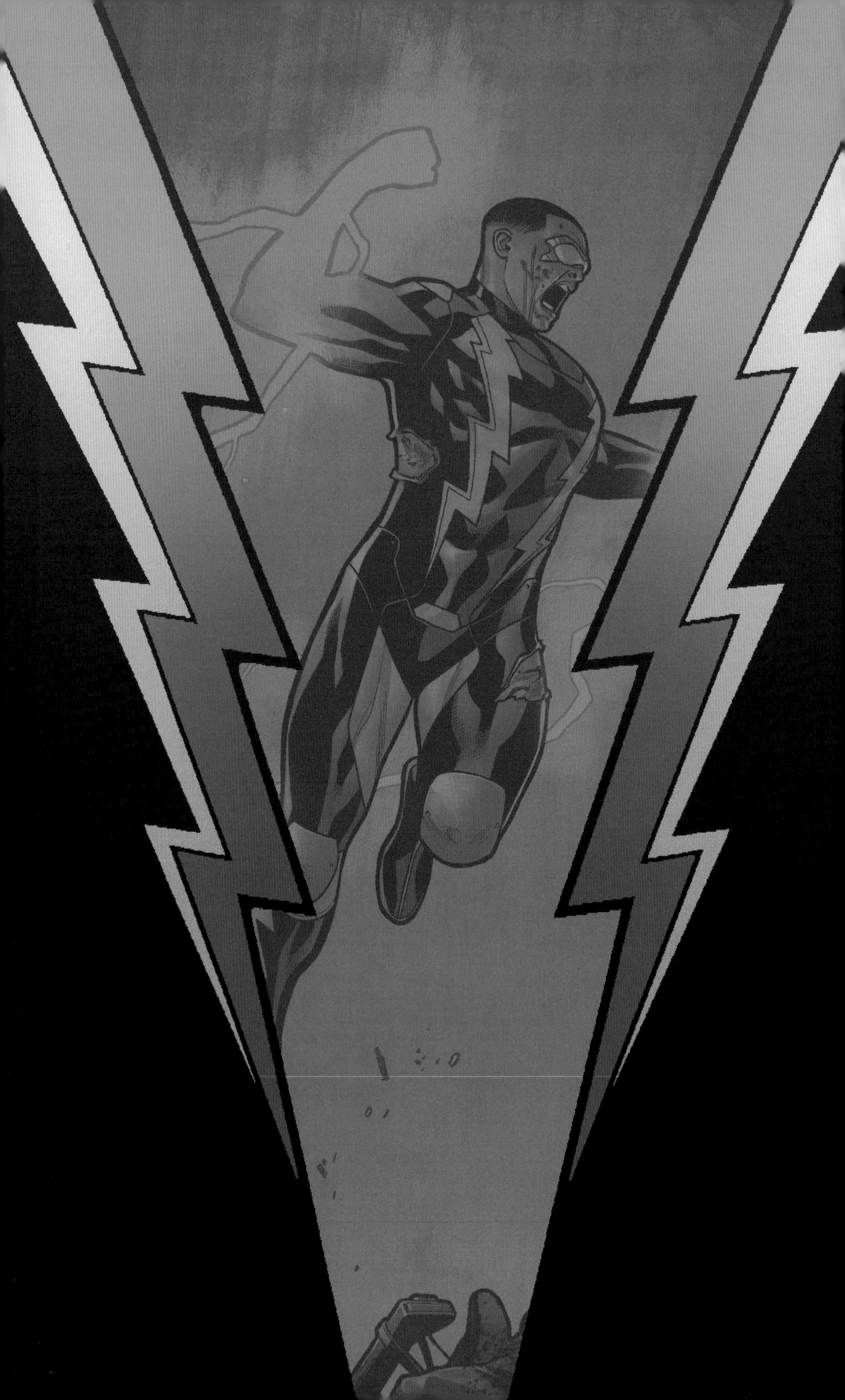

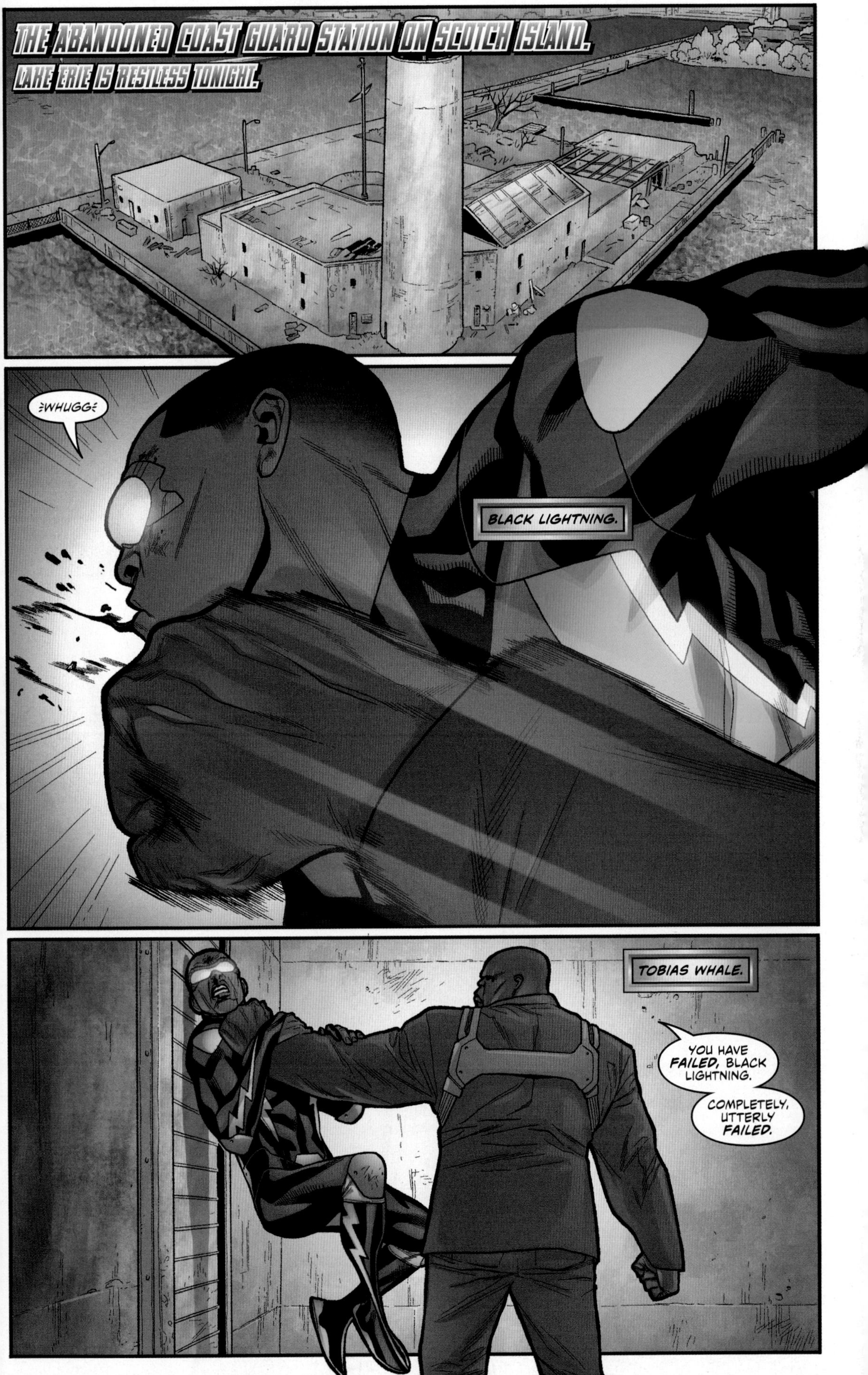
THE ABANDONED COAST GUARD STATION ON SCOTCH ISLAND.
LAKE ERIE IS RESTLESS TONIGHT.
WHUGG
BLACK LIGHTNING.
TOBIAS WHALE.
YOU HAVE FAILED, BLACK LIGHTNING.
COMPLETELY, UTTERLY FAILED.

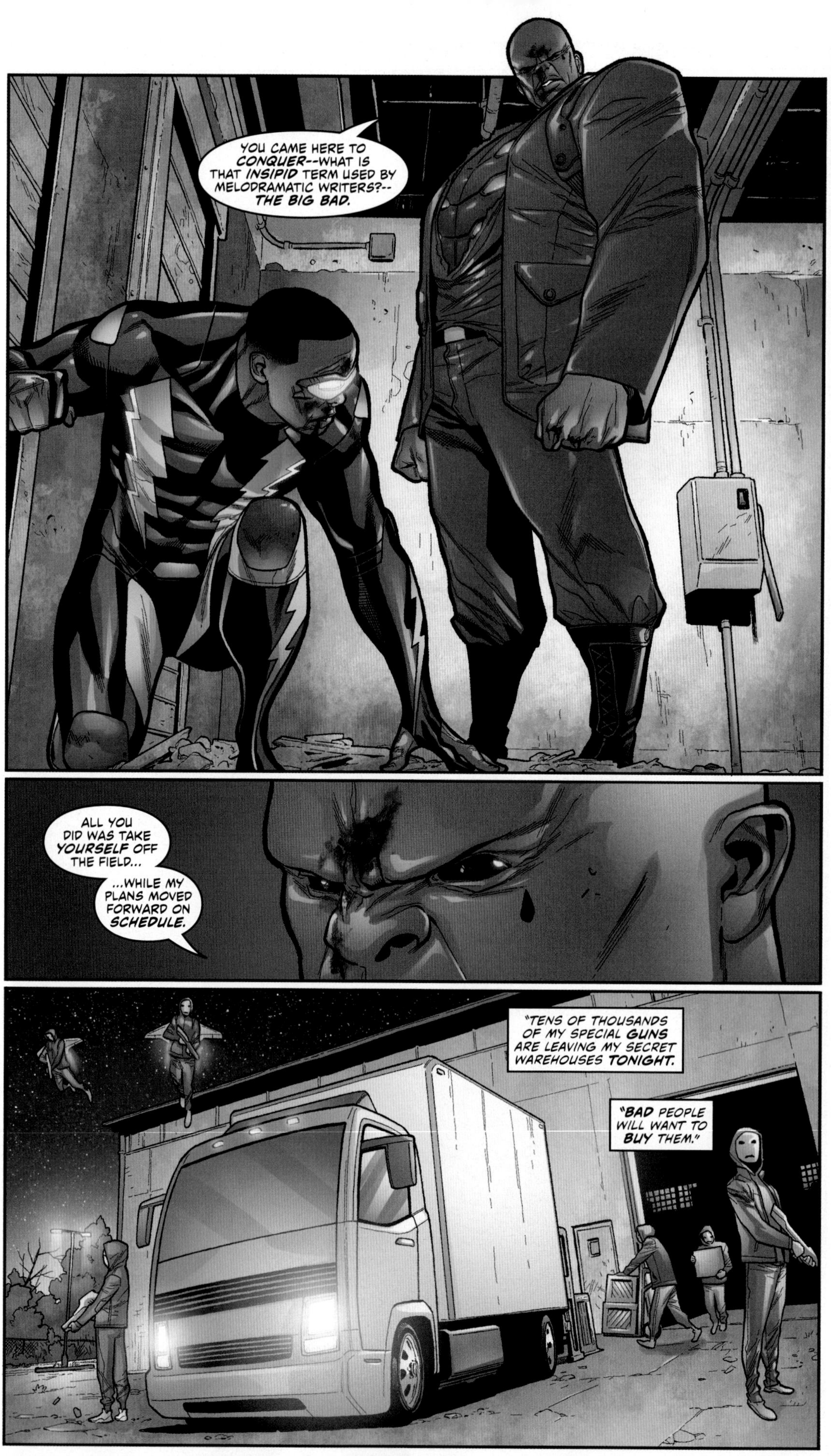
YOU CAME HERE TO CONQUER--WHAT IS THAT INSIPID TERM USED BY MELODRAMATIC WRITERS?-- THE BIG BAD.
ALL YOU DID WAS TAKE YOURSELF OFF THE FIELD...
...WHILE MY PLANS MOVED FORWARD ON SCHEDULE.
"TENS OF THOUSANDS OF MY SPECIAL GUNS ARE LEAVING MY SECRET WAREHOUSES TONIGHT.
"BAD PEOPLE WILL WANT TO BUY THEM."

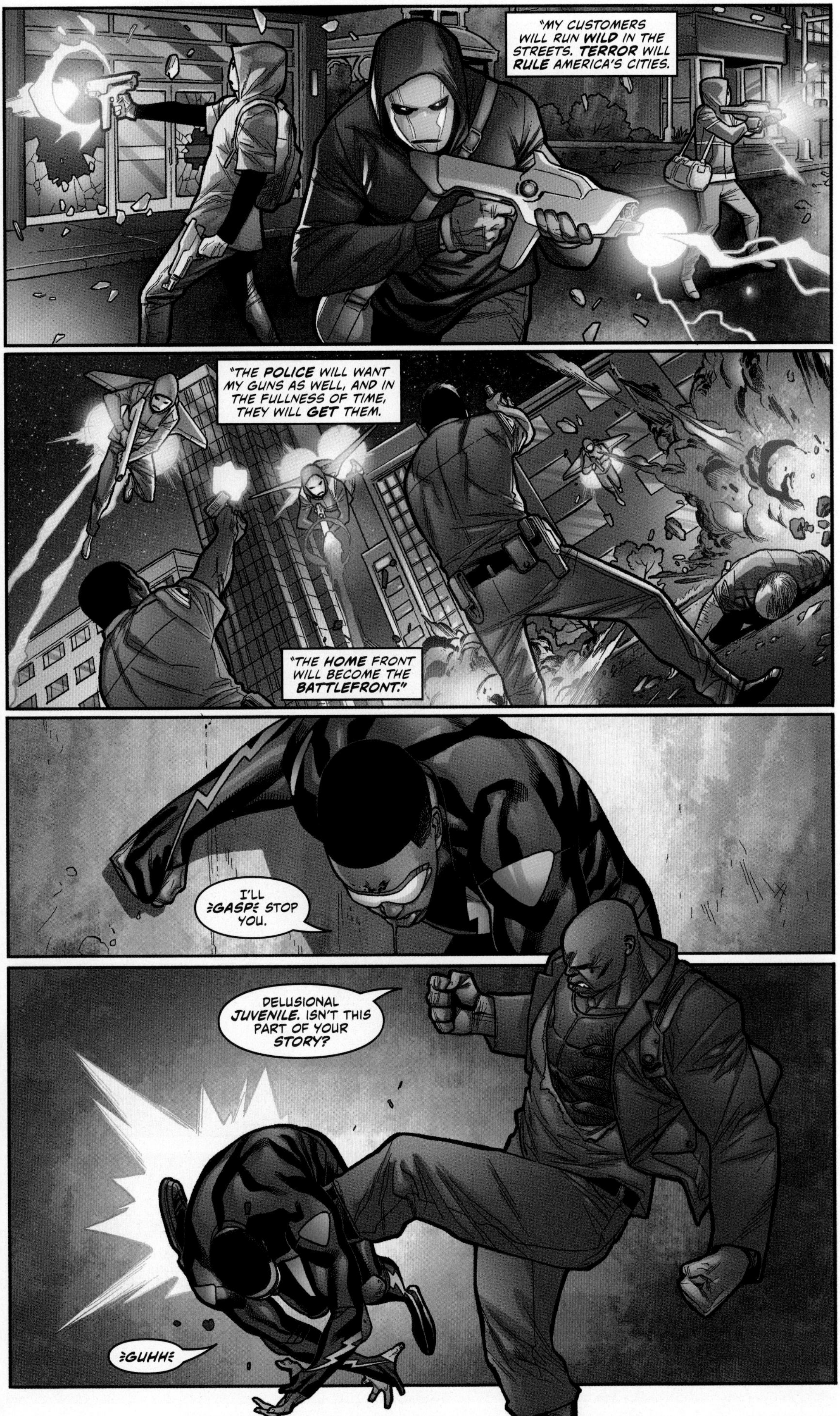
"MY CUSTOMERS WILL RUN WILD IN THE STREETS. TERROR WILL RULE AMERICA'S CITIES.
"THE POLICE WILL WANT MY GUNS AS WELL, AND IN THE FULLNESS OF TIME, THEY WILL GET THEM.
"THE HOME FRONT WILL BECOME THE BATTLEFRONT."
I'LL GASP STOP YOU.
DELUSIONAL JUVENILE. ISN'T THIS PART OF YOUR STORY?
GUHH

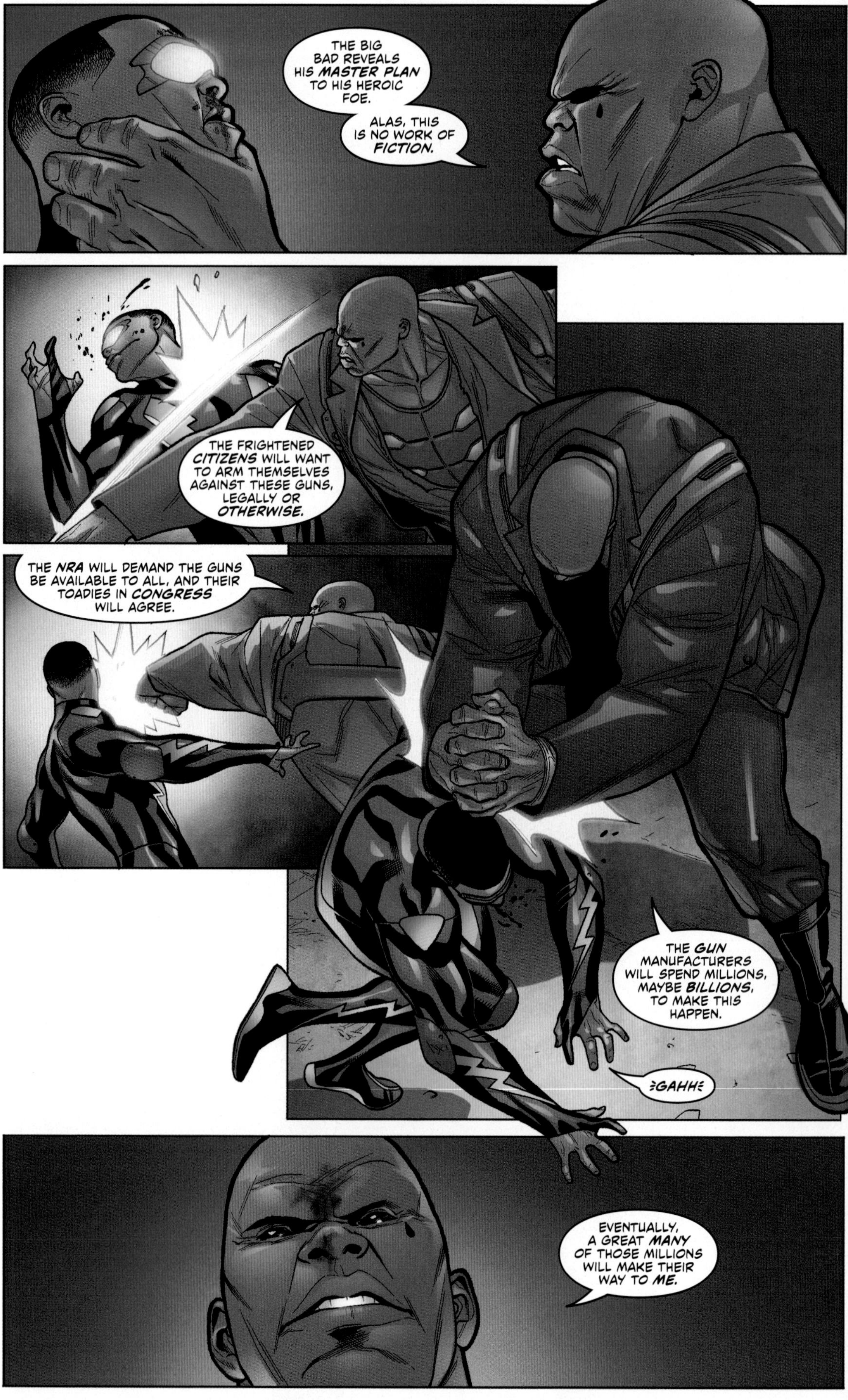
THE BIG BAD REVEALS HIS MASTER PLAN TO HIS HEROIC FOE.
ALAS, THIS IS NO WORK OF FICTION.
THE FRIGHTENED CITIZENS WILL WANT TO ARM THEMSELVES AGAINST THESE GUNS, LEGALLY OR OTHERWISE.
THE NRA WILL DEMAND THE GUNS BE AVAILABLE TO ALL, AND THEIR TOADIES IN CONGRESS WILL AGREE.
THE GUN MANUFACTURERS WILL SPEND MILLIONS, MAYBE BILLIONS, TO MAKE THIS HAPPEN.
GAHH
EVENTUALLY, A GREAT MANY OF THOSE MILLIONS WILL MAKE THEIR WAY TO ME.

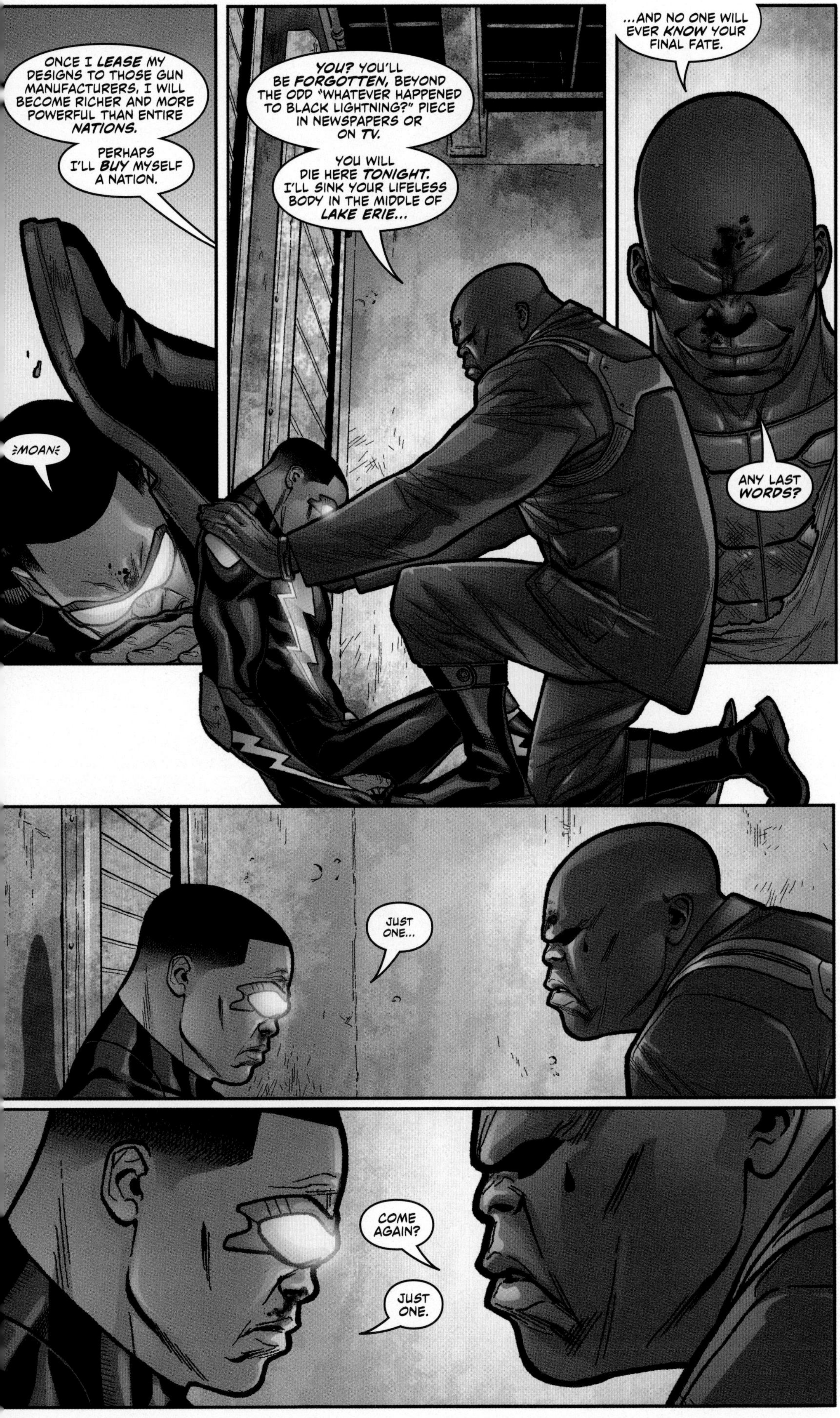
ONCE I *LEASE* MY DESIGNS TO THOSE GUN MANUFACTURERS, I WILL BECOME RICHER AND MORE POWERFUL THAN ENTIRE *NATIONS.*
PERHAPS I'LL *BUY* MYSELF A NATION.
YOU? YOU'LL BE *FORGOTTEN,* BEYOND THE ODD "WHATEVER HAPPENED TO BLACK LIGHTNING?" PIECE IN NEWSPAPERS OR ON *TV.*
YOU WILL DIE HERE *TONIGHT.* I'LL SINK YOUR LIFELESS BODY IN THE MIDDLE OF *LAKE ERIE...*
...AND NO ONE WILL EVER *KNOW* YOUR FINAL FATE.
MOAN
ANY LAST *WORDS?*
JUST ONE...
COME AGAIN?
JUST ONE.

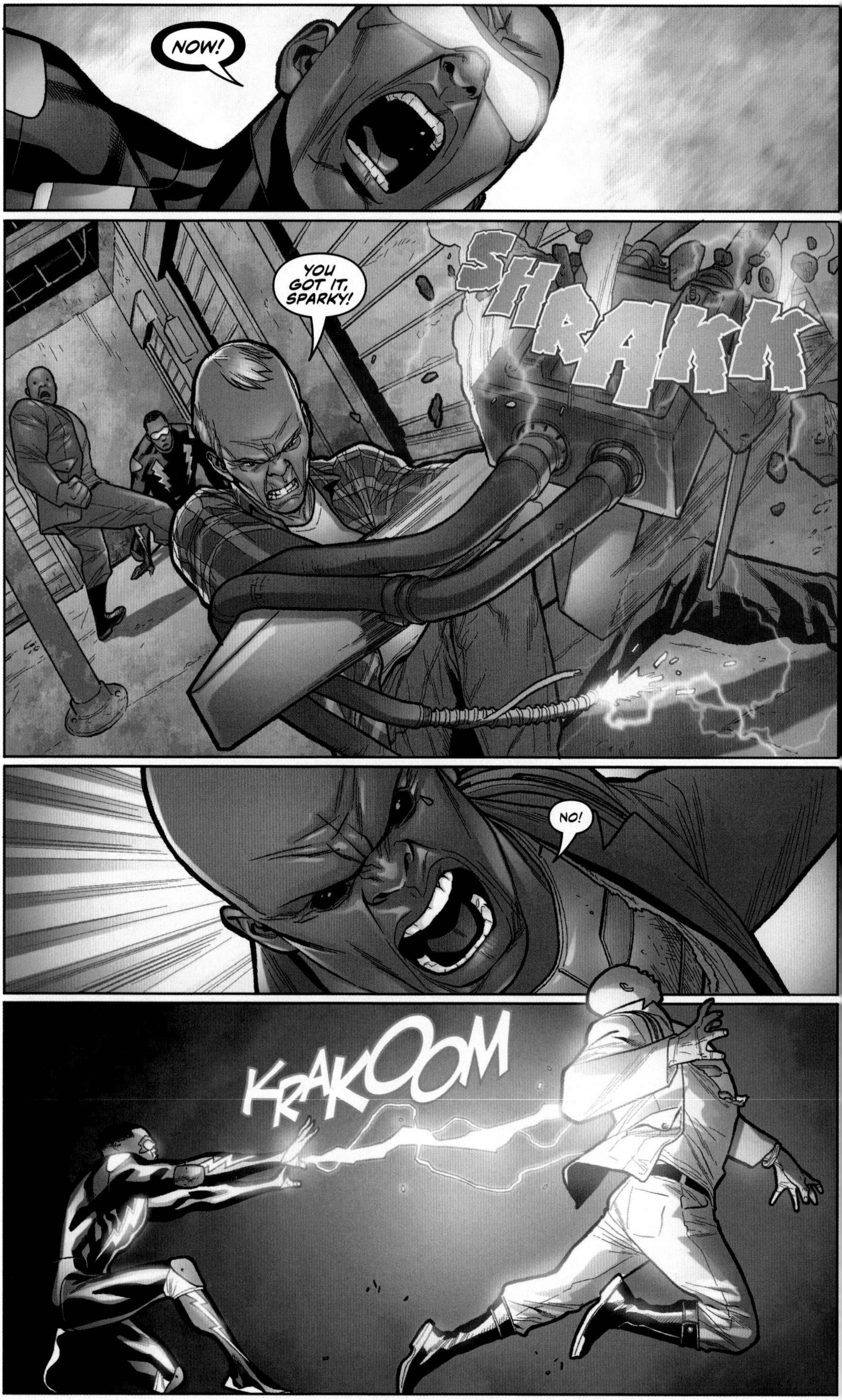
NOW!
YOU GOT IT, SPARKY!
SHRAKK
NO!
KRAKOOM

JEFFERSON PIERCE. A MAN WHO CAME HOME AND FOUND THAT HOME STRUGGLING WITH TROUBLES OLD AND NEW. NOW HE FIGHTS FOR THE FUTURE ON TWO FRONTS: IN THE CLASSROOM AS A DEDICATED TEACHER AND ON THE STREETS AS...

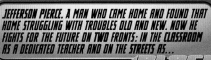

BLACK LIGHTNING

COLD DEAD HANDS

PART SIX: "SHOW US ANOTHER WAY"

I'M NOT GOING TO LIE.

THAT FELT GREAT.

| TONY ISABELLA writer | CLAYTON HENRY & YVEL GUICHET artists | PETE PANTAZIS colorist | JOSH REED letterer |

| CLAYTON HENRY & TOMEU MOREY cover | HARVEY RICHARDS associate editor | JIM CHADWICK group editor |

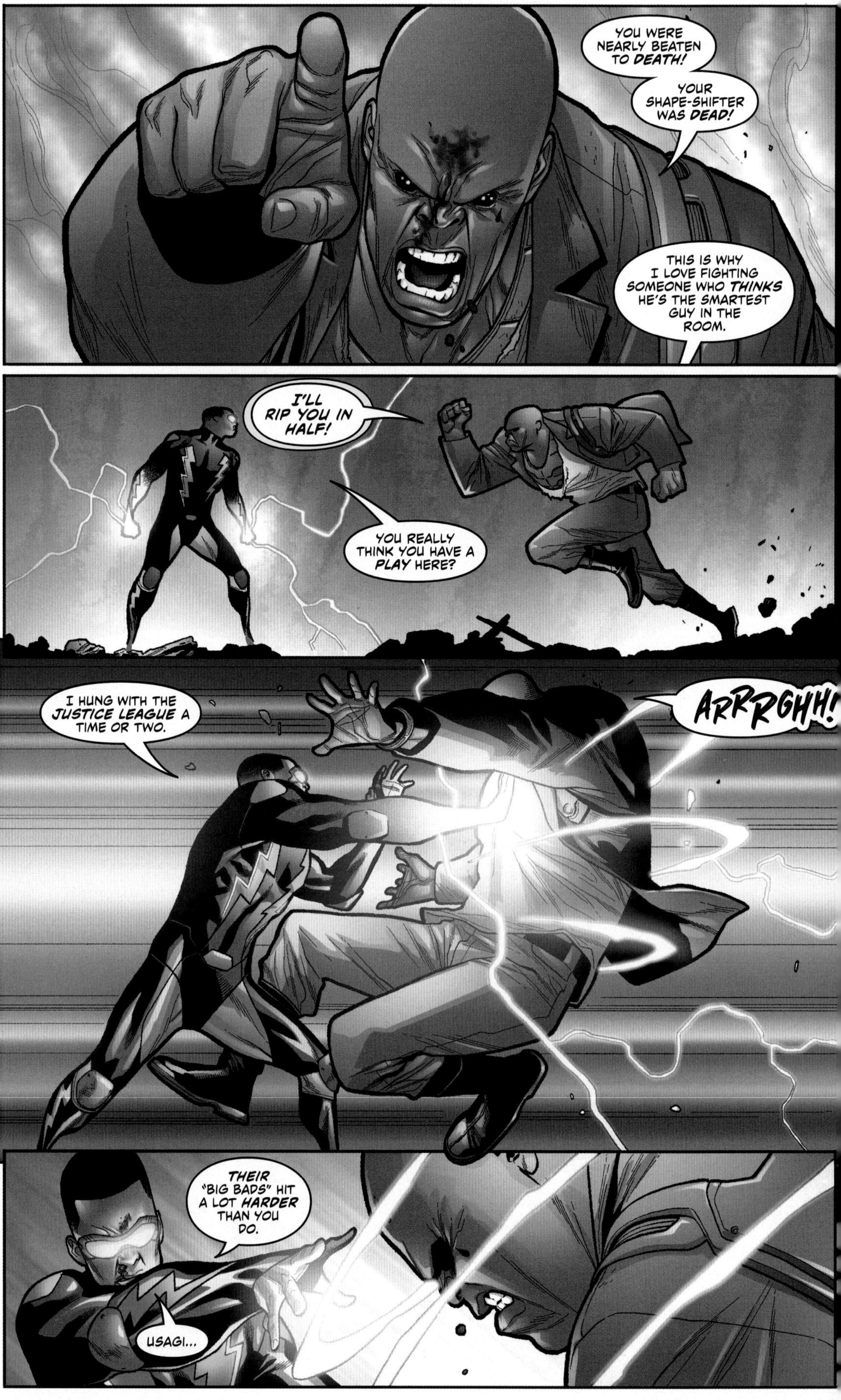
YOU WERE NEARLY BEATEN TO DEATH!
YOUR SHAPE-SHIFTER WAS DEAD!
THIS IS WHY I LOVE FIGHTING SOMEONE WHO THINKS HE'S THE SMARTEST GUY IN THE ROOM.
I'LL RIP YOU IN HALF!
YOU REALLY THINK YOU HAVE A PLAY HERE?
I HUNG WITH THE JUSTICE LEAGUE A TIME OR TWO.
ARRRGHH!
THEIR "BIG BADS" HIT A LOT HARDER THAN YOU DO.
USAGI...

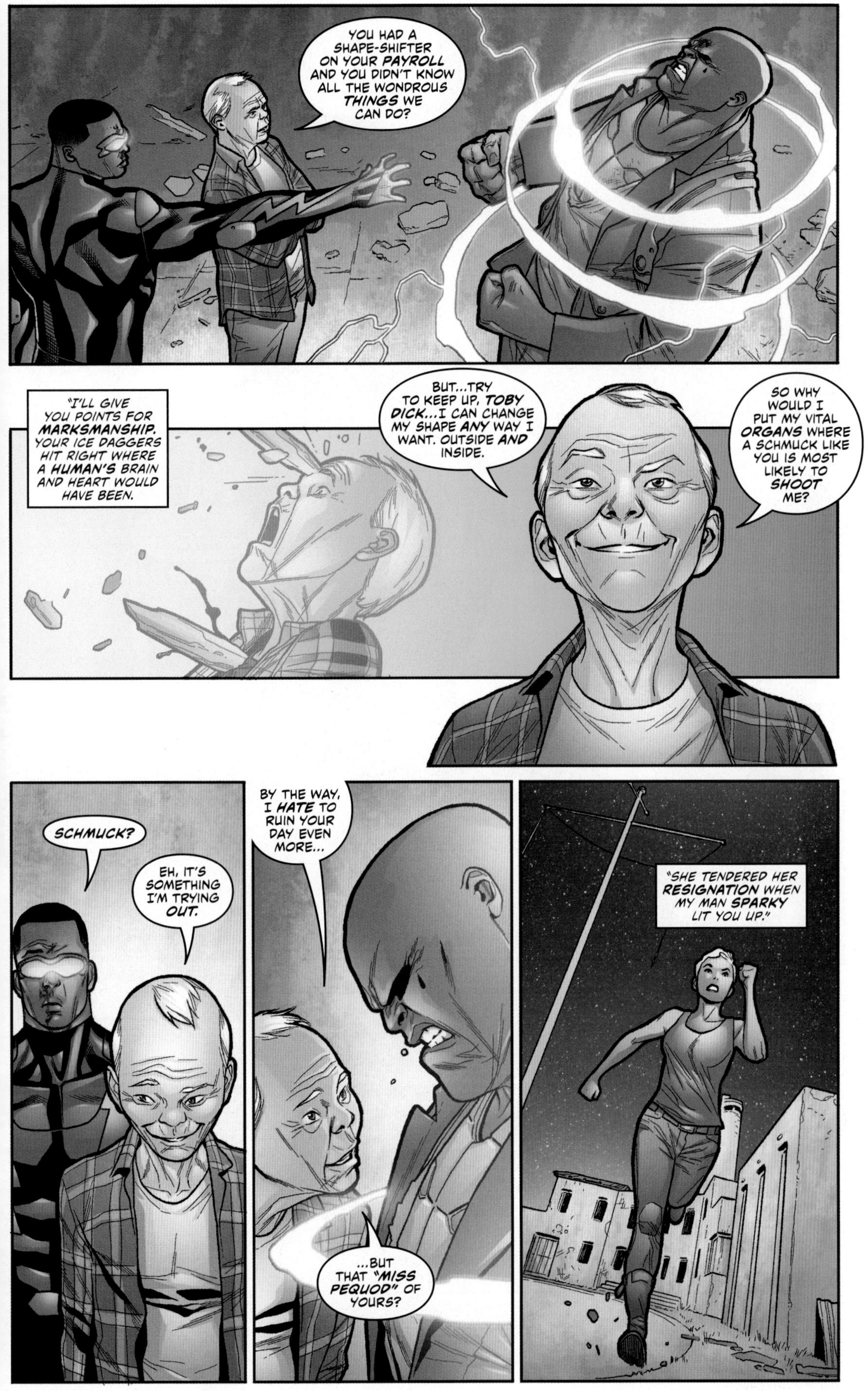
YOU HAD A SHAPE-SHIFTER ON YOUR PAYROLL AND YOU DIDN'T KNOW ALL THE WONDROUS THINGS WE CAN DO?
"I'LL GIVE YOU POINTS FOR MARKSMANSHIP. YOUR ICE DAGGERS HIT RIGHT WHERE A HUMAN'S BRAIN AND HEART WOULD HAVE BEEN.
BUT...TRY TO KEEP UP, TOBY DICK...I CAN CHANGE MY SHAPE ANY WAY I WANT. OUTSIDE AND INSIDE.
SO WHY WOULD I PUT MY VITAL ORGANS WHERE A SCHMUCK LIKE YOU IS MOST LIKELY TO SHOOT ME?
SCHMUCK?
EH, IT'S SOMETHING I'M TRYING OUT.
BY THE WAY, I HATE TO RUIN YOUR DAY EVEN MORE...
...BUT THAT "MISS PEQUOD" OF YOURS?
"SHE TENDERED HER RESIGNATION WHEN MY MAN SPARKY LIT YOU UP."

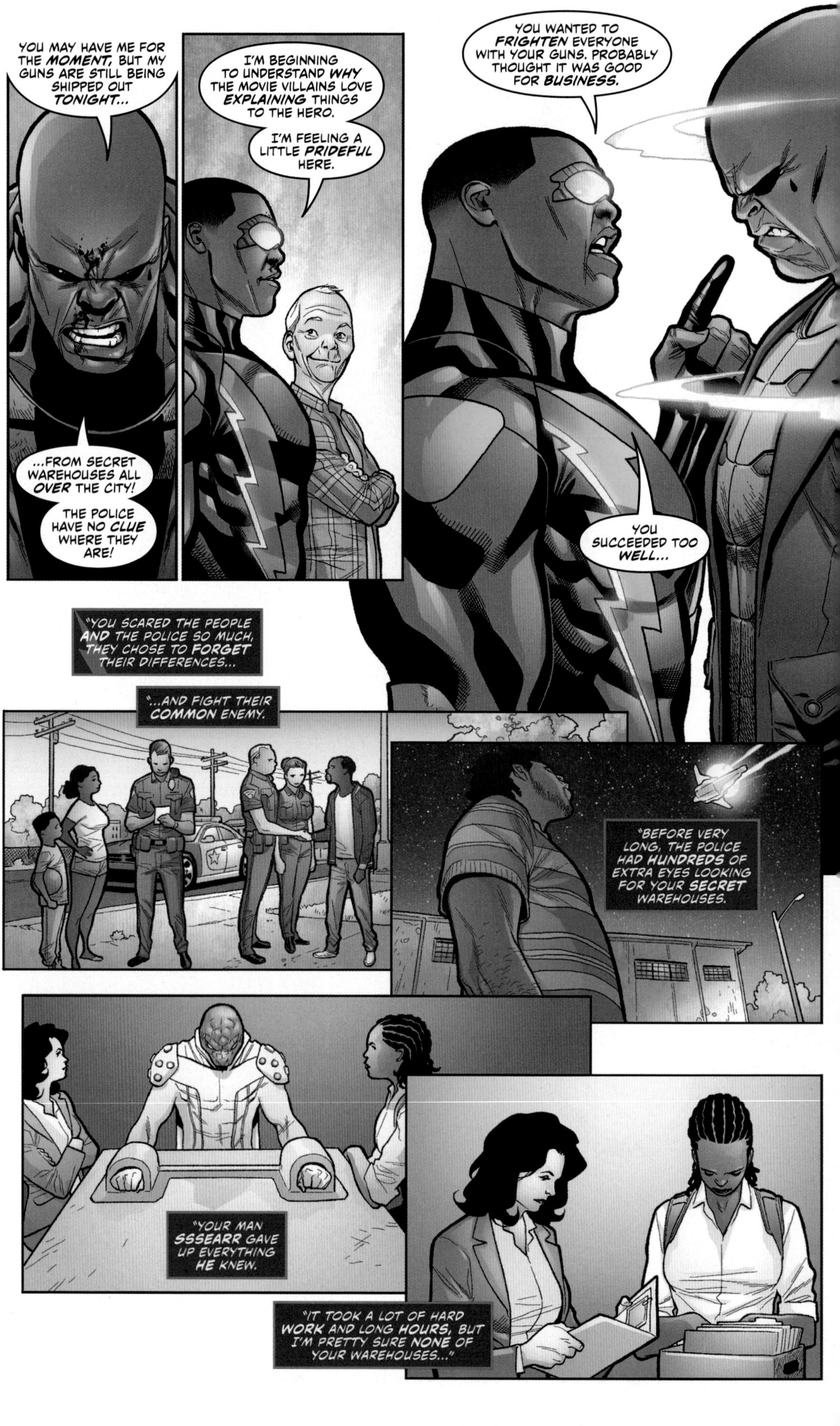
YOU MAY HAVE ME FOR THE MOMENT, BUT MY GUNS ARE STILL BEING SHIPPED OUT TONIGHT...
...FROM SECRET WAREHOUSES ALL OVER THE CITY!
THE POLICE HAVE NO CLUE WHERE THEY ARE!
I'M BEGINNING TO UNDERSTAND WHY THE MOVIE VILLAINS LOVE EXPLAINING THINGS TO THE HERO.
I'M FEELING A LITTLE PRIDEFUL HERE.
YOU WANTED TO FRIGHTEN EVERYONE WITH YOUR GUNS. PROBABLY THOUGHT IT WAS GOOD FOR BUSINESS.
YOU SUCCEEDED TOO WELL...
"YOU SCARED THE PEOPLE AND THE POLICE SO MUCH, THEY CHOSE TO FORGET THEIR DIFFERENCES...
"...AND FIGHT THEIR COMMON ENEMY.
"BEFORE VERY LONG, THE POLICE HAD HUNDREDS OF EXTRA EYES LOOKING FOR YOUR SECRET WAREHOUSES.
"YOUR MAN SSSEARR GAVE UP EVERYTHING HE KNEW.
"IT TOOK A LOT OF HARD WORK AND LONG HOURS, BUT I'M PRETTY SURE NONE OF YOUR WAREHOUSES..."

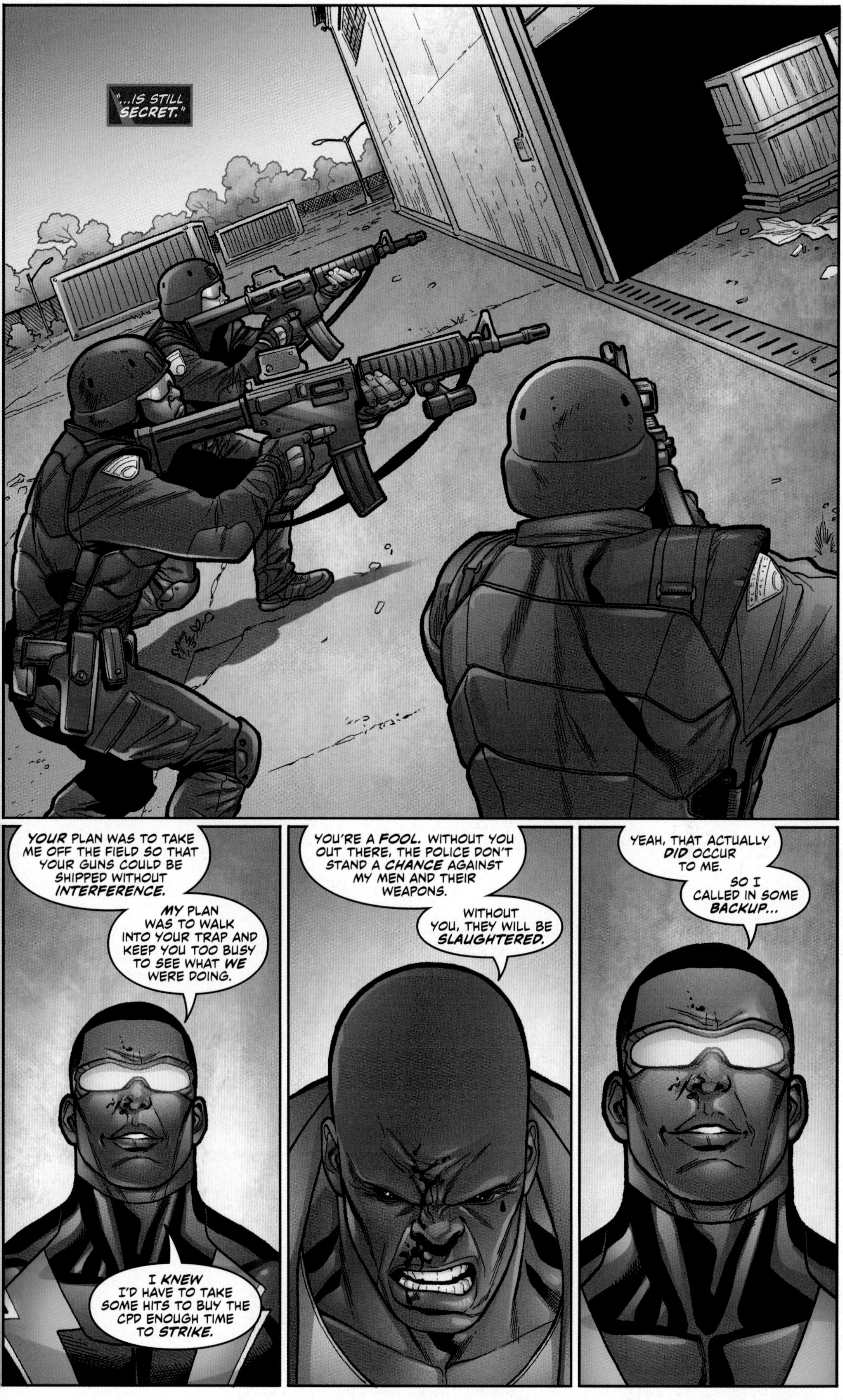
"...IS STILL SECRET."
YOUR PLAN WAS TO TAKE ME OFF THE FIELD SO THAT YOUR GUNS COULD BE SHIPPED WITHOUT INTERFERENCE.
MY PLAN WAS TO WALK INTO YOUR TRAP AND KEEP YOU TOO BUSY TO SEE WHAT WE WERE DOING.
I KNEW I'D HAVE TO TAKE SOME HITS TO BUY THE CPD ENOUGH TIME TO STRIKE.
YOU'RE A FOOL. WITHOUT YOU OUT THERE, THE POLICE DON'T STAND A CHANCE AGAINST MY MEN AND THEIR WEAPONS.
WITHOUT YOU, THEY WILL BE SLAUGHTERED.
YEAH, THAT ACTUALLY DID OCCUR TO ME.
SO I CALLED IN SOME BACKUP...

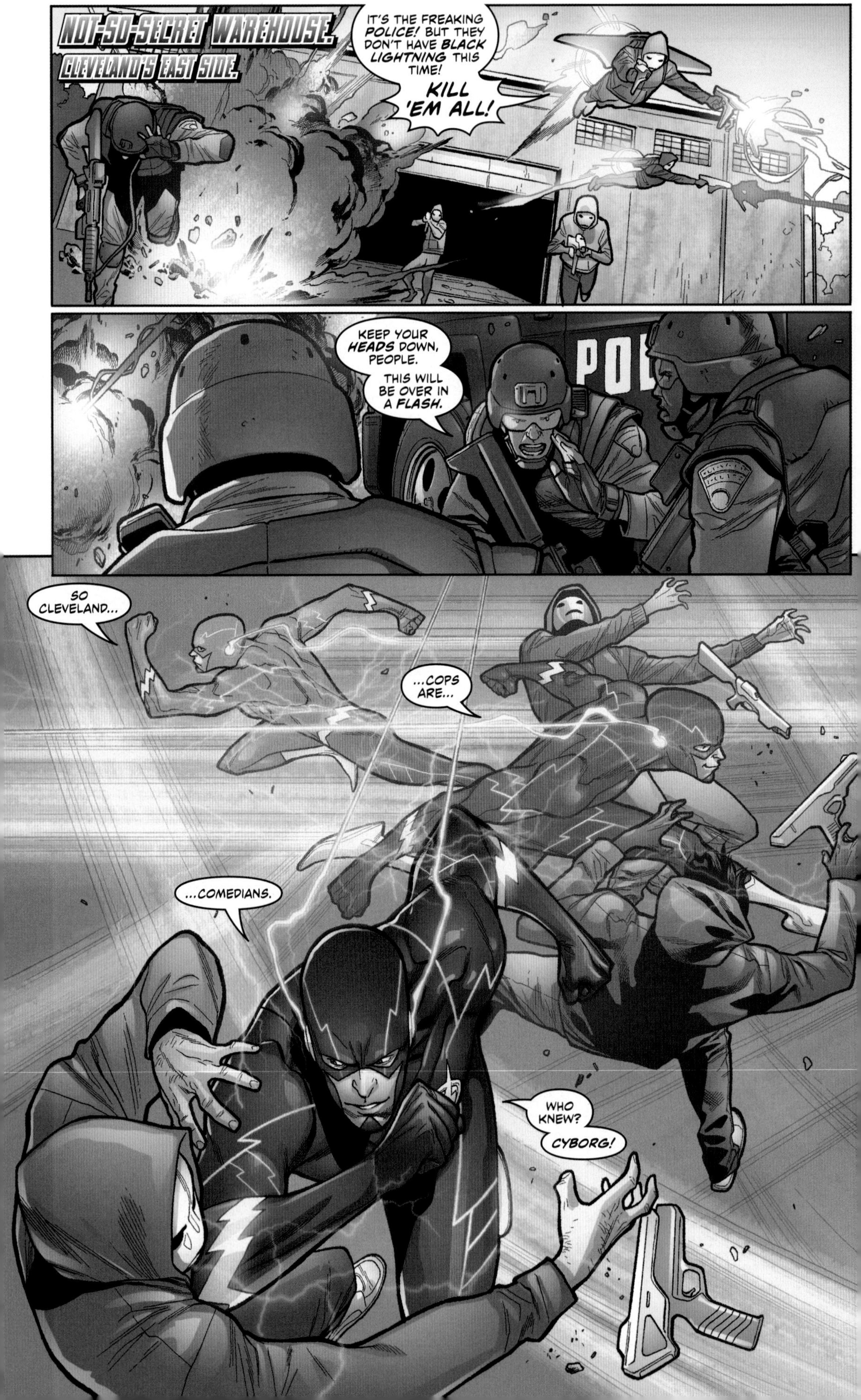
NOT-SO-SECRET WAREHOUSE.
CLEVELAND'S EAST SIDE.
IT'S THE FREAKING POLICE! BUT THEY DON'T HAVE BLACK LIGHTNING THIS TIME!
KILL 'EM ALL!
KEEP YOUR HEADS DOWN, PEOPLE.
THIS WILL BE OVER IN A FLASH.
POL
SO CLEVELAND...
...COPS ARE...
...COMEDIANS.
WHO KNEW?
CYBORG!

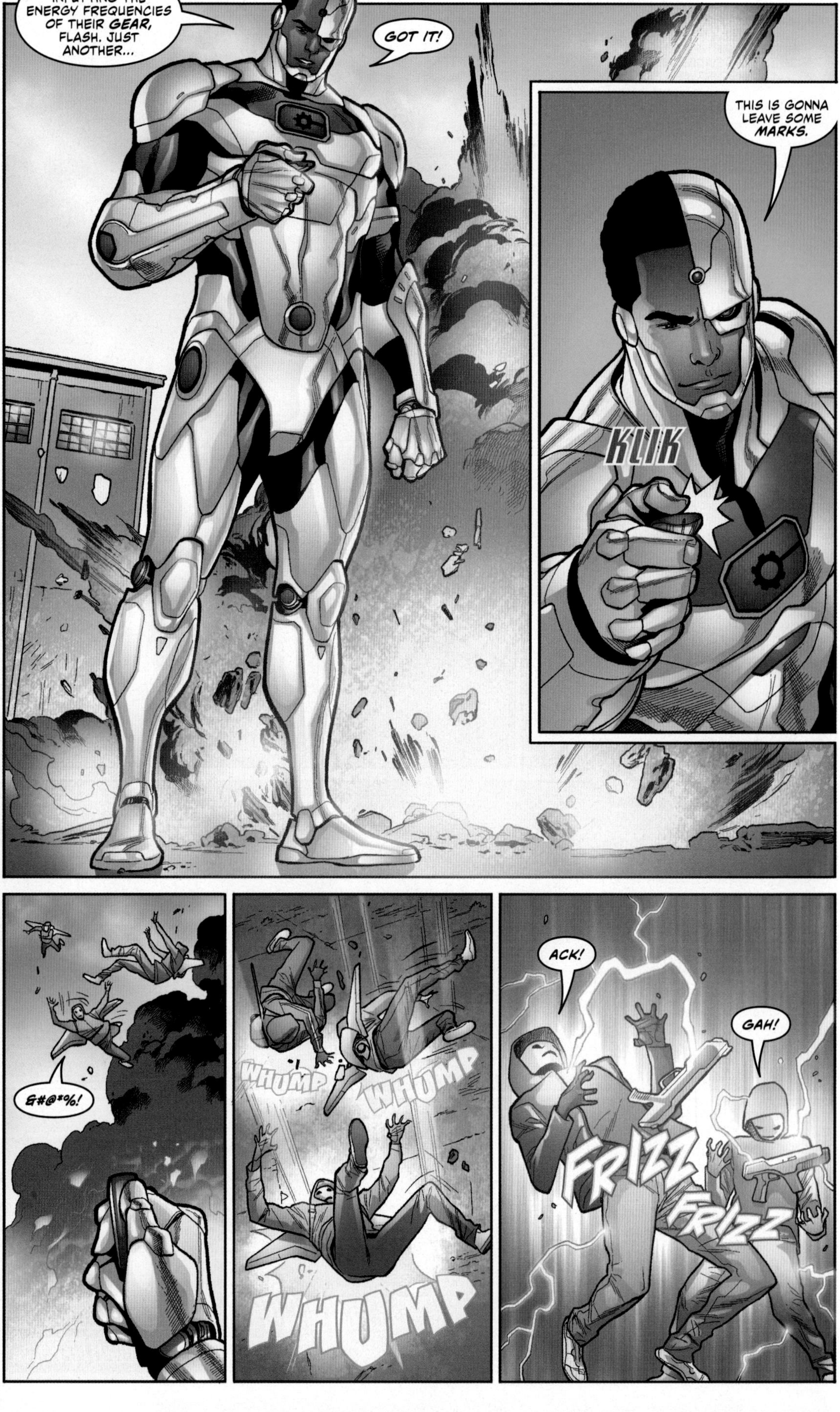
JUST INPUTTING THE ENERGY FREQUENCIES OF THEIR GEAR, FLASH. JUST ANOTHER...
GOT IT!
THIS IS GONNA LEAVE SOME MARKS.
KLIK
&#@*%!
WHUMP
WHUMP
WHUMP
ACK!
GAH!
FRIZZ
FRIZZ

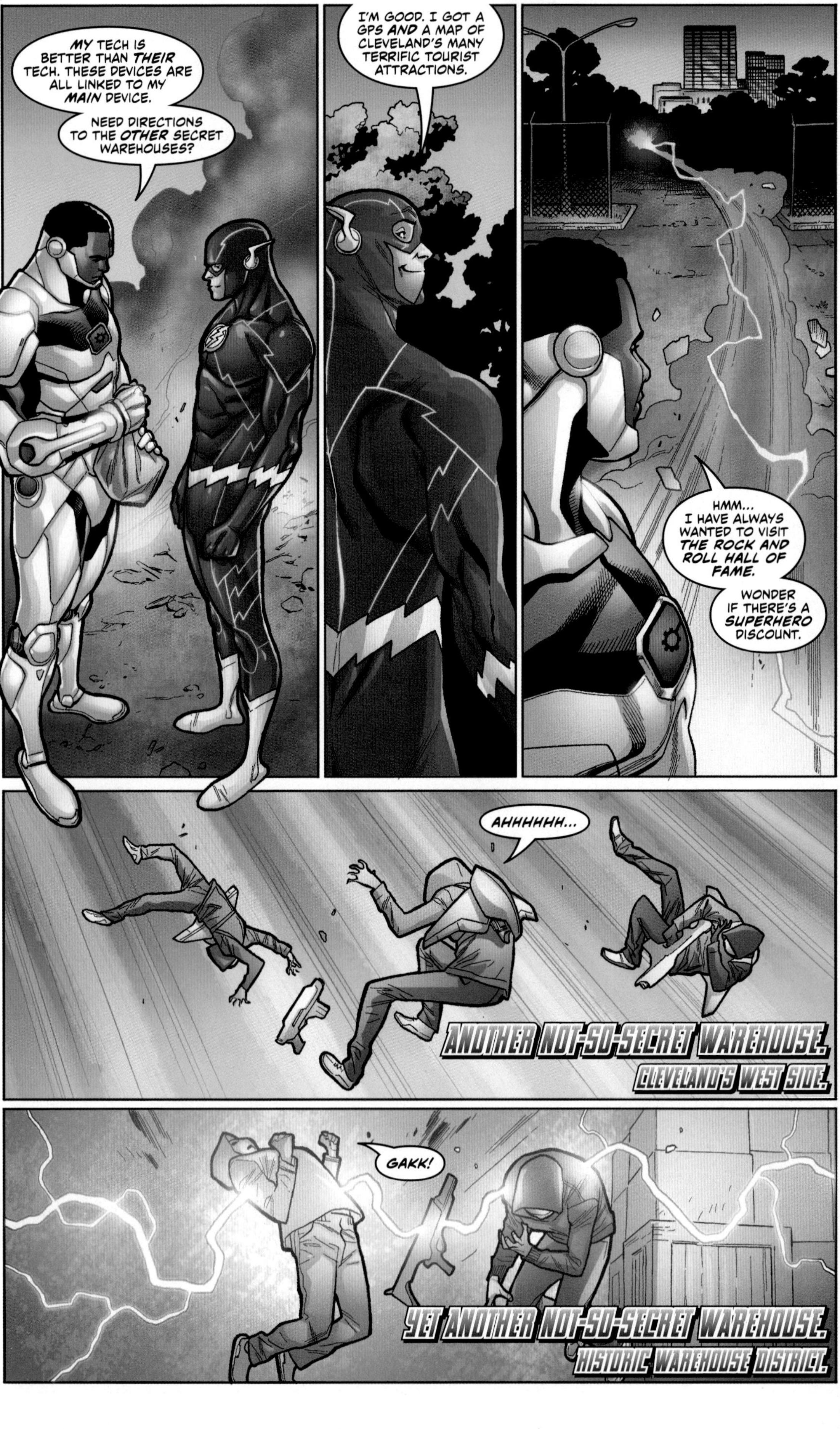
MY TECH IS BETTER THAN THEIR TECH. THESE DEVICES ARE ALL LINKED TO MY MAIN DEVICE.
NEED DIRECTIONS TO THE OTHER SECRET WAREHOUSES?
I'M GOOD. I GOT A GPS AND A MAP OF CLEVELAND'S MANY TERRIFIC TOURIST ATTRACTIONS.
HMM... I HAVE ALWAYS WANTED TO VISIT THE ROCK AND ROLL HALL OF FAME.
WONDER IF THERE'S A SUPERHERO DISCOUNT.
AHHHHHH...
ANOTHER NOT-SO-SECRET WAREHOUSE.
CLEVELAND'S WEST SIDE.
GAKK!
YET ANOTHER NOT-SO-SECRET WAREHOUSE.
HISTORIC WAREHOUSE DISTRICT.

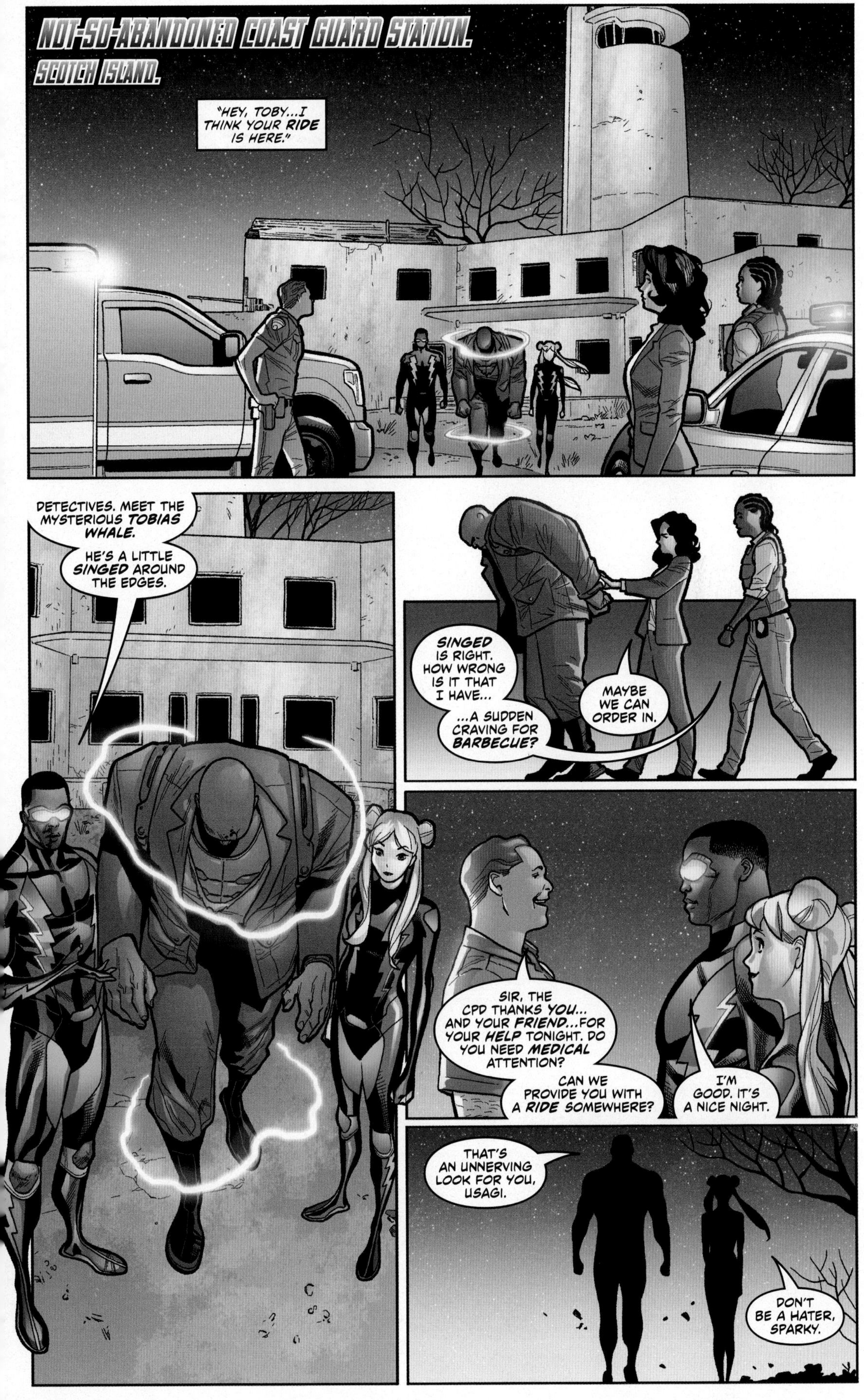
NOT-SO-ABANDONED COAST GUARD STATION.
SCOTCH ISLAND.
"HEY, TOBY...I THINK YOUR RIDE IS HERE."
DETECTIVES. MEET THE MYSTERIOUS TOBIAS WHALE.
HE'S A LITTLE SINGED AROUND THE EDGES.
SINGED IS RIGHT. HOW WRONG IS IT THAT I HAVE...
...A SUDDEN CRAVING FOR BARBECUE?
MAYBE WE CAN ORDER IN.
SIR, THE CPD THANKS YOU... AND YOUR FRIEND...FOR YOUR HELP TONIGHT. DO YOU NEED MEDICAL ATTENTION?
CAN WE PROVIDE YOU WITH A RIDE SOMEWHERE?
I'M GOOD. IT'S A NICE NIGHT.
THAT'S AN UNNERVING LOOK FOR YOU, USAGI.
DON'T BE A HATER, SPARKY.

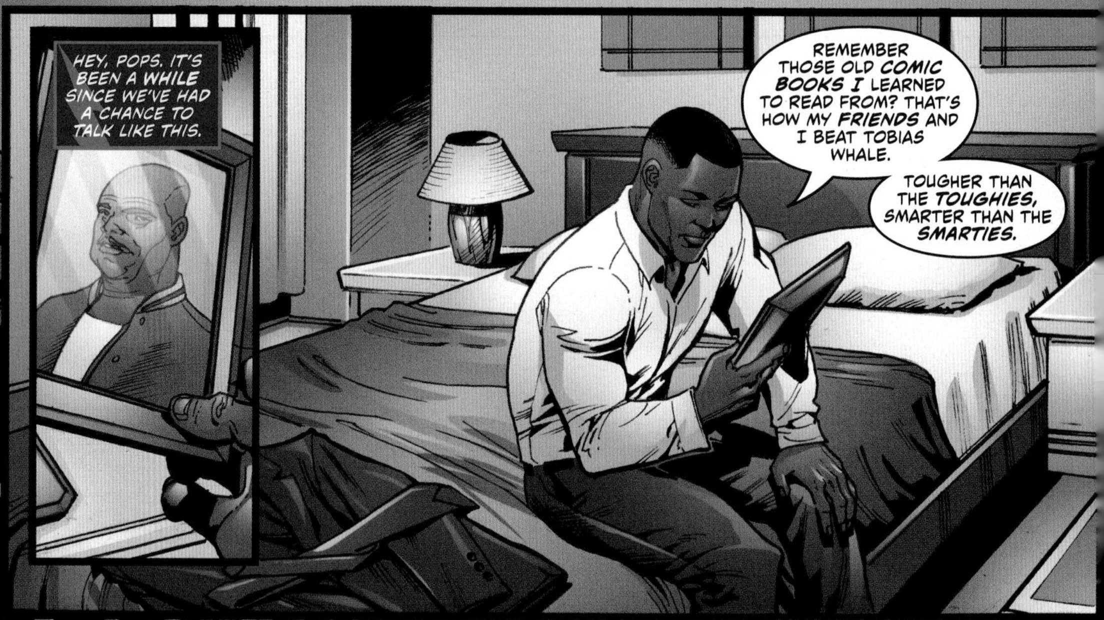
HEY, POPS. IT'S BEEN A WHILE SINCE WE'VE HAD A CHANCE TO TALK LIKE THIS.
REMEMBER THOSE OLD COMIC BOOKS I LEARNED TO READ FROM? THAT'S HOW MY FRIENDS AND I BEAT TOBIAS WHALE.
TOUGHER THAN THE TOUGHIES, SMARTER THAN THE SMARTIES.

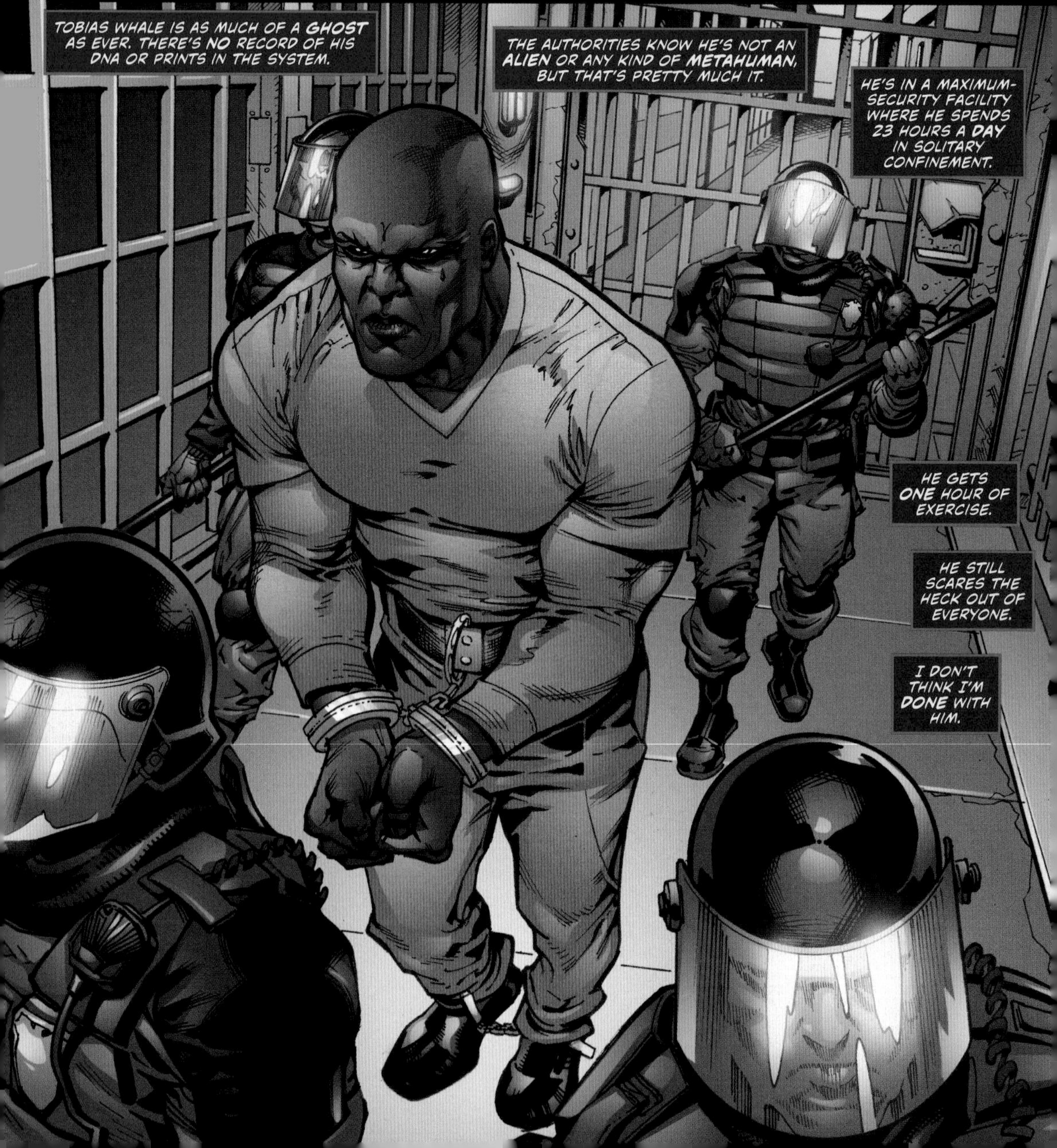
TOBIAS WHALE IS AS MUCH OF A GHOST AS EVER. THERE'S NO RECORD OF HIS DNA OR PRINTS IN THE SYSTEM.
THE AUTHORITIES KNOW HE'S NOT AN ALIEN OR ANY KIND OF METAHUMAN, BUT THAT'S PRETTY MUCH IT.
HE'S IN A MAXIMUM-SECURITY FACILITY WHERE HE SPENDS 23 HOURS A DAY IN SOLITARY CONFINEMENT.
HE GETS ONE HOUR OF EXERCISE.
HE STILL SCARES THE HECK OUT OF EVERYONE.
I DON'T THINK I'M DONE WITH HIM.

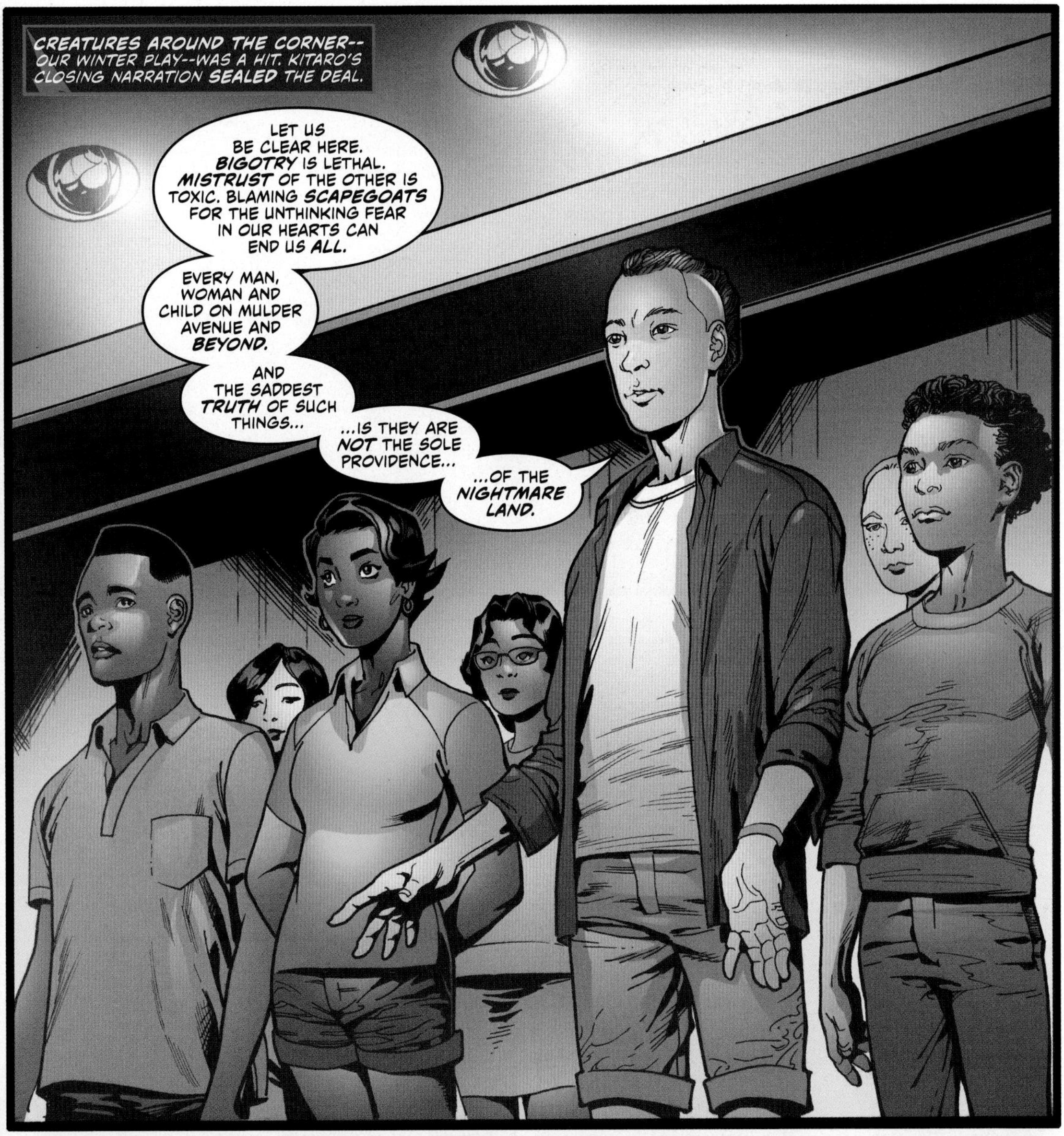
CREATURES AROUND THE CORNER--OUR WINTER PLAY--WAS A HIT. KITARO'S CLOSING NARRATION SEALED THE DEAL.
LET US BE CLEAR HERE. BIGOTRY IS LETHAL. MISTRUST OF THE OTHER IS TOXIC. BLAMING SCAPEGOATS FOR THE UNTHINKING FEAR IN OUR HEARTS CAN END US ALL.
EVERY MAN, WOMAN AND CHILD ON MULDER AVENUE AND BEYOND.
AND THE SADDEST TRUTH OF SUCH THINGS...
...IS THEY ARE NOT THE SOLE PROVIDENCE...
...OF THE NIGHTMARE LAND.

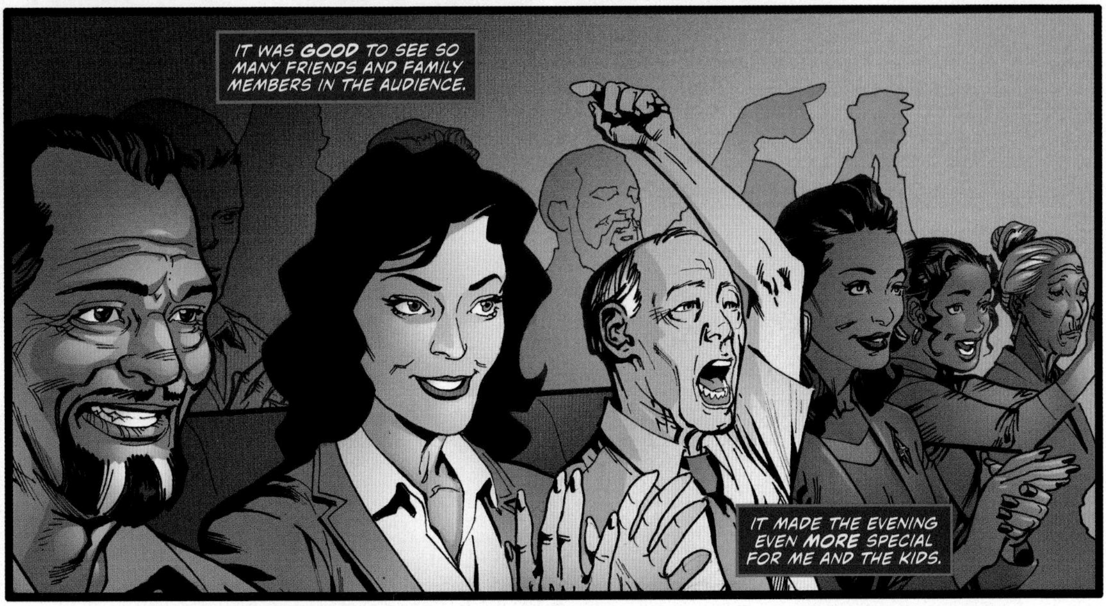
IT WAS GOOD TO SEE SO MANY FRIENDS AND FAMILY MEMBERS IN THE AUDIENCE.
IT MADE THE EVENING EVEN MORE SPECIAL FOR ME AND THE KIDS.

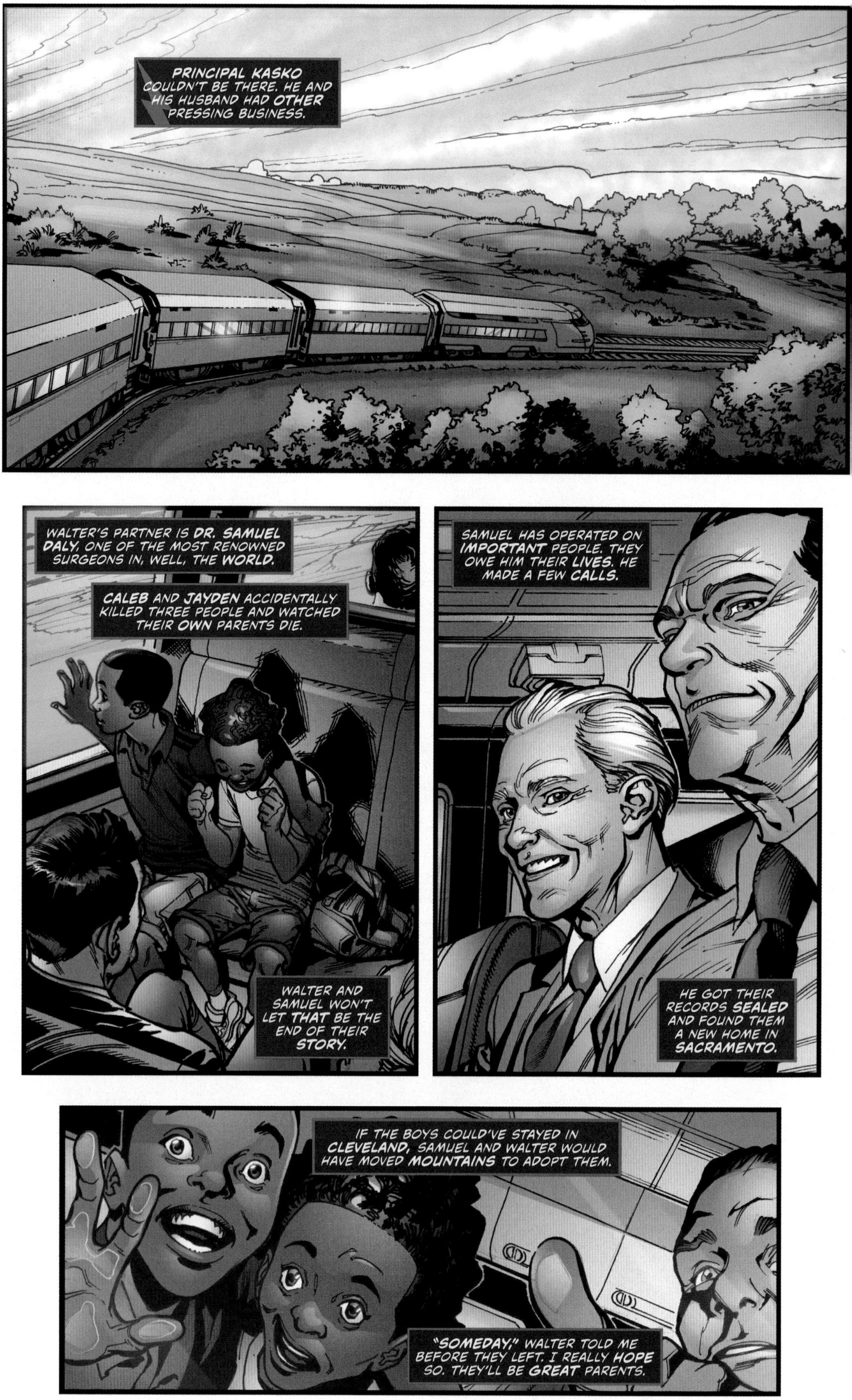
PRINCIPAL KASKO COULDN'T BE THERE. HE AND HIS HUSBAND HAD OTHER PRESSING BUSINESS.
WALTER'S PARTNER IS DR. SAMUEL DALY, ONE OF THE MOST RENOWNED SURGEONS IN, WELL, THE WORLD.
CALEB AND JAYDEN ACCIDENTALLY KILLED THREE PEOPLE AND WATCHED THEIR OWN PARENTS DIE.
WALTER AND SAMUEL WON'T LET THAT BE THE END OF THEIR STORY.
SAMUEL HAS OPERATED ON IMPORTANT PEOPLE. THEY OWE HIM THEIR LIVES. HE MADE A FEW CALLS.
HE GOT THEIR RECORDS SEALED AND FOUND THEM A NEW HOME IN SACRAMENTO.
IF THE BOYS COULD'VE STAYED IN CLEVELAND, SAMUEL AND WALTER WOULD HAVE MOVED MOUNTAINS TO ADOPT THEM.
"SOMEDAY," WALTER TOLD ME BEFORE THEY LEFT. I REALLY HOPE SO. THEY'LL BE GREAT PARENTS.

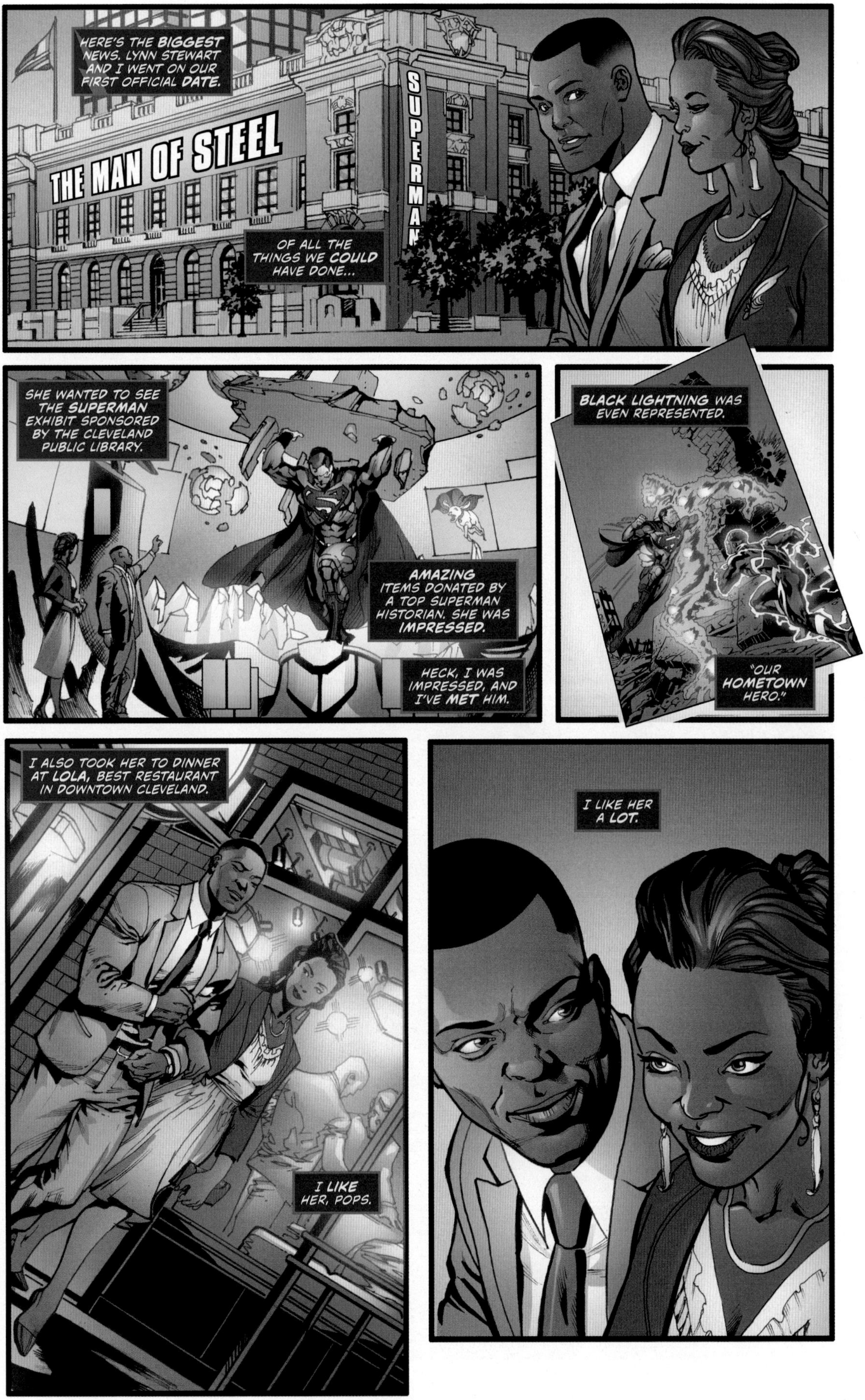
HERE'S THE BIGGEST NEWS. LYNN STEWART AND I WENT ON OUR FIRST OFFICIAL DATE.
THE MAN OF STEEL
SUPERMAN
OF ALL THE THINGS WE COULD HAVE DONE...
SHE WANTED TO SEE THE SUPERMAN EXHIBIT SPONSORED BY THE CLEVELAND PUBLIC LIBRARY.
AMAZING ITEMS DONATED BY A TOP SUPERMAN HISTORIAN. SHE WAS IMPRESSED.
HECK, I WAS IMPRESSED, AND I'VE MET HIM.
BLACK LIGHTNING WAS EVEN REPRESENTED.
"OUR HOMETOWN HERO."
I ALSO TOOK HER TO DINNER AT LOLA, BEST RESTAURANT IN DOWNTOWN CLEVELAND.
I LIKE HER, POPS.
I LIKE HER A LOT.

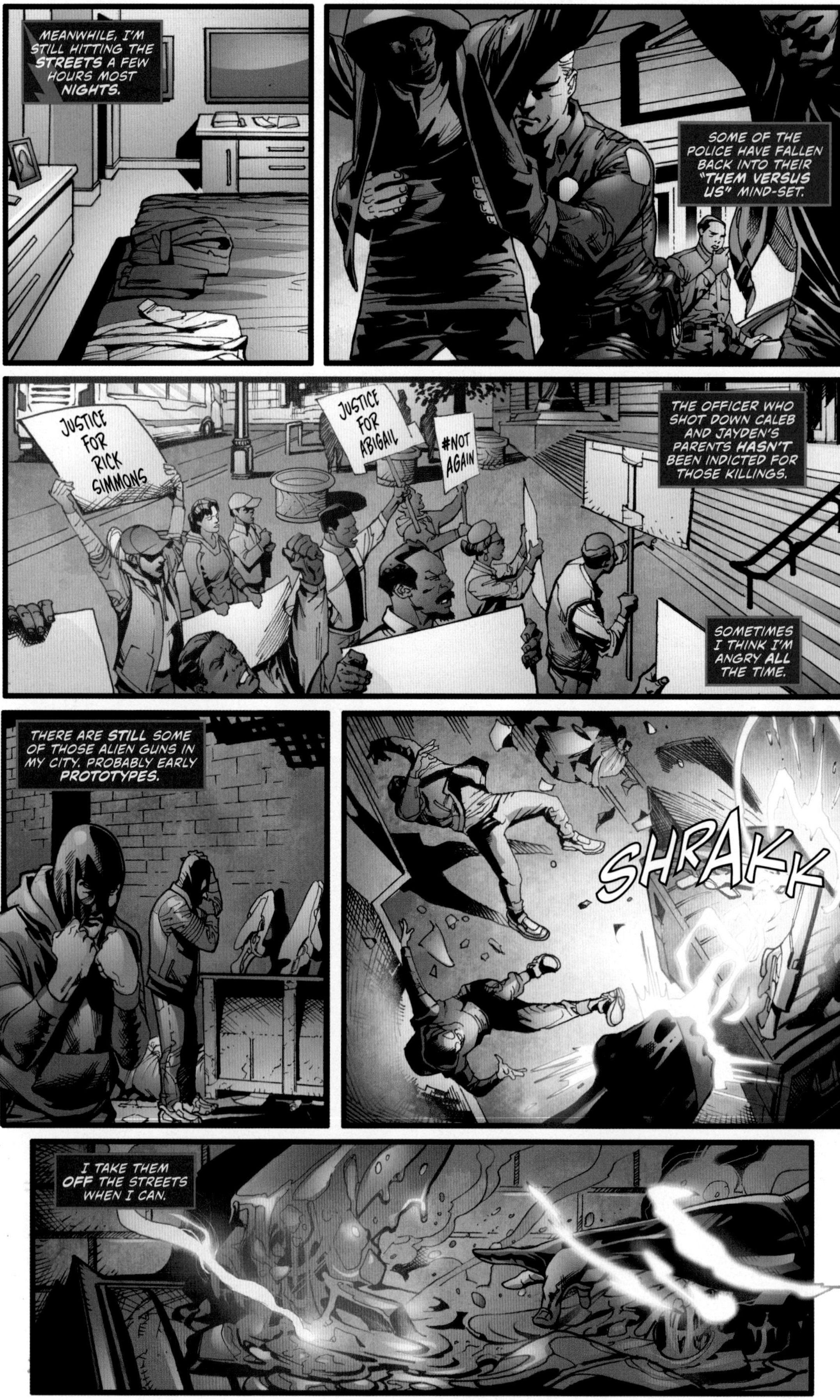
MEANWHILE, I'M STILL HITTING THE STREETS A FEW HOURS MOST NIGHTS.
SOME OF THE POLICE HAVE FALLEN BACK INTO THEIR "THEM VERSUS US" MIND-SET.
JUSTICE FOR RICK SIMMONS
JUSTICE FOR ABIGAIL
#NOT AGAIN
THE OFFICER WHO SHOT DOWN CALEB AND JAYDEN'S PARENTS HASN'T BEEN INDICTED FOR THOSE KILLINGS.
SOMETIMES I THINK I'M ANGRY ALL THE TIME.
THERE ARE STILL SOME OF THOSE ALIEN GUNS IN MY CITY. PROBABLY EARLY PROTOTYPES.
SHRAKK
I TAKE THEM OFF THE STREETS WHEN I CAN.

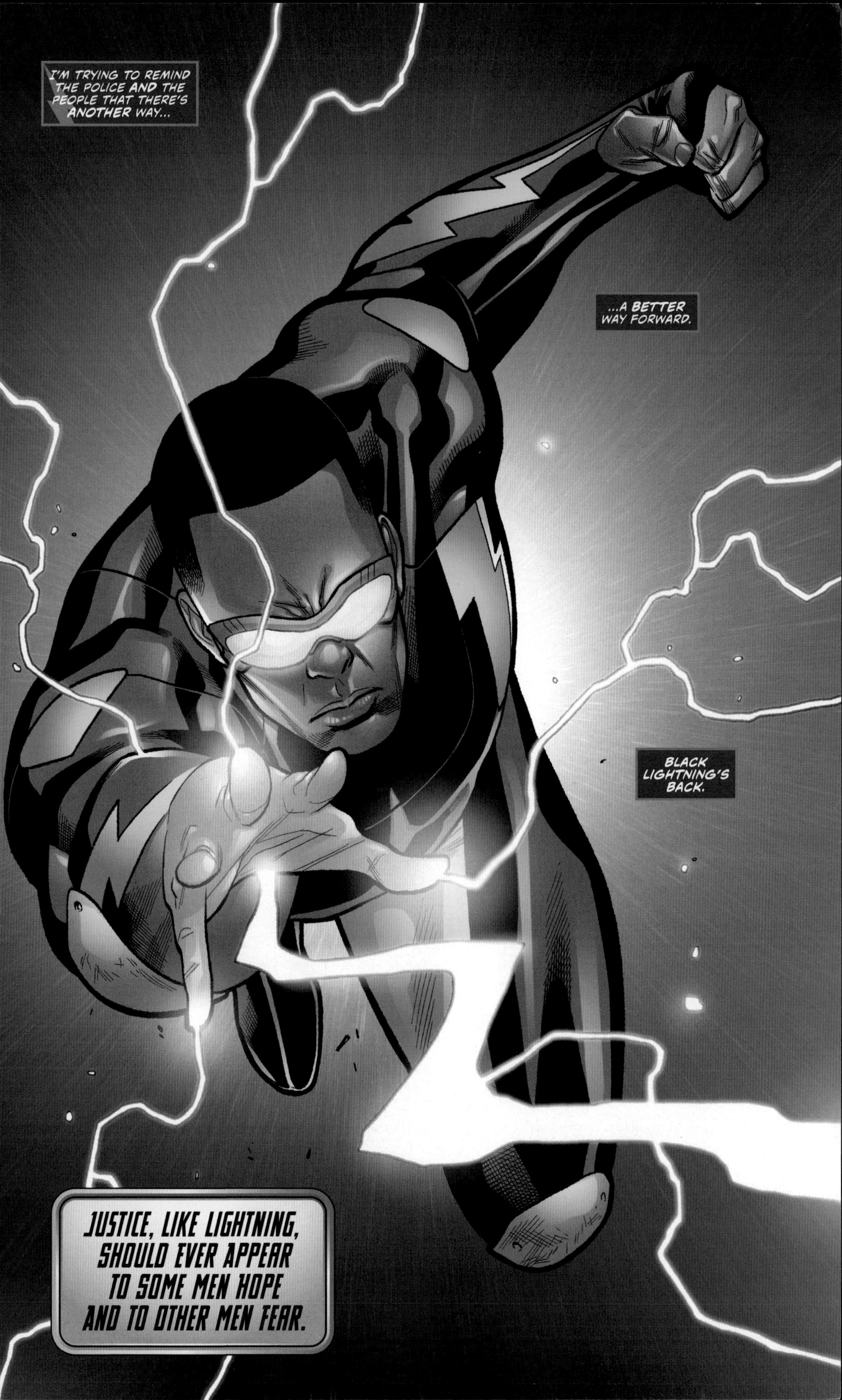
I'M TRYING TO REMIND THE POLICE AND THE PEOPLE THAT THERE'S ANOTHER WAY...
...A BETTER WAY FORWARD.
BLACK LIGHTNING'S BACK.
JUSTICE, LIKE LIGHTNING, SHOULD EVER APPEAR TO SOME MEN HOPE AND TO OTHER MEN FEAR.

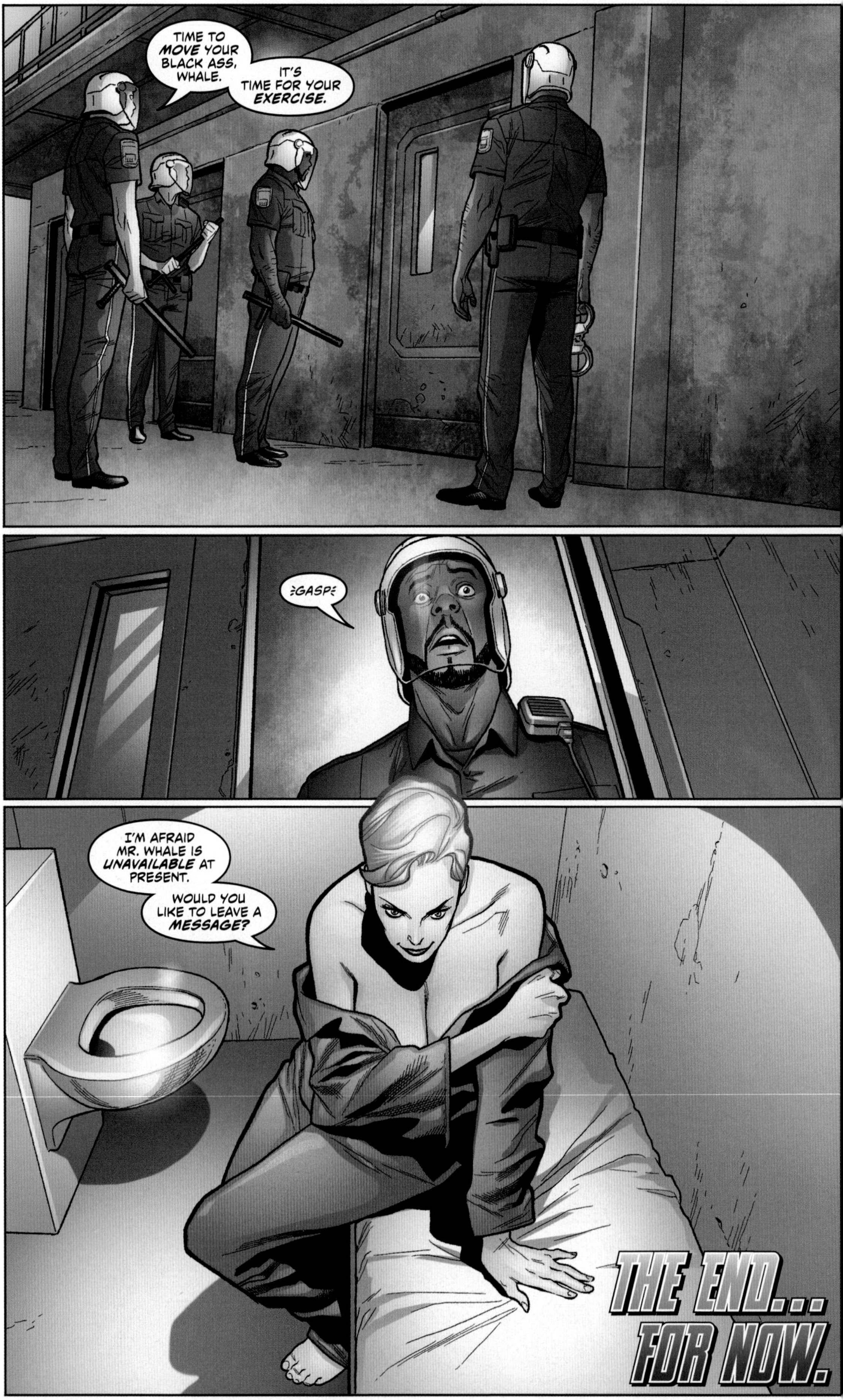
TIME TO MOVE YOUR BLACK ASS, WHALE.
IT'S TIME FOR YOUR EXERCISE.
GASP
I'M AFRAID MR. WHALE IS UNAVAILABLE AT PRESENT.
WOULD YOU LIKE TO LEAVE A MESSAGE?
THE END... FOR NOW.

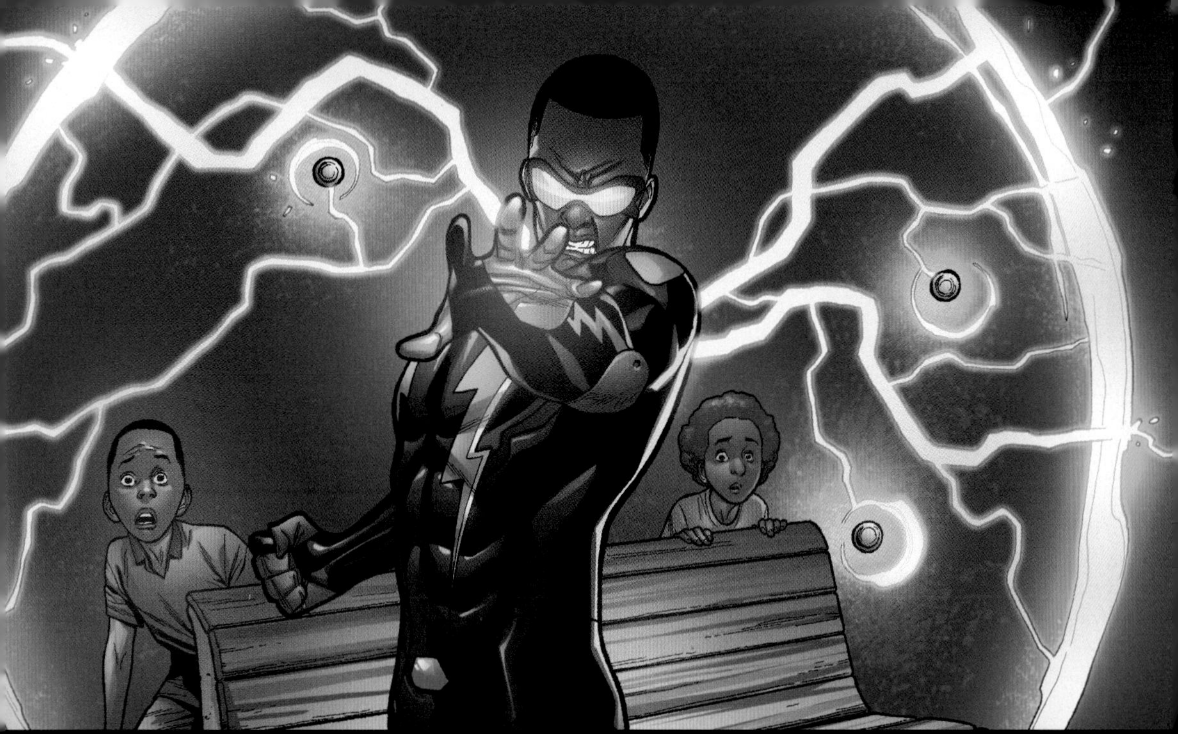

BLACK LIGHTNING'S BACK

Afterword by Tony Isabella

When DC publisher Dan DiDio asked if I'd be interested in writing a six-issue Black Lightning miniseries, I immediately said yes. That was an easy question. As I have often stated, I would like to write Black Lightning stories until they pry my keyboard from my cold dead hands.

The question I then asked Dan was...what version of Black Lightning do you want me to use? As is the nature of characters who exist in a shared Multiverse, Black Lightning and Jefferson Pierce are not always the same as they have appeared previously. I wrote them one way in my original 1970s series and another in my 1990s series. Other writers have put their own spins on my creation. That's the nature of the comics industry.

Dan said I could do whatever I wanted to do with the miniseries, which is a dangerous thing to tell a writer like me because I am all about going forward and not doing the same thing decade after decade. The result of Dan's answer and the faith shown in me by him and everyone else at DC is how we get to BLACK LIGHTNING: COLD DEAD HANDS, the kind-of-sort-of reboot of Black Lightning that you have just finished reading.

I wanted to reinvent Black Lightning and Jefferson Pierce, but also remain consistent with their core values. Jeff is a reluctant hero who becomes a costumed hero because he accepts the responsibility he has to his community. He would rather fulfill that responsibility as a teacher, but he lives in a world where people are menaced by alien invaders and super-villains as much as by more traditional criminals.

He is a man of faith because that's the core of his acceptance of his responsibility and because when we talk diversity in comics, this writer wants all of our readers to see themselves reflected in our characters. I wanted to tell stories reflecting contemporary social issues because our best comics have always reflected the real world around us.

These are the core values of Black Lightning and myself. All of the other stuff was me wanting to do things with my creation that I'd never done before.

This Jefferson Pierce is younger than I've ever written him before. He's smarter than any previous version. He reacts to situations thoughtfully (as when he realizes the downside of taking down a drug pusher on school grounds). Faced with new situations, he upgrades his tech to better deal with them.

This new take on Jefferson Pierce has honest-to-gosh family in his life. When I've written him before, he was an orphan with a knack for building families around him. This time he has a father, whose recent passing brought him back to his native Cleveland. He has a grandmother and two cousins. He has a sister from another mister. If I write more Black Lightning, you'll meet other family members.

He lives in a Cleveland as close to the real Cleveland as I could make it. I changed the names of places that play key roles in this story, but Clevelanders will recognize them all the same. Again, expect more of that from me.

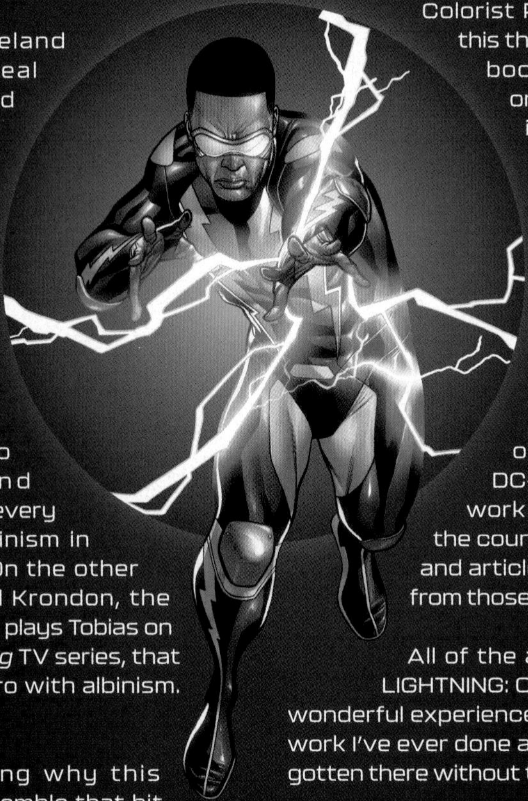

I didn't make Tobias Whale an albino this time around because just about every character with albinism in comics is a villain. On the other hand, I've promised Krondon, the wonderful actor who plays Tobias on the hit *Black Lightning* TV series, that I'll create a superhero with albinism. Fair's fair.

If you're wondering why this miniseries didn't resemble that hit TV series, it's because I started work on it before the great Salim and Mara Brock Akil were hired to be the showrunners of the *Black Lightning* TV show. Even with the obvious differences, both that TV series and this miniseries adhere to the core values I mentioned a few paragraphs back.

All through BLACK LIGHTNING: COLD DEAD HANDS, I was supported by some of the most talented people I've ever worked with in a career spanning five decades. Editors Jim Chadwick and Harvey Richards gave me the best notes I've ever received from any editors at any company. They didn't try to get me to write their stories. At all times, they worked to help me tell my stories better. From where I sit, they've raised the bar for every other editor I'll work with in the future.

Artist Clayton Henry drew both the superhero stuff and the human stuff brilliantly. Especially with a hero like Black Lightning, a hero so intrinsically tied to the real world, that ability is vital to what we did here. Thanks also to Yvel Guichet, who filled in on several pages when the deadlines got too close for comfort.

Colorist Pete Pantazis made this the best-colored comic book I've ever worked on. He was as involved in the issues as anyone, always striving to use his hues to further the story. Letterer Josh Reed made my words look real good. DC publicist Clark Bull worked hard to promote the series–as did many other fine people at DC–and continued that work on the other end of the countless interviews I did and articles that were written from those interviews.

All of the above made BLACK LIGHTNING: COLD DEAD HANDS a wonderful experience for me. It's the best work I've ever done and it would not have gotten there without these good folks.

The nature of comic books being what is, there's no guarantee I'll be writing more Black Lightning stories or that the others writing the character will follow my lead. But in this miniseries, I did exactly what I set out to do. I'm proud of this series. I hope I get the chance to continue creating comics that challenge me and help me grow as a writer.

Thanks for sharing this experience with me.

Tony Isabella
May 30, 2018

BLACK LIGHTNING: COLD DEAD HANDS #1 variant cover by **KEN LASHLEY** and **JUAN FERNANDEZ**

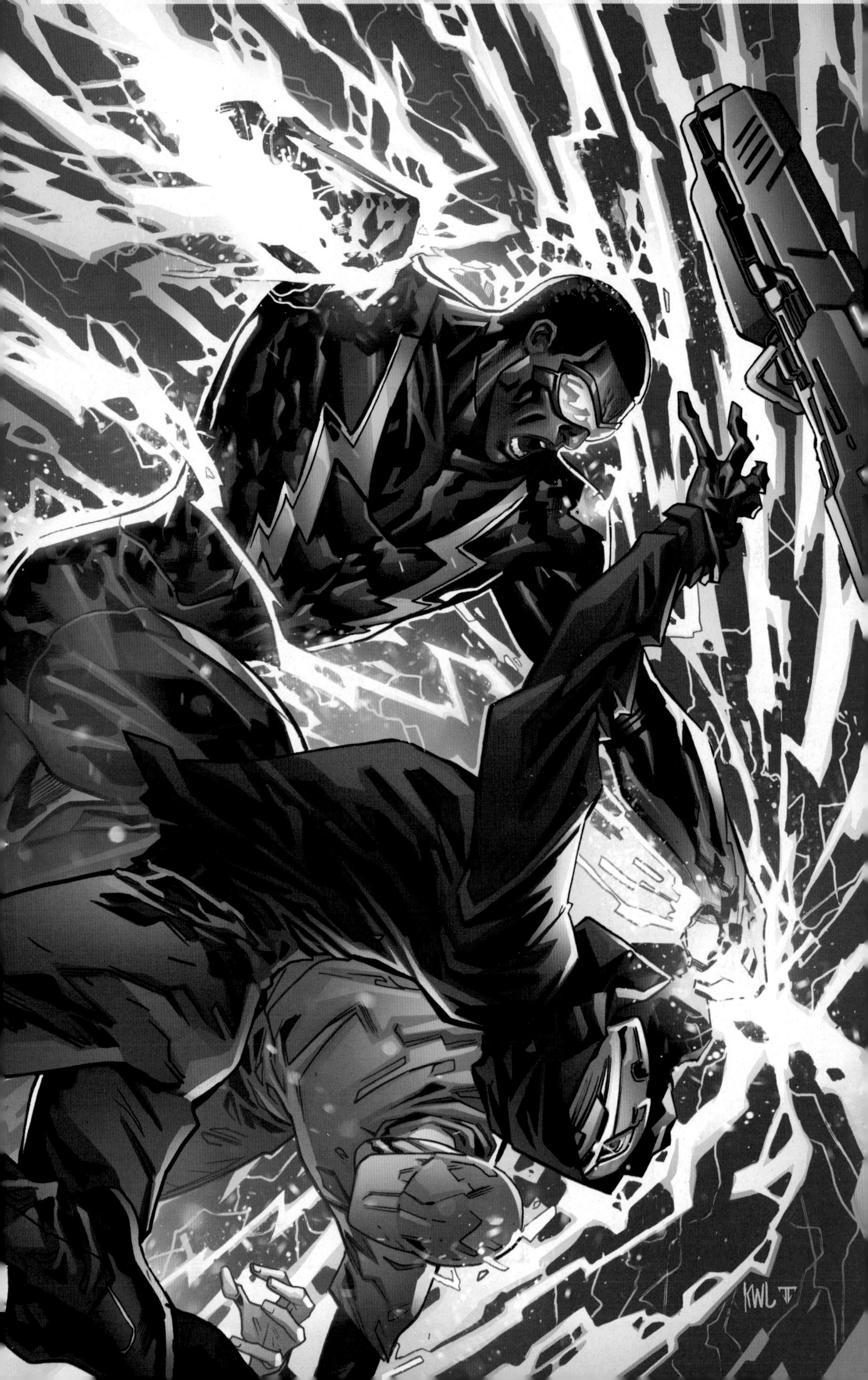

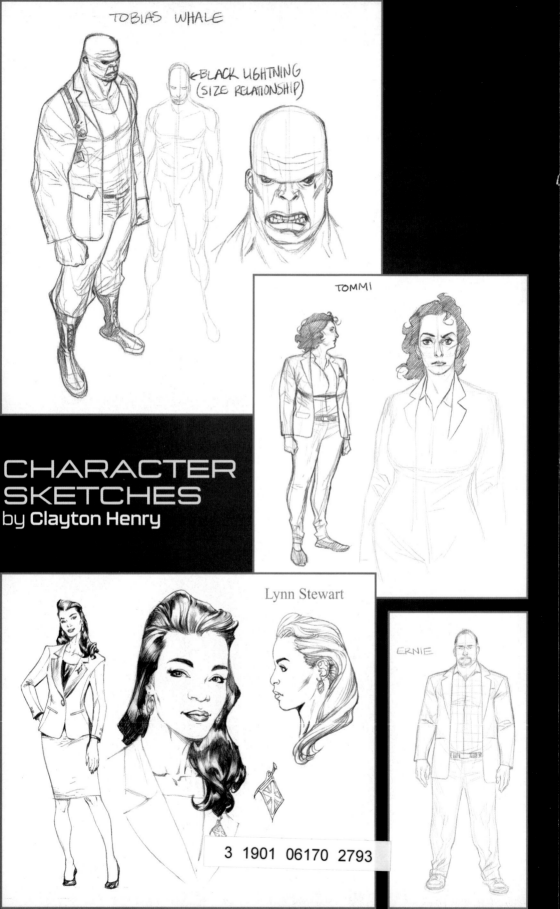

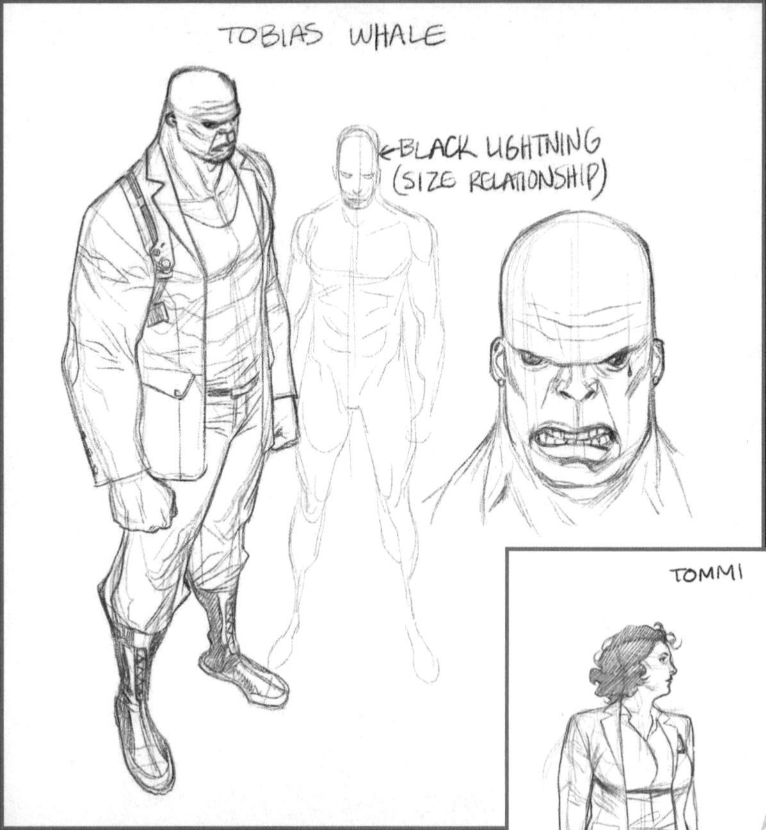
TOBIAS WHALE
←BLACK LIGHTNING
(SIZE RELATIONSHIP)

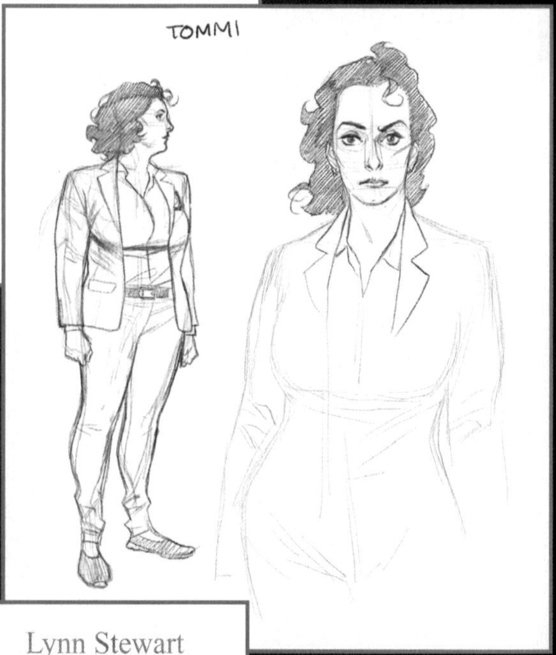
TOMMI

CHARACTER SKETCHES
by **Clayton Henry**

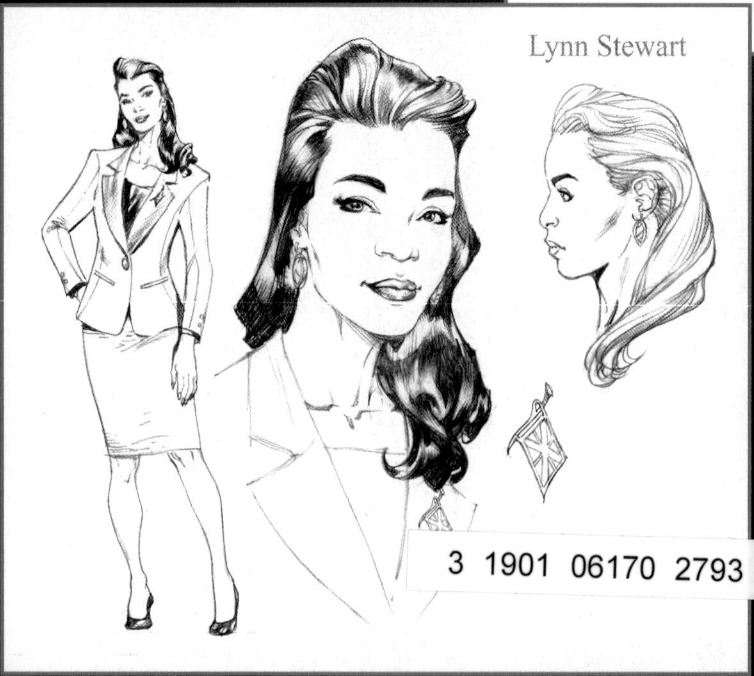
Lynn Stewart

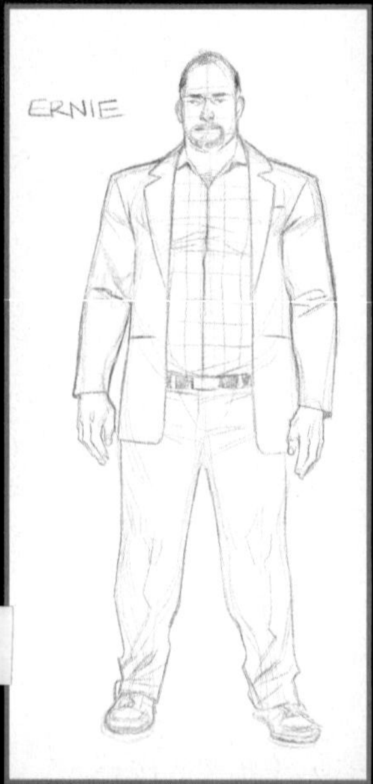
ERNIE